DUMBARTON OAKS
MEDIEVAL LIBRARY

Jan M. Ziolkowski, General Editor

CARMINA BURANA

VOLUME I

DOML 48

Carmina Burana

VOLUME I

Edited and Translated by

DAVID A. TRAILL

DUMBARTON OAKS
MEDIEVAL LIBRARY

HARVARD UNIVERSITY PRESS
CAMBRIDGE, MASSACHUSETTS
LONDON, ENGLAND
2018

Library of Congress Cataloging-in-Publication Data
Names: Traill, David A., 1942– editor, translator.

Title: Carmina Burana / edited and translated by David A. Traill.

Other titles: Carmina Burana (Traill) I Dumbarton Oaks medieval
library ; 48–49.

Description: Cambridge, Massachusetts : Harvard University Press,
2018. I

Series: Dumbarton Oaks medieval library ; 48–49 I Texts primarily in
Latin with English translations on facing pages ; some texts in Latin,
German, and French ; introduction and notes in English. I Includes
bibliographical references and index.

Identifiers: LCCN 2017018924 I ISBN 9780674660250 (v. 1, DOML 48 :
alk. paper) I ISBN 9780674980976 (v. 2, DOML 49 : alk. paper)

Subjects: LCSH: Latin poetry, Medieval and modern.

Classification: LCC PA8133.S8 C294 2018 I DDC 874/.0308 — dc23 LC
record available at https://lccn.loc.gov/2017018924

Contents

Introduction

Wine, Women and Song was the title John Addington Symonds chose in 1884 for his translation into English verse of a collection of "students' songs," which introduced to the English-speaking world a selection of poems from the *Carmina Burana* and other Medieval Latin sources. The title, racy by Victorian standards, offended the critics and probably hurt sales, but the book is still in print today. The translation is remarkable for Symonds's ingenuity in rendering the rhythms and rhyme patterns of the original. It was Helen Waddell, however, who above all brought this poetry to a wide audience in the twentieth century with her *Medieval Latin Lyrics* (1929).[1] Her verse translations, which charmingly combine a modern sensibility with a lingering romanticism, are much loved to this day.

The *Carmina Burana* is by far the largest and best-known anthology of Medieval Latin verse. It contains songs not only about springtime, love, sex, gaming, gambling, and drinking but also about crusading, the corruption of Rome, and the failings of the clergy; there are also plays about the birth of Christ and the events leading to his crucifixion and resurrection. The anthology provides fascinating insights into the values, attitudes, and social life of Europeans in the twelfth and thirteenth centuries. More than half of the poems in the *Carmina Burana* manuscript are not preserved elsewhere, though at least one of them is to be found in some three hundred manuscripts.

The collection includes some Middle High German, usually in the form of one or two stanzas added to the end of Latin poems. A few poems mix Latin and German, and three poems and one prose passage are entirely in German. The German content amounts to only about 7 percent of the total. In addition, one macaronic (mixed language) poem combines French and Latin. Finally, a few French words are scattered elsewhere.

The Manuscript

The Latin title *Carmina Burana* means "The Songs of Benediktbeuern." They are so called because the manuscript preserving them, often designated by the letter *B* for short, was found in the Bavarian abbey of Benediktbeuern (fifty kilometers south of Munich) and was initially assumed to have been written there. In 1803 the manuscript was moved to the state library (Bayerische Staatsbibliothek) in Munich, where it bears the shelf mark clm 4660 and is one of the library's most prized possessions. Careful study of the hands of the scribes, the German, and the physical appearance of the manuscript—including the placement of the wormholes—has revealed much of its complex history.

Many scholars have advanced our knowledge of the history of this important codex. In 1962 Peter Dronke corrected Schumann's dating of the core collection to the end of the thirteenth century by pointing out that the illustrations could be dated within narrow limits to around 1230.[2]

In 1939 Paul Lehmann maintained that the script showed Italian influence in the letter forms, indicating that the manuscript had originated in a German-speaking region much closer to Italy than Benediktbeuern. He suggested a scriptorium in South Tyrol. In 1967 Bernhard Bischoff, the leading paleographer of his day, agreed with Lehmann but proposed the Austrian region of Carinthia as a likelier alternative.[3] More recently, meticulous examination of the German dialectal forms has led to wide acceptance of Georg Steer's view that the manuscript was written in South Tyrol with the monastery of Novacella/Neustift (near Bressanone/Brixen) as the most likely scriptorium.[4] Olive Sayce, arguing that the emphasis on love poetry would "seem to rule out a monastic scriptorium as the main place of origin,"[5] maintains that the manuscript was not produced in a monastery but instead in the cathedral school of Bressanone.[6]

The core collection, which occupies 106 folios of the manuscript, was put together about 1230 and comprises some 228 items. These pieces (CB 1–228) vary in length from a Christmas play of three hundred lines to a two-line incantation of magical gibberish. Over the next hundred or so years a further twenty-six pieces were added. To signal their status as additions to the original collection, they are designated with a numeral followed by an asterisk: CB 1* to 26*. Some of these items were written in blank spaces in the manuscript and others on thirteen additional folios.[7]

The folios constituting the manuscript seem to have been left unbound for a time. When the codex was bound in the Middle Ages, some of the leaves had been lost. In the binding, the original ordering of the folios was not observed, so that instead of opening with poem 1, the first leaf contains poems 17 to 20. The leaves containing poems 1 to 16 were placed between those containing poems 92 and 93.[8] Accordingly, a reader consulting the codex today encounters the poems arranged in the following sequence: CB 17 to 92, 1 to 16, 93 to 228, then CB 7* to 26*.[9]

ARRANGEMENT OF THE POEMS

As happens in other Medieval Latin anthologies, the poems of the *Carmina Burana* manuscript are grouped thematically.[10] The poems of the core collection fall into four main groups: moral-satirical (1–55), love (56–186), tavern life (187–226), and religious plays (227–28). However, the compilers of *B* seem to have had a more ambitious program. In essence, they sought, at least at first, to break down the large groupings into smaller subgroups of rhythmical poems introduced by an appropriate heading and rounded off by short segments of metrical verse *(versus)* that offer commentary on the preceding rhythmical poems.[11] A modified version of the analysis in H-S-B's edition (1930–1970) of the relevant subgroups is to be found in the Notes to the Translation at the beginning of the main sections.[12]

AUTHORS

Except for three poems attributed to The Marner (3*, 6*, and 9*), the poems in the *Carmina Burana* manuscript are presented without any indication of authorship. Many of the poems, however, occur in other manuscripts, where the author's name *is* given, but even with plausible attributions made by modern scholars, roughly three-quarters of the Latin pieces remain anonymous.

LATIN AUTHORS

Archpoet

The Archpoet apparently earned his nickname because his employer, Rainald of Dassel, was both Archbishop of Cologne and Archchancellor of Italy. His actual identity is still in dispute.[13] Until recently, only ten poems were generally attributed to the Archpoet, but a convincing case has been made for adding to them CB 220/220a as a single poem, in accordance with its presentation in the manuscript.[14] All of the Archpoet's datable poems fall within the period 1162 to 1164, when he followed Rainald into and out of Italy. He delivered his masterpiece (CB 191) in Pavia, probably in November 1163. Since no trace of him can be detected after 1167, it has been suggested that he died in that year in the epidemic that killed many, including Rainald, belonging to the German army as it besieged Rome. (CB 191, 220)

Ausonius, Decimus Magnus (ca. 310–395)

A teacher of grammar and rhetoric in his native Bordeaux, Ausonius was summoned to Trier to teach Gratian, the son of the emperor, Valentinian I. Best known for his *Mosella,* a hexameter poem about the river Moselle and the towns and countryside it passes through, he also wrote many shorter poems. A twelve-line hexameter poem summarizing the twelve labors of Hercules is a fine example. (CB 64)

Disticha Catonis/Dicta Catonis (Sayings of Cato)

This collection of proverbial wisdom was compiled in the third century CE, was later attributed to Cato the Censor (234–149 BCE), and was widely used in education throughout the Middle Ages. (CB 221)

Godfrey of Saint Victor (ca. 1125/30–1194)

A philosopher, theologian, and poet, Godfrey followed in the mystical tradition of Hugh and Richard of Saint Victor. He was one of the last great names from the school of the Abbey of Saint Victor in Paris before it was eclipsed by the University of Paris. Godfrey arrived there in 1155/60, not long after the death of Adam of Saint Victor (late 1140s), who is reckoned among the best composers of religious sequences and whose influence is evident in Godfrey's lament of Mary, *Planctus ante nescia* (CB 14*). The lament was much admired and incorporated into the Passion play (CB 16*). (CB 14*, 16*)

Godfrey of Winchester (ca. 1050–1107)

Born in Cambrai, he came to England and rose to the level of prior in Winchester. He composed a book of proverbs in Latin *(Liber Proverbiorum)* in an epigrammatic style modeled on Martial. (CB 198)

Hugh Primas[15] (ca. 1093–1160)

Hugh's life is hard to reconstruct. An early practitioner of what has come to be known as goliardic verse, he owes his celebrity and nickname, Primas (foremost practitioner), to his achievements in satire. One of his poems, about the many metamorphoses of a cloak, was the model for the Archpoet's poem (CB 220) on the same topic. He seems to have been taught at Orléans, and his poems on themes drawn from classical mythology are perhaps to be attributed to this period. However, other poems of his suggest that he moved often among secular and ecclesiastical courts in northern France, including Tours, Le Mans, Reims, Amiens, Sens, and Paris. (CB 194 and mentioned at CB 215.8.6 and 220)

Marbod of Rennes (ca. 1035–1123)

Born in the region of Anjou, where he served as teacher and chancellor of the cathedral at Angers until appointed bishop of Rennes (1096–1123). A leading literary figure in eleventh-century France, he distinguished himself by his knowledge of classical Latin writers. His poem on precious stones (*De lapidibus*) was widely read. (CB 122a)

The Marner (ca. 1210–1270)

His German suggests origins in southern Germany; his Latin shows he had a good education. Poem 6* was written for performance in Carinthia, in Maria Saal or Seckau. (CB 3*, 6*, 9*)

Otloh of Saint Emmeram (1013–1072)

Born near Munich, he was educated in Tegernsee and Hersfeld and became a Benedictine monk in Regensburg, where he was soon entrusted with running the school. Well educated in the classics, he wrote a *Book of Visions* and a *Book about Temptations*, which offer insight into his inner life. In his later years he wrote a *Book of Proverbs*, in which he "christianized" pagan aspects of the *Dicta Catonis*. (CB 28, 32.2, 38, 125)

The Two Peters of Blois

Many excellent Latin lyrics written in the late twelfth century can be attributed to a Peter of Blois. Peter Dronke,

who believed that only one Peter of Blois of literary signifi-
cance existed at this time, ascribed these poems to the well-
known letter writer of that name (ca. 1135–1212), who served
as chancellor for three archbishops of Canterbury.[16] For the
last forty years most medievalists have followed Dronke—
wrongly in my opinion—in ascribing these poems to this
Peter of Blois.

Another literary figure named Peter of Blois was active
in the second half of the twelfth century (see *Lexikon des
Mittelalters* 6.1964). Richard Southern ("Two Peters") has ar-
gued, convincingly, that this Peter of Blois composed the
exquisite, though sometimes disturbingly violent, love po-
ems attributed to the other Peter of Blois. About this sec-
ond Peter of Blois ("the canonist"), we have only snippets of
information. Perhaps an uncle or older cousin of the first, he
seems to have been the tutor of his younger namesake, who
clearly viewed him as a better poet than himself, though he
deplored the racy content of some of his poems.[17] In the
early 1180s this second Peter of Blois dedicated his *Specu-
lum iuris canonici* (Mirror of Canon Law) to William of the
White Hands, archbishop of Reims, in whose entourage he
was then to be found.[18] In charters dated 1186 he appears as
Peter of Blois, archdeacon of Dreux. (CB 67, 72, 83, 84, 108)

Peter of Riga (ca. 1140–1209)

A canon of Reims, Peter wrote the *Aurora,* an oft-copied
summary of the Bible in verse. Besides summarizing the Bi-
ble, the *Aurora* incorporated commentary and allegorical in-
terpretations. Peter shows an extraordinary talent for sum-
marizing succinctly in verse, as in the two poems in the
Carmina Burana recently attributed to him (CB 99a and
102).[19]

Philip the Chancellor (ca. 1160–1236)

An illegitimate son of the archdeacon of Paris, Philip was assisted in his career by powerful family ties. Well educated, apparently in Paris, he was commissioned to write laments for the deaths of important personages closely connected to the French throne. Appointed archdeacon of Noyon from 1202, he became chancellor of Notre Dame in Paris in 1217 and soon found himself in the midst of prolonged wrangling between the young university and the bishop as the scholars sought to win its independence. Philip's facility for composing verse found expression in lyrics to accompany the efflorescence of music emanating from Notre Dame at this time. He is credited with inventing the motet.[20] (CB 14, 15, 21, 22, 23, 26, 27, 29, 31?, 33, 34, 36, 37?, 47, 63, 122, 131, 131a, 187, 189)

Walter of Châtillon (1130/40–1180/90)

A leading poet of the twelfth century, Walter was born near Lille and probably educated in Reims and later Paris. In the early 1160s he entertained the court of Henry I, count of Champagne, in Troyes. Disappointed in his hopes for a secure position there, he studied law in Bologna in 1164 but not long afterward returned to France without completing his legal studies. He was likely teaching at Châtillon-sur-Marne in 1176, when William of the White Hands, the new archbishop of Reims, brought him into his household as his secretary *(notarius)*. In 1178 Walter appears to have completed his *Alexandreis,* a hexameter epic on Alexander the Great, dedicating it to the archbishop. Shortly after 1179 he disappears from sight. He is said to have contracted leprosy. His datable poems all fall within the period 1160 to 1180. Besides epic, Walter was a master of satire, such as his *Propter*

Sion non tacebo (CB 41) on the corruption of the Roman Curia.[21] (CB 3, 8, 19, 41, 42, 123)

GERMAN AUTHORS[22]

Texts in the *Carmina Burana* by the authors listed below, except Freidank, are drawn from the corpus of *Minnesang*, songs with German lyrics about love, written between circa 1160 and circa 1300 for courtly audiences. Many of the singer-poets or, as they are known in German, *Minnesänger*, were themselves of noble birth.

Dietmar von Aist (second-half 12th century)

Dietmar may have been a member of, or a ministerial attached to, the baronial family von Aist, attested in Upper Austria from 1125. The songs gathered under his name, perhaps not all the work of a single poet, range in style from those characteristic of early, indigenous *Minnesang* to others closer to later, French-influenced models. The woman's openly expressed desire in CB 113a places it closer to the first group. (CB 113a)

Freidank (active ca. 1215–1233)

A professional writer, Freidank seems to have been in Acre in 1228/29 at the time of the Sixth Crusade. He may be the Fridancus magister whose death is noted in 1233 in the records of a Cistercian monastery near Donauwörth, Swabia. Freidank is known for a single work, *Bescheidenheit*—a word that designates the ability to judge correctly and draw proper conclusions. To foster this ability, Freidank offers an inventory of maxims and norms, mostly in epigrammatic couplets, drawn from the Bible, ancient and medieval writings, and oral tradition. The work, originally about 4,500 verses, was expanded, copied, and printed well into the sixteenth century and was even translated into Latin. (CB 17*)

Heinrich von Morungen (active ca. 1200)

One of the great *Minnesänger* from the period around 1200, Heinrich infuses the traditional forms and topoi with rich visual imagery, wide-ranging allusions, and rhythmic vitality; he highlights the demonic-magical power of love and the creative power of the poet. Linguistic and other evidence suggests that he was active in east central Germany. He may be the same Hendricus de Morungen who acted as witness to documents dated 1217 and 1218, a member of a ministerial lineage that took its name from the castle Morungen in Thuringia. (CB 150a)

Neidhart (active ca. 1210–ca. 1240)

Neidhart, who began his career in Bavaria, then moved to Austria sometime after 1230, is a great innovator of the love poetry known as *Minnesang.* While retaining many traditional forms and motifs, he replaced the cast of knights and ladies with unruly peasants. His work inspired adaptors and imitators well into the sixteenth century. Standing alone, as it does in the *Carmina Burana,* CB 168a looks like the opening of one of Neidhart's "summer songs," formally simple verse in which village women seek the favor of the knightly singer at an outdoor dance. It is actually the first strophe of a crusade song. (CB 168a)

Otto von Botenlauben (active probably ca. 1190–1200)

Count Otto of Henneberg, who took the name Botenlauben from a castle he acquired, is documented at the imperial court of Heinrich VI in 1197. He took part in the crusade of that year and, having married and acquired property in the Holy Land, spent most of his time there until 1220. Then he returned permanently to Germany, where he died about 1245. Nearly a third of his modest oeuvre comprises *Tagelieder,* or "dawn songs," a strophe from one of which appears in the *Carmina Burana.* (CB 48a)

Reinmar (active ca. 1200)

Second only to Walther von der Vogelweide in the estimation of his contemporaries, Reinmar wrote songs distinguished by their formal precision and thematic concentration. He is best known for the persona of a singer, disdained by his lady, who embraces his suffering and must deal with a public that has grown tired of his laments. CB 166a is a strophe from a song in this vein. However, Reinmar also wrote *Frauenlieder,* or "women's songs," in which ladies of the court reveal they are more sympathetic to their suitors than they dare admit. A lady of this kind speaks in CB 147a in dialogue with a messenger. A lament on the death of Duke Leopold V suggests Reinmar was at the Viennese court in summer 1195. There too he seems to have entered into a rivalry with Walter von der Vogelweide, who nevertheless wrote a poetic eulogy to his former rival, usually dated 1208/9. (CB 147a, 166a)

Walther von der Vogelweide (active ca. 1190–ca. 1230)

The greatest lyric poet of the German Middle Ages, Walther composed not only *Minnesang* but also *Sangsprüche*—strophic verse treating political, religious, social, and personal themes. Topical references in the latter allow many of them to be dated—the earliest 1198, the latest 1228. Walther says he "learned to sing in Austria," doubtless at the same court where Reinmar was active, but the *Sangsprüche* show that he had connections to many of the most important courts of the period. As a professional singer, he would have moved from one to another seeking patronage. In his *Minnesang*, Walther treats love from a variety of perspectives (some in direct challenge to those of Reinmar), and with an ethical seriousness, that were unprecedented. He employs traditional forms, but expands and enlivens them in new ways: the familiar flowers of May argue with each other (CB 151a); the lady's red lips, so often singled out for praise, are criticized for mocking laughter (CB 169a). (CB 151a, 169a, 211a)

METER, RHYTHM, AND RHYME

METRICAL VERSE

Most poems in the *Carmina Burana* are rhythmic/accentual, but every so often there is also verse written according to the familiar rules of classical Latin's quantitative metrics.[23] It is usually preceded by the word *versus* in the manuscript. Practically all the quantitative verse in the *Carmina Burana* is in either dactylic hexameters or elegiac couplets. One major departure from classical practice was the introduction of rhyme into hexameters and pentameters. The most common types of rhyming hexameters (or pentameters) are the following:

Leonine, in which the word at the caesura rhymes with the end of the line.
Caudate, in which the ends of successive lines rhyme with one another.

Rhythmical Verse

The patterns of rhythmical verse are more readily grasped by English speakers than those of the quantitative meters of classical poetry. The former consists of patterns of stressed and unstressed syllables, as in English poetry. If readers read the following stanza aloud as if it were an additional stanza of *Good King Wenceslas,* they will observe the correct rhythm perfectly:

> Meum est propositum   in taberna mori
> ut sint vina proxima   morientis ori.
> Tunc cantabunt laetius   angelorum chori:
> "Sit deus propitius   huic potatori."

Generally speaking, the stress falls on the natural word stress. Hence *Túnc cantábunt.* However, just as in English songs, a word may need to take a secondary stress in order to keep the alternating pattern of stressed and unstressed syllables. So just as we say (or sing) "Wénceslás," so we need to say (or sing) *propósitúm.* Also, natural word stress may be violated in the first part of the line but is strictly observed at the end, as in

> Sí linguís angélicís   lóquar ét humánis

where the stress in *linguis,* normally falling on the first syllable, has to fall on the second. Within a single poem, lines can vary both in the number of syllables and in whether the penultimate (second last) or antepenultimate (third last) syllable is stressed. Most lines range from three to eight syllables, though longer lines are occasionally found. The lines above are unusual in that they consist of thirteen syllables and yet conform to a commonly used rhythm, called goliardic. It will be noticed, however, that they always have a break after the seventh syllable, so that each line in fact has the feel of two lines.

The rhythmical pattern for most poems is indicated in the Notes to the Translation. I have used the notation devised by Dag Norberg. For example, the notation for a goliardic line is 7pp+6p. This means that the line consists of two parts, the first part comprising seven syllables and ending with the stress on the antepenult (pp), and a second part of six syllables with the stress on the penult (p). A complete stanza of four goliardic lines is accordingly 4x(7pp+6p).

Rhythmical poems come in three major forms: conductus, sequence, and descort:

> **Conductus:** the rhythmical pattern followed in the first stanza is used throughout the remaining stanzas of the poem (e.g., CB 1).
>
> **Sequence:** In the classical sequence, the stanzas are arranged in pairs sharing the same rhythmical pattern. Thus a poem of six stanzas would exhibit three different rhythmical patterns, with 1a rhythmically identical to 1b, 2a to 2b, and 3a to 3b (e.g., CB 63). Later, more complex patterns evolved that might incorporate a run of three or four short corresponding stanzas (versicles) and/or a single noncorresponding stanza (e.g., CB 60, 61). An elaborate sequence of this type is sometimes called a **lay.**
>
> **Descort:** In this form each stanza has its own rhythmical pattern (e.g., CB 98).

One final technical term that crops up, particularly in rhythmical verse, is **anacrusis** (upbeat). This denotes an extra syllable at the beginning of a line (or half line), which was not felt to interfere with the rhythm.

RHYMES

The Dumbarton Oaks Medieval Library's preference for normalized and classicizing rather than medieval orthography disguises the rhymes in some cases. For a brief explanation of how to appreciate rhymes that are not immediately obvious, see the Orthography and Rhymes section in the Note on the Text.

MUSIC

MEDIEVAL

Many poems in the *Carmina Burana* are accompanied by an early form of musical notation, which, unfortunately, does not indicate pitch and so does not allow us to reconstruct the melodies. Some poems, however, are found in later manuscripts with a more developed form of musical notation, which has enabled reconstruction and reproduction in modern notation of the melodies for forty-six poems.[24]

Carl Orff (1895–1982)

For most people today the name *Carmina Burana* conjures up the famous cantata by Carl Orff. In 1979 Orff described how, as a gift from *Fortuna* herself, the idea of composing his cantata came to him in 1934. He was reading the catalog of a Würzburg antiquarian book dealer, when he encountered the entry (in German): *Carmina Burana: Latin and German*

Songs and Poems of a Thirteenth-century Manuscript from Bene-diktbeuern. Edited by J. A. Schmeller. He ordered the book and received it on March 29, 1934. On the first page was an engraving of the manuscript's famous illustration of Fortune seated in her wheel and, immediately below, the opening lines of CB 17: "O Fortuna, / velut luna . . ."[25] The engraving and the words of the poem impressed him deeply: he had found his next musical project. Almost immediately he contacted Michael Hofmann, a state archivist in Bamberg, with whom he was acquainted and who became his collaborator and the translator of the selected texts. Orff planned his work to be a "scenic cantata" with elaborate, changing scenery and the choir and soloists variously costumed and singing, dancing, and acting onstage.

Though Orff and Hofmann were aware of the improved text in the H-S-B edition, it was not really very helpful, as only two (CB 16 and 17) of the twenty-four pieces selected for the cantata were to be found in the first (and only) text volume published in 1930 (containing CB 1–55). Hofmann's German translation was very free and concentrated on reproducing the rhythm rather than the meaning and so was of little help for those trying to understand the Latin.[26] Later productions used a revised text and translation by the distinguished classicist Wolfgang Schadewaldt.[27]

Immediately after World War II, when questioned by Americans about possible ties to the Nazi regime, Orff cited his *Carmina Burana* as evidence that he subscribed to "the idea of a 'European commonality' rather than a narrow-minded German nationalism. His use of Latin in *Carmina Burana,* he asserted, manifested this conviction and hence constituted an act of opposition."[28] He also maintained that "the work had been banned outright from 1936 to 1940 and had generally been declared 'undesirable' throughout the duration of Third Reich."[29] In fact, however, the premiere took place in Frankfurt in 1937 and, though Nazi-inspired critical reaction to the Frankfurt production was lukewarm at best, the general public was enthusiastic, and "the work became a roaring success after the beginning of World War II," being performed in Dresden, Essen, Cologne, Mainz, Görlitz, Frankfurt, Göttingen, Hamburg, Aachen, and Münster.[30] Yet although Orff has been called "a genuine sympathizer of the Third Reich," he never joined the party and in fact was "a quarter Jewish," had Jewish friends, and "thoroughly disliked most of the things that National Socialism and the Third Reich came to stand for."[31]

The truth, as often, is complicated. As a musician whose livelihood partly depended on the performance of his music under a regime that strictly censored public cultural events, Orff was careful not to offend those in power and indeed tried to curry favor with them. What has been seen as his most reprehensible act in this regard was his ready acceptance in 1938 of a substantial sum from the mayor's office of Munich to write incidental music for Shakespeare's *Midsummer Night's Dream* to replace Mendelssohn's, which had been banned in Nazi Germany because its composer had been a Jew by birth.[32]

Despite its somewhat dubious political background, Orff's *Carmina Burana* remains to this day one of the most popular items in the classical musical repertoire.[33] In fact, in 2009 its opening song *O Fortuna* topped a list of the "most played" classical pieces in the United Kingdom over the preceding seventy-five years.[34] Websites on *Carl Orff's O For-*

tuna in Popular Culture list the astonishing number of films, television shows, and commercials that have featured the song and the many bands that have covered it.

TRANSLATION

The prose translation has often been written in short lines to facilitate comparison with the Latin text on the facing page. The varying degree of formality or informality is intended to reflect the perceived tone of the Latin. Latin stage directions were normally given in the subjunctive ("Let Hamlet exit left"). To comply with normal English practice these subjunctives have been rendered by indicatives.

In closing, I would like to express my thanks to the many people who made this edition possible. First of all, I am indebted to Alfons Hilka, Otto Schumann, and Bernhard Bischoff, who produced the standard edition, and to the late Benedikt Konrad Vollmann, whose excellent edition was the first to include a commentary on all the poems. Another major figure who helped me better understand some of these difficult poems was the late P. G. Walsh. I would also like to thank Jan Ziolkowski for inviting me to do an edition of the *Carmina Burana* for the Dumbarton Oaks Medieval Library and for persuading me to include all the pieces and not just the love poems. I am most grateful too to Danuta Shanzer, the editor of the Latin series, and to Raquel Begleiter of DOML. I am especially thankful to David Townsend, Winthrop Wetherbee, Danuta Shanzer, and Peter Stotz for spending many hours reading over earlier versions of this book and saving me from numerous embarrassing errors, and to James Schultz, who not merely normalized the orthography of the Middle High German[35] but also composed his own elegant translations. I also appreciate his having supplied brief accounts of the German authors (above).

At the University of California at Davis I would like to thank the Research Committee, Ralph Hexter (our provost), and Jessie Ann Owens (until recently Dean of Humanities, Arts and Cultural Studies, for research support); my current and former Program Directors, Rex Stem and Emily Albu, for negotiating office space for me; all of my colleagues in Classics for their friendship and moral support; Lester Stephens, for entering the Latin text; and, last but not least, our wonderful IT group, Anthony Drown, Ryan Sokol, and Ross Norton.

Notes

1 Waddell's *The Wandering Scholars* (1927), which was intended to set out the cultural background for *Medieval Latin Lyrics,* proved immensely popular with the general public. Seven editions were printed between 1927 and 1934, and by 1949 there were seven reprints of the seventh edition. The success of *The Wandering Scholars* created a large audience ready for *Medieval Latin Lyrics.*

2 Dronke, "Latin Songs," 25–26, and his article cited there (note 1).

3 Bischoff, *Carmina Burana, Facsimile,* 30.

4 See Steer, *"Carmina Burana* in Südtirol," 34–37.

5 Sayce, *Plurilingualism,* 202.

6 The monastery is only about three kilometers from the cathedral.

7 Poems 1* to 6* were added in spaces left between the earlier poems. CB 7* to 26* were inscribed in the manuscript's six remaining blank folios (107–12) and in an additional seven separate leaves (I–VII), which became separated from the rest and whose significance was first realized by Wilhelm Meyer, who published their contents as the *Fragmenta Burana* in 1901;

these additional leaves are also in the Bayerische Staatsbibliothek (shelf mark clm 4660a). For a detailed breakdown of exactly where each poem is located in the manuscript, see Bischoff, *Carmina Burana, Facsimile,* 38–40.

8 CB 1 is not the first poem of the original collection but rather the first poem of the surviving part of the collection. Only the second half of its last stanza survives in *B*. We do not know what else, besides the rest of CB 1, has been lost, though it is probable that there were more moral-satirical poems and perhaps even a whole section devoted to hymns.

9 This is a simplified version of the arrangement that does not take into account a few minor discrepancies; for poems 1* to 6* and more details on the manuscript, see note 5 above and Bischoff, *Carmina Burana, Facsimile,* 19–40.

10 On the grouping of the poems in Saint-Omer 351, see Walter of Châtillon, *Shorter Poems,* xxi. In Arundel 384 (British Library) a group of love poems (1–16) is followed by religious hymns (17–23) and moral-satirical poems (24–27); see McDonough, *Arundel Poems,* 2–139.

11 For the distinction between rhythmical and metrical verse, see the section on Meter, Rhythm, and Rhyme below.

12 I have combined Schumann's first two subgroups, because Schumann suggests *De Avaritia* (On Avarice) as an appropriate heading for both his section 1 (CB 1–2) and section 2 (CB 3–5).

13 Recent research by R. Schieffer and J. Fried (see bibliography) has identified him with one or other of the notaries of Rainald. Schieffer's view has won over Peter Godman, though Peter Dronke remains unconvinced. See Godman, "The Archpoet and the Emperor," 31, and Dronke, "Hugh Primas and the Archpoet," xx–xxi.

14 See Wollin, "Mutabilität," 329–413, esp. 372–405. It has long been noticed that the first four stanzas are identical to four stanzas in the Archpoet's ninth poem (ed., Watenphul and Krefeld), but the rest of the poem was not thought to be his.

15 See *Arundel Lyrics/Poems of Hugh Primas,* ed. McDonough.

16 For fuller accounts of the life of this Peter of Blois, see Cotts, *The Clerical Dilemma;* Southern, *Medieval Humanism,* 10–133, his *Scholastic Humanism,* 2.178–216, and his article in the *Oxford Dictionary of National Biography* (under "Blois, Peter of").

17 See his letter 76 (dated ca. 1195 by Southern): "Furthermore, you com-

pose everything you write with marvelous skill and with the most exquisite felicity of observation and word choice . . . Don't proclaim your ignominy publicly . . . It is the mark of a madman to write poems about illicit amours and to boast that he is the seducer of young women" (PL 207.234C and 233C).

18 On the second Peter of Blois, see also, Southern, "Two Peters," esp. 109–12, and his *Scholastic Humanism,* 2.178–216, esp. 179–82, 184, 191–92, 204–7; and Traill, "Walter of Châtillon's *In Domino confido,*" 858.

19 Wollin, "Troiagedichte."

20 On Philip, see further in Payne, "Philip the Chancellor," in the *New Grove Dictionary of Music and Musicians,* 2nd ed. (New York, 2001), and his *Philip the Chancellor: Motets and Prosulas.*

21 For more on Walter's life, see Walter of Châtillon, *Shorter Poems,* xi–xxi.

22 For a succinct overview of the German in the *Carmina Burana,* see Cyril Edwards's article in *Carmina Burana: Four Essays,* edited by Martin Jones, 41–70.

23 A detailed account of classical usage is to be found in Halporn, Ostwald, and Rosenmeyer, *The Meters of Greek and Latin Poetry.*

24 See Clemencic, Müller, and Korth, *Carmina Burana.* For a more specialized treatment of some of Philip the Chancellor's contributions, see Payne, *Philip the Chancellor.*

25 Willnauer, *Carmina Burana von Carl Orff,* 61.

26 The evolution of the cantata can be followed in their correspondence: see Orff and Hofmann, *Briefe zur Entstehung der Carmina Burana,* which also includes the text and translation used in the premiere production in 1937.

27 Schadewalt's Latin text and German translation are to be found at Willnauer, *Carmina Burana von Carl Orff,* 106–43.

28 Kater, *Composers of the Nazi Era,* 111–12; Willnauer, *Carmina Burana von Carl Orff,* 87–88.

29 Kater, *Composers of the Nazi Era,* 111 and 125.

30 Hausmann, *Das Fach,* 47–49, and Kater, *Composers of the Nazi Era,* 122–23, 127–28.

31 Kater, *Composers of the Nazi Era,* 119, and Hausmann, *Das Fach,* 50.

32 Kater, *Composers of the Nazi Era,* 125. This is somewhat mitigated by the

fact that he had already tried his hand at writing music for *Midsummer's Night Dream* in 1917.

33 Evidence of its popularity is clear from the fact that there are several much visited postings of performances of the complete cantata on YouTube; the University of California, Davis, performance tops the list with over fourteen million "hits," as of February 2016.

34 BBC News item, dated December 28, 2009. The list was compiled from royalties collection data related to public performance of the pieces.

35 See Note on the Text, 481.

ORIGINAL COLLECTION

1. Manus ferens munera
    pium facit impium.
    Nummus iungit foedera,
    nummus dat consilium,
5   nummus lenit aspera,
    nummus sedat proelium.
        Nummus in praelatis
        est pro iure satis.
        Nummo locum datis
10   vos, qui iudicatis.

2. Nummus ubi loquitur,
    fit iuris confusio;
    pauper retro pellitur,
    quem defendit ratio,
5   sed dives attrahitur
    pretiosus pretio.
        Hunc iudex adorat,
        facit, quod implorat.
        Pro quo nummus orat,
10   explet, quod laborat.

3. Nummus ubi praedicat,
    labitur iustitia;
    et causam, que claudicat,
    rectam facit curia.

1. The hand that offers gifts
    makes a pious man impious.
    Money seals treaties,
    money gives advice,
    money smooths over rough spots,   5
    money stops a battle.
        When it comes to prelates,
        money is as good as the law on your side.
        And you who are judges,
        you make way before money.   10

2. When money talks,
    what is right becomes blurred.
    The poor man, whom common sense defends,
    is pushed to the rear,
    whereas the rich man is advanced,   5
    made precious for a price.
        The judge adores him
        and does what he asks.
        When money pleads for a man,
        it accomplishes what he strives for.   10

3. When money makes its plea,
    justice falls to the ground;
    a case that is shaky
    the court finds solid and upright.

3

5   Pauperem diiudicat
veniens pecunia.
    Sic diiudicatur,
    a quo nihil datur;
    iure sic privatur,
10   si nil offeratur.

4.   Sunt potentum digiti
trahentes pecuniam.
Tali praeda praediti
non dant gratis gratiam,
5   sed licet illiciti
censum censent veniam.
    Clericis non morum
    cura, sed nummorum;
    quorum nescit chorum
10   chorus angelorum.

5.   "Date, vobis dabitur"—
talis est auctoritas.
Danti pie loquitur
impiorum pietas,
5   sed adverse premitur
pauperum adversitas.
    Quo vult, ducit frena,
    cuius bursa plena.
    Sancta dat crumena;
10   sancta fit amoena.

6.   Haec est causa curiae,
quam daturus perficit.
Defectu pecuniae

4

When money comes into play,   5
it condemns the poor man.
 This is the way the man who gives nothing
 is condemned;
 he loses his rights
 if he has nothing to offer.   10

4. The fingers of the powerful
 are raking in the money.
 Enriched by this kind of booty,
 they don't grant favors for free,
 but rather assess pardon illicitly   5
 on the basis of wealth.
  The concern of clerics is not for morals
  but money;
  their entire community
  is to the community of angels quite unknown.   10

5. "Give and it will be given unto you" —
 so goes the biblical passage.
 The kindness of impious men
 speaks well for the donor,
 while the adversity of the poor   5
 is made more crushing.
  The man whose purse is full
  steers with its reins where he wants to go.
  His purse confers sacred promises;
  since it brings delight, it becomes holy.   10

6. The case the court finds for is the one
 wrapped up by the man who is ready to give.
 Codrus loses his case

causa Codri deficit.
5   Tale foedus hodie
defoedat et inficit
      nostros "ablativos,"
      qui absorbent vivos,
      moti per "dativos"
10   movent "genitivos."

2

Versus

"Responde, qui tanta cupis," mihi Copia dicit,
"Pone modum; que vis, addo." "Volo plena sit arca."
"Plena sit." "Adde duas." "Addo." "Si quattuor essent,
sufficeret." "Sic semper ais; cum plurima dono,
5 plus quaeris, nec plenus eris, donec morieris."

3

1.   Ecce! Torpet probitas,   virtus sepelitur,
fit iam parca largitas   parcitas largitur,

from lack of money.
Such is the pact 5
that today defiles and infects
   our "ablatival" men,
   who swallow people alive,
   and, prompted by the "dative" men,
   perform "genitival" acts. 10

2

Metrical Verses

"Tell me, you who want so much," Abundance said to me, "how much you need; I'll give you what you want." "I want my strongbox full." "Full let it be!" "Just two more!" "All right." "If there were four more, that would be enough." "That's what you always say. When I give you a lot, you ask for more—you will never be satisfied until you die." 5

3

1.   See! Integrity is fast asleep, virtue dead and buried, openhandedness in short supply, and tightfistedness

verum dicit falsitas,   veritas mentitur.
Ref. Omnes iura laedunt
5   et ad res illicitas   licite procedunt.

2.   Regnat avaritia,   regnant et avari;
mente quivis anxia   nititur ditari,
cum sit summa gloria   censu gloriari.
Ref. Omnes iura laedunt
5   et ad prava quaelibet   impie recedunt.

3.   Multum habet oneris   "do das dedi dare."
Verbum hoc prae ceteris   norunt ignorare
divites, quos poteris   mari comparare.
Ref. Omnes iura laedunt
5   et in rerum numeris   numeros excedunt.

4.   Cunctis est aequaliter   insita cupido.
Perit fides turpiter,   nullus fidus fido,
nec Iunoni Iupiter   nec Aeneae Dido.
Ref. Omnes iura laedunt
5   et ad mala devia   licite recedunt.

5.   Si recte discernere   velis, non est vita,
quod sic vivit temere   gens hec imperita;
non est enim vivere   si quis vivit ita.
Ref. Omnes iura laedunt
5   et fidem in opere   quolibet excedunt.

lavished round about, Falsehood speaks the truth and
Truth is telling lies.
Ref. Everyone mistreats the law
　　and legally resorts to criminal activity.　　　　　　5

2.　Greed reigns supreme and the greedy are in power.
　　Everyone is striving anxiously to enrich himself,
　　for the highest honor is to take pride in one's wealth.
　　Ref. Everyone mistreats the law
　　　　and impiously resorts to every kind of wrong.　　5

3.　Conjugating "to give" is extremely burdensome.
　　The rich, whom you can compare to the sea,
　　know how not to know this verb beyond all the rest.
　　Ref. Everyone mistreats the law
　　　　and in the number of possessions they surpass all　5
　　　　counting.

4.　Avarice is equally ingrained in everyone.
　　Trust is in shameful decline; no one is faithful to his
　　　　faithful comrade,
　　not Jupiter to Juno, not Dido to Aeneas.
　　Ref. Everyone mistreats the law
　　　　and legally resorts to devious schemes.　　　　　5

5.　If you wish to know the truth, it is not life
　　that these untutored people live brazenly in this way,
　　for it is not living if one lives like that.
　　Ref. Everyone mistreats the law
　　　　and breaks faith in every undertaking.　　　　　5

4

1. Amaris stupens casibus
        vox exultationis
    organa in salicibus
        suspendit Babylonis.
5   Captiva est Confusionis
        involuta doloribus,
    Sion cantica laeta sonis
        permutavit flebilibus.

2. Propter scelus perfidiae,
        quo mundus inquinatur,
    fluctuantis ecclesiae
        sic status naufragatur.
5   Gratia prostat et scortatur
        foro venalis curiae;
    iuris libertas ancillatur
        obsecundans pecuniae.

3. Hypocrisis, fraus pullulat
        et menda falsitatis,
    quae titulum detitulat
        vere simplicitatis.
5   Frigescit ignis caritatis,
        fides a cunctis exulat,
    aculeus cupiditatis
        quos mordet atque stimulat.

4

1.   Aghast at bitter misfortunes,
the voice of joy
hung its instruments
on the willows of Babylon.
As a captive of the "City of Confusion,"   5
Zion, shrouded in grief,
changed its joyful songs
to lamentations.

2.   Thanks to the crime of perfidy,
which stains the world,
the Church, storm-tossed,
is suffering shipwreck.
Grace prostitutes and whores itself   5
in the venal curia's marketplace.
The law's independence now does service,
working at the behest of money.

3.   Fraud and hypocrisy are spreading,
as is dishonesty's lying
which undoes any claim
to simple truth.
The fire of charity grows chill;   5
trustworthiness is not to be found
in any who have been stung and goaded
by the sting of greed.

5

Versus

1. Flete   perhorrete   lugete   pavete   dolete
   flenda   perhorrenda   lugenda   pavenda   dolenda.

2. Aetates   anni   vitium   peccata   tyranni
   Currunt   labuntur   remanet   crescunt   statuuntur.

3. Virtus   ecclesia   clerus   Mammon   simonia
   cessat   calcatur   ambit   regnat   dominatur.

4. Pontifices reges   proceres   sacraria   leges
   errant   turbantur   turbant   sordent   violantur.

5. Abbas   possessa   praebendam contio   fessa
   inflatur   vastat   minuit   declamitat   astat.

6. Militibus   laude   monachos   mundalia   fraude
   gaudet   inescatur   horret   colit   insidiatur.

7. Subiecti   stulti   gnari   contemptus   inulti
   dissiliunt gaudent   maerent   attollitur   audent.

8. Ordo   pudicitia   pietas   doctrina   sophia
   languet   sordescit   refugit   rarescit   hebescit.

9. Insons   pupillus   humilis   viduata   pusillus
   plectitur   artatur   teritur   premitur   spoliatur.

10. Ingenuus   servus   parasitus   scurra   protervus
    servit   honoratur   tonat   imperitat   dominatur.

5

Metrical Verses

1. Lament for the lamentable	feel terror at the terrifying	grieve for the grievous	fear what is fearful	feel pain for the painful.
2. Lives go by at a run	years glide by	vice stays put	sins increase	tyrants set themselves up.
3. Virtue is dwindling	the church is trampled	the clergy is self-seeking	Mammon is king	simony holds sway.
4. Bishops go astray	kings are troubled	magnates cause trouble	sacred objects are uncared for	laws are violated.
5. The abbot is puffed up	he ruins abbey lands	he reduces the benefices	the community complains	but wearily stands by.
6. He delights in knights	he feeds on praise	he shudders at monks	he worships the secular world	he is a slippery schemer.
7. Monks are quitting	fools are happy	the intelligent are sorrowful	the despised are promoted	the unpunished dare more.
8. The order languishes	morality is sullied	piety is disappearing	learning is becoming rarer	wisdom is losing its edge.
9. The innocent are suffering	orphans are locked up	the humble crushed	widows abused	children robbed.
10. The free are enslaved	slaves are honored	parasites thunder forth	fops issue orders	the impudent are in charge.

11. Helluo praestat	periurus ditatur	raptor viget	fallax excellit	Epicurus decoratur.
12. Deliciae Enervant	fastus turget	inimicitiae exercentur	tumor furit	astus urget.
13. Blandi- menta suadent	minae adduntur	rabies saevit	usura tractatur	rapinae aguntur.
14. Idcirco caedimur	pesti incidimus	detrimentum patimur	grave languescimus	maesti imus.
15. Aër tabet	languores adaugentur	incendia consumunt	mucro saevit	timores habentur.
16. Aurum fallit	censores falluntur	pravi praesunt	iusti desunt	meliores rapiuntur.
17. Giraldus praefuit	mores ornavit	deflendus ruit	ovile orbavit	dolores cumulavit.
18. Omnipotens Audi	poenis tollatur	hostis fugiat	paradisus pateat	amoenis foveatur.

6

1. Florebat olim studium,
   nunc vertitur in taedium;
   iam scire diu viguit,
   sed ludere praevaluit.

2. Iam pueris astutia
   contingit ante tempora,

11. Gluttons are to the fore	perjurers are enriched	robbers do well	cheats thrive	epicures receive honors.
12. High living saps strength	pride swells	enmity is all around	anger seethes	cunning is a constant threat.
13. Flattery is doing its work	threats follow	a wild madness rages	usury is being practiced	pillaging is rampant.
14. So we are being cut down	attacked by a pestilence	suffering attrition	gravely sick	sadly we go on our way.
15. The air is foul	diseases are on the increase	fires are causing destruction	swords flash angrily	fear is everywhere.
16. Gold corrupts	officials are deceived	the wicked are in charge	good men are lacking	the best men are seized.
17. Gerald was in charge	a model of virtue	lamentably he has met his end	bereaving his fold	adding to our sorrows.
18. Hear me, Almighty,	spare him punishment	may the devil flee from him	may paradise be open to him	may they cosset him in bliss.

6

1. Once learning was in vogue
    but now it's a bore;
    for a long time knowledge flourished
    but now gambling has gained the upper hand.

2. Now boys become smart
    before their time

qui per malevolentiam
excludunt sapientiam.

3. Sed retroactis saeculis
vix licuit discipulis
tandem nonagenarium
quiescere post studium.

4. At nunc decennes pueri
decusso iugo liberi
se nunc magistros iactitant;
caeci caecos praecipitant.

5. Implumes aves volitant,
brunelli chordas incitant,
boves in aula salitant,
stivae praecones militant.

6. In taberna Gregorius
iam disputat inglorius,
severitas Hieronimi
partem causatur oboli.

7. Augustinus de segete,
Benedictus de vegete
sunt colloquentes clanculo
et ad macellum sedulo.

8. Mariam gravat sessio
nec Marthae placet actio,
iam Liae venter sterilis,
Rachel lippescit oculis.

but their malevolence leaves them
no room for wisdom.

3.   But in times gone by
students could scarcely
take a rest even after
ninety years of study.

4.   But today ten-year-old boys
shake free from the yoke
and boast that they now are teachers;
the blind lead the blind over the cliff.

5.   Featherless fledglings try to fly,
asses try to strike up the lyre,
oxen try to dance at court
and plowshare loudmouths try to serve as knights.

6.   In the tavern an inglorious Gregory
holds forth in disputation,
while a stern Jerome
sues for a fraction of an obol.

7.   An Augustine discusses grain crops
and a Benedict vegetables,
as they talk together privately
and earnestly at the meat market.

8.   Remaining seated weighs heavily on Mary,
whereas Martha does not like activity.
Leah's womb is now sterile
and Rachel's eyes are clouded.

9.   Catonis iam rigiditas
convertitur ad ganeas
et castitas Lucretiae
turpi servit lasciviae.

10.   Quod prior aetas respuit
iam nunc clarius claruit.
Iam calidum in frigidum
et humidum in aridum,

11.   virtus migrat in vitium,
opus transit in otium.
Nunc cunctae res debita
exorbitant a semita.

12.   Vir prudens hoc consideret.
Cor mundet et exoneret
ne frustra dicat "Domine!"
in ultimo examine.
5   Quem iudex tunc arguerit,
appellare non poterit.

7

Versus

1.   Postquam nobilitas servilia coepit amare,
coepit nobilitas cum servis degenerare.

9.   Strict old Cato
     is turning to prostitutes
     and chaste Lucretia
     is a slave to shameful lasciviousness.

10. What an earlier age rejected
     is now highly regarded.
     Hot has now become cold,
     wet has become dry.

11. Virtue is turning into vice,
     and work into leisure.
     Nowadays everything strays
     from its appointed path.

12. The prudent man should reflect on this.
     He should cleanse and unburden his heart
     so that he does not say "My Lord!" in vain
     at the Last Judgment.
     No one on whom the judge then passes judgment   5
     will have recourse to appeal.

7

Metrical Verses

1.   When the nobility began to love servile things,
     it began to lower itself to the level of slaves.

2. Nobilitas quam non probitas regit atque tuetur,
    lapsa iacet, nullique placet, quia nulla videtur.

3. Nobilitas hominis mens et deitatis imago.
    Nobilitas hominis virtutum clara propago.
    Nobilitas hominis mentem frenare furentem.
    Nobilitas hominis humilem relevare iacentem.
5   Nobilitas hominis naturae iura tenere.
    Nobilitas hominis, nisi turpia, nulla timere.

4. Nobilis est ille quem virtus nobilitavit.
    Degener est ille quem virtus nulla beavit.

8

1. Licet aeger cum aegrotis,
    et ignotus cum ignotis,
    fungar tamen vice cotis,
    ius usurpans sacerdotis.
5   Flete, Sion filiae!
            Praesides ecclesiae
            imitantur hodie
                Christum a remotis.

2. Si privata degens vita
    vel sacerdos vel levita
    sibi dari vult petita,
    hac incedit via trita:
5   praevia fit pactio

2. Nobility that is not ruled and guarded by rectitude
    slips and lies unappreciated, because it seems ignoble.

3. Man's nobility lies in his mind and in God's image.
    Man's nobility is the brilliant progeny of his virtues.
    Man's nobility consists in restraining rage.
    Man's nobility consists in raising up the lowly.
    Man's nobility consists in observing the laws of nature.   5
    Man's nobility consists in fearing nothing but disgrace.

4. That man is noble whom virtue has ennobled.
    That man is base whom no virtue has blessed.

8

1. Though sick among the sick
    and a nobody among nobodies,
    I will nevertheless perform the role of whetstone,
    assuming the function of a priest.
        Weep, daughters of Zion!   5
        The leaders of the church
        follow Christ today
            from a long way off.

2. If a priest or deacon
    who lacks a benefice
    wants to get what he has asked for,
    this is the well-worn path he treads:
        first a deal is made   5

      Simonis officio,
      cui succedit datio,
          et sic fit Giezita.

3.   Iacet ordo clericalis
     in respectu laicalis.
     Sponsa Christi fit mercalis,
     —generosa, generalis.
5   Veneunt altaria,
        venit Eucharistia,
        cum sit nugatoria
           gratia venalis.

4.   Donum Dei non donatur,
     nisi gratis conferatur.
     Quod qui vendit vel mercatur,
     lepra Syri vulneratur.
5   Quem sic ambit ambitus,
        idolorum servitus,
        templo sancti spiritus
          non conpaginatur.

5.   Si quis tenet hunc tenorem,
     frustra dicit se pastorem;
     nec se regit ut rectorem
     renum mersus in ardorem.
5   Haec est enim alia
        sanguisugae filia,
        quam venalis curia
          duxit in uxorem.

under Simon's auspices;
   then comes the payment;
      and that's how a Gehazi is created.

3.   In the eyes of the laity
   the clergy lie prostrate.
   The bride of Christ is on the market
   —once noble, now notorious.
      For sale are altar fees,   5
      for sale the Eucharist,
      though grace that is for sale
         is worthless.

4.   God's gift is not bestowed
   unless it is conferred for free.
   Whoever sells or trades it
   is afflicted by the Syrian's leprosy.
      A man so hemmed in by greed   5
      and idol worship
      is not built to be a temple
         of the Holy Spirit.

5.   Anyone who sticks to this path
   claims in vain to be a pastor;
   nor does that man control himself like a moral guide
   who is plunged in the hot throes of lust.
      This is the other   5
      daughter of the leech
      that the venal curia
         has taken as a wife.

6.　In diebus iuventutis
　　　timent annum senectutis,
　　　ne fortuna destitutis
　　　desit eis splendor cutis;
5　　　　　et dum quaerunt medium,
　　　　　vergunt in contrarium,
　　　　　fallit enim vitium
　　　　　　　specie virtutis.

7.　Ut iam loquar inamoenum,
　　　sanctum chrisma datur venum,
　　　iuvenantur corda senum
　　　nec refrenant motus renum.
5　　　　　Senes et decrepiti,
　　　　　quasi modo geniti,
　　　　　nectaris illiciti
　　　　　　　hauriunt venenum.

8.　Ergo nemo vivit purus,
　　　castitatis perit murus,
　　　commendatur Epicurus,
　　　nec spectatur moriturus.
5　　　　　Grata sunt convivia;
　　　　　auro uel pecunia
　　　　　cuncta facit pervia
　　　　　　　pontifex futurus.

6.   In the days of their youth
        they fear the years of old age,
        anxious that fortune might abandon them
        and the sheen go off their skin;
               in seeking a middle course,   5
               they head for the opposite extreme,
               for vice sneaks in
                      under the guise of virtue.

7.   To tell you now an unpleasant truth,
        holy unction is up for sale.
        Old men's hearts are becoming young again
        and putting no restraint on their lustful urges.
               Like newborn babes,   5
               the old and decrepit
               are gulping down the venom
                      of forbidden nectar.

8.   So no one is living a pure life.
        Gone is the wall of chastity.
        Today's Epicurus wins praise
        and no one sees that he is doomed to die.
               Banquets earn favor.   5
               With gold or cash
               the bishop-to-be
                      makes everything possible.

9

1.   Iudas gehennam meruit,
   quod Christum semel vendidit.
   Vos autem mihi dicite,
   qui septies cotidie
5. corpus vendunt dominicum,
   quod superest supplicium?

2.   Perpendite subtiliter:
   cum vendant dissimiliter
   et peccent in alterutrum,
   sumendo plus vel modicum,
5. quod anhelant ad munera,
   finis est avaritia.

3.   Petrus damnato Simone
   gravi sub anathemate
   docuit, ut fidelibus
   non esset locus amplius
5. in donis spiritalibus
   ipsorum venditoribus.

4.   Multi nunc damnant Simonem
   Magum magis quam demonem.
   Heredes autem Simonis
   suis fovent blanditiis.
5. Simon nondum est mortuus
   sed vivit in heredibus.

9

1.   Judas deserved to go to hell
   because he sold Christ once.
   Tell me now—those people
   who sell the Lord's body
   seven times a day,   5
   what punishment is in store for them?

2.   Consider carefully:
   although they differ one from the other
   in their selling and their sinning,
   some taking more, others just a little,
   given that they are eager for payment,   5
   the end result is avarice.

3.   By condemning Simon
   with a heavy curse,
   Peter showed that the faithful,
   in the matter of spiritual gifts,
   should have no place any longer
   for those who sell them.   5

4.   Many now condemn Simon the Magician
   more vehemently than the devil.
   Yet with flattering words
   they foster Simon's heirs.
   Simon is not yet dead   5
   but rather lives through his heirs.

5.   Quamvis cogente Abraham
Ephron sumens pecuniam
agrum sepulchro tribuit,
Ephran vocari meruit.
5   Sic Ephranitas diceres
multos postea similes.

10

1.   Ecce, sonat in aperto
vox clamantis in deserto:

2.   "Nos desertum, nos deserti,
nos de poena sumus certi.
Nullus fere vitam quaerit
et sic omne vivens perit.

3.   Omnes quidem sumus rei.
Nullus imitator Dei,
nullus vult portare crucem,
nullus Christum sequi ducem.

4.   Quis est verax? quis est bonus?
vel quis Dei portat onus?
Ut in uno claudam plura,
Mors extendit sua iura.

5.   Iam Mors regnat in praelatis.
Nolunt sanctum dare gratis,
quod promittunt sub ingressu
sanctae mentis in excessu.

5.   Although it was at Abraham's insistence
     that Ephron took money
     when he sold a field for a burial place,
     he deserved to be called Ephran.
     Accordingly, you can call Ephranites   5
     many who have later proved similar.

IO

1.   Listen! It resonates in the open air—
     the voice of one crying in the wilderness

2.   "We are the desert; we are the deserted;
     we are certain of the penalty we will pay.
     Practically no one seeks Life
     and so every living creature perishes.

3.   We are all guilty.
     No one is a devoted follower of Christ,
     no one wishes to carry his cross,
     no one wants to follow Christ as their guide.

4.   Who is truthful, who is good?
     Or who is carrying Christ's burden?
     To summarize briefly—
     Death is extending his domain.

5.   Death now reigns among the prelates;
     they refuse to give the sacraments for free,
     as they promised to do at the outset
     in a rapture of piety.

6.   Postquam sedent iam securi,
       contradicunt sancto iuri;
       rosae fiunt saliunca,
       domus Dei fit spelunca.

7.   Sunt latrones, non latores
       legis Dei destructores.
       Simon sedens inter eos,
       dat magnates esse reos.

8.   Simon praefert malos bonis,
       Simon totus est in donis,
       Simon regnat apud Austrum,
       Simon frangit omne claustrum.

9.   Cum non datur, Simon stridet,
       sed, si datur, Simon ridet,
       Simon aufert, Simon donat,
       hunc expellit, hunc coronat.

10.   Hunc circumdat gravi peste,
       illum nuptiali veste,
       illi donat diadema,
       qui nunc erat anathema.

11.   Iam se Simon non abscondit;
       res permiscet et confundit.
       Iste Simon confundatur,
       cui tantum posse datur.

12.   Simon Petrus hunc elusit
       et ab alto iusum trusit.
       Dum superbit motus penna,
       datus fuit in gehenna.

6.   Once securely ensconced in their sees,
     they contradict divine law,
     roses become gorse
     and the house of God becomes a den of thieves.

7.   They are thieves, not donors,
     demolishers of God's law.
     When Simon sits among them,
     he makes the magnates sinners.

8.   Simon prefers evil men to good,
     Simon is wholly focused on gifts.
     Simon holds sway like the king of the south.
     Simon breaks every lock.

9.   When no gift is given him, Simon yells.
     But if he is given a gift, Simon smiles.
     Simon takes away and Simon bestows;
     one man he drives out, another he crowns.

10. One man he besets with a devastating disease,
     another he clothes in a wedding suit.
     To another, recently cursed,
     he gives a diadem.

11. Now Simon is no longer in hiding,
     he upsets things and throws them into confusion.
     Let this Simon be confounded,
     to whom so much power is given!

12. Simon Peter outwitted Simon Magus
     and brought him down from his place on high.
     While he prided himself on flying,
     he was cast down into hell.

13. Quisquis eum imitatur,
     cum eodem puniatur
     et sepultus in infernum
     poenas luat in aeternum!"

II

Versus de Nummo

In terra Nummus   rex est hoc tempore summus.
Nummum mirantur   reges et ei famulantur.
Nummo venalis   favet ordo pontificalis.
Nummus in abbatum   cameris retinet dominatum.
5 Nummum nigrorum   veneratur turba priorum.
Nummus magnorum   fit iudex conciliorum.
Nummus bella gerit   nec si vult, pax sibi deerit.
Nummus agit lites,   quia vult deponere dites.
Erigit ad plenum   de stercore Nummus egenum.
10 Omnia Nummus emit   venditque, dat et data demit.
Nummus adulatur,   Nummus post blanda minatur.
Nummus mentitur,   Nummus verax reperitur.
Nummus periuros   miseros facit et perituros.

13. May anyone who seeks to imitate him
     be punished in the same manner!
     May he be buried in hell
     and pay for his crime for all eternity!"

II

Metrical Verses about Money

The mightiest king on earth today is Money.
Kings admire Money and are slaves to it.
Money is what the venal order of bishops favors.
Money is the master in abbots' treasuries.
Money is what the crowd of black priors venerates.   5
Money is the judge at the great councils.
Money wages war and if it so chooses, it will make peace.
Money files lawsuits because it wants to bring down the
     rich.
Money lifts the poor man from the dunghill and brings him
     to plenty.
Money buys and sells everything; it gives and takes back   10
     what it has given.
Money flatters and after the sweet talk uses threats.
Money lies but Money is found to be telling the truth.
Money makes perjurers out of the unhappy and those about
     to die.

Nummus avarorum   deus est et spes cupidorum.

15 Nummus in errorem   mulierum ducit amorem.

Nummus venales   dominas facit imperiales.

Nummus raptores   facit ipsos nobiliores.

Nummus habet plures   quam caelum sidera fures.

Si Nummus placitat,   cito cuncta pericula vitat.

20 Si Nummus vicit,   dominus cum iudice dicit:

"Nummus ludebat,   agnum niveum capiebat."

Nummus, rex magnus,   dixit: "Niger est meus agnus."

Nummus fautores   habet astantes seniores.

Si Nummus loquitur,   pauper tacet; hoc bene scitur.

25 Nummus maerores   reprimit relevatque labores.

Nummus corda necat   sapientum, lumina caecat.

Nummus, ut est certum,   stultum docet esse disertum.

Nummus habet medicos,   fictos acquirit amicos.

In Nummi mensa   sunt splendida fercula densa.

30 Nummus laudatos   pisces comedit piperatos.

Francorum vinum   Nummus bibit atque marinum.

Nummus famosas   vestes gerit et pretiosas.

Nummo splendorem   dant vestes exteriorem.

Nummus eos gestat   lapides, quos India praestat.

35 Nummus dulce putat,   quod eum gens tota salutat.

Nummus et invadit   et quae vult oppida tradit.

Nummus adoratur,   quia virtutes operatur:

hic aegros sanat,   secat, urit, et aspera planat.

Vile facit carum,   quod dulce est, reddit amarum

40 et facit audire   surdum claudumque salire.

De Nummo   quaedam maiora prioribus edam:

Money is the god of misers and the hope of the greedy.
Money leads women's love down the wrong path.   15
Money makes prostitutes out of emperors' wives.
Money makes even nobles robbers.
Money has more thieves than the sky has stars.
If Money goes to trial, it quickly bypasses all dangers.
If Money wins, the master says along with the judge: 20
"Money played and took a snow-white lamb."
Money, the mighty king, said: "My lamb is black."
Money has its supporters, the older men standing by.
If Money talks, the poor man falls silent; this is well known.
Money checks sorrow and eliminates and relieves toil.   25
Money kills the hearts of wise men and blinds their eyes.
Money, it is certain, teaches a stupid man how to be
    eloquent.
Money has doctors and acquires feigned friends.
On Money's table the dishes are wonderful and abundant.
Money eats prized fish spiced with pepper.   30
Money drinks French and imported wine.
Money wears fabulous, expensive clothes.
With Money's help clothes provide a splendid appearance.
Money makes a show of the gems that India provides.
Money finds it gratifying that the whole world respects it.   35
Money enters and hands over any towns it wants.
Money is highly regarded because it does good things:
it heals the sick, cuts, burns, or smooths rough bits;
it makes attractive what is ugly or makes disagreeable what
    is pleasant;
it makes the deaf hear and the lame leap.   40
I will now point out some more important things about
    Money:

vidi cantantem   Nummum, missam celebrantem;
Nummus cantabat,   Nummus responsa parabat;
vidi quod flebat,   dum sermonem faciebat
45 et subridebat,   populum quia decipiebat.
Nullus honoratur   sine Nummo, nullus amatur.
Quem genus infamat,   Nummus: "Probus est homo!"
    clamat.
Ecce patet cuique,   quod Nummus regnat ubique,
sed quia consumi   poterit cito gloria Nummi,
50 ex hac esse schola   non vult Sapientia sola.

12

1.   Procurans odium   effectu proprio
     vix detrahentium   gaudet intentio.
     Nexus est cordium   ipsa detractio.
     Sic per contrarium   ab hoste nescio
5   fit hic provisio.
     In hoc amantium   felix conditio.

2.   Insultus talium   prodesse sentio.
     Tollendi taedium   fulsit occasio.
     Suspendunt gaudium   pravo consilio;
     sed desiderium   auget dilatio.
5   Tali remedio
     de spinis hostium   uvas vindemio.

I have seen Money singing and celebrating mass.
Money was singing, Money was preparing the responses.
I have seen it weeping while it was giving a sermon
and smiling because it was deceiving the people.   45
No one without Money is honored or loved.
If a man's lineage confers infamy, Money shouts, "He's an
    upright man!"
See! It is clear to everyone that Money is king everywhere,
but because Money's glory can quickly be used up,
Wisdom alone refuses to be a member of that school.   50

12

1. Though the goal of detractors is to produce contempt
    they can hardly rejoice when they actually bring this
        about.
    The very act of maligning creates a bonding of hearts.
    So it is that, contrarily, there comes assistance
                            from the unwitting enemy.   5
    The happiness of lovers is dependent on this truth.

2. I believe that the quarrels of lovers are beneficial.
    An opportunity for dispelling monotony flashes like
        lightning.
    Evil counsel brings a lull to their joy;
    but the interlude enhances their longing for one
        another.
                            By the same token,   5
    I harvest grapes from the thorns of my enemies.

13

Versus

1. Invidus invidia comburitur intus et extra.

2. Invidus alterius rebus macrescit opimis.
   Invidia Siculi non invenere tyranni
   maius tormentum. Qui non moderabitur irae,
   infectum volet esse, dolor quod suaserit aut mens.

3. Invidiosus ego, non invidus esse laboro.

4. Iustius invidia nihil est, quae protinus ipsos
   corripit auctores excruciatque suos.

5. Invidiam nimio cultu vitare memento.

14

1. O varium
Fortunae lubricum,
   dans dubium
tribunal iudicum,
   non modicum
paras huic praemium,
   quem colere

5

13

Metrical Verses

1. The envious man burns inside and out with envy.

2. Another's good fortune withers the envious man.
   Sicilian tyrants devised no greater torture than envy.
   He who does not control his anger will want
   undone what his pain or passion made him do.

3. I strive to be an object of envy rather than envious.

4. There is no greater justice than envy, for it immediately
   upbraids its own practitioners and tortures them.

5. Remember to avoid envy with exceptional diligence.

14

1. Ah, the slippery fickleness
   of Fortune!
   You create an unpredictable
   tribunal of judges
   and make ready a huge reward   5
   for the person
   you wish to cultivate

tua vult gratia,
    et petere
10 rotae sublimia,
    dans dubia
tamen, praepostere
    de stercore
pauperem erigens,
15   de rhetore
consulem eligens.

   2. Aedificat
Fortuna, diruit.
    Nunc abdicat,
quos prius coluit,
5   quos noluit,
iterum vindicat,
    hac opera
sibi contraria
    dans munera
10 nimis labilia.
    Mobilia
sunt Sortis foedera,
    quae debiles
ditans nobilitat
15   et nobiles
premens debilitat.

   3. Quid Dario
regnasse profuit?
    Pompeio
quid Roma tribuit?
5   Succubuit

with your favor
and would have climb
to the top of the wheel. 10
However, you cause instability
by preposterously
raising a poor man
from the dunghill
and picking a rhetorician 15
as consul.

2. Fortune builds up
and tears down.
She now abjures
those she earlier cultivated,
while those she once rejected 5
she champions again,
bestowing
by this contradictory behavior
gifts
that are far from certain. 10
The arrangements that Fortune makes
are in a state of flux,
for she enriches the weak
and makes them nobility
and oppresses the nobles 15
and makes them weak.

3. Of what use was it to Darius
that he had once been king?
What did control of Rome
bring Pompey?
Both succumbed 5

uterque gladio.
    Eligere
media tutius,
    quam petere
10 rotae sublimius,
    et gravius
a summo ruere.
    Fit gravior
lapsus a prosperis
15   et durior
ab ipsis asperis.

    4. Subsidio
Fortunae labilis
    cur proelio
Troia tunc nobilis,
5   nunc flebilis
ruit incendio?
    Quis sanguinis
Romani gratiam,
    quis nominis
10 Graeci facundiam,
    quis gloriam
fregit Carthaginis?
    Sors lubrica,
quae dedit, abstulit,
15   haec unica,
quae fovit, perculit.

    5. Nil gratius
Fortunae gratia,
    nil dulcius

42

to the sword.
It is safer to choose
a middle course
than to aim for
the high point of the wheel   10
and plummet
more heavily from the top.
The fall from prosperity
is heavier
and harsher   15
from its very bitterness.

4.   Why, with the help
of fickle Fortune,
did Troy, once noble
in battle,
now pitiable,   5
collapse in flames?
Who was it
who destroyed
the high regard
for Roman birth,   10
the Greeks' fame for eloquence,
or the glory of Carthage?
Slippery Fortune
and none other;
she gave and took away,   15
she cherished and she smote.

5.   Nothing would be more welcome
than the welcoming smile of Fortune,
nothing sweeter

est inter dulcia
5   quam gloria,
si staret longius,
  sed labitur
ut holus marcidum
  et sequitur
10 agrum nunc floridum,
  quem aridum
cras cernes. Igitur
  improprium
non edo canticum—
15   "o varium
Fortunae lubricum."

15

1. Caelum, non animum
   mutat stabilitas,
 firmans id optimum
   quod mentis firmitas
5 praebet cum animi
   tamen iudicio.
 Nam si turpissimi
   voti consilio
 vis scelus imprimi
10   facto nefario,
 debet haec perimi
   facta promissio.

among sweet things
than glory   5
if it stayed long with us,
but it fades away
like a wilted vegetable
and follows the example
of the field which now is blooming   10
but tomorrow
you will see parched.
So it is a fitting song
I sing—
"Oh the slippery fickleness   15
of Fortune!"

15

1.   Steadfastness changes the sky,
      but not the mind,
      when it confirms that the best
      is what a stout heart provides,
      yet with the soul's   5
      understanding.
      For if you agree that a crime
      abetted by a promise
      you most shamefully made
      is to be labeled a nefarious act,   10
      then this promise ought
      to be withdrawn.

2.   Non erat stabilis
      gradus, qui cecidit,
pes eius labilis
      domus quae corruit.
5   Hinc tu considera,
      quid agi censeas.
Dum res est libera,
      sic sta, ne iaceas.
Prius delibera,
10   quod factum subeas,
ne die postera
      sero paeniteas.

3.   Facti dimidium
      habet qui coeperit,
coeptum negotium
      si non omiserit,
5   non tantum deditus
      circa principia,
nedum sollicitus
      pro finis gloria.
Nam rerum exitus
10   librat industria,
subit introitus
      praeceps incuria.

4.   Coronat militem
      finis, non proelium;
dat hoc ancipitem
      metam, is bravium.
5   Iste quod tribuit
      dictat stabilitas;

2. The man who has fallen
    was not of firm footing
    and the foundation of the house
    that collapsed was insecure.
    Reflect, therefore,   5
    on what you think is to be done.
    While the situation is still fluid,
    adopt a position that will not lead to a fall.
    Consider beforehand
    what you are about to do   10
    to ensure that you don't regret it too late
    the following day.

3. The man who has begun
    has half of the work done
    provided he does not set aside
    the task undertaken,
    that is, if he is not so focused   5
    on the beginning
    that he is not concerned
    about the glory of the finish.
    It is hard work that determines
    the outcome of things,   10
    while reckless abandon
    approaches the entrance into them.

4. It is the end of the war, not a battle,
    that wins glory for the soldier;
    the battle provides the uncertain turning point;
    the finish of the war is the prize.
    What he contributes   5
    is determined by his steadfastness;

istud quod metuit
  inducit levitas.
Nam palmam annuit
10   mentis integritas,
quam dari respuit
  vaga mobilitas.

5. Mutat cum Proteo
      figuram levitas;
    assumit ideo
      formas incognitas.
5   Vultum constantia
      conservans intimum,
    alpha principia
      et o novissimum
    flectens fit media,
10   dat finem optimum,
    mutans invaria
      caelum non animum.

16

1. Fortunae plango vulnera   stillantibus ocellis,
    quod sua mihi munera   subtrahit rebellis.
    Verum est quod legitur: fronte capillata,
    sed plerumque sequitur   Occasio calvata.

a lack of resolve
brings on what he fears.
Singleness of purpose
earns the victory   10
which cannot be vouchsafed
by feckless wavering.

5.   Irresolution keeps changing
its outward appearance like Proteus;
so it takes on
unfamiliar shapes.
Steadfastness maintains   5
its inner countenance
and, as it works on the alpha beginnings
and the final omega,
it follows a moderate course
and achieves an excellent result,   10
while, itself unchanging, it alters
the sky overhead but not the mind within.

16

1.   I weep for the wounds Fortune has inflicted, my eyes
          brimming with tears,
     because she has turned against me and is taking from
          me the gifts she gave.
     It is true what we read: opportunity comes
     with long tresses in front, but is often bald at the back.

2.   In Fortunae solio   sederam elatus,
prosperitatis vario   flore coronatus.
Quicquid tamen florui   felix et beatus,
nunc a summo corrui   gloria privatus.

3.   Fortunae rota volvitur,   descendo minoratus.
Alter in altum tollitur   nimis exaltatus.
Rex sedet in vertice,   caveat ruinam!
nam sub axe conspice   Hecubam reginam!

17

1. O Fortuna,
velut luna
statu variabilis,
semper crescis
5   aut decrescis,
vita detestabilis.
Nunc obdurans
et tunc curans
ludo mentis aciem,
10   egestatem,
potestatem
dissolvis ut glaciem.

2. I sat on the throne of Fortune, beside myself with joy,
   crowned with the varied flowers of success.
   But for all that I flourished, rich and happy,
   now I have tumbled down from the top, stripped of
       my glory.

3. The wheel of Fortune keeps turning; down I go, my
       status diminished.
   Another is lifted up on high, supremely exalted.
   He sits as king at the very top—he should beware of
       his downfall!
   For look, beneath the axle—Queen Hecuba!

17

1. Oh, Fortune,
   like the moon
   that is constantly changing,
   you are always waxing
   or waning,   5
   despicable for your changeful nature.
   For your amusement you now harden,
   now soften
   the keen edge of your intentions,
   melting poverty   10
   or power
   like ice.

2. Sors immanis
   et inanis,
rota tu volubilis,
   status malus,
5   vana salus,
semper dissolubilis.
   Obumbrata
   et velata
mihi quoque niteris;
10   nunc per ludum
   dorsum nudum
fero tui sceleris.

3. Sors salutis
   et virtutis
mihi nunc contraria.
   Est affectus
5   et defectus
semper in angaria.
   Hac in hora
   sine mora
chordis pulsum tangite;
10   quod per sortem
   sternit fortem
mecum omnes plangite.

2. Fortune, you are monstrous
    and vacuous,
    you are a revolving wheel,
    an unsure foothold,
    a treacherous refuge,   5
    always ready to melt away.
    Shadowy
    and veiled,
    you exercise your power on me too;
    my back is now bare   10
    from gambling
    thanks to your villainy.

3. My fortunate position
    of safety and strength
    has now been turned upside down.
    Success
    or failure   5
    are now always dependent on my service to another.
    Now
    without delay,
    strum the lutes!
    Join with me, all of you, in lamenting   10
    that Fortune has arbitrarily brought
    a strong man down.

18

Versus

1. O Fortuna levis,   cuivis das omnia quaevis,
     et cuivis quaevis   auferet hora brevis.

2. Passibus ambiguis Fortuna volubilis errat,
     et manet in nullo certa tenaxque loco;
   sed modo laeta manet, modo vultus sumit acerbos
     et tantum constans in levitate manet.

3. Dat Fortuna bonum   sed non durabile donum,
     attollens pronum,   faciens et de rege colonum.

4. Quos vult Sors ditat,   et quos vult sub pede tritat.

5. Qui petit alta nimis,   retro lapsus ponitur imis.

18a

Regnabo; regno;   regnavi; sum sine regno.

18

Metrical Verses

1. Oh, fickle Fortune! You give anything you want to anyone and a brief hour will take away anything from anyone.

2. With uncertain steps Fortune wanders around unsteadily and nowhere remains secure and firmly fixed; one moment she happily stays put, the next she takes on a grim look and remains steadfast only in her fickleness.

3. The gift that Fortune gives is good but not lasting. She raises up one who is down and turns a king into a tenant farmer.

4. Luck enriches whom she will and crushes underfoot whom she will.

5. He who strives to fly too high slips back and is put at the bottom.

18a

I will be king, I am king, I was king; I have no kingdom.

19

1.   Fas et nefas ambulant   paene passu pari.
     Prodigus non redimit   vitium avari.
     Virtus temperantia   quadam singulari
         debet medium
5   ad utrumque vitium   caute contemplari.

2.   Si legisse memoras   ethicam Catonis,
     in qua scriptum legitur   "Ambula cum bonis,"
     cum ad dandi gloriam   animum disponis
         supra cetera
5   primum hoc considera,   quis sit dignus donis.

3.   Dare non ut convenit,   non est a virtute.
     Bonum est secundum quid,   sed non absolute.
     Digne dare poteris   et mereri tute
         famam muneris,
5   si me prius noveris   intus et in cute.

4.   Vultu licet hilari,   verbo licet blando
     sis aequalis omnibus,   unum tamen mando:
     si vis recte gloriam   promereri dando,
         primum videas
5   granum inter paleas   cui des et quando.

5.   Si prudenter triticum   paleis emundas,
     famam emis munere.   Sed caveto, cum das,
     largitatis oleum   male non effundas.
         In te glorior,
5   quia Codro Codrior   omnibus abundas.

19

1. Right and Wrong proceed almost in lockstep. The prodigal does not redeem the vice of the miser. Virtue ought to use exceptional moderation and carefully keep its eye on the mean between opposing vices.   5

2. If you recall reading Cato's ethical work, in which we find the words "Walk with good men," then, when you become disposed to the glorious act of giving, first, above anything else, consider who is worthy of gifts.   5

3. Giving unsuitably is not giving virtuously. The good in giving depends on circumstances and is not absolute. You will be able to give in a worthy manner and be sure of earning good report for your gift if you first get to   5 know me inside out.

4. Though you show a cheerful face and offer encouraging words to everyone alike, nonetheless I pass on one piece of advice: if you want to earn glory the right way through giving, first discern the wheat among the chaff and take care to whom you give and when.   5

5. If you prudently sift the grain from the chaff, you buy a reputation with your gift. But take care when you give you do not pour out carelessly the oil of largess. I take pride in you because, though you out-Codrus Codrus, you are rich in everything.   5

20

Versus

1. Est modus in verbis, duo sunt contraria verba:
    "do, das" et "teneo" contendunt lite superba.
    Per "do, das" largi conantur semper amari
    sed "teneo, tenui" miseri potiuntur avari.

2. Sicut ad omne quod est mensuram ponere prodest,
    sic sine mensura non stabit regia cura.

3. Virtus est medium vitiorum utrimque reductum.
    Et mala sunt vicina bonis; errore sub illo
        virtus pro vitio crimina saepe tulit.

4. Dum stultus vitat vitia, in contraria currit,
    Fallit enim vitium specie virtutis et umbra.

21

1. Veritas veritatum,
        via, vita, veritas,
    per veritatis semitas
        eliminans peccatum,

20

Metrical Verses

1. Words have their limits. There are two contradictory words: "I give, you give," and "I hold" compete in proud contention. By "I give, you give" generous men always try to be loved, but wretched misers grab on to "I hold, I held."

2. Just as it is good to impose a limit on every existing thing, so unlimited royal power cannot stand.

3. Virtue is the midpoint between two vices, equidistant from both. Evil is not far removed from the good; thanks to this confusing fact virtue has often been inculpated as a vice.

4. In avoiding vices, the fool runs to the opposite extreme. For vice deceives under the guise and semblance of virtue.

21

1. You who are the truth of truths,
   the way, the life, and the truth,
   who banish sin
   by the ways of truth,

5   te Verbum incarnatum
clamant Fides, Spes, Caritas.
    Tu primae pacis statum
    reformas post reatum.
Tu post carnis delicias
10   das gratias,
      ut facias
       beatum.
O quam mira potentia!
      Quam regia
15   vox principis,
cum aegrotanti praecipis:
     "surge, tolle grabatum!"

2. Omnia sub peccato
    clausit Adae meritum,
dum pronior in vetitum
    non paruit mandato.
5   De statu tam beato
nos dedit in interitum.
    De morsu venenato
    fel inhaesit palato
per hoc culpae dispendium
10   in vitium
     nascentium
      translato.
Mortis amarae poculum
     in saeculum
15   transfunditur,
nil cui dulce bibitur
    de vase vitiato.

Faith, Hope and Charity proclaim 5
you the Word incarnate.
You restore the condition of original peace
after sin.
After our pleasures of the flesh
you offer grace 10
to create
blessedness.
Ah, what wonderful power!
How regal
your voice is, my prince, 15
when you tell the sick man,
"Arise, pick up your pallet!"

2. Adam's wrong imprisoned
the world in sin,
for all too inclined to the forbidden,
he did not obey the commandment.
From such a blessed state 5
he consigned us to death.
The gall from the envenomed bite
stuck to his palate, and
was transformed
into the sinfulness 10
of succeeding generations
thanks to the loss occasioned by Adam's transgression.
The draft of bitter death
was poured out
over the world, 15
for which nothing drunk
from a tainted vessel is sweet.

3.   Spiritus veritatis,
       spiritus consilii
modo poenam supplicii
       non reddit pro peccatis,
5   ut timor castitatis,
quo reverentur filii,
       castiget in praelatis
       fermentum vetustatis.
Sed quando sponsus veniet,
10   inveniet
        quid faciet
         ingratis.
Non huic poenam abstulit,
       cui distulit,
15   sed animam
nunc impinguat ad victimam
       adeps iniquitatis.

4.   Tarditas praelatorum
       iudicem exasperat,
sed his qui solus reserat
       medullas animorum,
5   a fructibus eorum
novit eos et tolerat,
       quos extra viam morum
       fert impetus errorum.
Sed "Ecce," clamat, "venio
10   cum gladio
        flagitio
         malorum!"
Et cum purgabit aream,

3.   The spirit of truth,
the spirit of good counsel
does not now pay the penalty
of torment for sins,
so that the kind of pious fear   5
with which sons revere their fathers
may rebuke the old leaven
among the prelates.
But when the bridegroom comes,
he will find   10
what he will do
to the ungrateful.
He has not done away with punishment,
when he has deferred it for someone;
rather, the fullness of that man's iniquity   15
is now fattening up his soul
to become a victim.

4.   The dilatoriness of the prelates
angers the judge.
But it is he alone who can unlock
their inmost thoughts
and knows them by their fruits   5
and tolerates those
who are led off the path of good behavior
by the onset of error.
He calls out: "See, I come
with my sword   10
to punish
evil men!"
When he cleans up the threshing floor,

tunc paleam
15   abiciet.
Sic erit, quando veniet
ille Sanctus Sanctorum.

5.   Cecidit in praeclaris
hominum funiculus.
Sed nostrae mentis oculus
per vias huius maris
5   ad viae singularis
metam contendit sedulus.
Sed luxus saecularis
per ministros altaris
nunc solis vacat opibus
10   patentibus
hiatibus
avaris.
Sic per praelatos Mammonae
mors animae
15   concipitur,
dum cunctis male vivitur
ad formam exemplaris.

22

Homo, quo vigeas
vide!
Dei

he will throw away
the chaff.   15
This is how it will be
when the Holiest One comes.

5.   A glorious lot of land
has come down as inheritance to mankind.
But our spirit's eye
eagerly hurries over the paths of this sea
to its goal—   5
the one true path.
Yet worldly decadence
that prevails among the ministers at the altar
has time now only for wealth,
which they pursue   10
with greedy maws
gaping wide.
In this way, thanks to the prelates of Mammon,
death of the soul
spreads like a disease,   15
since everyone lives badly,
following their example.

22

Mankind, consider
what gives you strength.
Abide

fidei
5 adhaereas!
In spe gaudeas
et in fide
intus ardeas,
foris
10 luceas!
Turturis retorqueas
os ad ascellas.
Docens ita
verbo, vita,
15 oris
vomere
de cordibus fidelium
evellas
lolium;
20 lilium
insere
rosae
ut alium
per hoc corripere
25 speciose
valeas.
Virtuti
saluti
omnium
30 studeas.
Noxias
delicias
detesteris.
Opera

by your faith
in God! 5
Take joy in hope
and burn inwardly
with faith
and on the outside
be radiant! 10
Twist the dove's head
back under its wings.
Teaching in this way
by word and way of life,
with the plowshare 15
of your mouth
tear up the weeds
from the hearts
of the faithful;
graft 20
the lily
on the rose,
so that you can
thereby,
gracefully 25
reform another.
Focus
on the good
and the salvation
of all. 30
Abhor
harmful
pleasures.
Reflect on

35   considera,
     quae si non feceris,
            damnaberis.
               Hac in via
                  milita
40   gratiae
            et praemia
                  cogita
                  patriae
            et sic tuum
45   cor in perpetuum
                  gaudebit.

23

1.   Vide, qui nosti litteras
     et bene doces vivere,
     quid sit doctrina Litterae,
     de quo et ad quid referas.
5   Diligenter considera,
     si sis doctor, quid doceas;
     et quod doces, hoc teneas,
     ne tua perdant opera
     "aeterna Christi munera."

2.   Vide, qui colis studium
     pro Dei ministerio,
     ne abutaris studio

the good works   35
whose omission
will cause your damnation.
Soldier
along this path
of grace   40
and ponder
the rewards
of your homeland
and in this way
your heart will find   45
everlasting joy.

23

1.   You who are skilled in letters
      and teach the good life, ponder
      the teaching of the Letter, what it means,
      what you discuss and to what end.
      If you are to teach, carefully consider   5
      what it is you teach;
      and abide by what you teach
      or else your good works may lose
      "Christ's everlasting gifts."

2.   You who cultivate learning
      for the service of God,
      don't waste your study time,

suspirans ad dispendium
5   lucri, nec te participes
coniuge vitae vitio.
Namque multos invenio
qui sunt huius participes
"Ecclesiarum principes."

3.   Vide, qui debes sumere
religionis gloriam
summi per Dei gratiam,
ne te possit decipere,
5   nec trudat in interitum
Philisteus improvide,
   —namque prodent te Dalidae—
ut non amittas meritum,
"Deus, tuorum militum."

24

Iste mundus   furibundus   falsa praestat gaudia,
quia fluunt   et decurrunt   ceu campi lilia.
Laus mundana,   vita vana   vera tollit praemia,
nam impellit   et submergit   animas in Tartara.
5   Lex carnalis   et mortalis   valde transitoria;
fugit, transit,   velut umbra   quae non est corporea.
Quod videmus   vel tenemus   in praesenti patria,
dimittemus   vel perdemus   quasi quercus folia.
Fugiamus,   contemnamus   huius vitae dulcia

sighing over loss of income,
and take no part in vice,   5
life's tenacious companion.
Many, I find,
who participate in this, are
"leaders of the Church."

3.   You who are due to assume
      the honor of religious office
      through the grace of almighty God,
      make sure no Philistine
      can unexpectedly deceive you   5
      and thrust you to your death
      —for Delilahs will betray you—
      so that you do not lose the service,
      "God, of your soldiers."

24

This mad world offers only joys that are false; they ebb and
run their course like lilies of the field. Worldly glory and a
misguided life rob us of our true rewards, for they drive our
souls to Tartarus and plunge them into its depths. The law   5
that is carnal and mortal is completely transitory; it flees
and slips away like an insubstantial shadow. What we see or
possess here on earth we shall let go or lose, as an oak tree
loses its leaves. Let us flee from this life's pleasures and

10 ne perdamus   in futuro   pretiosa munera.
Conteramus,   confringamus   carnis desideria,
ut cum iustis   et electis   in caelesti gloria
gratulari   mereamur   per aeterna saecula!
Amen.

25

Versus

1.   Vivere sub meta   lex praecipit atque propheta.

2.   Est velut unda maris   vox, gloria, laus popularis.

3.   Omnia sunt hominum tenui pendentia filo.

4.   Qui differt poenas,   peccandi laxat habenas.

5.   Nil fieri stulte   credit qui peccat inulte.

6.   Discit enim citius meminitque libentius illud,
quod quis deridet quam quod probat et veneratur.

scorn them to ensure we don't lose precious gifts in the fu- 10
ture. Let us trample and crush the desires of the flesh so
that we may deserve to live happily in celestial glory with
the righteous and the chosen for ever and ever!

Amen.

25

Metrical Verses

1. The law and the prophets instruct us to live a life within
    proper limits.

2. The cries, glory, and applause of the people are like a
    wave of the sea.

3. All human affairs hang from a slender thread.

4. He who postpones punishment gives rein to sin.

5. He who sins with impunity foolishly believes there are
        no consequences.

6. A man learns faster and more readily remembers
    what people laugh to scorn than what they approve
        and revere.

26

De Correctione Hominum

1.   Ad cor tuum revertere,
condicionis miserae
homo! Cur spernis vivere?
Cur dedicas te vitiis?
5   Cur indulges malitiis?
Cur excessus non corrigis,
nec gressus tuos dirigis
in semitis iustitiae,
sed contra te cottidie
10   iram Dei exasperas?
In te succidi metue
radices ficus fatuae,
cum fructus nullos afferas.

2.   O condicio misera!
Considera,
quam aspera
sit haec vita, mors altera,
5   quae sic immutat statum.
Cur non purgas reatum
sine mora,
cum sit hora
mortis tibi incognita,
10   et invita caritas
—quae non proficit—

26

The Improvement of Mankind

1. Return to your senses, mankind,
    your condition is wretched!
    Why spurn eternal life?
    Why dedicate yourself to vice?
    Why indulge your evil ways?   5
    Why do you not curb your excesses
    and direct your steps
    in the paths of justice
    but rather provoke God's anger
    against yourself every day?   10
    Have a fear that the roots of the sterile fig tree
    within you will be cut away
    since you bear no fruit!

2. Ah how wretched your condition!
    Consider
    how harsh
    this life is—a second death—
    which changes so drastically.   5
    Why not purge your guilt
    without delay,
    since the hour of your death
    is unknown to you
    and a grudging act of charity   10
    —and so of no avail—

prorsus aret et deficit,
nec efficit
beatum.

3. Si vocatus ad nuptias
advenias
sine veste nuptiali,
a curia regali
5   expelleris,
et obviam si veneris
sponso lampade vacua,
es quasi virgo fatua.

4. Ergo vide, ne dormias,
sed vigilans aperias
Domino, cum pulsaverit.
Beatus, quem invenerit
5   vigilantem, dum venerit.

27

1. Bonum est confidere
in dominorum Domino.
Bonum est spem ponere
in spei nostrae termino.
5   Qui de regum potentia,
non de Dei clementia,
spem concipis,
te decipis,
et excipis

dries up, fails completely,
and wins
no blessedness?

3.   If, invited to the wedding,
you arrive
without wedding attire,
you are sent away
from the king's court,   5
and if you meet the bridegroom
with your lamp empty,
you are like a foolish virgin.

4.   So make sure you don't sleep
but stay awake and open the door
for the Lord when he knocks!
Blessed is he whom he finds awake
when he comes.   5

27

1.   It is good to place your trust
in the Lord of lords.
It is good to place your hope
in the goal of all our hoping.
If you base your hope   5
on the power of kings,
not on God's mercy,
you deceive yourself
and exclude yourself

10   ab aula summi principis.
    Quid in opum aggere
    exaggeras peccatum?
    In Deo cogitatum
        tuum iacta.
15   Prius acta
    studeas corrigere.
    In labore manuum
    et in sudore vultuum
    pane tuo vescere.

2.   Carnis ab ergastulo
    liber eat spiritus
    ne peccati vinculo
        vinciatur
5   et trahatur
    ad inferni gemitus,
    ubi locus flentium,
    ubi stridor dentium,
ubi poena gehennali
10 affliguntur omnes mali
    in die novissimo,
    in die gravissimo,
    quando iudex venerit,
    ut trituret aream
15   et exstirpet vineam,
    quae fructum non fecerit.
    Sic granum a palea
        separabit
        congregabit
20   triticum in horrea.

from the court of the prince on high.   10
Why pile up sin
with a pile of money?
Direct your thoughts
to God.
Strive to put right   15
your past actions.
Eat your bread
thanks to the work of your hands
and the sweat of your brow!

2.   Let your spirit go free
      from the workhouse of the flesh
      for fear that it may be bound
      by the bonds of sin
      and dragged off   5
      to the groans of hell,
      which is the place of weeping
      and gnashing of teeth,
      and where all evil souls
      are punished with hellish punishment   10
      on the last day,
      on the grimmest day,
      when the judge comes
      to trample the threshing floor
      and uproot the vineyard   15
      which has produced no fruit.
      In this way he will separate
      the grain from the chaff
      and gather
      the wheat into the granary.   20

3.   O beati
       mundo corde,
       quos peccati
       tersa sorde
5   vitium non inquinat,
     scelus non examinat,
       nec arguunt peccata,
       qui Domini mandata
              custodiunt
10   et sitiunt!
   Beati qui esuriunt
   et confidunt in Domino
   nec cogitant de crastino!
   Beati qui non implicant
15   se curis temporalibus,
     qui talentum multiplicant
     et verbum Dei praedicant
     omissis saecularibus!

28

Versus

Laudat rite Deum,   qui vere diligit illum.
Lumbos praecingit,   qui carnis vota restringit.

3.   Blessed are those
pure in heart,
for once the stain of sin
has been quite wiped away,
no fault stains them,   5
no crime makes them questionable
and no sins accuse,
and they keep
the Lord's commandments
and thirst after them!   10
Blessed are those who are hungry
and put their trust in the Lord
and do not think about tomorrow!
Blessed are those who do not become involved
in worldly concerns,   15
who multiply their talent
and, passing over the things of this world,
preach the word of God.

28

Metrical Verses

The man who truly loves God, duly praises him.
The man who restrains the desires of the flesh girds up his
     loins.

Maxime quaerendum,   quod semper erit retinendum.
Nil peccant oculi,   si mens velit his dominari.
5 Ne tardare velis,   si quem convertere possis.
Nisus stultorum   par semper erit sociorum.
Omne quod est iustum,   merito dici valet unum.
Os quod mentitur,   animam iugulare probatur.
O quantis curis   mens indiget omnibus horis!
10 Peccans cotidie   studeat mox se reparare.

29

De Conversione Hominum

1.   In lacu miseriae
et luto luxuriae
volveris, inutile
tempus perdens, Pamphile.
5   Cur offensas numinum
aut derisum hominum
        non metuis,
        dum destruis

That which will be worth keeping forever is to be sought
    above all else.
The eyes commit no sin if the mind chooses to control
    them.
Do not be slow if you can put someone on the right path.   5
The striving of fools will always copy that of their
    companions.
All that is just can truly be said to be a single whole.
The mouth that lies is found to throttle the soul.
How much careful attention the mind needs at every
    moment!
May the sinner strive every day to put himself on the right   10
    track soon.

29

The Conversion of Mankind

1.   You wallow, Pamphilus,
    in a pool of wretchedness
    and a mire of lust,
    senselessly wasting time!
    Why no fear   5
    of offending heaven
    or of the mockery of men
    as you ravage

corpus, rem et animam?
10   Salva saltem ultimam
vitae portiunculam,
offerens caelestibus,
pro iuventae floribus,
senectutis stipulam.

2.   Forsan ludo Veneris
ultra vires ureris,
ut amoris taedium
tibi sit remedium.
5   Sed si te medullitus
exsiccatum penitus
        exhaurias,
        ut febrias,
nihil tamen proficis,
10   dum ad tempus deficis,
nam insurget artius
Hydra multiplicior,
et post casum fortior
surget Terrae filius.

3.   Ut stes pede stabili
sine casu facili,
cave praecipitium
devitando vitium.
5   sed si te vexaverit
aut si comprehenderit
        Aegyptiaca,
        mox pallia
fugitivus desere,
10   nec lucteris temere,

body, property, and soul?
Save at least   10
the last little portion of your life,
offering to those in heaven
for the flowers of youth
the stubble of old age.

2.   Perhaps Venus's game makes you burn
     so far beyond your strength
     that love's tedium
     becomes your cure.
     But though you drain yourself   5
     to the marrow,
     completely dry,
     to the point of becoming feverish,
     it still does you no good
     when you fail at the critical moment,   10
     for the Hydra will tower up
     with a denser array of heads
     and the son of Earth will arise
     stronger after his fall.

3.   To stand with steady footing
     without danger of falling,
     stay away from the precipice
     by avoiding sin.
     But if the Egyptian woman   5
     pesters you
     or grabs hold of you,
     quick, run away
     and leave your cloak behind!
     Don't be rash and struggle,   10

nam resistens vincitur
in hoc belli genere,
et qui novit cedere
fugiendo, fugitur.

30

1. Dum iuventus floruit,
   licuit   et libuit
   facere, quod placuit:
   iuxta voluntatem
5 currere,   peragere
   carnis voluptatem.

2. Amodo sic agere,
   vivere   tam libere,
   talem vitam ducere,
   viri vetat aetas,
5 perimit   et eximit
   leges assuetas.

3. Aetas illa monuit,
   docuit,   consuluit,
   sic et aetas annuit:
   "Nihil est exclusum!"
5 Omnia   cum venia
   contulit ad usum.

for in warfare of this kind
he who resists is the loser,
and when a man knows how to yield
by running away, they flee from him.

30

1. In the flourishing days of my youth
   it was permitted—and a joy—
   to do whatever I wanted:
   to run around at will
   and exhaust   5
   all the pleasures of the flesh.

2. To behave like this today
   to live with such freedom,
   to lead such a life
   the years of a full-grown man forbid,
   putting an end to, and sundering me from,   5
   my accustomed ways.

3. My earlier years advised,
   taught, counseled
   and gave assent to this dictum:
   "Nothing is off limits!"
   They gave permission to try anything   5
   and be forgiven.

4.   Volo resipiscere,
     linquere,   corrigere
     quod commisi temere.
       Deinceps intendam
5   seriis,   pro vitiis
       virtutes rependam.

31

1.   Vitae perditae
        me legi
       subdideram,
    minus licite
5   dum fregi,
       quod voveram,
sed ad vitae vesperam
    corrigendum legi
quicquid ante perperam
10   puerilis egi.

2.   Rerum exitus
       dum quaero
      discutere,
    falsum penitus
5   a vero
      discernere,
falso fallor opere,
    bravium si spero

4.   I want to change my ways,
       to leave behind and put right
       my rash behavior.
       Then I will focus on
       serious matters and for my vices   5
       compensate with virtues.

31

1.   I gave myself up
       to the practice of pursuing
       a decadent life,
       illicitly
       breaking   5
       my vows.
       But toward the evening of my life
       I have chosen to amend
       all the earlier waywardness
       of my youth.   10

2.   While I sought
       to debate
       the end of the world,
       to distinguish clearly
       the true   5
       from the false,
       I was greatly mistaken
       if I hoped

me virtutum metere,
10   vitia dum sero.

3.   Non sum duplici
                perplexus
            itinere,
        nec addidici
5   reflexus
            a Venere,
    nec fraudavi temere
        coniugis amplexus.
    "Dalidam persequere,
10   ne fraudetur sexus."

4.   Famem siliqua
                porcorum
            non abstulit,
        quae ad lubrica
5   errorum
            me contulit,
    sed scriptura consulit,
        viam intrem morum,
    quae praelarga protulit
10   pabula donorum.

5.   Dum considero,
                quid Dinae
            contigerit,
        finem confero
5   rapinae.
                Quid luerit,
    scio: vix evaserit

      to reap the prize for virtue
      while sowing sins.   10

3.   I was not puzzled
      by a fork
      in the road.
      I neither learned
      to turn away   5
      from Venus
      nor did I rashly steal
      a wife's embraces.
      "Pursue Delilah to ensure
      that your manhood is not cheated."   10

4.   Husks fed to swine
      did not allay
      the hunger
      that swept me
      down the slippery path   5
      of sin.
      Rather, scripture counseled me
      to start on a path of virtue,
      which proffered a generous feast
      of satisfying rewards.   10

5.   When I consider
      what happened
      to Dinah,
      I compare the outcome
      to rape.   5
      I know what sin
      she expiated:

mens corrupta fine
diu quam contraxerit
10   maculam sentinae.

6.   Praeter meritum
me neci
non dedero,
si ad vomitum
5   quem ieci
rediero.
Nec a verbo aspero
liberum me feci,
servus si serviero
10   vitiorum faeci.

7.   Viae veteris
immuto
vestigia.
Ire Veneris
5   refuto
per devia.
Via namque regia
curritur in tuto;
si quis cedit alia,
10   semper est in luto.

8.   Croesi solium,
Sinonis
astutiam,
confer Tullium,
5   Zenonis
prudentiam,

a corrupted heart can, in the end,
hardly escape the stain
contracted over a long period.   10

6.   I shall be consigning myself
     to a death
     that is not undeserved
     if I return
     to the vomit   5
     I have thrown up.
     Nor have I freed myself
     from harsh words
     if, like a slave, I serve
     the cesspool of vice.   10

7.   I am changing
     my former
     path.
     I refuse
     to proceed along   5
     the byways of Venus.
     The royal road is traveled
     in safety—
     anyone who takes another road
     always finds himself in filth.   10

8.   Give me the throne of Croesus,
     the craftiness
     of Sinon,
     the eloquence of Cicero,
     the wisdom of Zeno—   5
     I will feel I am abusing these gifts

nil conferre sentiam
    his abutens bonis,
ni fugiendo fugiam
10   Dalidam Samsonis.

9.   Ergo veniam
        de rei
      miseria,
    ut inveniam
5   de Dei
      clementia,
haec et his similia
    quod peregi, rei
sola parcens gratia
10   miserere mei.

32

Versus

1.   Cur homo torquetur?   ne fastus ei dominetur.
    Cur homo torquetur?   Ut ei meritum cumuletur.
    Cur homo torquetur?   ut Christus glorificetur.

and making no contribution,
unless I drive away
Samson's Delilah
and shun her.   10

9. Accordingly, that I may win
pardon from God's mercy
for the wretchedness
of my case,
have mercy on me, a sinner,   5
for committing
these sins
and sins like them,
sparing me
by your grace alone.   10

32

Metrical Verses

1. Why does man suffer torture?   So that he not be
mastered by pride.
Why does man suffer torture?   So that his merit may
be increased.
Why does man suffer torture?   So that Christ may be
glorified.

Cur homo torquetur?   ut poenis culpa pietur.
5   Cur homo torquetur?   ut dupliciter crucietur.

2.   Gratia sola Dei,   quos vult facit alta mereri.

33

De ammonitione praelatorum

1.   Non te lusisse pudeat,
        sed ludum non incidere,
        et quae lusisti temere,
        ad vitae frugem vertere
5   magistra morum doceat
                        te ratio,
        ut dignus pontificio
        divini dono numinis,
        ad laudem Christi nominis
10   fungaris sacerdotio.

2.   Sis pius, iustus, sobrius,
        prudens, pudicus, humilis,
        in lege Dei docilis,
        et ne sis arbor sterilis,

Why does man suffer torture?   To expiate his guilt by
    punishment.
Why does man suffer torture?   So that his torment   5
    may be doubled.

2.   God's grace alone makes those it chooses earn a lofty
    reward.

33

The Admonition of Prelates

1.   There should be no shame in having played around,
    only in failing to cut short the game
    and as for your brash foolery,
    let reason, teacher of character,
    show you how to turn it around   5
    to the betterment of your life
    that you may be worthy of the episcopate,
    and, as a gift to the divinity,
    fulfill your role as priest
    to the glory of Christ's name.   10

2.   Be pious, just, and self-controlled,
    wise, modest, humble,
    and eager to learn God's law,
    and, to avoid becoming a sterile tree,

5   tuo te regas aptius
              officio.
       Expulso procul vitio,
       munderis labe criminis,
       ut mundus mundae Virginis
10   ministres in altario.

3.   Pius protector pauperum
       omni petenti tribue.
       Malos potenter argue,
       manusque sacras ablue
5   a sordidorum munerum
              contagio;
       nullus te palpet praemio,
       quaesita gratis gratia
       largire beneficia,
10   sed dignis beneficio.

4.   Non des ministris scelerum
       non tua sed ecclesiae.
       Sub pietatis specie
       non abutaris impie
5   commisso tibi pauperum
              suffragio.
       Nil a te ferat histrio,
       et tibi non allicias
       infames amicitias
10   de Christi patrimonio.

5.   Ministros immunditiae
       a te repellas longius.
       Bonorum vitam fortius

govern yourself as befits   5
        your office.
Drive vice far away from you.
and cleanse yourself of the stain of sin
that you may serve unsullied
at the altar of the unsullied Virgin.   10

3.   As a kind protector of the poor,
    give to all who ask.
    Vigorously punish the wicked!
    Wash clean your sacred hands
    of any contagion   5
    from tainted gifts;
    let none seduce you with a bribe,
    but when your favor is freely sought,
    bestow your benefices liberally
    but only on those who deserve them.   10

4.   Don't give to the servants of sin
    what belongs not to you but the church.
    Under the guise of piety
    do not impiously abuse
    the protection of the poor   5
    entrusted to you.
    Don't employ entertainers
    and don't attract
    notorious friendships
    with the patrimony of Christ.   10

5.   Keep sinful assistants
    at a far remove.
    Bad company powerfully corrupts

pravus depravat socius,
5 et afficit infamiae
dispendio.
Sic trahitur praesumptio
a convictu similium.
Praelati vita vilium
10 vilescit contubernio.

6. Caute dispone domui.
Pauca sed vera loquere,
verba confirmes opere,
quia non decet temere
5 os sacerdotis pollui
mendacio.
Prudentium consilio
te frui non displiceat,
nec te sinistre moveat
10 salubris exhortatio.

7. Teneris, ut abstineas
ab omni mala specie.
Sub freno temperantiae
magistra pudicitiae
5 sobrietate floreas,
nec vario
vagoque desiderio
declines ad illecebras,
sed caecae mentis tenebras
10 purga virtutis radio.

the lives of the righteous
and affects them with the loss   5
of their good name.
This is the way arrogance is contracted
—from association with arrogant men.
A prelate's life is debased
by association with base men.   10

6. Carefully manage your household.
    Speak few words but true
    and follow up your words with action,
    because the mouth of a priest
    should not be rashly corrupted   5
    with lying.
    See fit to draw on
    wise men's advice
    and don't let well-meant counsel
    provoke you adversely.   10

7. You are obligated to abstain
    from every form of evil.
    Under moderation's curb
    may you flourish in self-restraint,
    modesty's teacher.   5
    Do not,
    through fickle and inconstant desire,
    give way to temptations
    but rather, purge the darkness of murky thoughts
    with the bright ray of virtue.   10

34

1. Deduc Sion uberrimas
velut torrentem lacrimas,
namque pro tuis patribus
nati sunt tibi filii,
5   quorum dedisti manibus
tui sceptrum imperii,
fures et furum socii.
Turbato rerum ordine
abutuntur regimine
10   pastoralis officii.

2. Ad corpus infirmitas
    capitis descendit,
singulosque gravitas
    artus apprehendit.
5   Refrigescit caritas,
    nec iam se extendit
ad amorem proximi.
Nam videmus opprimi
    pupillum a potente,
10   nec est qui salvum faciat,
vel qui iustum eripiat
    ab impio premente.

3. Vide, deus ultionum,
    vide, videns omnia,
quod spelunca vespillonum
    facta est ecclesia,
5   quod in templum Salomonis

34

1. Zion, let a flood of tears
    stream down like a torrent,
    for the sons born to you
    to replace your fathers,
    into whose hands you have given   5
    the scepter of your sway,
    are robbers and friends of robbers.
    Confusing the order of things,
    they abuse the prescribed role
    of their pastoral office.   10

2. A disease of the head
    descends to the body
    and a heaviness takes hold
    of the limbs, one after another.
    Love grows cold   5
    and no longer extends
    to love of one's neighbor.
    We see a ward
    exploited by his powerful guardian
    and there is no one to protect him   10
    or to rescue the just man
    from his impious oppressor.

3. See, God of vengeance!
    See, you who see all things—
    the Church has become
    a den of thieves,
    that the Prince of Babylon has entered   5

venit princeps Babylonis,
et excelsum sibi thronum
    posuit in medio.
    Sed arrepto gladio
10 scelus hoc ulciscere.
    Veni, Iudex gentium,
    cathedras vendentium
    columbas evertere.

35

1. Magnus, maior, maximus,
    parvus, minor, minimus —
    gradus istos repperi,
    per quos gradus comperi
5   augeri et conteri
    gradus status hominis,
    prout datur dignitas,
    dignitatum quantitas
    quantitasque nominis.

2. Magni parvus extiti,
    parvi magnus meriti.
    Parvaeque sunt gratiae
    diviti contrariae.
5   Cui plus datur hodie,
    magis est obnoxius,
    quique minus habuit

the temple of Solomon
and placed his lofty throne
in the middle!
Seize your sword
and avenge this crime!   10
Come, Judge of the world,
to overturn
the dove sellers' benches!

35

1. Great, greater, greatest,
    small, smaller, smallest—
    these are the degrees I have found
    through which, I have learned,
    a man's rank   5
    waxes and wanes,
    depending on the standing of his office,
    the number of offices,
    and the extent of his fame.

2. I have been a little man of great merit
    and a great man of little merit.
    Paltry thanks
    are not the rich man's way.
    The man given more today   5
    is all the more in thrall,
    while the man who has received less

et minus attribuit,
minus reddit gratiae.

3.   Viri fratres praesules,
rationis consules,
me non imitemini
nec sic operemini
5   super gregem Domini!
Pervigil sit animus;
sit lumen in manibus,
praesit custos renibus
magnus maior maximus.

36

1a.   Nulli beneficium
iustae paenitudinis
amputatur.
Nulli maius vitium
5   quam ingratitudinis
imputatur.
Ergo, praesul confitens,
esto vere paenitens,
quia nil confessio
10   lavat, cui contritio
denegatur.

1b.   Si confessus fueris
ore, fit confessio

and contributed less
is less grateful.

3.   Men, brothers, bishops,
princes of reason,
do not copy me
and do not treat the Lord's flock
as I have done!   5
Keep your mind awake,
and the lamp in your hands lit;
set a guard in control of your passions,
that is great, greater, greatest!

36

1a. No one is deprived
of the benefit
    of a genuine repentance.
No one is charged
with a greater vice   5
    than ingratitude.
So in your confession,
bishop, be truly penitent,
because confession
fails to wash away sin,   10
    if there is no contrition.

1b. If you make an oral confession,
the confession counts

ad salutem,
corde si contereris.
5   Animi contritio
dat virtutem
ut salutem habeas.
Ut virtutem teneas,
relictis prioribus
10   tuam orna moribus
iuventutem.

2a.   Virtute, non sanguine
decet niti
sub honorum culmine.
Corde miti
5   foveas innoxium.
Reprime flagitium
superbi et impii.
Supremi iudicii
memor iuste iudica;
10   praedicans, non claudica.

2b.   Tuum sit contemnere
contemnentes
et fovere munere
nil habentes.
5   Relevato debiles
et exaltes humiles.
In te sit humilitas,
cui mixta sit gravitas,
ut lene corripias
10   et serene lenias.

> toward salvation
> if you are contrite in your heart.
> Contrition 5
>   confers virtue
> so that you can win salvation.
> To maintain your virtue
> abandon your earlier ways
> and enhance your youth 10
>   with good character.

2a. You ought to strive for high office
>   with your virtue
> not by your blood ties.
>   With a gentle heart,
> foster the blameless. 5
> Check the outrageous behavior
> of the man who is proud and impious.
> Ever mindful of the Last Judgment,
> judge with justice;
> don't falter in your preaching. 10

2b. Let it be your goal to have contempt
>   for the contemptuous
> and to assist with a gift
>   those who have nothing.
> Raise up the weak 5
> and exalt the humble.
> May there be humility in you
> combined with solemn dignity
> so that you may gently chide
> or soothe with calm serenity. 10

3a.   Cui magis committitur,
        ab eo plus exigitur.
        Quid Domino retribuis
        pro tot quae tibi tribuit,
5   quod lac et lanam eligis
        gregis, cui constituit
                te pastorem?
        Sed cave, ne dum venerit,
        te districte tunc conterat
10   ut raptorem!
        Districtus iudex aderit,
        nunc sustinens considerat
            peccatorem.

3b.   Cum subiectis ne pereas,
        exempla prava timeas
        in subiectos transfundere.
        Nam quanto gradus altior
5   cum graviori pondere,
        tanto labenti gravior
            lapsus datur.
        Ne desperes, si criminis
        in latens praecipitium
10   pes labatur,
        nam iustae paenitudinis
        nemini beneficium
          amputatur.

3a.　More is demanded of the man
　　　to whom more is entrusted.
　　　What do you give to the Lord in return
　　　for all that he has given you,
　　　namely, the milk and the wool you take　　　　　5
　　　from the flock whose shepherd
　　　　　he made you?
　　　Take care when he comes,
　　　that he not crush you severely,
　　　　　as he would a robber!　　　　　　　　　　10
　　　A stern judge will he be then!
　　　Now he waits,
　　　　　pondering the sinner.

3b.　Lest you perish along with your flock,
　　　take care you don't pass on to them
　　　an evil example.
　　　The higher and weightier the rank,　　　　　5
　　　the heavier your fall
　　　　　if you slip.
　　　Don't lose all hope if your foot
　　　should slip into a hidden crevasse
　　　　　of wrongdoing,　　　　　　　　　　　10
　　　for no one is denied
　　　the benefit
　　　　　of a genuine repentance.

37

1. In Gedeonis area
       vellus aret extentum,
    et demolitur tinea
       regale vestimentum.
5   Superabundat palea,
       quae sepelit frumentum,
       et loquitur iumentum,
    nec redit bos ad horrea
       sed sequitur carpentum.

2. Exit rumor discriminis
       de Grandimontis cella,
    quae tam sanctae dulcedinis
       late fundebat mella.
5   Praeposteratur ordinis
       plantatio novella,
       dum movet in se bella,
    bases in summo culminis
       ponens, non capitella.

3. Quod sanctum sacerdotium,
       quod unctio regalis
    se curvet ad imperium
       et vocem subiugalis,
5   humanum est mysterium
       et furor laicalis.
       Favor tamen venalis,
    qui non intrat per ostium,
       fovet eos sub alis.

37

1. On Gideon's threshing floor
    the splayed fleece remains dry
    and the moth destroys
    the garment of the king.
    There is a surfeit of chaff   5
    burying the grain,
    the ass speaks,
    and the ox, instead of returning to the granary,
    follows the wagon.

2. Out of Grandmont monastery,
    which used to spread far and wide
    honey of such divine sweetness,
    there comes word of a crisis.
    The propagation of the order   5
    is turning things upside down,
    provoking internecine war,
    and setting the bases, not the capitals,
    at the top of the columns.

3. That the sacred priesthood
    and royal unction
    should bend to the command
    of a beast of burden
    is a human mystery   5
    and layman's madness.
    But the venal patronage
    of one who does not enter by the door
    protects them under its wings.

4. Clausa quondam religio
    vel otium secretum
nunc subiacet opprobrio
    per vulgus indiscretum,
5 quod tali tirocinio
    non erat assuetum.
    Et quod format decretum,
non legis patrocinio
    nec litteris est fretum.

5. Sub brevi doctus tempore
    stultus dum incappatur,
pleno prophetat pectore,
    ructans interpretatur
5 et disputat cum rhetore,
    qui tacet et miratur,
    quod vir iustus tollatur,
et assumptus de stercore
    sententias loquatur.

6. Vae vae, qui regis filiam
    das in manum lenonis!
Vae, qui profanas gloriam
    tante devotionis!
5 Qui cellam pigmentariam
    et opus Salomonis
    fraude rapis praedonis,
si certius inspiciam
    ad rem conditionis.

4.   What once was a cloistered religious life
      or sequestered contemplation
      is now open to the taunts
      of an undiscerning crowd
      unaccustomed   5
      to its new role.
      As for the decree it has laid down,
      it is not supported
      by the authority of law or official letter.

5.   When a fool has received a little instruction
      and is cowled,
      he utters prophecies from his inspired breast,
      belches forth interpretations,
      and enters into disputation with a rhetorician   5
      who keeps silent, amazed
      that a righteous man has been removed
      and a man taken from a dunghill
      is pronouncing judgments.

6.   Shame on you, who placed
      a king's daughter in the hands of a pimp!
      Shame on you, who profane the glory
      of such devotion!
      You plunder the fragrant chamber   5
      and temple of Solomon
      like a marauding bandit,
      if I look at the reality
      of the situation closely.

38

Versus

Doctrinae verba paucis   prosunt sine factis.
Eloquium sanctum   pretiosum fit super aurum.
Expers doctrinae   tenebras patietur ubique.
Est quasi vas vacuum,   cui cura deest animarum.

39

1. In huius mundi patria
    regnat idolatria;
    ubique sunt venalia
    dona spiritalia.
5   Custodes sunt raptores
    atque lupi pastores.
    Principes et reges
    subverterunt leges.
    Hac incerta domo
10 insanit omnis homo.
    Sed ista cum vento
    transibunt in momento.

2. Lia placet lipposa,
    sed Rachel flet formosa,

38

Metrical Verses

Words of instruction without deeds are helpful to few.
Holy Scripture is more precious than gold.
An uneducated man will encounter darkness everywhere.
He whose care for souls is deficient is like an empty vessel.

39

1.　In this world
　　idolatry rules;
　　spiritual gifts
　　are on sale everywhere.
　　The guardians are plunderers　　　　　　5
　　and the shepherds are wolves.
　　Kings and princes
　　have overturned the laws.
　　In this uncertain home of ours
　　everyone is mad.　　　　　　　　　　　10
　　But all this will pass in a moment
　　with the wind.

2.　Cloudy-eyed Leah finds favor,
　　while beautiful Rachel weeps.

quae diu manens sterilis
ob inmanitatem sceleris,
5   generat anicilla.
Nam Raab ancilla
navem mundi mersit;
discordia dispersit
mortis seminaria
10   et mundi luminaria
luminant obscure.
Pauci vivunt secure.

3.   Doctores apostolici
et iudices Catholici
quidam colunt Albinum
et diligunt Rufinum;
5   cessant iudicare
et student devorare
gregem sibi commissum.
Hi cadunt in abyssum.
Si caecus ducit caecum,
10   in fossam cadit secum.
Hi tales subsannantur
et infra castra cremantur.

4.   Episcopi cornuti
conticuere muti.
Ad praedam sunt parati,
et indecenter coronati.
5   Pro virga ferunt lanceam,
pro infula galeam,
clipeum pro stola
—haec mortis erit mola—

Long remaining infertile
because of the immensity of the crime,
she gave birth only as an old woman.   5
The slave-girl Rahab
has plunged the world's ship beneath the waves.
Discord has spread far and wide
the seedbeds of death,
and the lamps of the world   10
give only a shrouded light.
Few live free from care.

3. As for the apostolic teachers
    and Catholic judges,
    some worship Albinus
    and love Rufinus;
    they give up acting as judges   5
    and concentrate on devouring
    the flock entrusted to them.
    They fall into the abyss.
    If one blind man leads another,
    the one falls into the ditch with the other.   10
    Such men are mocked
    and become burned offerings within the camp.

4. The horned bishops
    have fallen silent;
    they are ready for their prey,
    with their heads inappropriately crowned.
    Instead of a crozier they carry a lance,   5
    a helmet instead of a miter—
    a shield instead of a stole
    —this will be their millstone of death—

119

loricam pro alba
10 —haec occasio calva—
pellem pro humerali,
pro ritu seculari.

5. Sicut fortes incedunt
et a Deo discedunt,
ut leones feroces
et ut aquilae veloces,
5 ut apri frendentes
exacuere dentes,
linguas ut serpentes
pugnare non valentes,
mundo consentientes
10 et tempus redimentes,
quia dies sunt mali
iure imperiali.

6. Principes et abbates
ceterique vates,
ceteri doctores

< four lines missing>

iura deposuerunt,
canones ac decreta.
10 Sicut scripsit propheta,
Deum exacerbaverunt,
et Sanctum blasphemaverunt.

7. Monachi sunt nigri,
et in regula sunt pigri,
bene cucullati

a breastplate instead of an alb,
— this prefigures Fortune's bald back view —   10
a hide instead of a humeral veil,
to perform secular rituals.

5. They move onward like strong warriors,
and distance themselves from God,
like fierce lions,
or swift-flying eagles,
or boars, gnashing their teeth   5
to sharpen them,
or snakes, flashing their tongues
to attack their impotent prey,
living in harmony with this world,
and making full use of their time   10
because times are bad
under imperial rule.

6. Princes, and abbots
the rest of the bishops
and the rest of the teachers

<four lines missing>

have set aside Roman law,
canons, and decrees.
As the prophet wrote,   10
they have provoked God
and blasphemed the Holy One.

7. There are the black monks,
laggards in following the rule.
They are well hooded

et male coronati.
5   Quidam sunt cani
et sensibus profani.
Quidam sunt fratres,
et verentur ut patres;
dicuntur Norpertini
10 et non Augustini.
In cano vestimento
novo gaudent invento.

39a

1. In huius mundi domo
miser qui vivis homo,
quod cinis es, memento.
Transibis in momento;
5   post carnem cinis eris
atque morte teneris.
Cinis et origo.
Sit tibi formido,
cum spiritus cadit
10 et ad Dominum vadit,
qui eum dedit.
Miser, qui hoc non credit.

2. Vanitatum vanitas
et omnia vanitas!
Est animalis homo

and badly tonsured.
There are some white monks,   5
profane in their sentiments.
Some are brothers
and are revered as fathers.
They are called Norbertians
and not Augustinians.   10
They take joy
in their newly devised white robes.

39a

1. You who live wretchedly
    in the house that is this world,
    remember that you are ashes.
    You will pass away in a moment;
    after flesh you will be ashes   5
    and held in death's thrall.
    Ashes are also what you came from.
    Fear the time
    when your spirit dies
    and goes to the Lord   10
    who bestowed it.
    Wretched is he who does not believe this.

2. Vanity of vanities!
    Everything is vanity!
    In the house that is this world

in huius mundi domo.
5   Cuncta, que sub sole,
assimilantur molae,
nam omnia volvuntur:
quaedam dissolvuntur,
quaedam ad vitam crescunt,
10   et omnia decrescunt.
Sed spiritalis homo
Dei regnat in domo.

39b

Cum vadis ad altare
missam celebrare,
te debes praeparare,
vetus expurgare
5 de corde fermentum.
Sic offers sacramentum:
invoca Christum,
psalmum dicas istum:
Iudica teque ipsum
10 praeiudica; Israel et Iuda,
cordis mala denuda.

man is a creature driven by his senses.
Everything under the sun 5
is like a mill wheel,
for everything is cyclical:
some things are broken down
and some grow into living things
and everything fades away. 10
But spiritual man
reigns in the house of God.

39b

When you go to the altar
to celebrate mass,
you ought to prepare yourself
and clean out the old leaven
from your heart. 5
This is how you offer the sacrament:
call on Christ,
sing this psalm,
Pass judgment and first
judge yourself. Israel and Judah, reveal 10
all the evil in your heart!

40

Versus

1. Quicquid habes meriti, praeventrix gratia donat,
   nil Deus in nobis praeter sua dona coronat.

2. Agricolis fessis   cum venerit ultima messis,
   semina dant fructum,   detergunt gaudia luctum.

3. Os habet immite,   qui non fert gaudia vitae.

41

1. Propter Sion non tacebo,
   sed ruinas Romae flebo,
      quousque iustitia
   rursus nobis oriatur,
5 et ut lampas accendatur
      iustus in ecclesia.

2. Sedet vilis et in luto
   princeps facta sub tributo.
      Quod solebam dicere—
   Romam esse derelictam,
5 desolatam et afflictam—
      expertus sum opere.

40

Metrical Verses

1. Any merit you have, prevenient grace gave you.
   What God crowns in us are simply his own gifts.

2. When the end of harvest comes for weary farmers,
   the seeds bear fruit; joy wipes away sadness.

3. He has a harsh mouth who brings no joy to life.

41

1. For Zion's sake I will not keep silent.
   I will weep over the ruins of Rome
   until we see justice
   arising again
   and a just man blazing like a torch   5
   in the church.

2. She sits in the mud, despised,
   once queen, now forced to pay tribute.
   What I used to say in the past—
   that Rome was abandoned,
   desolate and afflicted—   5
   I now know from personal experience.

3. Vidi, vidi caput mundi
   instar maris et profundi
     vorax guttur Siculi.
   Ibi mundi bithalassus,
5 ibi sorbet aurum Crassus
     et argentum saeculi.

4. Ibi latrat Scylla rapax
   et Charybdis auri capax
     potius quam navium.
   Ibi pugna galearum,
5 et conflictus piratarum,
     id est, cardinalium.

5. Syrtes insunt huic profundo
   et Sirenes, toti mundo
     minantes naufragium.
   Os humanum foris patet,
5 in occulto cordis latet
     informe daemonium.

6. Habes iuxta rationem
   bithalassum per Franconem.
     Quod ne credas frivolum.
   Ibi duplex mare fervet,
5 a quo non est qui reservet
     sibi valens obolum.

7. Ibi venti colliduntur,
   ibi panni submerguntur,
     byssus, ostrum, purpurae.
   Ibi mundus sepelitur,
5 immo totus deglutitur
     in Franconis gutture.

3.　I have seen it, I have seen the capital of the world,
　　a gullet as voracious
　　as the sea and the Sicilian deep.
　　There two seas of the world come together,
　　there Crassus sucks down　　　　　　　　　　5
　　the gold and silver of all mankind.

4.　There yelps rapacious Scylla,
　　there lurks Charybdis, swallowing gold
　　instead of ships.
　　There you hear the clash of galleys
　　and the brawling of pirates,　　　　　　　　　5
　　that is, the cardinals.

5.　In these deep waters there are Syrtes
　　and Sirens that threaten to shipwreck
　　the entire world.
　　A human face shows on the outside,
　　but deep in their hearts　　　　　　　　　　5
　　lurks hideous devilry.

6.　By all accounts, you have
　　a dangerous stretch past Franco.
　　Don't think it a simple matter.
　　A treacherous sea seethes there.
　　No one can safely keep　　　　　　　　　　5
　　an obol from him for himself.

7.　There winds collide,
　　there woven cloths go under—
　　fine sheets of crimson and purple.
　　There the world is buried
　　or rather swallowed whole　　　　　　　　　5
　　down Franco's gullet.

8.   Franco nulli miseretur,
    nullum sexum reveretur,
      nulli parcit sanguini.
    Omnes illi dona ferunt,
5   illuc enim ascenderunt
      tribus, tribus Domini.

9.   "Canes Scyllae" possunt dici
    veritatis inimici,
      advocati Curiae,
    qui latrando falsa fingunt,
5   mergunt simul et confringunt
      carinam pecuniae.

10.   Iste probat se legistam,
    ille vero decretistam,
      inducens Gelasium;
    ad probandum quaestionem,
5   hic intendit actionem
      regundorum finium.

11.   Nunc rem sermo prosequatur:
    hic Charybdis debacchatur,
      id est cancellaria,
    ubi nemo gratus gratis,
5   nulli datur absque datis
      Gratiani gratia.

12.   Plumbum, quod hic informatur,
    super aurum dominatur
      et massam argenteam.
    Aequitatis fantasia
5   sedet teste Zacharia
      super bullam plumbeam.

8.   Franco takes pity on no one,
      has no respect for either sex,
      and spares no bloodline.
      All bring their gifts to him,
      for the tribes have all gone up there,   5
      the tribes of the Lord.

9.   The lawyers of the Curia
      you can call "The Dogs of Scylla,"
      enemies of the truth,
      for they bark and make up falsehoods,
      while they smash and sink   5
      a shipload of money.

10.   One proves himself an expert
      in civil law, another in canon law,
      citing Gelasius;
      to test an issue,
      a third brings an action   5
      to determine limits.

11.   Now let my words reflect the reality.
      Here Charybdis, that is, the chancellery,
      raves like a madwoman;
      here no one is welcomed without a fee
      and the grace of Gratian is given   5
      only after gifts.

12.   Lead, which here they shape into a seal,
      lords it over gold
      and a mass of silver.
      According to Zechariah,
      a mere fantasy of justice   5
      sits on the lead seal.

13. Qui sunt Syrtes vel Sirenes?
    Qui sermone blando lenes
        attrahunt Byzantium.
    Spem praetendunt lenitatis,
5   sed procella parcitatis
        supinant marsupium.

14. Dulci cantu blandiuntur,
    ut Sirenes, et loquuntur
        primo quaedam dulcia:
    "Frare, ben je te cognosco,
5   certe nihil a te posco,
        nam tu es de Francia.

15. Terra vestra bene cepit
    et benigne nos recepit
        in portu concilii,
    nostri estis, nostri—cuius?
5   sacrosanctae sedis huius
        speciales filii.

16. Nos peccata relaxamus
    et laxatos collocamus
        sedibus aethereis.
    Nos habemus Petri leges
5   ad ligandos omnes reges
        in manicis ferreis."

17. Ita dicunt cardinales,
    ita solent di carnales
        in primis allicere.
    Sic instillant fel draconis
5   sed in fine lectionis
        cogunt bursam vomere.

13. Who are the Syrtes or the Sirens?
    Those who gently and with coaxing words
    draw the Bezant toward themselves.
    They hold out hopes of calm weather ahead,
    but with a howling gale of greed   5
    blow the purse flat.

14. They soothe you with their sweet songs
    like Sirens, and at first
    they say nice things to you:
    "I know you well, brother.
    I'm not going to ask you for a penny,   5
    for you're from France.

15. Your land kindly took us in
    and warmly welcomed us
    at the council's safe harbor.
    You are our children—whose?
    You are the special children   5
    of this Holy See.

16. We forgive sins
    and place the forgiven
    in heavenly abodes.
    We have the laws of Peter
    to enable us to bind all kings   5
    in iron manacles."

17. So say the cardinals,
    so the gods of the flesh
    usually start the process of enticement.
    In this way they instill the viper's venom,
    and at the end of the day   5
    they force your purse to spew forth.

18. Cardinales, ut praedixi,
     novo iure Crucifixi
         vendunt patrimonium,
     Petrus foris, intus Nero,
5   intus lupi, foris vero
         sicut agni ovium.

19. Tales regunt Petri navem,
     tales habent eius clavem,
         ligandi potentiam.
     Hi nos docent, sed indocti
5   hi nos docent et nox nocti
         indicat scientiam.

20. In galea sedet una
     mundi lues importuna
         camelos deglutiens.
     Involuta canopeo
5   cuncta vorat sicut leo
         rapiens et rugiens.

21. Hic piratis principatur—
     et Pilatus appellatur—
         sedens in insidiis
     ventre grosso, lota cute,
5   grande monstrum nec virtute
         redemptum a vitiis.

22. Maris huius non est dea
     Thetis mater Achillea,
         de qua saepe legimus;
     immo mater Sterlingorum,
5   sancta soror loculorum,
         quam nos Bursam dicimus.

18. The cardinals, as I have said before,
  by a strange, new right
  are selling Christ's patrimony—
  Peter on the outside, but Nero on the inside,
  wolves on the inside, but on the outside   5
  just like newborn lambs.

19. Such are the men who steer Peter's ship,
  such are the men who hold his key,
  the power to bind.
  These are our teachers, but they teach us,
  themselves untaught, and darkness reveals   5
  its knowledge to darkness.

20. In one galley sits
  a chronic scourge of the world,
  swallowing camels.
  Covered by a canopy,
  it devours everything, plundering   5
  and roaring like a lion.

21. He is the pirates' king—
  and Pilate is his name—
  sitting there in ambush,
  a big-bellied man with pampered skin,
  a huge monster, his vices   5
  unredeemed by any virtue.

22. This sea's goddess
  is not Thetis, mother of Achilles,
  about whom we have often read;
  rather, it is the mother of the Sterling boys,
  the holy sister of the wallets,   5
  whom we call Purse.

23. Haec dum praegnat, ductor ratis
     epulatur cum piratis
         et amicos reperit.
     Sed si Bursa detumescit;
5   surgunt venti, mare crescit
         et carina deperit.

24. Tunc occurrunt cautes rati,
     donec omnes sint privati
         tam nummis quam vestibus.
     Tunc securus fit viator,
5   quia nudus et cantator
         it coram latronibus.

25. Qui sunt cautes? Ianitores,
     per quos, licet saeviores
         tigribus et beluis,
     intrat dives aere plenus,
5   pauper autem et egenus
         pellitur a ianuis.

26. Quod si verum placet scribi,
     duo tantum portus ibi,
         duae tantum insulae,
     ad quas licet applicari,
5   et iacturam reparari
         confractae naviculae.

27. Petrus enim Papiensis,
     qui electus est Meldensis,
         portus recte dicitur;
     nam cum mare fluctus tollit,
5   ipse solus mare mollit
         et ad ipsum fugitur.

23. When Purse is pregnant,
    the ship's captain feasts with the pirates
    and finds friends.
    But if Purse loses her bulge,
    winds get up, the sea rises   5
    and the ship is destroyed.

24. At that point a ship encounters rocks
    until everyone is stripped
    of cash and clothes.
    Then the traveler goes his way, free from care,
    for if he comes face to face with robbers,   5
    he is naked and singing.

25. Who are the rocks? The doorkeepers,
    through whom, though they are fiercer
    than tigers and sharks,
    the rich man, full of cash, gains entrance,
    while the man who is poor and needy   5
    is driven from the door.

26. But if you wish the truth to be told,
    there are just two harbors there,
    just two islands,
    where you can put in
    and repair the damage   5
    to your broken ship.

27. Peter of Pavia,
    who was elected bishop of Meaux,
    is rightly called a harbor,
    for when the sea churns up its waves,
    he alone brings calm,   5
    and people turn to him for refuge.

28. Est et ibi maior portus,
     fetus ager, florens hortus,
        pietatis balsamum,
     Alexander ille meus,
5   meus inquam, cui det Deus
        paradisi thalamum.

29. Ille fovet litteratos;
     cunctos malis incurvatos,
        si posset, erigeret.
     Verus esset cultor Dei,
5   nisi latus Elisei
        Giezi corrumperet.

30. Sed ne rursus in hoc mari
     me contingat naufragari,
        dictis finem faciam,
     quia, dum securus eo,
5   ne submergar, ori meo
        posui custodiam.

42

1. Utar contra vitia   carmine rebelli.
    Mel proponunt alii,   fel supponunt melli.
    Pectus subest ferreum   deauratae pelli
    et leonis spolium   induunt aselli.

28. There is another, still greater harbor there,
    a fertile field, a flowering garden,
    compassion's balm,
    that is, my own dear Alexander.
    May God grant my Alexander   5
    a room in paradise!

29. He cherishes men of letters;
    if he could, he would raise up
    all those crushed by misfortune.
    He would be a true worshipper of God,
    if Gehazi were not corrupting   5
    Elisha's side.

30. But so as not to be shipwrecked
    in this sea again,
    I will put an end to my poem,
    because, while I now go carefree,
    I have put a guard on my mouth   5
    lest I be plunged beneath the waves.

42

1. I will employ a poem that fights back against vices.
   Others offer honey but conceal gall under the honey.
   Beneath a golden hide there beats an iron heart
   and it is asses that cover themselves with a lion's skin.

2. Disputat cum animo   facies rebellis.
    Mel ab ore profluit,   mens est plena fellis.
    Non est totum melleum,   quod est instar mellis;
    facies est alia   pectoris quam pellis.

3. Vitium in opere,   virtus est in ore,
    tegunt picem animi   niveo colore.
    Membra dolent singula   capitis dolore
    et radici consonat   ramus in sapore.

4. Roma mundi caput est,   sed nil capit mundum,
    quod pendet a capite,   totum est immundum.
    Trahit enim vitium   primum in secundum:
    et de fundo redolet,   quod est iuxta fundum.

5. Roma capit singulos   et res singulorum,
    Romanorum Curia   non est nisi forum.
    Ibi sunt venalia   iura senatorum,
    et solvit contraria   copia nummorum.

6. In hoc consistorio   si quis causam regat
    suam vel alterius,   hoc inprimis legat:
    nisi det pecuniam,   Roma totum negat;
    qui plus dat pecuniae,   melius allegat.

7. Romani capitulum   habent in decretis,
    ut petentes audiant   manibus repletis.
    Dabis aut non dabitur,   petunt quando petis;
    qua mensura seminas,   hac eadem metis.

8. Munus et petitio   currunt passu pari.
    Opereris munere,   si vis operari.
    Tullium ne timeas,   si velit causari;
    nummus eloquentia   gaudet singulari.

2. Their faces fight with their minds. Honey flows from their mouths, while their thoughts are full of gall. Not all that looks like honey is honey-sweet; the face is not bonded to the heart.

3. Vicious in what they do, virtuous in what they say, they hide the pitch in their hearts under a snow-white exterior. When the head is sick, so too are all the limbs; and the quality of the branch matches that of the root.

4. Rome is the capital of the world but contains nothing clean. Everything that depends on the head is unclean. The first vice leads to the second and what is next to the bottom smacks of the bottom.

5. Rome takes individuals and their property. The Roman Curia is nothing other than a marketplace. There the rulings of the senators are up for sale and a large chunk of cash eliminates opposition.

6. Anyone in charge of a case before this assembly, his own or someone else's, should first read this: unless he gives money, Rome says no to everything; he who gives more money makes the better case.

7. The Romans have a clause in their decrees that they will hear only those petitioners whose hands are full. You will give or it will not be given unto you. They ask, when you ask. As you sow, so do you reap.

8. Gift and petition go in lockstep. If you want to achieve your goal, do so with a gift. Do not be afraid of a Cicero, should he choose to plead; money enjoys outstanding eloquence.

9. Nummis in hac Curia   non est qui non vacet;
crux placet, rotunditas   et albedo placet,
et cum totum placeat   et Romanos placet,
ubi nummus loquitur,   et lex omnis tacet.

10. Si quo grandi munere   bene pascas manum,
frustra quis obiceret   vel Iustinianum
vel sanctorum canones,   quia tamquam vanum
transeunt has paleas,   et imbursant granum.

11. Solam avaritiam   Romae nevit Parca;
parcit danti munera,   parco non est parca,
nummus est pro numine   et pro Marco marca,
et est minus celebris   ara quam sit arca.

12. Cum ad papam veneris,   habe pro constanti:
non est locus pauperi,   soli favet danti,
vel si munus praestitum   non sit aliquanti,
respondet: "haec tibia   non est mihi tanti."

13. Papa, si rem tangimus,   nomen habet a re,
quicquid habent alii,   solus vult papare,
vel si verbum gallicum   vis apocopare,
"Paies! Paies!" dist li mot   si vis impetrare.

14. Porta quaerit, chartula   quaerit, bulla quaerit,
papa quaerit etiam,   cardinalis quaerit,
omnes quaerunt; et si des,   si quid uni deerit,
totum mare falsum fit,   tota causa perit.

15. Das istis, das aliis,   addis dona datis
et cum satis dederis,   quaerunt ultra satis.

9. There is no one in this Curia not focused on money. They like the cross, the roundness, and the silvery hue. Since Romans like everything about it and it soothes them, when money talks, even every law is silent.

10. Were you to feed a hand to good effect with a large gift it would be useless for anyone to cite either the Justinian code or the canons of our sainted fathers because they pass over this chaff as worthless and pocket the wheat.

11. The only thing Fate has spun for Rome is greed. She spares the giver of gifts and spares no one who fails to give. The denarius is her deity, and the mark is her Mark and the altar is celebrated less than the strongbox.

12. When you come before the pope, bear this in mind: it is no place for a poor man; only the donor he favors. If the gift presented to him is not of significant value, he replies: "I don't think this flute is worth much."

13. To be frank, the pope takes his name from his role; whatever others have, he wants to swallow whole himself, or if you want to abbreviate the French word, "Pay! Pay!" the word says, if you wish to win your plea.

14. The gate asks for a tip, the charter asks, the seal asks; the pope asks too, and so does the cardinal; everyone asks and if you pay and one comes up short, then the whole sea turns treacherous and everything is lost.

15. You give to one group, then to another. You add to the gifts you gave and when you have given enough, they

O vos bursae turgidae,   Romam veniatis,
Romae viget physica   bursis constipatis.

16. Praedantur marsupium   singuli paulatim.
    Magna, maior, maxima   praeda fit gradatim.
    Quid irem per singula?   Colligam summatim:
    omnes bursam strangulant,   et exspirat statim.

17. Bursa tamen Tityi   iecur imitatur.
    Fugit res, ut redeat,   perit, ut nascatur.
    Et hoc pacto loculum   Roma depraedatur,
    ut, cum totum dederit,   totus impleatur.

18. Redeunt a Curia   capite cornuto;
    ima tenet Iupiter,   caelum regit Pluto,
    et accedit dignitas   animali bruto,
    tamquam gemma stercori   vel pictura luto.

19. Divites divitibus   dant, ut sumant ibi,
    et occurrunt munera   relative sibi.
    Lex est ista celebris,   quam fecerunt scribi:
    "si tu mihi dederis,   ego dabo tibi."

43

1. Roma tuae mentis oblita sanitate
   desipis, cum resipisceris tarditate.
   Lampas caret oleo, male sed mercatur,
   sponsus et cum venerit, salus obumbratur,

ask for more. Bloated purses, come to Rome! Rome abounds in medicine for constipated purses.

16. One by one they gradually prey on your purse. Slowly their booty becomes big, bigger, very big. Why go into detail? I will cut the story short: they all strangle your purse and it promptly breathes its last.

17. Your purse, however, imitates the liver of Tityus. The money slips away only to return; it perishes only to be reborn. Rome makes such depredations on your purse that when it has given its all, it all fills up again.

18. They come back from the Curia, horns on their heads. A Jupiter rules the lowest depths, a Pluto rules the sky. High office is given to a brainless brute, as one might add a jewel to a dunghill or put a painting in the mud.

19. The rich give to the rich to take on the spot and gifts flow back and forth between them. This is the famous law that they caused to be written: "You give to me and I will give to you."

43

1. Rome, since you have taken leave of your senses and are slow to recover, you are floundering. Your lamp lacks oil, which cannot easily be bought, and when the bridegroom comes, your salvation will be in the shadows

5 pietas nec audit supernae civitatis,
  foris dum inclamitat vox calamitatis.

2. O sedes apostolica,
  quae vix lates catholica,
  convertere, convertere!
  Iam mundus languet opere.

      3. Perit lex,
       manet faex.
       Bibit grex
       virus hoc letale.
5   Pastor cedit,
       lupus redit,
       morsu laedit
        permale.

4. Claudicat ecclesia patribus orbata.
  Sternitur iustitia capite truncata.
  Princeps tenebrarum se sentit gloriari
  orbis fluxa, miseri student quem sectari.

5. Ludit ad interitum rerum coniectura
  quodam vili schemate, docet ut natura.
  Basem rei publicae, sortem senatorum
  machina corrodit praesentium malorum.
5 Sed si de qua viguit stirpe solidatur,
  huius et propagine solium laetatur.

      6. O decus exaltabile
       saluti collaudabile,
       complectere, complectere!
       Iam languet mundus opere.

and the compassion of the heavenly city does not hear   5
when calamitous cries are raised outside the gate.

2.   Ah Apostolic See,
      you that are universal and can scarcely remain hidden,
      change your ways, change your ways!
      The world is now really sick.

3.   Law has gone,
      a polluted mess remains.
      The flock drinks
      this lethal poison.
      The shepherd departs,   5
      the wolf returns
      and with his bite
      inflicts severe wounds.

4.   The Church limps, deprived of its fathers. Justice has
      been laid low, its head lopped off. The Prince of Dark-
      ness sees he is winning glory from the world's flux, for
      wretched mortals are eager to follow him.

5.   The entire world amuses itself in the face of its own
      destruction after the vulgar fashion that nature teaches.
      The siege engine of our present ills is corroding the
      state's foundation and the fate of its leaders. But if it   5
      gains strength from the stock from which it has drawn
      its vigor, the throne will prosper with its descendants
      also.

6.   O glory to be exalted,
      to be praised for our salvation,
      embrace us, embrace us!
      The world is now really sick.

7.   Sed cum sis
     plena vis,
     cedat lis
vitia premantur,
5   orbe laeto,
     tristi spreto,
     iure freto,
pellantur.

8.   Aruit spes aestuans   diuturnitate,
     saecula iam pereunt   imbecillitate.
     Ordo principalium   mente discrepata
     volvitur, miseria   mundo non piata.
5 Falso quoque veritas convincitur augurio,
nec altus est in Israel fidem dans centurio.

44

Ewangelium

Initium sancti evangeli secundum marcas argenti.

In illo tempore dixit papa Romanis: "Cum venerit filius ho-
minis ad sedem maiestatis nostrae, primum dicite: "Amice,
ad quid venisti?" At ille si perseveraverit pulsans, nil dans

7. Since you are
    a full force,
    let strife depart
    and our vices be crushed
    and driven   5
    from a world filled with joy,
    where sadness has been banished
    and reliance is placed on the law.

8. Hope has dried up in the long, sweltering heat. The
    world is coming to an end in its weak old age. Those
    who constitute our leadership are divided in their opin-
    ions and vacillate, while the world's misery remains un-
    mitigated. Truth is defeated by false prophecy, nor has   5
    a centurion who inspires confidence been raised in
    Israel.

44

Gospel

The Beginning of the Holy Gospel according to
Marks of Silver.

At that time the pope said to the Romans: "When the Son
of man comes to the seat of our majesty, first say to him:
"Friend, why have you come?" If he persists in knocking at

vobis, eicite eum in tenebras exteriores." Factum est autem, ut quidam pauper clericus veniret ad Curiam Domini Pape, et exclamavit dicens: "Miseremini mei saltem vos, ostiarii papae, quia manus paupertatis tetigit me. Ego vero egenus et pauper sum; ideo peto ut subveniatis calamitati et miseriae meae." Illi autem audientes indignati sunt valde et dixerunt: "Amice, paupertas tua tecum sit in perditione. Vade retro, Satanas, quia non sapis ea, quae sapiunt nummi. Amen, amen, dico tibi: non intrabis in gaudium domini tui, donec dederis novissimum quadrantem." Pauper vero abiit et vendidit pallium et tunicam et universa quae habuit et dedit cardinalibus et ostiariis et camerariis. At illi dixerunt: "Et hoc, quid est inter tantos?" Et eiecerunt eum ante fores, et egressus foras flevit amare et non habens consolationem.

Postea venit ad Curiam quidam clericus dives, incrassatus, impinguatus, dilatatus, qui propter seditionem fecerat homicidium. Hic primo dedit ostiario, secundo camerario, tertio cardinalibus. At illi arbitrati sunt inter eos, quod essent plus accepturi. Audiens autem dominus papa cardinales et ministros plurima dona a clerico accepisse, infirmatus est usque ad mortem. Dives vero misit sibi electuarium aureum et argenteum et statim sanatus est. Tunc Dominus Papa ad se vocavit cardinales et ministros et dixit eis, "Fratres, videte, ne aliquis vos seducat inanibus verbis. Exemplum enim do vobis, ut, quemadmodum ego capio, ita et vos capiatis."

the gate without offering you anything, throw him out into the outer darkness." Now it came to pass that a certain poor cleric came to the Curia of the Lord Pope. He cried aloud, saying: "Take pity on me, you who are the pope's gatekeepers, because the hand of poverty has touched me. I am poor and in need; for this reason I ask you to come to my assistance in my calamity and misfortune." The gatekeepers, however, when they heard this, were very indignant and said: "Friend, to hell with you and your poverty. Get thee behind me, Satan, because you do not smell like money. Verily, verily I say unto you, you will not enter into the joy of your master until you have given your last penny." The poor man went away and sold his outer garment and his tunic and everything he had and gave the proceeds to the cardinals and the gatekeepers and the chamberlains. They said to him: "And what is this among so many?" and they threw him out in front of the gate and he went away and wept bitterly and inconsolably.

Later a rich cleric came to the Curia, all fattened up, stout, and puffed up. He had committed homicide over a quarrel. First of all, he gave something to the gatekeeper, then to the chamberlain, and then to the cardinals. They thought among themselves that they would get more. Now the Lord Pope, hearing that the cardinals and his servants had received very many gifts from the cleric, became sick to the point of death. So the rich man sent him a pill of gold and silver and at once he was cured. Then the Lord Pope called his cardinals and ministers to him and said to them: "My brothers, make sure that no one sways you with empty words. I am setting this example for you, so that just as I receive, so shall you receive."

45

Versus

1. Roma, tenens morem   nondum satiata priorem,
   donas donanti,   parcis tibi participanti.
   Sed miser immunis   censetur, eum quia punis.
   "Accipe," "sume," "cape"   tria sunt gratissima papae,
5.   "Nil do," "nil praesto"   nequeunt succurrere maesto.
   Non est Romanis   curae legatus inanis.
   Si dederis marcas,   et eis impleveris arcas,
   poena solveris   quacumque ligatus haberis.
   Ergo non nosco,   quamvis cognoscere posco,
10.   in quo papalis   res distet et imperialis.
   Rex capit argentum,   marcarum milia centum;
   et facit illud idem   paparum Curia pridem.
   Rex facit audenter,   Dominus sed Papa latenter.
   Ergo pari poena,   rapientes sic aliena
15.   condemnabuntur,   quia Simonis acta sequuntur.

2. Curia Romana   non curat ovem sine lana.

3. Roma manus rodit;   si rodere non valet, odit.

45

Metrical Verses

1. Rome, sticking to your old ways and still not satisfied, you give to those who give to you but are stingy toward those entitled to a share. But the man without a gift you consider a wretch, because you punish him. "Accept," "take," and "receive" are the three words most welcome to the pope. "I have nothing to give," "I have 5 nothing to offer" cannot help the dejected petitioner. An empty-handed envoy is of no interest to the Romans. If you give marks and fill their chests with them, you will be absolved from any penalty for which you are bound and held. So I don't know, though I seek to know, in what respect papal and imperial transactions 10 differ. The king takes money—a hundred thousand marks. The papal Curia has long been doing exactly the same. The king takes brazenly, while the Lord Pope does so secretly. Accordingly, since both plunder in this way what belongs to others, they will be condemned 15 to the same punishment because both imitate Simon's deeds.

2. The Roman Curia does not care for a sheep without wool.

3. Rome gnaws hands; if it can't gnaw, it hates.

46

De Cruce Signatis

1.   Fides cum Idolatria
       pugnavit teste Gratia,
       agresti vultu turbida,
       mundi non quaerens tegmina,
5   sed forti fidens pectore,
       dives una cum paupere.

2.   Propheta teste, misera
       tu Babylonis filia.
       Beatus est qui parvulos
       petrae collidit tuos!
5   Prisci das poenas sceleris
       Chaldaea nunc metropolis.

3.   Iohannes super bestiam
       sedere vidit feminam
       ornatam, ut est meretrix,
       in forma Babylonis.
5   Sed tempus adest calicis
       faeces usque sceleris.

4.   Princeps vocatur principum,
       qui colla premit gentium.
       Costam scandat tetragoni
       sedentis ut aeterni
5   sub Herculis memoria
       vexilla ponens rosea.

46

About Crusaders

1. Rough and disordered in her appearance,
   Faith fought with Idolatry
   with Grace as witness,
   not looking for worldly protection,
   but rather trusting in her stout heart,   5
   the rich along with the poor.

2. As the prophet bears witness,
   daughter of Babylon, your lot is wretched.
   Blessed is he who smashes
   your little children against the rock!
   You are paying the penalty for the crime of old,   5
   you who are now capital of Chaldea.

3. John saw a woman
   sitting on a beast,
   adorned like a prostitute,
   symbolizing Babylon.
   Now is the time to drink   5
   the cup for your crime to the lees.

4. He who crushes the necks of the nonbelievers,
   is called the Prince of Princes.
   Let him climb the side of the rectangle
   that is forever seated there
   and place the rose-colored standards   5
   to commemorate Hercules.

5.   Quem Deus ponet hominem
       navis in artemonem,
       cuius regat pulcherrimum
       velum triangulatum.
5   Hinc militum tripudio
       laetetur Pacis Visio!

6.   Confusionis Civitas
       decepit te, Gentilitas.
       Inniteris harundini,
       cladem laturae manui.
5   Revertere, revertere!
       Factoris opus respice.

7.   Qui colunt cacodaemones,
       non fiunt illis similes,
       qui fibris non utuntur,
       dum illis insculpuntur,
5   nec vox inest nec ratio,
       nec locus in arbitrio?

8.   Beati sunt mucrones,
       quos portant Christi milites,
       suffulti crucis tegmine,
       sub cuius gaudent robore,
5   quorum felix atrocitas
       constringit te, Gentilitas.

9.   De viis atque saepibus
       et mundi voluptatibus
       compellimur intrare:
       "Nunc nuper epulare,
5   gusta saepe medullitus
       quam suavis sit Dominus!"

5. God will set up this man
    as the ship's foremast
    to control its beautiful
    triangular topsail.
    So let the Vision of Peace rejoice   5
    in the soldiers' exultation!

6. The City of Confusion
    has deceived you, nonbelievers.
    You are leaning on a reed,
    a hand that will bring disaster.
    Go back, go back!   5
    Consider the work of the Creator.

7. Don't those who worship demons
    become like those
    who cannot use their muscles,
    though invested with them,
    and have no voice or power of reasoning,   5
    and where they stand is not theirs to decide?

8. Blessed are the swords
    that Christ's soldiers carry,
    relying on the protection of the cross,
    in whose strength they rejoice;
    their fortunate ferocity, non-believers,   5
    keeps you in check.

9. From the pathways, hedgerows,
    and pleasures of the world,
    we are driven to go inside:
    "Feast just now,
    savor often deep within,   5
    how sweet the Lord is!"

10. Nam panis filiorum
    fit cibus catulorum
    sub mensa pii domini
    de verbis evangelii.
5   Gaude, Syrophoenissa,
    iam valet tua filia!

11. Forum est Ierosolymis
    in campo libertatis,
    quod Rex regum instituit.
    Mercator prudens aderit.
5   Qui vitam velit emere,
    festinet illuc currere!

12. Non tamen ita properet,
    quin coniugi provideat
    de rebus necessariis
    una cum parvis liberis.
5   Quod quidem nisi faciat,
    ignoro quid proficiat.

13. Sepulchrum gloriosum
    prophetis declaratum
    impugnatur a canibus,
    quibus sanctum non dabimus.
5   Nec porcis margaritae
    mittuntur deridendae.

14. Ad multas mansiones
    in domo Patris stabiles
    nummi trahit conventio.
    Nec gravet operatio,
5   pondus diei praeterit,
    merces perennis aderit.

10. The children's bread
    becomes food for the young dogs
    under the table of a kindly master,
    as the words of the gospel tell us.
    Rejoice, Phoenician woman of Syria,   5
    your daughter is now in good health!

11. There is a market in Jerusalem
    in the field of freedom,
    which the King of Kings has established.
    The prudent merchant will be there.
    May whoever wants to buy eternal life   5
    make haste to hurry there!

12. Let him not, however, be in such a hurry
    that he does not provide for his wife
    and his little children
    regarding life's necessities.
    Should he fail in this,   5
    I don't know what he accomplishes.

13. The tomb of glory
    described by the prophets
    is being attacked by dogs
    but we will not give them what is holy.
    Pearls are not cast before swine   5
    only to be mocked.

14. The wages agreed upon take you
    to the many everlasting mansions
    in the house of the Father.
    Don't let the work weary you.
    The day's burden passes,   5
    the lasting reward will remain.

15. Novissimus fit primus,
et primus fit novissimus.
Dispar quidem vocatio,
sed par remuneratio,
5   dum cunctis laborantibus
vitae datur denarius.

16. Non hic mutatur sedes,
non corrumpuntur aedes,
non maior hic minori,
non pauper ditiori,
5   non obstat alter alteri,
nec locus hic opprobrii.

47

1. Crucifigat omnes
Domini crux altera,
nova Christi vulnera!
Arbor salutifera
5   perditur; sepulchrum
gens evertit extera
violente.   Plena gente
sola sedet civitas.
Agni foedus   rapit haedus,
10   plorat dotes perditas
sponsa Sion. Immolatur
Ananias, incurvatur

15. The last will be first,
and the first will be last.
The hour of summons varies
but the reward is the same,
since the wage of eternal life   5
is given to all the laborers.

16. Here there is no change of residence,
here the houses do not decay,
here the great man is not at odds with the lesser,
nor the poor man with the rich man,
nor any man with another,   5
nor is there any scope for recrimination.

47

1. May our Lord's second cross
and Christ's fresh wounds
crucify us all!
Lost is the Tree that brings salvation!
A foreign people   5
has violently overthrown his tomb.
The city, once full of people,
sits abandoned.
A goat has seized the Lamb's covenant,
Zion the bride, mourns   10
her lost dowry.
Hananiah is sacrificed,

cornu David. Flagellatur
   mundus,
15 ab iniustis abdicatur,
per quem iuste iudicatur
   mundus.

2. O quam dignos luctus!
  Exulat rex omnium!
  Baculus fidelium
  sustinet opprobrium
5   gentis infidelis!
  Cedit parti gentium
pars totalis. Iam regalis
  in luto et latere
elaborat tellus, plorat
10 Moysen fatiscere.
Homo, Dei miserere!
Fili, Patris ius tuere!
In incerto certum quaere;
   ducis
15 ducum dona promerere
et lucrare lucem verae
   lucis.

3. Quisquis es signatus
  fidei charactere,
  fidem factis assere;
  rugientes contere
5   catulos leonum.
  Miserans intuere
corde tristi damnum Christi.
  Longus Cedar incola,

and the power of David bent low.
One who is innocent,
by whom the world is rightly judged,   15
is being scourged
and abjured by the unrighteous!

2.   How fitting the grief!
The king of the world is exiled!
The staff of the faithful
endures the jeers
of the infidels!   5
The entire region yields
to the side of the nonbelievers.
Now the royal land
toils with mud and bricks, and laments
the helplessness of its Moses.   10
Mankind, take pity on God!
Son, protect your Father's rights!
In a time of uncertainty seek what is certain;
earn the gifts
of the Lord of lords   15
and gain the light
of the true light.

3.   All you who are marked
with the stamp of faith,
assert that faith with deeds;
crush the roaring
lion cubs!   5
Gaze with pity
and a saddened heart on Christ's loss.
You who long have lived in Kedar, arise!

surge! Vide   ne de fide
10   reproberis frivola!
Suda martyr in agone!
Spe mercedis et coronae
derelicta Babylone
           pugna
15 pro caelesti regione!
Aqua vitae te compone
           pugna!

47a

1.   Curritur ad vocem
      nummi vel ad sonitum;
      haec est vox ad placitum.
      Omnes ultra debitum
5   (ut exempla docent)
      nitimur in vetitum.
      Disce morem   et errorem
        fac et tu similiter!
      Hac in vita   nihil vita;
10   vive sic, non aliter!
      Cleri vivas ad mensuram,
      qui pro censu das censuram
      quando iacis in capturam
           rete.
15   Messem vides iam maturam,
      et tu saltem per usuram
           mete!

See that they don't accuse you
of a frivolous faith!   10
Sweat like a martyr in the throes of death!
With the expectation of a crown as a reward
leave Babylon behind
    and fight
for the kingdom of Heaven!   15
Compose yourself with the water of Life
    by fighting!

47a

1.   When money calls
or clinks, we run.
This is a sound we like.
All of us strive more than we should
(as we learn from examples)   5
for what is forbidden.
Learn men's ways, mistakes and all,
and go and do likewise!
Shun nothing in this life!
This is the way to live — no other way!   10
Follow the example of the clergy
in tailoring your judgments to a person's wealth
when you cast your net
to capture your prey!
You see that the harvest is now ripe,   15
make sure you reap too —
    with interest!

2. Si quis in hoc artem
    populo non noverit,
    per quam mundus vixerit,
    omnia cum viderit,
5   eligat hanc partem,
    aut nihil decreverit:
    quod vis, aude   dolo, fraude.
            Mos gerendus Thaidi,
    mundo gere   morem! Vere
10   nil vitandum credidi.
            Legi nihil sit astrictum,
    iuri nihil sit addictum.
    Sanciatur hoc edictum
                    tibi:
15 ubi virtus est delictum,
    Deo nihil est relictum
                    ibi.

48

1. Quod spiritu   David praecinuit,
                    nunc exposuit
    nobis Deus,   et sic innotuit.
    Sarracenus   sepulchrum polluit,
5   quo recubuit
    qui pro nobis   crucifixus fuit.
    Quantum nobis   in hoc condoluit,
    quantum nobis   propitius fuit,

2.   If there is anyone in this nation,
     who is unfamiliar with the tricks
     by which the world lives,
     he should, once he has seen everything,
     assume this role   5
     or make no decision:
     dare to go after what you want—by guile or deceit!
     You have to humor Thais;
     humor the world! I have truly come to believe
     that nothing is to be shunned.   10
     There should be no strict observance of the law,
     no slavish adherence to what is right!
     Let this pronouncement be sacred
     for you:
     where virtue is a crime,   15
     there is no place left
     for God there.

48

1.   What David foretold mystically,
          God has now
     revealed to us and so it has become known:
     the Saracen has profaned the tomb,
          where he reposed   5
     who was crucified for us.
     How much compassion he felt for us in doing this!
     How great was his benevolence toward us

dum sic voluit
10   mortem pati   cruce, nec meruit!
Ref. Exsurgat Deus!

2.   Et dissipet   hostes, quos habuit,
postquam praebuit
Sarracenis   locum, quo iacuit.

\<three lines missing\>

7   Duo ligna   diu non habuit,
Sarreptina,   quibus ut caruit,
semper doluit
10   et dolebit,   dum rehabuerit.
Ref. Exsurgat Deus!

3.   Sunamitis   clamat pro filio,
qui occubuit,
nec Giezi   sanare potuit:
"Helisaeus   nisi met venerit
5   non surrexerit,
et os ori   recte coniunxerit."
Helisaeus   nisi nunc venerit,
ni peccata   compassus tulerit,
non habuerit
10   ecclesia   crucem, qua caruit.
Ref. Exsurgat Deus!

4.   Et adiuuet   in hoc exercitu,
quos signaverit
signo crucis,   qua nos redemerit.
Iam veniae   tempus advenerit,
5   quo potuerit

when he so chose
to suffer undeserved death on the cross!　　　　10
　　Ref. May God rise up!

2.　　Let him scatter the enemies he acquired
　　　　　　when he granted
　　　the Saracens the place where he lay,

　　　\<three lines missing>

　　　The widow of Zarephath did not have her two sticks　　7
　　　for long and when she lost them,
　　　　　　she constantly grieved for them
　　　and will grieve for them until she has them again.　　10
　　　　　　Ref. May God rise up!

3.　　The Shunamite woman called out for her son
　　　　　　when he died
　　　and Gehazi could not heal him:
　　　"If Elisha does not come himself
　　　and duly apply mouth to mouth,　　　　5
　　　　　　he will not rise again."
　　　If an Elisha does not come today,
　　　and with compassion take our sins from us,
　　　　　　the church will not regain
　　　the cross it has lost.　　　　10
　　　　　　Ref. May God rise up!

4.　　May he come to assist those in this army
　　　　　　he has marked
　　　with the sign of the cross with which he redeems us.
　　　The time for forgiveness will soon be here
　　　　　　when salvation　　　　5

se salvare,   qui crucem ceperit.
Nunc videat   quisque, quid fecerit,
quibus et quot   Deum offenderit.
              Quod si viderit,
10   et se signet,   his solutus erit.
              Ref. Exsurgat Deus!

5.   Exsurrexit!   Et nos assurgere
                  ei propere
iam tenemur   atque succurrere.
Ierusalem   voluit perdere,
5   ut hoc opere
sic possemus   culpas diluere;
nam si vellet   hostes destruere
absque nobis   et terram solvere
                  posset propere,
cum sibi nil   possit resistere.
10   *Ref.* Exsurgat Deus!

48a

"Hœrstu, friunt, den wahter, an der zinne,
wes sîn sanc verjach?
wir müezen uns scheiden nû, lieber man.
alsô schiet dîn lîp nû jungest hinnen,
5   dô der tac ûf brach
unde uns diu naht sô flühteclîchen tran.
naht gît senfte, wê tuot tac.

can be won by everyone who takes up the cross.
Now let each reflect on what he has done,
with what acts—and how many—he has offended
  God. If he reflects on this
and takes the cross, he will be freed from these sins. 10
  Ref. May God rise up!

5. He has risen up! We too are now bound
   to rise up for him in haste
 and hurry to his assistance.
 He chose to destroy Jerusalem
   so that by undertaking this task, 5
 we could wash away our sins;
 for if he wished, he could quickly
 destroy the enemy without our help
   and set the land free,
 for nothing can stand up to him. 10
  Ref. May God rise up!

48a

"Do you hear, my friend, the watchman on the battlement?
Do you hear what his song proclaimed?
We must part now, dear man.
Just so, not long ago, you left this place
when day broke 5
and night slipped away from us like a fugitive.
The night brings comfort, the day brings sorrow.

owê, herze liep, in mac
dîn nû verbergen niht.
10 uns nimet diu freude gar daz grâwe lieht.
stant ûf, riter!"

49

1. Tonat evangelica   clara vox in mundo:
"Qui dormis in pulvere,   surge de profundo!
Luce sua Dominus   te illuminabit
et a malis omnibus   animam salvabit."

2. Memor esto, iuvenis,   tui creatoris.
Crux Christi te moneat   omnibus in horis.
Cape mente, cogita   corde de futuris,
quod ad radicem arboris   sit posita securis.

3. Senes et decrepiti,   vobis est oblata
vera paenitentia   cruce Christi data.
Dies vestra desiit   et est inclinata,
nam ad umbram vergitur   fine desperata.

4. Ecce cum fiducia   venit regnum Dei.
Illud primum quaerite   vos qui estis rei.
Carnem crucifigite   famulantes ei
et in psalmis dicite: "Miserere mei!"

5. O peccatrix anima,   si vis dealbari
et ab omni crimine   penitus mundari,
te in cruce Domini   oportet gloriari
et in ipsa penitus   ab hoste liberari.

Ah, my heart's true love,
I can no longer hide you.
The gray light robs us of all our joy.   10
Rise up, my knight!"

49

1.   The clear voice of the gospel thunders in the world:
"Arise from the depths, you who sleep in the dust! The
Lord will make his light shine upon you and will save
your soul from all evils."

2.   Be mindful, young man, of your creator. Let the cross
of Christ be your guide at all times. Grasp it with your
mind; reflect in your heart on the future, recalling that
an ax has been placed at the root of the tree.

3.   You who are old and broken, you have been offered
true repentance as the gift of Christ's cross.
Your day has passed and is now on a downward slope
for it is headed for the darkness, despairing of its end.

4.   See! The kingdom of God comes with the help of faith!
Seek that first, you who are guilty of sin.
Crucify the flesh, you who are slaves to it,
and sing with the psalms "Take pity on me!"

5.   Ah, sinful soul, if you wish to be washed white as snow
and completely cleansed of every sin, you ought to
glory in the cross of the Lord and through it completely
free yourself from the enemy.

6. Iacob scalae summitas   altera calcatur,
  in qua Christi passio   nobis reseratur.
  Tyrus alta desinit,   in se reprobatur;
  in Iudea Domini   mons uber adoratur.

7. O fidelis anima,   clama de profundis!
  De terrenis fugito   rebus et immundis!
  Cruce Christi naviga   velis in secundis
  ne te ventus turbinis   suffocet in undis.

8. Cum per ignem venerit   nos iudicaturus
  homo Dei Filius,   nulli parcens, durus,
  eius omnis crucifer   erit tunc securus
  gratulans cum angelis,   candidus et purus.

9. In die iudicii   cum sol obscuratur
  et lumen fidelibus   crucis Christi datur,
  tunc in peccatoribus   hostis dominatur,
  sed ab hoste crucifer   tunc omnis liberatur.

10. Ergo Christi milites,   fugite beati
  huius mundi gloriam   cruce iam signati,
  in qua Christus moriens   mortem superavit,
  atque suo sanguine   peccata nostra lavit.

11. Quid erit, cum stabimus   ante tribunal Christi?
  Pandens sua vulnera   dicet: "Quid fecisti?
  Pro te crucem subii;   quare non subisti
  hanc loco paenitentiae?   Vade, iam peristi!"

6. We are reaching the top of a second Jacob's ladder, whereby Christ's passion is revealed to us. Lofty Tyre is nearing its end, condemned out of its own mouth. The fertile hill of the Lord is worshipped in Judea.

7. Faithful soul, cry out from the depths! Flee from things that are of this world and unclean! Steer your course by Christ's cross under billowing sails to ensure that no storm wind engulfs you under the waves.

8. When the man who is the Son of God comes in fire
   to judge us, stern and sparing none,
   then everyone who bears his cross will be safe,
   white and pure, rejoicing with the angels.

9. On Judgment Day, when the sun is darkened,
   and the light of Christ's cross is given to the faithful,
   then the enemy holds dominion over sinners
   but everyone who bears the cross he then sets free.

10. So, blessed soldiers of Christ, flee from this world's glory, for you are now marked with the cross on which Christ conquered death by dying and with his blood washed away our sins.

11. What will happen when we stand before Christ's judgment seat? He will show his wounds and say "What have you done? I endured the cross for you; why did you not take it up by way of repentance? Away with you! You are done for!"

12. Ergo foetens Lazarus   ducatur in exemplum
digne paenitentibus,   ut sint eius templum,
in quo virtus habitet   suae passionis,
hoc impleat et muniat   ipse suis donis!

50

1. Heu voce flebili   cogor enarrare
facinus, quod accidit   nuper ultra mare,
quando Saladino concessum est vastare
terram, quam dignatus est   Christus sic amare.

2. Exeunte Iunio   anno post milleno
centum et octoginta   iunctis cum septeno,
quo respexit Dominus   mundum sorde pleno
erigens de stercore   pauperem ac caeno,

3. Malus comes Tripolis   mentem ferens ream
magna cum tyrannide   tenens Tiberiam
Turcos suis fraudibus   ducit in Iudaeam
atque primum occupat   totam Galilaeam.

4. Saladinus convocat   barbaros per gyrum
habitantes Phrygiam,   Pontum usque Tyrum,
Agarenos populos,   Arabem et Syrum,
ab Aegypti finibus   usque in Epirum.

12. So let Lazarus, smelling of the grave, be adduced as an example for those who are properly repentant, so that they may be his temple in which the power of his Passion may dwell; may he fill and fortify this temple with his gifts.

50

1. Alas I am forced to recount, in a tearful voice,
a crime that recently occurred overseas,
when Saladin was allowed to lay waste
the land that Christ had the grace to love so much.

2. At the end of June in the one hundred and eighty-seventh year after the millennium, when the Lord cast his gaze on our world filled with filth, seeking to raise the poor man from the dunghill and the mire,

3. the evil count of Tripoli, who ruled Tiberias with a tyrannical hand, his heart filled with criminal intent, treacherously brought the Turks into Judea, first seizing the whole of Galilee.

4. Saladin gathered his barbarian troops from all around, inhabitants of Phrygia, Pontus, and as far south as Tyre, the peoples descended from Hagar, the Arab and Syrian, from the land of Egypt as far as west as Epirus.

5. Veniunt Turcomili   atque Trogoditae,
   Mauri atque Gaetuli,   Barbari et Scythae,
   filii Moab, Ammon   et Ismahelitae,
   atque cum his omnibus   sunt Amalechitae.

6. Turcos ac Massagetas   praecipit adesse;
   Tatari atque Sarmates   nolunt hinc abesse;
   currunt Quadi, Vandili,   Medi atque Persae,
   undique conveniunt   gentes sic diversae.

7. Terram intrant inclitam,   cuncta devastantes,
   capiunt Christicolas,   senes et infantes,
   et, ut ferae pessimae   sanguinem amantes,
   iugulant puerulos,   dividunt praegnantes.

8. Saladino igitur   terram sic ingresso
   rex atque Templarii   currunt ex adverso,
   totis obstant nisibus   barbaro perverso
   cupientes populo   subvenire presso.

9. Turci pugnant acriter,   iacula mittentes,
   Christianos vulnerant,   cedunt resistentes,
   et, ut malae bestiae   dentibus frementes,
   territant sonipedes   tubis perstrepentes.

10. Nostri se dum sentiunt   ita praegravatos
    et a malis gentibus   undique vallatos,
    stringunt suis manibus   enses deauratos
    atque truncant fortiter   barbaros armatos.

5. The Turkmens came and the Troglodytes,
    the Mauri and Getulians, the Berbers and Scythians,
    the sons of Moab and Ammon, and the Ishmaelites,
    and in addition to all these there were the Amalekites.

6. The Turks and Massagetae he ordered to attend; the
    Tatars and Sarmatians had no wish to be absent. The
    Quadi, Vandals, Medes and Persians hurried to join
    him. Such were the diverse peoples who gathered from
    all sides.

7. They invaded the famous land, devastating everything.
    They captured Christians, old and infants alike, and
    like savage, bloodthirsty wild beasts they slit children's
    throats and cut open pregnant women.

8. When Saladin invaded the land in this way, the king
    and Templars hurried to oppose him and strove by ev-
    ery means to block the malevolent barbarian, seeking
    to aid the oppressed people.

9. The Turks fought fiercely, hurling their spears; they
    wounded the Christians, cut down those who resisted,
    and, like evil beasts gnashing their teeth, terrorized the
    horses with trumpet blasts.

10. When our men felt themselves thus hard-pressed
    and hemmed in on all sides by hostile nonbelievers,
    they took their gilt swords in their hands
    and bravely hacked away at the armed barbarians.

11. Plus quam decem milia   erant Christiani,
     sed pro uno quolibet   ter centum pagani;
     sic pugnando comminus   Bactri et Hyrcani,
     vix ex nostris aliqui   evaserunt sani.

12. Rex cum cruce capitur,   alii truncantur,
     ter centum Templarii   capti decollantur,
     quorum nulla corpora   sepulturae dantur,
     sed a Christo animae   caelo coronantur.

13. Nostrae postquam acies   ita sunt confractae,
     currunt crudelissimae   gentes illa parte,
     urbem Acrim capiunt   absque ullo Marte
     atque omnes alias   manu, simul arte.

14. Surim solam liberat   navita marinus
     marchio clarissimus   vere palatinus,
     cuius vires approbat   Graecus et Latinus,
     timet quoque plurimum   ferox Saladinus.

15. Latro ille pessimus   terrae devastator,
     per quam suis pedibus   transiit Salvator,
     natus qui ex virgine   omnium creator
     in praesepi ponitur   caeli fabricator.

16. Inde siccis pedibus   maria calcavit,
     et ex quinque panibus   multos satiavit,
     quem Iohannes praedicans   digito monstravit,
     et Iordanis sentiens   post retrogradavit.

17. Cruci demum fixus est   Deus homo natus,
     aquam atque sanguinem   sparsit eius latus
     quo ac tali pretio   mundus est salvatus,
     qui per primum hominem   fuerat damnatus.

11. There were more than ten thousand Christians but for each Christian there were three hundred pagans; so it was that as Bactrians and Hyrcanians fought them hand to hand, only a few of our men escaped unscathed.

12. The king was captured along with the cross; others were mutilated; three hundred Templars were captured and beheaded and none of their bodies were buried, but their souls are crowned by Christ in heaven.

13. After they broke through our ranks in this way, the nonbelievers moved over the land with great speed and cruelty. They captured Acre without a fight and all the other towns by force and guile.

14. Tyre alone was liberated—by a naval man, a most distinguished count, a true paladin, whose prowess won the approval of Greeks and Latins alike. Fierce Saladin particularly feared him.

15. That vile brigand, plunderer of the land over which the feet of our Savior traversed, who, though creator of all, was born of a virgin, and, though maker of heaven, was placed in a crib.

16. Then he trod the sea dry-shod and satisfied the hunger of a multitude with five loaves. While preaching, John the Baptist pointed him out and when the Jordan felt his body, it flowed backward.

17. In the end he was crucified, God born a man,
    water and blood spurted from his side.
    Such was the price he paid for the salvation of the
    world, which the first man had damned.

18. Heu, terra inclita,   terra vere bona,
    sola digna perfrui   florida corona,
    terra, cui dederat   Deus tanta dona,
    heu, quantum impia   te nunc cingit zona!

19. Heu, heu, Domine,   gloria iustorum,
    angelorum bonitas,   salus peccatorum,
    ecce, canes comedunt   panes filiorum,
    velut aqua funditur   sanguis nunc sanctorum.

20. Flete, omnes populi,   flete, et non parum,
    graves luctus facite   planctum et amarum,
    flumina effundite,   undas lacrimarum;
    sic ruinam plangite   urbium sanctarum.

21. Flete amarissime   omnes auditores,
    magni atque minimi,   fratres et sorores!
    Mutate in melius   vitam atque mores,
    nam de caelo prospicit   Deus peccatores.

22. Dat flagella impiis,   punit delinquentes,
    et per tempus corrigit   stulta praesumentes;
    humiles glorificat,   deicit potentes,
    recipit ut filios   digne paenitentes.

23. Sic iratus Dominus   quondam Israheli
    iudicans ex nubibus   et de alto caeli
    arcam testamenti accensus igne zeli
    tradidisse legitur   populo crudeli.

18. Alas, famous land, truly noble land
    which alone has deserved to wear a garland of flowers,
    land on which God bestowed so many gifts,
    alas, how impious the girdle that encloses you now!

19. Alas, alas, Lord, glory of the righteous,
    source of goodness for angels and salvation for sinners!
    See, dogs are eating your children's bread
    and the blood of the saints is now flowing like water!

20. Weep, all nations of the world, and weep abundantly,
    let your mourning be grief-stricken, your lamentation
    bitter, shed streams of tears, wave on wave;
    so mourn the plight of the holy cities.

21. Weep most bitterly, all you who hear this,
    the great and the lowly, brothers and sisters!
    Change your lives and your ways for the better,
    for from heaven God watches for sinners.

22. He whips the impious and punishes wrongdoers and
    eventually puts in their place the foolishly presump-
    tuous; he glorifies the humble and casts down the
    powerful and welcomes as his children the truly
    repentant.

23. The Lord was once so angered at Israel, we read, as he
    judged them from the clouds and high heaven, that,
    burning with passion, he handed over the ark of the
    covenant to a cruel people.

24. Sed et quamvis viribus   haec putabant acta,
sunt compulsi plangere   statim sua facta.
Coegerunt reddere   munera cum arca,
nam illorum viscera   stabant putrefacta.

25. Convertamur igitur   et paeniteamus,
mala que commisimus   fletu deleamus,
atque Deo munera   digne offeramus,
ut placatus lacrimis   donet quod rogamus.

51

1. Debacchatur mundus pomo,
quod comedit primus homo.
Demonstratur nobis tomo,
quod privamur nostra domo.
    Ref. Proh dolor!
Moyses et Aaron,
rex David et Salomon,
Ierusalem et Gion,
5   mundus plorat et Sion.

2. Ecce tempus, tempus maestum,
propter plebem fit infestum,
patet enim manifestum,
quod plebs temptat inhonestum.
    Ref.

24. But although the Philistines thought their strength had won them this, they were soon compelled to lament what they had done. The Israelites forced them to return the ark and give gifts as well, for the mettle of the Philistines had atrophied.

25. So let us change our ways and repent; let us undo with our tears the evil we have done and make due offering of gifts to God so that he may be placated by our tears and give us what we ask for.

51

1. The world went mad because of the apple
   that the first man ate.
   It is shown to us by the Bible
   that we are robbed of our home.
         Ref. Alas, alas!
   Moses and Aaron,
   King David and Solomon,
   Jerusalem and Gihon,
   the world laments and Zion with it.   5

2. Behold the times, sad times.
   Because of the people they become unsafe,
   for it is quite clear
   that the people engage in dishonorable conduct.
         Ref.

3. Alteratur creatura,
   fit naevosa pro natura.
   Quid superbit limatura,
   de qua summis nulla cura?
      Ref.

4. Homo reus captivatur,
   dum hic vagus exulatur;
   non de iure gratulatur,
   dum hic brevis moriatur.
      Ref.

51a

1. Imperator rex Grecorum
   minas spernens paganorum
   auro sumpto thesaurorum
   parat sumptus armatorum.
      Ref. Ayos
   o theos athanatos,
   ymas sather yskyros.
   Miserere, kyrios.
5   Salva tuos famulos.

2. Almaricus, miles fortis,
   rex communis nostrae sortis,
   in Aegypto fractis portis
   Turcos stravit dirae mortis.
      Ref.

3. All creation is undergoing change;
    its natural state is giving way to a flawed one.
    Why is a creature of mud, for whom those on high
    care nothing, so arrogant?
        Ref.

4. Guilty man remains a captive
    as long as he wanders in exile here;
    he has no right to joy
    since after a brief stay here he dies.
        Ref.

51a

1. The emperor-king of the Greeks,
    unconcerned by the threats of the pagans,
    took gold from his treasuries
    and makes ready the cost of an army.
        Ref. Holy
    is immortal God,
    our mighty savior.
    Take pity on us, Lord!
    Save your servants!   5

2. Almaric, brave knight,
    king of our shared inheritance
    broke the gates of grim death in Egypt
    and laid low the Turks.
        Ref.

3. Omnis ergo Christianus
   ad Aegyptum tendat manus.
   Semper ibi degat sanus.
   Destruatur rex paganus!
     Ref.

52

1. Nomen a solemnibus   trahit Solemniacum;
   solemnizent igitur   omnis praeter monachum,
   qui sibi virilia   resecavit Serracum.
   Illum hinc excipimus   tamquam demoniacum.
5 Ipse solus lugeat   reus apud Aeacum.

2. Exultemus   et cantemus   canticum victoriae,
   et clamemus   quas debemus   laudes regi gloriae,
   qui salvavit   urbem David   a paganis hodie.
   Ref. Festum agitur;
        dies recolitur,
      in qua Dagon frangitur
   et Amalec vincitur,
5   natus Hagar pellitur,
        Ierusalem eripitur,
   et Christianis redditur;
   diem colamus igitur.

3. Haec urbs nobilissima   prima regem habuit.
   In hac urbe maxima   Domino complacuit,
   in hac propter hominem   crucifigi voluit.
   Hic super apostolos   spiritus intonuit.
     Ref.

3.   So let every Christian
     stretch out his hands to Egypt.
     Let him stay there, forever unharmed!
     May the pagan king be destroyed!
          Ref.

52

1.   Solignac takes its name from its solemnities
     So let everyone observe these solemnities
     except the monk Serracus, who cut off his manhood.
     We except him as one possessed by a demon.
     Let him weep as he stands alone, guilty before Aeacus.   5

2.   Let us rejoice and sing a song of victory
     and shout out the praises we owe the King of Glory,
     who today saved the city of David from the heathens!
               Ref. There is a festival today.
               We commemorate the day
               on which Dagon was broken
               and Amalec defeated,
               the son of Hagar driven back,   5
               Jerusalem was rescued
               and restored to Christians;
               so let us celebrate this day!

3.   This most noble city had a king at first.
     The Lord took pleasure in this mighty city.
     In it he chose to be crucified for man's sake.
     Here the Holy Spirit thundered above the disciples.
          Ref.

4. Urbs insignis,   ad quam ignis   venit annis singulis,
   quo monstratur,   quod amatur   omnibus in saeculis
   honoranda,   frequentanda   regibus et populis!
   Ref.

5. Urbs sacrata caelitus   adamata superis,
   legis tabernaculum,   templum arcae foederis,
   hospitale pauperum   et asylum miseris.
   Non timebis aliquod,   dum in ea manseris.
   Ref.

6. Tanta lucis claritate   superatur sol et luna;
   tanta vicit sanctitate   omnes urbes haec urbs una.
   Non elegit frustra locum   Iebuseus Areuna.
   Ref.

53

1. Anno Christi   incarnationis
   anno nostrae   reparationis
                   millesimo
                   centesimo
5   septuagesimo
                       septimo
           rex aeternae gloriae
           dono suae gratiae

4. City of distinction, to which fire comes every year, which shows that the city has been loved at all times, a city to be honored and to throng with kings and peoples!

   Ref.

5. It is a city consecrated from on high, beloved by those that dwell in heaven, the tabernacle of the Law, temple of the ark of the covenant, shelter for the poor, and refuge for the wretched. You will have nothing to fear as long as you remain in it.

   Ref.

6. The brilliant clarity of its light surpasses that of the sun and moon; in its great holiness this one city has out-stripped all others. Araunah the Jebusite did not choose its site in vain.

   Ref.

53

1. In the eleven-hundred
   and seventy-seventh year
   of our salvation
   since the incarnation of Christ,
   the king of everlasting glory   5
   with the gift of his grace
   banished
   the dark cloud

tenebrosam nebulam
10   schismatis fugavit
quassamque naviculam
Simonis salvavit.

2.   Hoc chaos orbem obduxerat,
immo infecerat
annis quater quinis
schismatum pruinis;
5 scintilla caritatis alserat
facta iam cinis.

3.   Hoc decus concordiae
sanxit flos Saxoniae,
noster felix pontifex
Wichmannus, omnis pacis artifex,
5   mira gratia,
per quem talia
fiunt consilia,
quae hunc errorem
valent reducere
10   sic ad pacis honorem.

4.   Victor imperatoris
ensis cum mucrone
Petri prisci moris
unitate dimicans
5 feliciter maioris
vim resecat erroris.

5.   Gaude, mater Roma triumphalis!
Ecce, nauta iam universalis
de profundo maris

of the schism,
and saved   10
Simon's
shaken ship.

2.   This confusion had cast a shadow
over the earth and blighted it
for twenty years
with the frost of the schism;
the spark of charity had grown cold   5
and had now become ash.

3.   It was our blessed bishop
Wichmann, flower of Saxony,
and facilitator of all peace,
who with wonderful grace
sanctioned this honorable agreement.   5
Thanks to him
policy was adopted
that was able to bring
this aberration
to an honorable peace in this way.   10

4.   The victorious sword
of the emperor,
fighting in age-old union
with the sword of Peter,
has successfully cut back   5
the virulence of the great error.

5.   Rejoice, triumphant mother Rome.
See, in the storm the world's helmsman
reached the harbor of peace

193

hieme remige integro
5   portum pacis adiit,
dum pietatis dexteram tetigit.

6. Felix acumen huius mentis,
qui cum tribus elementis
aliis hanc dirimit litem
pacis ligamentis.

7. Nunc Sion laetetur gens,
quia Dominus exsurgens
miserans cor lenit,
tempus enim venit.

8. Huius anni magnalia
sunt iubilaei gaudia.
Exstirpantur zizania,
flavet seges triticea,
5   et paleae de area
ventantur foras horrea.

9. Hoc decus concordiae
canat vox ecclesiae!
Haec nova tripudia
requirat casta Sion filia!

     from the deep sea with his crew intact,
     when he grasped the right hand   5
     piously extended.

6.   Blessed is the acumen of this man's mind,
     who, with the help of three other parties,
     put an end to this strife
     with the bonds of peace.

7.   Now let the people of Zion rejoice
     because our risen Lord
     has softened his heart in compassion,
     for the time has come.

8.   This year's great events
     are like the joyful return of the jubilee year.
     The weeds have been ripped out,
     the wheat fields are golden
     and the straw from the threshing floor   5
     is being winnowed from the granary.

9.   Let the church raise its voice
     to hymn this honorable agreement.
     Let the chaste daughter of Zion
     encourage this joyous celebration.

53a

1. Passeres illos, qui transmigrant supra montes, Alexan-
der tertius sagax et fidelis archivenator illaqueavit.

2. Vulpes, quae demoliuntur vineas, captivavit,
      anguem stravit,
      qui disseminavit
discolum virus, quod infrigidavit
5   igniculum fidei, quique caecavit.

54

1. Omne genus daemoniorum
          caecorum,
          claudorum
   sive confusorum,
5   attendite iussum meorum
et vocationem verborum.

2. Omnis creatura phantasmatum,
quae corroboratis principatum
   serpentis tortuosi,
      venenosi,
5   qui traxit per superbiam
stellarum partem tertiam,
      Gordan,

53a

1. Those sparrows that fly over mountains, Alexander the Third, the astute and faithful master of the hunt, has trapped.

2. He captured the foxes destroying the vineyards
   and flattened the snake
   which spread
   the bitter poison that brought a chill
   to the spark of faith and put it out.   5

54

1. Demons of every kind—those that cause
   blindness,
   lameness,
   and confusion—
   pay heed to my commands   5
   and the summons I make!

2. All you of the world of phantoms,
   who lend support to the leadership
   of the twisted,
   venomous snake
   that in his pride brought down   5
   a third of the stars,
   Gordan,

Ingordin et Ingordan,
per sigillum Salomonis
10 et per magos Pharaonis
omnes vos coniuro,
omnes exorcizo
per tres magos, Caspar,
Melchior et Balthasar,
15 per regem David,
qui Saul sedavit,
cum iubilavit
vosque fugavit.

3. Vos attestor,
vos contestor
per mandatum Domini,
ne zeletis,
5 quem soletis
vos vexare, homini,
ut compareatis
et post discedatis,
et cum desperatis
10 chaos incolatis.

4. Attestor,
contestor
per timendum,
per tremendum
5 diem iudicii,
aeterni supplicii,
diem miseriae,
perennis tristitiae,
qui ducturus est

Ingordin and Ingordan,
I conjure you all,
by the seal of Solomon   10
and by the Pharaoh's wise men
and exorcize you all
in the name of the three Magi,
Caspar, Melchior and Balthasar,
and in the name of King David,   15
who soothed Saul
when he played his music
and put all of you to flight.

3.   I make this proclamation
and, on the Lord's instructions,
I call on you to bear witness:
do not cast an evil eye
on mankind,   5
whom you are accustomed to harass.
I call on you to appear
and then depart
and go dwell in the abyss with those
who have abandoned hope.   10

4.   I make this proclamation,
and call on you to bear witness:
by the fearful,
by the awful
Judgment Day   5
for eternal punishment,
a day of misery
and lasting sadness,
which will send you

10   vos in infernum,
        salvaturus est
            nos in aeternum.

5.   Per Nomen mirabile
      atque ineffabile
      Dei tetragrammaton,
          ut expaveatis
5   et perhorreatis,
              vos exorcizo,
                      Larvae,
                      Fauni,
                      Manes,
10   Nymphae,
                Sirenae,
                Hamadryades
                  Satyri,
                  Incubi,
15   Penates,
        ut cito abeatis,
          chaos incolatis,
          ne vas corrumpatis
          Christianitatis.

6.   Tu nos, Deus, conservare ab hostibus digneris.

55

Amara tanta tyri   pastos sycalos sycaliri
ellivoli scarras   polili posylique lyvarras.

to hell   10
and save us
forever more:

5.   By the wonderful
and unspeakable Name,
the tetragrammaton of God,
I warn you: you should be full of dread
and terror-struck.   5
I exorcise all of you,
ghosts,
fauns,
spirits of the dead,
nymphs,   10
Sirens,
Hamadryads,
satyrs,
incubuses,
Penates.   15
Quickly, away with you
to dwell in the abyss
so that you do not corrupt
a Christian soul!

6.   God, save us, please, from our enemies.

55

Amara tanta tyri   pastos sycalos sycaliri
elliuoli scarras   polili posylique lyvarras.

56

1.   Ianus annum circinat,
      ver aestatem nuntiat,
      calcat Phoebus ungula,
      dum in Taurum flectitur,
5   Arietis repagula.
  Ref. Amor cuncta superat,
      Amor dura terebrat.

2.   Procul sint omnia
           tristia!
           Dulcia
           gaudia
5 sollemnizent Veneris gymnasia!
       Decet iocundari
   quos militare contigit
       Dionaeo lari.
  Ref. Amor cuncta superat,
      Amor dura terebrat

3.   Dum alumnus Palladis
          Cythereae scholam
   introissem, inter multas
           bene cultas
5   vidi unam solam
         facie

56

1. Janus brings the year full circle,
    spring heralds summer,
    with his horses' hooves Phoebus kicks away
    the barriers of Aries,
    as he bends his course into Taurus.   5
    Ref. Love conquers all.
            Love bores a way through difficulties.

2. Away with everything
        sad!
        Sweet
        are the joys
    that the exercises of Venus celebrate!   5
    Those whose luck it is
    to serve in Dione's domain
    should enjoy themselves.
    Ref. Love conquers all.
            Love bores a way through difficulties.

3. When I was a student of Pallas
    and entered the school of the Cytherean,
    I saw among many
    chic ladies
    one alone   5
    who is second only

Tyndaridi
ac Veneri
secundam,
10 plenam elegantiae
et magis pudibundam.
Ref. Amor cuncta superat,
Amor dura terebrat

4.   Differentem omnibus
amo differenter.
Novus ignis in me furit,
et adurit
5   indeficienter.
Nulla magis nobilis,
habilis,
pulchra vel amabilis;
nulla minus mobilis,
10   instabilis,
infrunita reperitur
vel fide mutabilis.
Eius laetum vivere
est meum delectari.
15   Diligi si merear,
hoc meum est beari.
Ref. Vincit Amor omnia,
regit Amor omnia.

5.   Parce, puer, puero!
Fave, Venus, tenero
ignem movens,
ignem fovens,
5 ne mori sit quod vixero,

to Helen
and Venus
in her appearance,
very elegant   10
and more modest.
Ref. Love conquers all.
    Love bores a way through difficulties.

4.   My love for her is different,
    for she differs from all the others.
    A strange new fire rages within me
    and burns away
    and does not die.   5
    No woman is more noble,
    more amenable,
    more beautiful or more lovable;
    none is less capricious,
    less flighty,   10
    less silly,
    or less fickle in her loyalty.
    Her joie de vivre
    is my delight.
    If I earn her love,   15
    that is my blessing.
    Ref. Love conquers all,
        Love rules everything.

5.   Youthful Cupid, spare me for I am young!
    Venus, look with favor on my inexperience
    by starting up a fire
    and nursing that fire
    so that the life I lead will not be a death   5

nec sit ut Daphne Phoebo
cui me ipsum dedo.
Olim tiro Palladis
nunc tuo iuri cedo.
Ref. Vincit Amor omnia,
regit Amor omnia.

57

1. "Bruma veris aemula
sua iam repagula
dolet demoliri,
demandat Februario,
5 ne se a solis radio
sinat deliniri.

2. Omnis nexus elementorum
legem blandam sentit amorum,
sed Hymenaeus eorum
iugalem ordinat torum
5 votis allubescens deorum
piorum.

3. Sed Aquilonis
ira praedonis
elementis officit,
ne pariant,
nec tamen in hoc proficit;
5 sed Hymaeneus obicit

and so that she to whom I dedicate myself
will not be as Daphne was to Apollo.
Once apprenticed to Pallas,
I now yield to your rule.
Ref. Love conquers all
Love rules everything.

57

1. "Winter, begrudging spring,
   grieves that its barriers
   are being demolished;
   it bids February
   not to let itself be softened   5
   by the sun's rays.

2. Every combination of elements
   feels the pleasant laws of love,
   but Hymen arranges
   their marriage bed,
   humoring the wishes   5
   of the kindly gods.

3. Yet the wrath
   of the ravaging North Wind
   tries to hinder the elements
   from giving birth
   and yet makes no headway;   5
   yet Hymen

eius se turbini,
in hoc enim numini
deserviunt Dionae.

4.   Felicibus stipendiis
Dione freta gaudiis
gaudet suos extollere,
qui se suo iugo libere
5   non denegant submittere.
Quam felici vivere
vult eos pro munere!

5.   Optat Thetis
auram quietis,
ut caelo caput exserat,
suosque fructus proferat.
5 Ceres quoque secus undam cursitat,
et tristia sollicitat
inferorum numina
pro surrepta Proserpina.

6.   Elementa supera
coeunt et infera.
Hinc illis vocabula
sunt attributa mascula,
5   istis vero feminina
congrue sunt deputata nomina,
quia rerum semina
concipiunt ut femina.

7.   Sol, quia regnat in Piscibus
caclestibus,
dat copiam

opposes himself to its turbulence;
as a result the elements
serve the will of Dione.

4. Trusting in happy rewards,
Dione enjoys
raising her followers to joy,
who freely choose
to submit to her yoke.   5
How pleasant the service
for which she wants them to live!

5. Thetis looks for
a quiet breeze
to expose her head to the sky
and bring forth the fruits of the sea.
Ceres too hurries along beside the water   5
and makes her plea
to the gloomy gods of the nether world
for her Proserpine, stolen from her.

6. The elements of the upper
and lower worlds come together.
Hence it is that words
attributed to the former are masculine,
whereas feminine nouns   5
are fittingly applied to the latter,
because they conceive the seeds of things
like a woman.

7. Because he is king
in Pisces's stretch of sky,
the sun gives rich abundance

          plenariam
5   piscationi,
reddens formam turbidae Iunoni."

8a. Ista Phrison decantabat
      iuxta regis filiam,
aegram quae se simulabat,
     dum perrexit per viam

8b. desponsari. Sed haec nanus
     notans sponso retulit.
Mox truncatur ut profanus
    tandem sponso detulit.

58

1.   Iam ver oritur.
Veris flore variata
     tellus redimitur.
Excitat in gaudium
5 cor concentus avium
     voce relativa
Iovem salutantium.
    In his Philomena
Tereum reiterat,
10   et iam fatum
     antiquatum
   querule retractat
sed, dum fatis obicit

to fishing parties
as he restores beauty 5
to disordered Juno."

8a. Such was the song Phrison sang
to the king's daughter,
who pretended to be sick
as she continued on her way

8b. to be married. The dwarf took note of all this
and reported it to the bridegroom.
He was promptly mutilated when he eventually
made his disloyal denunciation to the bridegroom.

58

1. Spring is now showing itself.
The earth is garlanded with spring flowers
of many colors.
The singing of birds
greeting the sky 5
stirs joy in the heart
with their calls to one another.
Among them the nightingale
repeats the name of Tereus,
plaintively going over 10
the fateful events
of long ago,
but while she rebukes the Fates

Itym perditum,
15 merula
choraulica
 carmina
  coaptat.

2. Istis insultantibus
   casibus
  fatalibus
in choreae speciem
5   res reciprocatur.
His autem conciliis
noster adest Iupiter
  cum sua Iunone,
  Cupido cum Dione,
10 post hos Arcas stellifer
et Narcissus floriger,
Orpheusque plectriger,
Faunus quoque corniger.

3. Inter haec solemnia
   communia
alterno motu laterum
lascive iactant corpora
5   collata
  nunc occurrens,
  nunc procurrens
 contio pennata.

for her lost Itys,
the blackbird,   15
joins in
with a flutelike
song.

2.   While these birds revile
their fateful
misfortunes,
there comes a response
in the form of a chorus.   5
In attendance at this assembly
are our Jupiter
with his wife Juno,
Cupid with Dione,
and behind them star-studded Arcas,   10
and Narcissus wreathed with flowers,
Orpheus holding his plectrum,
and horned Faunus.

3.   Participating in these shared
solemnities
and, crowded together,
playfully swaying and tossing
their bodies this way and that,   5
now flying up to one another,
now pressing forward,
is a flock of birds.

4. Mergus aquaticus,
aquila munificus,
  bubo noctivagus,
  cygnus flumineus,
5   phoenix unica,
  perdix lethargica,
hirundo domestica,
columba turtisona,
upupa galigera,
10   anser sagax,
    vultur edax,
psittacus gelboicus,
milvus girovagus,
alaudula garrula,
15 ciconia rostrisona.

5. His et consimilibus
    paria
   sunt gaudia,
demulcet enim omnia
5 haec concors consonantia.

6. Tempus est laetitiae.
  Verno tempore
   vernant flores
  in pratis virentibus
5   et suis rebus
  decus auget Phoebus
  in nostris finibus.

4. The gull that loves the water,
   the gift-bearing eagle,
   the owl that flies by night,
   the river-dwelling swan,
   the solitary phoenix,   5
   the drowsy partridge,
   the common swallow,
   the dove with its soft, throbbing cry,
   the crested hoopoe,
   the wise goose,   10
   the hungry vulture,
   the yellow parrot,
   the circling kite,
   the chattering lark
   and the stork with clattering beak.   15

5. These birds and birds like them
   all share
   an equal joy,
   for this harmonious hubbub
   creates a soothing calm everywhere.   5

6. It is a time for rejoicing.
   In springtime,
   flowers bloom
   in the green meadows,
   and with his power   5
   Phoebus enhances the beauty
   in our land.

59

1. Ecce, chorus virginum   tempore vernali,
dum solis incendium   radios aequali
moderatur ordine,   nubilo semoto
frondem pansat tiliae   Cypridis in voto!
    Ref. Cypridis in voto!
frondem pansat tiliae   Cypridis in voto!

2. In hac valle florida   floreus, flagratus
inter saepta lilia   locus purpuratus.
Dum garritus merulae   dulciter alludit,
philomena carmine   dulcia concludit.
    Ref.

3. Acies virginea   redimita flore!
Quis enarret talia?   Quantoque decore
praenitent ad libitum   Veneris occulta!
Dido necis meritum   proferat inulta.
    Ref.

4. Per florenta nemorum   me fortuna vexit.
"Arcum Cupidineum"   vernula retexit,
quam inter Veneream   diligo cohortem.
Langueo, dum videam   libiti consortem.
    Ref.

5. Quaestio per singulas   oritur honesta:
potior quae dignitas,   casta vel incesta?
Flora consors Phyllidis   est sententiata:
"Castae non est similis   turpiter amata."
    Ref.

59

1. Look, there's a chorus of young women in springtime,
   when the sun's fire disposes its rays
   equally over the world, banishes the clouds,
   and opens the linden's foliage in homage to Venus!
   Ref. In homage to Venus!
   It opens the linden's foliage in homage to Venus!

2. In this blossoming vale there is an expanse of crimson,
   flowery and fragrant, amid the rows of lilies. While a
   blackbird's chatter keeps pleasant accompaniment, a
   nightingale completes the charm with her song.
   Ref.

3. A line of young women wreathed in flowers! Who could
   describe it? With what beauty the hidden charms of
   Venus gleam forth to my heart's desire! Dido could
   reveal with impunity what earned her her death!
   Ref.

4. Fortune carried me through the blossoming glades.
   A little servant girl has uncovered her Cupid's bow;
   among Venus's band she is the one I love.
   I languish to see her as partner of my lust.
   Ref.

5. A question of honor arose among several of them:
   which status is worthier for a woman, chaste or un-
   chaste? Flora, Phyllis's companion, expressed her opin-
   ion: "She who has been loved shamefully differs from
   the chaste woman."
   Ref.

6. Iuno, Pallas, Dione,   Cytherea dura
    affirmant interprete   Flora verbi iura:
    "Flagrabit felicius   nectare mellito
    castam amans potius   quam in infinito."
        Ref.

7. Iura grata refero   puellarum puris:
    vigeant in prospero   pudice futuris!
    Actibus temeritas   nulla salutaris.
    Contingat iocunditas   spes adulta caris.
        Ref.

60

1a. Captus amore gravi
     me parem rebar avi
     sede revinctae suavi,
     quae procul aethra videt
5   nec modulando silet;
     inde perire libet.

1b. <At tu diligis quidem>
     psallere, virgo, pridem
     non semper hic ibidem,
     quam scrutabundus Amor
5   notarat et amator.
     Hinc ortus ille clamor.

6.   Juno, Pallas, Dione, and the harsh Cytherean confirm,
     according to Flora, the prescriptions of the saying:
     "He who loves a chaste woman will smell more blissfully
     of honeyed nectar than the man who loves indiscrim-
     inately."
     Ref.

7.   I report the welcome judgment to young virgins: may
     they flourish and prosper in chastity for the future.
     Brazenness in sexual intercourse never brings salvation!
     May joy, their hope come to fruition, fall to the lot of
     the men they love!
     Ref.

60

1a. Held fast by an oppressive love,
     I likened myself to the bird
     tied to its sweet home
     that sees the heavens far off
     and refuses to cease singing —   5
     happy to die from the effort.

1b. But you have long delighted
     to sing, my girl —
     not always here, in the same place,
     and ever-watchful Love
     and your lover observed you.   5
     From this that hue and cry arose.

2. Est bilis amarissima,
    qualem gignit Sardonia,
    in incentivo Veneris
    eiusque miri generis
5   militiam proponere
    nec posse votum solvere!
    Haec, ecce, virgo inclita,
    tibi notabis edita.

3. Amor instillat, quare
    te, virgo, salutare
    velim, sed onus grave
    videris acerbare,

4. dum effluis in meritum,
    grave ferens imperium,
    vilipendens obloquium,
    me minans in interitum,
5   fidem promittens alteri,
    contradicendo Cypridi.

5a. Ecce querimonia,
    quam genuit Amor.
    Me misit in suspiria
    Venereus favor.

5b. Cuncta sprevi virginum
        ego tripudia,
    te volens mihi iungere.
        Modo diludia

2. It is the bitterest gall,
    like that which Sardinia produces,
    to pledge service
    in response to the promptings
    of Venus and her wonderful son   5
    and then to be unable to fulfill the vow!
    This, my lady, you will note,
    is your doing!

3. Love instills in me the desire
    to pay my respects to you,
    but you seem to make a duty,
    already onerous, quite unpleasant,

4. for you give yourself over to making money,
    finding my commands oppressive,
    making light of my rebukes,
    driving me to my grave,
    promising your love to another   5
    and opposing the will of Cypris.

5a. That is the litany of woes
    that Love caused me!
    Venus's blessing
    led me to sighs of grief.

5b. I spurned all delights
    with young women,
    wanting to win you.
    Recently you looked for a break

5c. \<quaeris\> inique gratiam;
    sed iam alterius
captas benevolentiam.
    Quo nil deterius

6a. queo fari.
Nec solari
me curat Glycerium.

6b. Me fastidit
et allidit,
aestimans inglorium.

6c. Bella gero
cum severo,
Cypridis ob meritum.

7a. Dum mens una \<rem\> recolit,
famaque nefas coperit,
pupilla fletum protulit.
    Iam expedit,
5   ut vera \<nos\> loquamur.

7b. Amaveram prae ceteris
te, sed amici veteris
es iam oblita; superis
    vel inferis
5   ream te criminamur.

8a. Dolor, fletus,
irae, metus
tremebundis artubus
simul incubuere.

5c.　and I came into favor.
　　　But now you are chasing after
　　　the goodwill of another.
　　　There's nothing worse than this

6a.　that I can say.
　　　And Glycerium does not care
　　　to offer me solace.

6b.　She spurns me
　　　and dashes my hopes,
　　　thinking me of no account.

6c.　I am waging war
　　　with a stern rival to be deemed worthy
　　　of the Cyprian's reward.

7a.　As long as it was only my thoughts reflecting on the
　　　affair and what was said concealed your unspeakable
　　　behavior, my eyes were filled with tears.
　　　It is now the time
　　　　for me to speak the truth.

5

7b.　I loved you above all others
　　　but you have forgotten your former lover.
　　　Before the powers above
　　　and those below,
　　　I charge your guilt.

5

8a.　Grief, tears,
　　　anger, and fear
　　　have swept over my trembling limbs
　　　all at the same time.

8b.   Prae dolore
      verso more
      canticum conticuit.
      Nil restat nisi flere.

8c.   Sorte dira
      pendet. Pyra
      structa luet. Atropos
      filum cessavit nere.

9.   Me mergis hic,
      cum sis illic.
      Natando sic
      non stabis hic.

10.   Sed lubrica contagia
            te gaudes insectari.
      Prostibulum patibulo
            iam meruit piari.
5   En, oro te per superos,
      tibi ames obnoxios.
      Reclude secretarios,
      quos nil iuvat amari.

11.   Si lethargum vitae
      insectabor lite,
      hunc <tu> colis rite.
            Cum ego te
5   in soliloquiorum
            carmine canebam,
      te unam cupiebam,
      idque ius tenebam
            <ut bearer,>
10   sed nihil audis horum.

224

8b. My grief has changed me,
    my singing has ceased.
    There is nothing left to do
    but weep.

8c. She will pay for this;
    her fate will be grim. On a raised pyre
    she will atone. Atropos
    has stopped the spinning of her thread.

9. When you are there,
    you drown me here.
    You fluctuate like this
    and won't stay put here.

10. Instead, you take joy
    in chasing after your unsavory contacts.
    Prostitution has rightly
    been punished with the gallows!
    I beg you in the name of the gods   5
    to love those who are devoted to you.
    Shut out any confidants
    who take no joy in being loved!

11. If I pursue at law
    a man who shows no zest for life,
    he's the one you duly cultivate,
    When I sang about you
    in a soliloquizing song   5
    it was only you
    I desired
    and I considered it right
    that I should find happiness
    but you didn't want to hear any of this.   10

12. Mihi te subdideras,
    et amore iunxeras
fallentis vitae semitas,
et te ita subverteras,
5 ut redimam me vivere!
Praesumptuosa, temere
amores vis transponere,
et cor meum conterere?

13a. Usque quo te perferam,
        quam premit aemulatio?

13b. Ut quid agis perperam,
        o dira simulatio?

14a. Ex fraudibus alternis
        et ignominia
    cur aemula superbis,
        bifrons, ingloria?

14b. Cum foedera discerpis,
        o praeceps nimia,
    te funditus evertis
        ceu Bachanaria.

15. Si balbi more veritus
    nil ausim fari penitus,
    obnixerim emeritus,
    quem captat hinc interitus.

16. O Cypris alma, conspice
    tuae clientem operae,
    poenamque nobis exime,
    quam patimur indebite.

12. You gave yourself to me
     and united in love the paths
     of our uncertain lives
     and yet went back on your word
     so completely that I now reclaim my life.   5
     Is it your wish, presumptuous woman,
     brazenly to transfer your affections
     and break my heart?

13a. How long am I to put up with you,
      afflicted as you are with rivalry?

13b. Why do you behave so perversely,
      you complete sham?

14a. Given your serial cheating
      and notoriety,
      why pride yourself, two-faced pretender,
      on disgrace?

14b. When you tear up your commitments,
      all too hasty,
      like a Bacchant
      you lead yourself to complete ruin.

15. If, fearful, like a stammerer,
     I dared not speak a word,
     I would still fight, though retired,
     when death shuffles me off.

16. Kindly Venus, have a care
     for a devoted servant of your work
     and free me from the punishment
     which I suffer undeservedly.

5   Tu lamiam intercipe,
       eiusque rixas opprime.

17.   Cupido mentem gyrat,
       telumque minans vibrat,
       Favonius aspirat
       nectar, quo venas inflat.

18.   <two lines missing >
       medullitus; id teneris
       pergratum est in feminis,
5   quas alit affabilitas
       atque cordis simplicitas.

19a.   Semel opto, basia
               michi quod offerat,
       quam sorte de infantia
               Natura venustat.

19b.   Post hanc nulla complacet,
               quam sic assumpserim,
       cum potius amabiles,
               te propter spreverim.

20a.   Iam odorus
       noster torus
       demoratur. Inscia

20b.   es optata;
       sed vocata
       non occurris intima.

21a.   Gaude, proles regia,
       quae vitae privilegia

Remove this witch and put an end   5
to the trouble she causes.

17. Cupid turns my heart around,
brandishing his weapon threateningly.
Favonius breathes out the nectar,
with which he puffs up the veins.

18. \<two lines missing\>
deep within. This is most welcome
in the case of inexperienced young women
of an approachable nature   5
and guileless heart.

19a. Just once I want
to be offered kisses
by the woman Nature picked by fortunate choice
to bestow her charms on from childhood.

19b. There is no second to her,
whom I would care to take up with,
for I have spurned all the more attractive ones
because of you.

20a. Now our fragrant couch
stands waiting.
Though you are unaware of this,

20b. I long for you;
but when I invite you
you don't come inside to me.

21a. Rejoice, my princess,
for you enjoy the privileges of life.

gestas. Ecce! Venerea
   collegia
5   per te floruerunt.

21b. Si iam detur optio,
   tuo quod utar osculo,
   haec noctis in crepusculo
     sub otio
5   aspera non erunt.

22a. Matutini sideris
    iubar praeis
      et lilium
    rosaque periere.

22b. Micat ebur dentium
      per labium,
     ut Sirium
  credat quis enitere.

22c. <four lines missing>

23.   Si Maenalus   fatidicus
     virginibus
    mihi det omen fari:
     Aetna mons occiduus
5 ponti ferat minas prius
  quam desinat, virgo, tuus
     honor laudari.

24.   Amores ergo fidibus
  canendi sunt his rudibus
  cibentur ut his fructibus;
  stipendium erit Venus.

See! You have made
the community of Venus
flourish.   5

21b. Should my wish be granted
to enjoy your kisses,
this tryst at twilight,
idling at our ease,
will not be disagreeable.   5

22a. Your radiance
surpasses that of the morning star,
and the lily and the rose
have given way before you.

22b. The ivory of your teeth flashes
so brightly between your lips
that one might believe
that it is Sirius shining.

22c. <four lines missing>

23.   If Maenalus,
soothsayer to young women,
might allow me to utter a prophecy:
May Mount Etna collapse
and endure the threats of the deep,   5
before, my lady, praise of your honor
ceases.

24.   Accordingly, I must sing of my beloved
on this rough lyre
so that she may feast on these fruits.
Lovemaking will be my reward.

25.   Amore quando linit
        Venus, quae corda ferit,
        incitamentum Veneris
        fastidium est ceteris.
5   Quod laudis mihi titulum
        clarumque det obsequium!

26.   Intemerata virginum,
          serena respice,
     et generosa supplici
          iam vota perfice!

61

1a.   Siquem Pieridum ditavit contio,
      nulli Teieridum aptetur otio.
            Par Phoebi citharae
            sum verno nectare.

1b.   Cui prae cunctis virginum oboedio,
      me potest alere vel mortis taedio,
           si decus intimum
           mavult potissimum.

1c.   Terminum vidit brumae desolatio.
      Gaudent funditus in florum exordio
           qui norunt Cypridem
           plaudentes eidem.

25. When Venus strikes our hearts
     and anoints them with love,
     others find disagreeable
     her goading to lovemaking.
     But let it give me my claim to glory   5
     and distinguished service!

26. Most chaste of young women,
     regard with serene indulgence
     and now generously bring to fruition
     the prayers of your suppliant.

61

1a. If the company of the Muses has blessed someone with
     a gift, he should not try to match the leisure of the
     followers of Anacreon. The nectar of spring puts me
     on a par with the lyre of Apollo.

1b. She whom I obey beyond all other young women
     can sustain me even in the gloom of death,
     if she prefers
     a particularly intimate distinction.

1c. Winter's desolation has seen its end.
     As flowers begin to bloom, those who know Cypris
     rejoice from the bottom of their hearts
     and applaud her.

1d. Nunquam tanti cordis fui, pro Iupiter,
     de spe Venerea, opinor; iugiter
               me vitae fertilis
               alit spes stabilis.

2a. Me risu linea
     regit virginea;
     nunc ergo tinea
     maeroris pellitur,
5   dolor avellitur,
     tremor percellitur.

2b. Cui tanta claritas
     ac mira caritas,
     fecunda largitas
     semper et undique
5   arrident utique—
     hanc opto denique.

3.   Ne miretur ducis tantae
         quis sublimitatem,
     quae me sibi vi praestante
     doctum reddit plus quam ante,
5   stillans largitatem!

4a. O decora
     super ora
         belli Absalonis,
     et non talis,
     ut mortalis
5   sis condicionis.

1d. By Jupiter, never, I think, have I been so encouraged
in my hopes for success in Venus's realm; I am always
nourished with a firm hope
for a fruitful life.

2a. The maiden's lineage
controls me through her smile;
so the moth of my sadness
is now dispelled,
my pain taken from me,   5
and my trembling overcome.

2b. She whose shining presence,
marvelous kindness,
and endless generosity
smile always and everywhere,
without fail—   5
she is the one I desire.

3.   No one should be surprised
at the majesty of such a leader,
for with her remarkable power
she makes me more skilled than I was before,
by infusing her largesse.   5

4a. You, whose beauty
surpasses
the comeliness
of fair Absalon—
it cannot be   5
that you are mortal.

4b. Mihi soli,
  virgo, noli
    esse refragata!
  Quaeso finem,
5 ut reclinem
    a re desperata.

5. Tuum praestolor nuntium,
  dele maerorem conscium,
  mundani decus iubaris,
  o verecunda Tyndaris.

6a. Apollo mire vinctus est
    Peneide respecta;
  sic meus amor tinctus est
    re veteri deiecta.

6b. Magnetem verum iterat
    virgo mire perfecta,
  attractu crebro superat
    me gratia directa.

6c. Miranda de Priamide
    rememorantur gesta,
  qui militavit floride.
    Sic valent mea festa.

7. Florenti desolatio
  non esset conturbatio,
  sed eo plus tremit ratio,
  quo Dionaea sit dilatio:
5   quid facio?

4b. Don't be dismissive
     of me in my loneliness,
          my lady.
     The goal I seek
     is to be released   5
     from my despair.

5.   I await a message from you.
     End my sorrow that is conscious of my wrongdoing,
     you who are the beautiful, shining light of the world,
     a blushing Helen!

6a. Apollo was miraculously bound
     when he caught sight of Daphne;
     so too my love received its baptism
     when my old affair was cast aside.

6b. A young woman of marvelous perfection,
     she is a true magnet;
     her unaffected grace frequently
     overwhelms me with its power to attract.

6c. Wonderful exploits of Priam's son
     are told again and again.
     His military campaigns were glorious.
     My banquets are equally brilliant.

7.   If things were going well for me, my financial ruin
     would not upset me
     but my thoughts become all the more fearful,
     the longer the joys of Venus are delayed.
     What am I to do?   5

237

8a.　　　Gratia,
　　　solacia
　　donato menti languidae,
　　　mea dos,
5　　　amorum flos,
　　morigerata vivide.

8b.　Amantum lis,
　　te, quicquid vis,
　　da laudi bene placide.
　　　Nil tibi par,
5　　electe lar
　　laetitiae fervidae.

9a.　Te visa primitus
　　exarsi penitus,
　　proinde gemitus
　　durat perenniter.
5　　Tu deme leniter
　　illatum duriter.

9b.　Istaec est dira sors,
　　nec durior est mors.
　　Non meae vitae fors
　　stat ritu prospero
5　　Quam soli confero,
　　repugnat tenero.

10.　Huic me corde flagrante
　　　nosco intricatum,
　　cuius nutu me versante
　　et ad votum conspirante
5　　　me fero beatum.

8a. You who are grace itself,
     grant solace
     to my languishing heart—
     my treasure,
     my choicest love,   5
     good-natured and filled with life.

8b. You, over whom suitors quarrel,
     whatever your choice may be,
     serenely give yourself up to praise.
     You are without peer,
     the choice home   5
     of ebullient joy.

9a. Since I first saw you,
     I have been completely on fire;
     and so my sighing
     goes on forever.
     Please extinguish gently   5
     the fire so brusquely set.

9b. This fate of mine is grim.
     Not even death is harsher.
     My life's destiny
     is not on a happy course.
     She whom I compare to the sun   5
     resists her young admirer.

10. I realize that my burning heart
     has entangled me with her
     but if with a nod she turns me around
     by acquiescing in my wishes,
     I am in bliss.   5

11a. Aptiorem,
  dulciorem
    nollem reperire,
  quam elegi
5   meae legi
    si dat subvenire.

11b. Plus amarem,
  plus optarem
    sui verbi dona,
  quam si mundi
5   vi rotundi
    fungerer corona.

12.   \<four-line stanza missing\>

13a. Sed primum exaltandus est
    risus clarificatus,
  a quo Iovis secundus est
    mihi significatus.

13b. Effectum si non invenit,
    ut me velit amare.
  pie rogo, quod convenit,
    me queat alterare.

13c. Sed si nos, Discordia,
    tuo more disponis,
  mutabo iam primordia
    meae professionis.

11a. I would not want to find
      a more agreeable
      and congenial partner
      than the one I have chosen,
      if she is willing to yield   5
      to my authority.

11b. I would much rather have,
      much rather choose,
      the gift of her word,
      than win by force
      the crown   5
      of the entire world.

12.   <four-line stanza missing>

13a. But first I must exalt
      the brilliant smile
      meant for me,
      which puts Jove's smile in second place.

13b. If she cannot find it
      in her heart to love me,
      I humbly ask, as is fitting,
      that she may succeed in changing me.

13c. But if you, Discord, set us apart
      after your fashion,
      I will withdraw the profession of love
      I have begun.

14. Ergo, nitidior sidere,
    respice, si me vis vivere,
    nam flores constat emergere.
    Tuo me solatum foedere
5   da ludere.

62

1. Dum Dianae vitrea
   sero lampas oritur,
   et a fratris rosea
   luce dum succenditur,
5 dulcis aura Zephyri,
   spirans omnes aetheri
                nubes tollit;
                sic emollit
   vis chordarum pectora,
10   et immutat
                cor, quod nutat,
   ad amoris pignora.

2. Laetum iubar Hesperi
                gratiorem
                dat humorem
   roris soporiferi
5 mortalium generi.

14. Therefore, you who shine brighter than any star,
    have regard for me if you want me to live,
    for flowers are springing up, as all can see.
    Console me with your pledge
    and let me enjoy love's play.   5

62

1. When Diana's crystal lamp
   rises in the evening
   and is suffused
   with her brother's rosy light,
   Zephyr's soft breeze   5
   breathes away all the clouds
   from the sky;
   just so does the power of the lyre
   relax the mind
   and turn   10
   the hesitant heart
   toward pledges of love.

2. The Evening Star's joyful beam
   bestows the welcome moisture
   of a dew
   that wafts sleep
   to mortals.   5

3.   O quam felix est antidotum soporis,
quod curarum tempestates sedat et doloris!
    Dum surrepit clausis oculorum poris,
gaudio aequiparat dulcedini amoris.

4.   Orpheus in mentem
    trahit impellentem
ventum lenem segetes maturas,
murmura rivorum per harenas puras,
5 circulares ambitus   <per se> molendinorum,
qui furantur somno   lumen oculorum.

5.   Ex alvo laeta fumus evaporat,
    qui capitis tres cellulas irrorat.
            Hic infumat oculos
            ad soporem pendulos
5   et palpebras sua fumositate
replet, ne <sic> visus exspatietur late.
Unde ligant oculos virtutes animales,
    quae sunt magis visae ministeriales.

6.   Post blanda Veneris commercia
    lassatur cerebri substantia.
    Hinc caligant mira novitate
oculi nantes in palpebrarum rate.
5 Hei, quam felix transitus amoris ad soporem;
sed suavior <et gratior> regressus ad amorem!

3. Ah! How welcome is the antidote of sleep, which calms
    the storms of pain and passions! Once it has slipped
    past the closed portals of the eyes, it matches the
    sweetness of love in the joy it brings.

4. Orpheus draws into the mind a gentle wind,
    driving the ripened grain,
    the murmuring of streams
    past banks of untouched sand
    and mill wheels circling of their own accord,   5
    that steal the light from our eyes with sleep.

5. From the well-fed stomach a vapor arises,
    which bedews the three chambers of the brain.
    It clouds the eyes,
    drooping to sleep,
    and fills the eyelids with its mist   5
    so that vision does not roam abroad.
    Hence the eyes are closed by bodily forces
    which have rather been thought to be subordinate.

6. After the sweet exchanges of Venus
    the brain becomes languid.
    Then with a wonderful strangeness the eyes mist over,
    floating on the raft of the eyelids.
    Ah! How happy is the transition from love to sleep;   5
    but sweeter and more welcome is a renewal of love.

62a

1. Fronde sub arboris amoena,
    dum querens canit philomena,
        suave est quiescere,
        suavius ludere
5   in gramine
                    cum virgine
                    speciosa.
            Si variarum
            odor herbarum
10   spiraverit,
                    si dederit
                    torum rosa,
    dulciter soporis alimonia
    post Veneris defessa commercia
15   captatur,
            dum lassis instillatur.

2. O in quantis
        animus amantis
        variatur vacillantis!
    Ut vaga ratis per aequora,
5   dum caret ancora,
    fluctuat inter spem metumque dubia,
        sic Veneris militia.

62a

1.   Under a tree's pleasant branch,
     with a nightingale singing its plaintive song,
     it is sweet to take one's rest,
     but it is sweeter to play
     on the grass   5
     with a pretty
     maiden.
     If varied herbs
     breathe
     their fragrance   10
     and roses
     make a bed,
     the nourishment of sleep
     comes softly
     after the exhausting exchanges of Venus,   15
     distilling itself into weary bodies.

2.   Ah! In what turmoil
     the mind of the vacillating lover
     is tossed!
     It is buffeted like a boat adrift on the sea
     without an anchor,   5
     uncertain whether to hope or fear.
     Such is the service of Venus!

63

1a.   Olim sudor Herculis
     monstra late conterens,
     pestes orbis auferens,
     claris longe titulis
5   enituit.
     Sed tandem defloruit
     fama prius celebris
     caecis clausa tenebris,
     Ioles illecebris
10   Alcide captivato.
     Ref. Amor famae meritum
              deflorat.
     Amans tempus perditum
              non plorat,
15   sed temere
         diffluere
         sub Venere
           laborat.

1b.   Hydra damno capitum
     facta locupletior
     omni peste saevior
     reddere sollicitum
5   non potuit
     quem puella domuit.
     Iugo cessit Veneris
     vir qui maior superis
     caelum tulit humeris

63

1a.   Hercules's efforts long ago
     in subduing monsters far and wide,
     clearing the world of plagues,
     entitled him to far-flung fame
     of brilliant luster.   5
     But the bloom of his renown,
     once so bright, faded in the end,
     shrouded in gloomy darkness,
     when he, Alcaeus's grandson,
     was captivated by Iole's charms.   10
     Ref. Love takes the bloom
     from well-earned fame.
     The lover does not lament
     the time he's lost
     but rashly   15
     struggles
     to wallow
     in Venus's power.

1b.   The Hydra, who was only enhanced
     with the loss of her heads
     and more savage than any plague,
     could not
     upset him,   5
     though a girl subdued him.
     He submitted to Venus's yoke,
     a man, who, surpassing the gods,
     bore the sky on his shoulders

10   Atlante fatigato.
        Ref.

2a.   Caco tristis halitus,
        vel flammarum vomitus,
        vel fuga Nesso duplici
                non profuit.
5   Geryon Hesperius
        ianitorque Stygius,
        uterque forma triplici
                non terruit
        quem captivum tenuit
10   risu puella simplici.
        Ref.

2b.   Iugo cessit tenero
        somno qui letifero
        horti custodem divitis
                implicuit,
5   frontis Acheloiae
        cornu dedit Copiae.
        Apro, leone domitis
                emicuit,
        Thraces equos imbuit
10   cruenti caede hospitis.
        Ref.

3a.   Antaei Libyci
        luctam sustinuit,
        casus sophistici
        fraudes cohibuit,
5   cadere dum vetuit.

when Atlas became weary.   10
Ref.

2a. Foul exhalations
and blasts of fire from his mouth
were of no help to Cacus; no more was flight
to duplicitous Nessus.
Geryon from the Hesperian shore   5
and the Stygian gatekeeper,
both of triform shape,
did not alarm him,
but a girl held him captive
with her artless smile.   10
Ref.

2b. He yielded to the tender yoke,
the man who shrouded
in deadly sleep the guardian
of the rich garden
and gave Abundance   5
the horn from Achelous's brow.
After subduing the boar and the lion
he quickly rose to prominence
and soaked the Thracian horses
with the gore of his cruel host.   10
Ref.

3a. He endured the wrestling match
with Libyan Antaeus,
checking the trickery
of the bogus fall
by stopping him from falling.   5

Sed qui sic explicuit
   luctae nodosos nexus,
vincitur, et vincitur,
      dum labitur
10   magna Iovis soboles
      ad Ioles
         amplexus.
   Ref.

3b. Tantis floruerat
   laborum titulis,
   quem blandis carcerat
   puella vinculis
5 et dum lambit osculis
nectar huic labellulis
   Venereum propinat.
Vir solutus otiis
   Venereis
10 laborum memoriam
     et gloriam
       inclinat.
   Ref.

4a. Sed Alcide fortior
     aggredior
pugnam contra Venerem.
     Ut superem,
5   hanc fugio,
in hoc enim proelio
fugiendo fortius
    et melius
      pugnatur;

But the mighty son of Jupiter
who so disentangled
the knotted entanglements of their wrestling,
was conquered and bound,   10
when he fell for the embraces
of Iole.
Ref.

3b. Such were the Labors
that won him great renown,
but a girl made him her captive
with sweet shackles
and when she kissed him,   5
her lips gave him
the nectar of Venus.
When a man gives way
to love affairs
he mars the memory   10
and glory
of his deeds.
Ref.

4a. But braver than Hercules,
   I go forward
into battle against Venus.
   In order to win,
   I flee from her,   5
for in this battle
it is by fleeing that you fight
   more vigorously
      and with greater skill;

10   sicque Venus vincitur.
           Dum fugitur,
              fugatur.
Ref.

4b.   Dulces nodos Veneris
          et carceris
  blandi seras resero.
        De cetero,
5   ad alia
  dum traducor studia,
  o Lycori, valeas,
       et voveas
          quod vovi:
10   ab amore spiritum
       sollicitum
         removi.
Ref.

63a

Ni fugias tactus, vix evitabitur actus.

this is the way to beat Venus:
   when you flee from her
   she is put to flight.   10
Ref.

4b.   I am undoing Venus's sweet knots
     and unlocking
the locks of her pleasant prison.
    From this day forward
    I will be drawn   5
to other pursuits
and, Lycoris, I take my leave of you
    and hope you vow,
       as I have vowed:
I have distanced my troubled   10
            heart
             from love.
Ref.

63a

If you don't run away when touched, you will hardly escape
   being molested.

64

De XII virtutibus Herculis

Prima Cleonaei tolerata aerumna leonis.
Proxima Lernaeam ferro et face contudit Hydram.
Mox Erymantheum vis tertia perculit aprum.
Aeripedis quarto tulit aurea cornua cervi.
5 Stymphalidas pepulit volucres discrimine quinto.
Threiciam sexto spoliavit Amazona balteo.
Septima in Augeis stabulis impensa laboris.
Octava expulso numeratur adoria tauro.
In Diomedeis victoria nona quadrigis.
10 Geryone extincto decimam dat Iberia palmam.
Undecimo mala Hesperidum districta triumpho.
Cerberus extremi supremaque meta laboris.

65

1. Quocumque more motu volvuntur tempora,
    eadem fretus eucrasi pulso tympana.

2a.   Seu Philogaeus
             in imis moretur,

64

The Twelve Labors of Hercules

The first Labor he undertook was that of the Nemean Lion.
He next defeated the Lernaean Hydra with sword and torch.
His third feat was to overcome the Erymanthian boar.
For the fourth he carried off the bronze-hoofed stag's
    golden antlers.
In the fifth contest he drove off the Stymphalian birds.   5
In the sixth he stripped the Thracian Amazon of her girdle.
His seventh labor was performed in the Augean stables.
Driving out the bull counts as his eighth achievement.
His ninth victory was over Diomedes's four-horse team.
Iberia awarded him his tenth when he killed Geryon.   10
In his eleventh triumph he gathered the apples of the
    Hesperides.
Cerberus was his last and culminating labor.

65

1.   However the seasons roll past,
    I beat my drum to the same rhythm.

2a.   Whether Philogaeus
    lingers in the lower regions

aut Erythraeus
solito vernali semine rubens notetur,
5 vel dum coruscus Actaeon aestivo lumine repletur,
sive Lampas radians autumni copia ditetur,
ab uno semper numine mihi salus debetur.

2b.   Brevi spectata
Pasithea immisit,
                quod expectata
tempore tanto Euryale tandem subrisit.
5 Sola Euphrosyne, strictrici aemula, fautrix mihi sit,
cui Dione nudula per quandam dulciter arrisit;
        nam Allotheta cecinit hoc carmen, quod promisit.

3a. Cypris barbata
gaudeat occultu,
      iam renovata
maturo tumultu.
5 Virgo dudum feminae
habitum mentita,
nec fallit in virgine
Veneris perita.
Nomine pudico palliat
10   Venereum libamen
provida, ne palam ebulliat
        expertae rei famen.
Devirginata tamen
non horruit, cum iteravit naturae luctamen.

3b. Fautor sis, Paris,
Veneris agonis!
Venus, fruaris

or Erythraeus makes his appearance,
ruddy with the customary burgeoning of spring
or Actaeon sparkles, filled with summer's light,   5
or Lampas sends his rays, rich with autumn's bounty,
I always look for my salvation from just a single deity.

2b. Pasithea, glimpsed only briefly,
has signaled that Euryale,
so long awaited,
has finally smiled. If only Euphrosyne, who rivals
any witch, favors me, for a naked little Dione   5
in the form of a certain woman, smiled sweetly at me;
for Allotheta sang this song, as promised.

3a. May the bearded Venus,
now brought back to us
by the hurrying crowd,
take joy in her secret!
Long since as a virgin   5
she falsely donned woman's garb
but it does not go unnoticed when a virgin
is experienced in sex.
She concealed her sexual initiation
under the chaste term,   10
seeking to ensure that word of her expertise
should not burst out into the open.
Nonetheless, after losing her virginity, she has shown
no reluctance in repeating the struggle of nature.

3b. Paris, may you show your support
for the tussle of Venus!
Venus, may you enjoy

amplexibus Adonis!
5 Myrtum libans Indicam
   fanis Cithaeronis
testem ponam pedicam
  meae conditionis.
  Delio liberior immobili
10   non superor cohorte.
Spes lassam rem impulit, dum nobili
        fruar tori consorte,
        nec admittetur "forte,"
nam intra seram militavi virginalis portae.

4a. Pallerem, nisi me Veneri miranda decore
                virgo probaret,

4b. Marcerem, nisi spe veteri fuscata timore
                me stimularet.

5a. Inclita res ita cognita, perdita dat mihi fata,
                namque rogavi,

5b. Cui pia basia, dulcia, suavia congeminata
                multiplicavi.

6a. Hac bibo pocula vitae;
    hoc decus est mihi mite.

6b. Quae satis est mihi culta
    obvia saecula multa.

7a. Sat modo mature
    sum confessus eam.

7b. Claudit opus ture
    dum complector meam.

the embraces of Adonis!
Offering Indian myrtle   5
at your sanctuary on Cithaeron
I will hang up my fetter
as testimony of my status.
I am freer than Apollo
and unsurpassed by his unmoving entourage.   10
Hope has banished lassitude
provided I enjoy a noble bed partner—
and there will be no "perhaps" about it, for I have
waged my campaign within the virgin's locked door.

4a.   I would be pale were it not that a young woman, whose beauty deserves Venus's admiration, approves of me.

4b.   I would be wasting away were it not that she arouses in me hope tinged with inveterate fear.

5a.   Our wonderful lovemaking, so familiar to me, if lost, will be the death of me, for it was I who sought it.

5b.   Her gentle kisses, sweet and sensual, I have redoubled and multiplied.

6a.   Thanks to her I drink deep drafts of life; this is my peaceful glory.

6b.   Worship of her is enough for me for many years to come.

7a.   I have now confessed rather hurriedly my allegiance to her.

7b.   She envelops our lovemaking in a cloud of incense when I embrace my loved one.

8a.   Gratia laetitiae
      iure cupita,

8b.   moribus et facie
       tam redimita

9a.   flosculo praesignis
       dote leporis,

9b.   foveat me signis
       dulcis amoris!

10a. Haec memor corde serva,
      quod te mea Minerva,
      nunc prudens nunc proterva
  multiformi hactenus   declarat harmonia
5 prosa, versu, satira   psallens et rhythmachia
  te per orbem intonat   scolaris symphonia.

10b. Siquis versat quod verso
      amans et e converso,
      corde nihil diverso
  petat, optet, supplicet,   ut duret amor meus.
5 Ego vicem replicans   non ero fraudis reus,
  ut tali freto foedere   sit annus iubilaeus.

8a. Rightly desired
    for her joyful spirit,

8b. and so gracefully adorned
    in character and appearance,

9a. surpassing the best
    in charm and wit,

9b. I want her to hold me close
    with tokens of her sweet love!

10a. Keep this safe in your heart and remember it:
     it is you that my Muse, now serious, now playful,
     has been describing as she sings
     in a complex harmony—in prose, meter, satire,
     and rhythmical verse—a full scholarly symphony,   5
      proclaiming you throughout the world.

10b. If anyone treads the path I tread,
     one who loves and is loved in return,
     may he in similar vein beg, wish, and pray
     for my love to endure. I will return the favor
     and will keep my word so that for anyone   5
     relying on such a pact it will be a jubilee year.

66

Versus de Eodem

Actaeon, Lampos, Erythreus et Philogaeus—
istis nominibus poterit spectare peritus
quemque diem tantum tempus retinere quaternum.
Actaeon primum Graeci dicunt rubicundum,
5   nam sol purpureum iam mane novum tenet ortum.
Post graditur Lampos, est qui cognomine fulgens,
nam tunc splendorem sentimus sole micantem.
Ardens Erythreus sequitur, sic iure vocatus,
est nam quisque dies medius fervore repletus.
10   Post hoc extremus procedit tunc Philogaeus,
dictus "Amans terram," quod vespere tendit ad illam,
nam vult occasum terris inducere certum.

67

1a.   A globo veteri
cum rerum faciem
traxissent superi,
mundi quae seriem
5   prudens explicuit
        et texuit,

66

Metrical Verses on the Same Topic

Actaeon, Lampos, Erythraeus and Philogaeus —
from these names the scholar can see
that every day has just four segments.
The Greeks call Actaeon, who comes first, "ruddy,"
for the rising sun in the early morning has a reddish tinge.　　5
Then comes Lampos, whose name means "radiant,"
for then we feel the sun's shining splendor.
Burning Erythraeus follows, rightly so called,
for the middle of each day is filled with burning heat.
Then after this, last of all, Philogaeus comes to the fore,　　10
called "Earth-lover," for in the evening he sinks toward her,
as he wants to bring a predetermined sunset to the world.

67

1a.　When the gods had drawn forth
　　the elements,
　　from the original round mass,
　　Nature,
　　who prudently unraveled and wove together　　5
　　the array of phenomena

Natura
iam praeconceperat
quod fuerat
10   factura.

1b.   Quae causas machinae
mundanae suscitans,
de nostra virgine
iam dudum cogitans,
5   plus hanc excoluit,
plus praebuit
decoris,
dans privilegium
et praemium
10   laboris.

2a.   In hac prae ceteris
totius operis
Naturae lucet opera.
Tot munera
5   nulli favoris contulit,
sed extulit
hanc ultra cetera.

2b.   Et quae puellulis
avara singulis
solet partiri singula,
huic sedula
5   impendit copiosius
et plenius
formae munuscula.

that constitute the world,
had already
conceived
what she would create.   10

1b. As she summoned up the processes
     by which the world's fabric was put together,
     she had long been thinking
     about my young woman;
     on her she lavished extra care,   5
     on her bestowed
     more beauty,
     applying to the task
     exceptional skill
     and her best efforts.   10

2a. In this girl, beyond all the other works
     of her creation,
     the careful work of Nature shines.
     On nothing else did she bestow
     so many tokens of her favor,   5
     raising her high
     above everything else.

2b. And Nature, who normally gives,
     grudgingly,
     one mark of beauty
     to each girl,
     eagerly lavished   5
     in rich profusion
     her gifts of loveliness on her.

3a.   Naturae studio
     longe venustata
contendit lilio
     rugis non crispata
5   frons nivea.
     Simplices siderea
     luce micant ocelli.

3b.   Omnes amantium
     trahit in se visus,
spondens remedium
     verecunda risus
5   lascivia.
Arcus supercilia
     discriminant gemelli.

4a.   Ab utriusque luminis
        confinio
moderati libraminis
        indicio
5   naris eminentia
      producitur venuste
quadam temperantia,
nec nimis erigitur,
     nec premitur
10   iniuste.

4b.   Allicit verbis dulcibus
        et osculis,
castigate tumentibus
        labellulis
5   roseo nectareus

3a.   Her snowy brow,
      unmarred by wrinkles,
      much embellished
      by Nature's care,
      rivals the lily.   5
      Her eyes that know no guile
      flash with starry light.

3b.   She attracts
      all lovers' glances,
      promising them
      relief from their pain
      with the modest playfulness   5
      of her laugh. Twin arches
      form her eyebrows.

4a.   From the corner
      of either eye,
      creating an effect
      of perfect symmetry,
      the rise of her nose   5
      runs down charmingly
      and with due restraint,
      neither coming up too high
      nor remaining
      too low.   10

4b.   The nectar-like fragrance
      that pervades her rosy mouth
      entices with her sweet words
      and kisses,
      while her lips swell   5

odor infusus ori.
Pariter eburneus
sedet ordo dentium
  par nivium
10   candori.

5a. Certant nivi, micant lene
pectus, mentum, colla, genae
sed ne candore nimio
evanescat in pallorem,
5 praecastigat hunc candorem
rosam maritans lilio
 prudentior Natura,
ut ex his fiat aptior
 et gratior
10   mixtura.

5b. Rapit mihi me Coronis,
privilegiata donis
et Gratiarum flosculis.
Nam Natura, dulcioris
5 alimenta dans erroris,
dum in stuporem populis
 hanc omnibus ostendit,
in risu blando retia
 Veneria
10   tetendit.

modestly.
Her set of ivory teeth
is evenly balanced
and matches the whiteness
of snow.   10

5a. Also rivaling snow and gleaming softly
are her breast, chin, neck and cheeks
but to ensure that this whiteness
does not dissolve through excess, into pallor,
farsighted Nature   5
restrained the whiteness
by marrying the rose to the lily
so that there might be a blending of the two
that would be more harmonious
and pleasing.   10

5b. Coronis, richly endowed with the gifts
and charming qualities of the Graces,
robs me of my senses.
For when Nature offered
a cause for sweet dalliance   5
by presenting her
for all the world to marvel at,
she stretched
the nets of Venus
over her winning smile.   10

68

1. Saturni sidus lividum Mercurio micante
    fugatur ab Apolline Risum Iovis nudante,
    redit ab exilio Ver coma rutilante.

2. Cantu nemus avium
    lascivia canentium
            suave delinitur,
            fronde redimitur;
5   vernant spinae floribus
            micantibus,
            signantibus
    Venerem, quia spina pungit, flos blanditur.

3. Mater Venus subditis amori
                            dulcia
                        stipendia
                        copia
5   largiri delectatur uberiori.

4. Dulcis aura Zephyri
        spirans ab occidente
    Iovis favet sideri
        alacriori mente,
5   Aquilonem carceri
            Aeolo nolente
    deputans. Sic ceteri
    glaciales spiritus diffugiunt repente,
                    redit calor aetheri,
10 dum caligo nubium rarescit sole Taurum tenente.

68

1.   As Mercury sparkles, the pale star of Saturn
   is put to flight by Apollo, who uncovers Jupiter's Smile.
   Spring, with his russet hair, returns from exile.

2.   The woods,
   pleasantly soothed
   by the playful singing of birds,
   are decked with foliage.
   The thorny bushes bloom   5
   with dancing flowers
   that signify Venus, because the thorn pricks
   and the flower offers blandishments.

3.   Mother Venus takes delight
   in bestowing
   sweet rewards
   in rich abundance
   on those who surrender themselves to love.   5

4.   The Zephyr's sweet breath,
   blowing gently from the west,
   favors Jupiter's star
   of livelier mood,
   while, against the will of Aeolus,   5
   it relegates the North Wind to prison.
   As a result, the rest of the icy breezes suddenly
   flee away and warmth returns to the sky,
   as the mist of clouds thins out
   now that the sun is in Taurus.   10

5.   Sic beari spes, halitus fragrans oris tenelli
                              dum acclinat basium,
                              scindit nubem omnium
                              curarum, sed avelli
5   nescit, ni congressio sit arcani medica duelli.

6.   Felix hora huius duelli,
       cui contingit nectar adunare melli!
                       Quam felix unio,
              cuius suavitatis poculo
5   sopiuntur sensus et ocelli!

69

1.   Aestas in exilium
                       iam peregrinatur,
       laeto nemus avium
                       cantu viduatur,
5   pallet viror frondium,
                       campus defloratur.
                       Exaruit
                       quod floruit,
              quia felicem statum nemoris
10   vis frigoris
                       sinistra denudavit,
              et aethera silentio
                       turbavit,
                       exilio
15   dum aves relegavit.

5. Just so does the prospect of a blissful encounter,
    when sweet breath from a tender mouth offers a kiss,
    break up the cloud of all my cares—but the cloud
    cannot be dispersed unless we come together
    in the secret tussle that brings healing.   5

6. Happy is the hour of this struggle
    for the man lucky enough to encounter nectar
    mixed with honey! How happy is our union,
    when we drink a draft of its sweetness,
    and our senses and eyes are lulled to sleep!   5

69

1. Summer is now gone,
    off into exile,
    the woods are bare
    of the joyful song of birds,
    the green foliage   5
    is turning pale,
    the fields have lost their flowers.
    What once bloomed
    has now withered
    because the baleful power of frost   10
    stripped away
    the happy state of the woods
    and upset the sky
    with the silence
    when it exiled the birds.   15

2.   Sed amorem,
       qui calorem
 nutrit, nulla vis frigoris valet attenuare,
              sed ea reformare
 5   studet, quae corruperat brumae torpor, amare.
                                   Crucior,
                                   morior
                    vulnere, quo glorior.
                    Eia, si me sanare
10   uno vellet osculo,
                 quae cor felici iaculo
                         gaudet vulnerare!

3.   Lasciva, blandi risus,
      omnes in se trahit visus.
                  Labia
                  Veneria
 5   tumentia—
      sed castigate—dant errorem
                  leniorem,
             dum dulcorem
 instillant, favum mellis, osculando,
10 ut me mortalem negem aliquando.
         Laeta frons tam nivea,
         lux oculorum aurea,
         caesaries subrubea,
         manus vincentes lilia
15   me trahunt in suspiria:
                  rideo,
              cum video
      cuncta tam elegantia,

2.   But no power of frost
can diminish
the love that generates heat;
rather, love strives to restore the beauty
that winter's torpor disfigured.   5
I am tortured,
I am dying
from the wound I glory in.
Ah! if only she who takes joy in wounding
my heart with her welcome shaft   10
were willing to heal me
with a single kiss!

3.   Playful and with a seductive laugh,
she draws all eyes to her.
Her lips
are those of Venus —
full,   5
but not too full —
and cause mild discomposure
when they instill the sweetness of a honeycomb
with their kisses so that at times
I say I am no longer mortal.   10
Her snowy brow that radiates joy,
the golden light in her eyes,
her chestnut hair,
her hands paler than lilies,
all cause me to sigh.   15
I smile
when I see
all these details, so elegant,

tam regia,
20   tam suavia,
tam dulcia.

70

1.   Aestatis florigero tempore
sub umbrosa residens arbore,
avibus canentibus in nemore,
sibilante serotino frigore,
meae Thisbes adoptato
5   fruebar eloquio,
colloquens de Veneris
blandissimo commercio.

2.   Eius vultus,   forma, cultus
prae puellis,   ut sol stellis,
sic praelucet.   O, inducet
hanc nostra ratio,
5   ut dignetur suo
nos beare consortio?

3.   Nil ergo restat satius,
quam caecam mentis flammam
denudare diffusius.
Audaces fortuna iuvat penitus.
5   His ergo sit introitus:

so regal,
so attractive,   20
so charming.

70

1. Summertime was abloom with flowers
    and I was sitting under a shady tree,
    while birds sang in the woods
    and a cool evening breeze rustled by.
    I was enjoying the conversation   5
    I had taken up with my Thisbe,
    about the delightful business of love.

2. Her face, her beauty, her fine toilette
    make her outshine all other girls,
    as the sun outshines the stars.
    Ah! Will my arguments
    persuade her to consent   5
    to bless me by sharing her love with me?

3. No better course is available to me
    than to reveal more fully
    the flame hidden in my heart.
    Fortune always favors the bold.
    So let's begin with these words: 5

4a. "Ignem caecum sub pectore
     longo depasco tempore,
     qui vires miro robore
     toto diffundit corpore.

4b. Quem tu sola percipere,
     si vis potes extinguere
     hoc meum semivivere
     felici ligans foedere."

4c. "Amoris spes est dubia,
     aut verax aut contraria.
     Amanti necessaria
     virtutis est constantia.

5a. Prae ceteris virtutibus
          est patientia
          amoris famulantia.

5b. Sed et ignem, qui discurrit
          per praecordia,
          fac extinguat alia.

5c. Noster amor non furtiva,
          non fragilia
          amplexatur gaudia."

6a. "Ignis quo crucior,
     immo quo glorior,
     ignis est invisibilis.

6b. Si non extinguitur
     a qua succenditur
     manet inextinguibilis.

4a. "I have long been feeding
      a hidden fire deep in my heart,
      which spreads its strength with amazing power
      throughout my entire body.

4b. You alone can perceive it
      and, if you will, extinguish it,
      by uniting this half-life I lead
      in a happy bond with yours."

4c. "In love what we hope for is never certain;
      it turns out either true or not.
      What is essential for a lover
      is to remain steadfast to his ideal.

5a. More than any of the other virtues
      patience is the handmaiden
      of love.

5b. And as for the fire which runs through
      your inner being,
      have another woman extinguish it!

5c. My love does not embrace joys
      that are furtive
      and unlikely to last."

6a. "The fire that tortures me
      or rather the fire I glory in
      is an unseen fire.

6b. If it is not put out
      by the one who set it alight,
      it cannot be put out.

7a.   Est ergo tuo munere
      me mori vel me vivere."

7b.   "Quid refert pro re pendula
      vitae pati pericula?

8a.   Est pater, est mater,
      est frater, qui quater
      die me pro te corripiunt,

8b.   et vetulas per cellulas
      et iuvenes per speculas
   deputantes, nos custodiunt.

9.   Argumque centioculum
      plus tremo quam patibulum.

10.   Est ergo dignum
         virum benignum
         vitare signum,
         unde malignum
5   murmur cursitat per populum."

11a. "Times in vanum;
      tam est arcanum,
      quod nec Vulcanum
   curo cum sophisticis catenis.

11b. Stilbontis more
      Lethaeo rore
      Argum sopore
   premam oculis clausis centenis."

7a. So it is up to you
     whether I live or die."

7b. "What use is it for me to put my life in danger
     for something uncertain?

8a. I have a father, a mother
     and a brother who scold me about you
     four times a day,

8b. and by setting up old women in little rooms
     and young men in watchtowers
     they are keeping a wary eye on us.

9.   And I fear Argus the Hundred-Eyed
     more than the gallows.

10. So it is right and proper
     that a man of good intent
     should avoid giving any indication
     that could lead to malevolent gossip
     spreading quickly among the people."   5

11a. "Your fears are groundless;
     our affair is so secret
     that I am not even concerned
     about Vulcan and his ingenious chains.

11b. Like Mercury
     I will close Argus's hundred eyes
     and put him to sleep
     with the water of Lethe."

12a. "In trutina mentis dubia
        fluctuant contraria
      lascivus amor et pudicitia.

12b. Sed eligo quod video,
        collum iugo praebeo,
      ad iugum tamen suave transeo."

13.   "Non bene dixeris
       iugum secretum Veneris,
          quo nil liberius,
     nil dulcius,   nil melius.

14a. O quam dulcia
        sunt haec gaudia!
      Veneris furta sunt pia.

14b. Ergo propera
        ad haec munera:
      carent laude dona sera."

15.   "Dulcissime,
      totam tibi subdo me."

71

1a.   Axe Phoebus aureo
         celsiora lustrat
       et nitore roseo
          radios illustrat.

12a. "In the wavering scales of my mind
two contrary desires contend:
sexual attraction and restraint.

12b. But I choose what I see before me;
I offer my neck to the yoke
but it is under a pleasant yoke that I pass."

13. "You are wrong to call
Venus's mystery a yoke.
There is nothing more liberating,
nothing sweeter, nothing better.

14a. Ah, how pleasant
these joys are!
Stolen moments of love are acts of piety!

14b. So hurry
to give these gifts.
Late gifts are not well received."

15. "Sweetest love,
I give myself wholly up to you."

71

1a. Phoebus in his golden chariot
is traversing higher tracts of heaven
and making his rays
shine with a rosy gleam.

1b. Venustata Cybele
    facie florente
  florem nato Semelae
    dat Phoebo favente.

2a. Aurarumve suavium
    gratia iuvante
  sonat nemus avium
    voce modulante.

2b. Philomena querulae
    Terea retractat,
  dum canendo merulae
    carmina coaptat.

3a. Iam Dionaea
    laeta chorea
sedulo resonat   cantibus horum.

3b. Iamque Dione
    iocis, agone
relevat, cruciat,   corda suorum.

4a. Me quoque subtrahit   illa sopori,
  invigilareque   cogit amori.

4b. Tela Cupidinis   aurea gesto,
  igne cremantia   corda molesto.

5a. Quod mihi datur
    expaveo,
  quodque negatur,

1b. Cybele, beautifully decked out,
    her face full of flowers,
    brings bloom to Semele's son
    with Phoebus's assistance.

2a. With gentle breezes
    graciously assisting,
    the wood echoes
    with the melodious sounds of birds.

2b. Philomena plaintively goes over
    again and again the deeds of Tereus,
    while she attunes her song
    to the blackbird's.

3a. Now Dione's
    joyful chorus
    responds to their songs
    in eager counterpoint.

3b. Now Dione
    lightens and tortures
    the hearts of her followers
    with pleasant games and agony.

4a. I am one of those she keeps from sleep
    and forces to stay awake for love.

4b. I carry Cupid's golden arrows
    and trouble my heart that burns with their fire.

5a. What is offered me
    causes me great fear,
    and what is denied me

        hoc aveo
5   mente severa.

5b. Quae mihi cedit,
      hanc caveo.
    Quae non oboedit,
      huic faveo,
5   sumque revera

6a. infelix, seu peream,
    seu relever per eam.
    Quae cupit, hanc fugio,
    quae fugit, hanc cupio.

6b. Plus renuo debitum,
    plus feror in vetitum;
    plus licet illibitum,
    plus libet illicitum.

7a. O metuenda
Dionae decreta.
    O fugienda
venena secreta!
5   Fraude verenda
doloque repleta.

7b. Docta furoris
in aestu punire
    quos dat amoris
amara subire,
5   plena livoris
urentis et irae.

I crave
passionately.   5

5b. If a woman yields to me,
I am wary of her.
But if she does not do what I ask,
I like her
and am really   5

6a. wretched, whether she be the death of me
or may give me relief.
The woman who desires me I run from.
The woman who runs from me I desire.

6b. The more I turn from what I ought to do,
the more I am attracted to what is forbidden;
the more what I dislike is permitted,
the more I like what is not permitted.

7a. Ah, the decrees of Dione
that we need to fear!
Ah, her hidden poisons
we need to flee!
Her deceptiveness makes her formidable   5
and she is full of guile.

7b. She is skilled in punishing
in an onset of fury
those whom she causes
to experience the bitterness of love;
she is full   5
of burning envy and rage.

8a. Hinc mihi metus
  abundat,
hinc ora fletus
  inundat.

8b. Hinc mihi pallor
  in ore
est, quia fallor
  amore.

72

1a. Grates ago Veneri,
   quae prosperi
mihi risus numine
   de virgine
5   mea gratum
   et optatum
  contulit trophaeum.

1b. Dudum militaveram,
   nec poteram
hoc frui stipendio;
   nunc sentio
5   me beari,
   serenari
  vultum Dionaeum.

8a. This is why I am filled
with fear;
this is why tears
flow down my cheeks.

8b. This is why my face
is pale:
because I am cheated
in love.

72

1a. I give thanks to Venus,
who by the power
of her propitious smile
has granted me
a welcome   5
and longed-for victory
over my girl.

1b. I had campaigned for a long time
without being able
to enjoy this
reward; now I feel
handsomely recompensed,   5
and that Dione's face
is beaming.

2a. Visu, colloquio,
        contactu, basio
frui virgo dederat,
                sed aberat
5 linea posterior
                et melior
                        amoris,
quam nisi transiero
                de cetero,
10 sunt quae dantur alia
                materia
                        furoris.

2b. Ad metam propero,
        sed fletu tenero
mea me sollicitat,
                dum dubitat
5 solvere virguncula
                        repagula
                                pudoris.
Flentis bibo lacrimas
                        dulcissimas;
10 sic me plus inebrio
                        plus haurio
                                fervoris.

3a. Delibuta lacrimis
        oscula plus sapiunt.
        Blandimentis intimis
        mentem plus alliciunt.
5   Ergo magis capior
                et acrior

2a. The woman had allowed me to enjoy
     seeing her, talking with her,
     touching and kissing her
     but the final
     and best   5
     stage of love
     was missing
     and unless I crossed that line
     in the future
     other favors granted   10
     were fuel
     for madness.

2b. I hurry toward the goal,
     but with tender tears
     my girl implores me,
     since she is hesitant
     to undo   5
     the barrier
     of her chastity.
     As she weeps I drink
     her delicious tears
     and the more intoxicated I become in this way,   10
     the more passion
     I imbibe.

3a. Kisses tinged with tears
     have more savor.
     They entice the heart
     more than intimate protestations of love.
     So I am the more captivated   5
     and the heat of the flame

vis flammae recalescit.
Sed dolor Coronidis
se tumidis
10   exerit singultibus
nec precibus
mitescit.

3b. Preces addo precibus
basiaque basiis.
Fletus illa fletibus,
iurgia conviciis,
5   meque cernit oculo
nunc aemulo
nunc quasi supplicanti.
Nam nunc lite dimicat,
nunc supplicat,
10   dumque prece blandior,
fit surdior
precanti.

4a. Vim nimis audax infero.
Haec ungue saevit aspero,
comas vellit,
vim repellit
5   strenua.
Sese plicat
et intricat
genua
ne ianua
10   pudoris resolvatur.

burns more fiercely.
But Coronis's anguish
reveals itself
in heaving sobs   10
and does not yield
to my entreaties.

3b. I add prayers to prayers,
     and kisses to kisses.
     She adds tears to tears,
     reproaches to recriminations
     and looks at me   5
     now with an eye that challenges,
     now with an eye that is almost begging.
     At one moment she is disputing with me,
     at the next she is entreating me,
     and when I coax her with prayers,   10
     she becomes deaf
     to my pleas.

4a. All too boldly I press my attack.
     She fights back fiercely with her sharp nails,
     pulls my hair,
     and resists my assault
     vigorously.   5
     She curls up
     and crosses
     her legs
     to prevent the door of her chastity
     from being opened.   10

4b. Sed tandem ultra milito,
     triumphum do proposito.
         Per amplexus
         firmo nexus
5   brachia
         eius ligo,
         pressa figo
         basia.
         Sic regia
10   Diones reseratur.

5a. Res utrique placuit,
     et me minus arguit
     mitior amasia,
         dans basia
5   mellita

5b. et subridens tremulis
     semiclausis oculis,
     veluti sub anxio
         suspirio
5   sopita.

73

1a. Clauso Cronos et serato
        carcere ver exit;
    risu Iovis reserato
        faciem detexit.

4b. But finally I take my campaign further
and win the triumph I planned for.
With embraces
I entwine her firmly
and bind   5
her arms
and press kisses
upon her.
In this way I unlock
the palace of Dione.   10

5a. We both enjoyed the encounter,
and a gentler lover
checked her accusations,
giving me kisses
sweet as honey   5

5b. and smiling,
with fluttering,
half-closed eyes,
as if lulled to sleep
with an anxious sigh.   5

73

1a. With Cronus shut up and the prison locked,
spring is coming forth;
with the unlocking of Jupiter's smile
it has shown its face.

1b. Coma caelum rutilante
      Cynthius emundat
et terrena secundante
      aere fecundat.

2a. Purpurato   flore prato
      ver tenet primatum
ex argenti   renitenti
      specie renatum.

2b. Iam odora   Rheam Flora
      chlamyde vestivit,
quae ridenti   et florenti
      specie lascivit.

3a. Vernant veris ad amoena
    thyma, rosae, lilia.

3b. His alludit philomena,
    merops et luscinia.

4a. Satyros hoc excitat
    et Dryadum choreas,
redivivis incitat
    hoc ignibus Napaeas.

4b. Hoc Cupido concitus,
    hoc amor innovatur,
hoc ego sollicitus,
    hoc mihi me furatur.

5a. Ignem alo tacitum,
amo, nec ad placitum,
ut qui contra libitum
cupio prohibitum.

1b.   With his russet hair
       Apollo is clearing the sky
       and, with the help of the lower air,
       is bringing fertility to the earth.

2a.   The fields are crimson with flowers,
       and spring, reborn
       from the gleaming beauty of the silver urn,
       holds pride of place.

2b.   Flora has clothed Rhea
       in a fragrant dress.
       With an appearance now smiling and blooming,
       Rhea becomes playful.

3a.   Responding to the pleasant warmth of spring,
       thyme, roses, and lilies put forth new growth.

3b.   Among them dart playfully
       the swallow, bee-eater, and nightingale.

4a.   Spring rouses the Satyrs
       and the troupes of dancing Dryads.
       and stirs the glade nymphs
       with renewed passion.

4b.   Spring stirs up Cupid
       and makes love begin anew;
       spring makes me anxious
       and robs me of my self-control.

5a.   Feeding a silent flame,
       I am in love but not of my own choosing;
       rather, as one who against his wishes
       desires what is forbidden.

5b.   Votis Venus meritum
rite facit irritum,
trudit in interitum
quem rebar emeritum.

6a.   Si quis amans per amare mereri   posset amari
posset Amor mihi velle mederi   dando beari.

6b.   Quot faciles   mihi cerno medelas   posse parari
tot steriles   bi perdo querelas   absque levari.

7a.   Imminet exitus   igne vigente
morte medullitus   ossa tenente.

7b.   Quod caro praedicat   haec macilenta,
hoc sibi vendicat   usque perempta.

8a.   Dum mala sentio, summa malorum,
pectora saucia, plena furorum,
pellere semina nitor amorum.

8b.   Ast Venus artibus   usa nefandis,
dum bene palliat   aspera blandis,
unguibus attrahit   omnia pandis.

9.   Parce dato pia,   Cypris agone,
et quia vincimur,   arma repone!
Et quibus es Venus,   esto Dione!

5b.   The merit I have earned by my vows
      Venus duly treats as worthless
      and pushes me to my destruction,
      when I thought I had retired from her service.

6a.   If any lover could by his love deserve to be loved,
      Love could choose to heal me by according me bliss.

6b.   But for all the easy remedies that I see can be adduced
      for me, I waste useless complaints and win no relief.

7a.   The fire is gathering strength and my end is near,
      for death has its grip on my bones deep within me.

7b.   The fate that this emaciated body of mine forebodes
      is what it claims as its own after its endless wasting.

8a.   I feel the pain, excruciating pain,
      my heart wounded and filled with passion,
      and I struggle to drive out the seeds of love.

8b.   But Venus employing her evil skills, cleverly
      cloaks her harshness with soft words
      and drags all toward her with curved claws.

9.   Cyprian goddess, you have caused me pain. Be kind
      and spare me. We are beaten; lay down your arms!
      And toward those to whom you are Venus, be Dione!

74

1. Laetabundus rediit
   avium concentus,
   ver iucundum prodiit;
   gaudeat iuventus
5   nova ferens gaudia!
   Modo vernant omnia;
   Phoebus serenatur,
   redolens temperiem,
   novo flore faciem
10   Flora renovatur.

2. Risu Iovis pellitur
   torpor hiemalis.
   Altius extollitur
   cursus aestivalis
5   solis, beneficio
   cuius omnis regio
   recipit teporem.
   Sic ad instar temporis
   nostri Venus pectoris
10   reficit ardorem.

3. Aestivantur Dryades,
   colle sub umbroso
   prodeunt Oreades,
   coetu glorioso.
5   Satyrorum contio
   psallit cum tripudio
   Tempe per amoena;

74

1. The cheerful chorus
   of birds has returned.
   and joyous spring has come forth.
   Let the young people rejoice
   as they experience new joys!   5
   Everything now shows signs of spring;
   Phoebus is serene and clear,
   emitting a warm fragrance,
   Flora makes over her appearance.
   with new flowers.   10

2. Winter's torpor
   has been driven off by Jove's smile.
   The sun's summer path
   is mounting higher
   and thanks to its kindness   5
   every region
   is warming up.
   This is how, in keeping with the season,
   Venus is stoking
   the ardor of my heart.   10

3. The Dryads avoid the heat
   beneath a shady hill,
   while the mountain nymphs come forth
   in glorious procession.
   A band of satyrs   5
   sings and dances
   in the pleasant vale of Tempe.

his alludens concinit,
cum iocundi meminit
10   veris, philomena.

4.   Aestas ab exilio
        redit exoptata.
     Picto ridet gremio
        tellus purpurata.
5   Miti cum susurrio
     suo domicilio
        gryllus delectatur.
     Hoc canore, iubilo,
     multiformi sibilo
10   nemus gloriatur.

5.   Applaudamus igitur
        rerum novitati!
     Felix qui diligitur
        voti compos grati,
5   dono laetus Veneris,
     cuius ara teneris
        floribus odorat.
     Miser e contrario
     qui sublato bravio
10   sine spe laborat.

A nightingale accompanies them
in song, as she recalls
the pleasantness of spring.   10

4.   The longed-for summer
is returning from exile.
The earth, turned crimson,
is smiling, its bosom aglow with color.
With its gentle buzz   5
the cricket shows its delight
in its home.
The woods exult melodiously
in this joyful song,
with a multitoned rasping.   10

5.   Let us therefore welcome
the newness of the world!
Happy is the man who is loved,
for he has achieved his heart's desire,
rejoicing in the gift of Venus,   5
whose altar is fragrant
with tender flowers.
Wretched, on the other hand, is the man
who, after the prize has been carried off,
struggles on without hope.   10

75

1. Omittamus studia,
    dulce est desipere,
    et carpamus dulcia
    iuventutis tenerae!
5   Res est apta senectuti
        seriis intendere.
    Res est apta iuventuti
        laeta mente ludere.
    Ref. Velox aetas praeterit.
        Studio detenta,
    lascivire suggerit
        tenera iuventa.

2. Ver aetatis labitur,
    hiems nostra properat.
    Vita damnum patitur:
    cura carnem macerat,
5   sanguis aret, hebet pectus,
        minuuntur gaudia.
    Nos deterret iam senectus
        morborum familia.
    Ref.

3. Imitemur superos
    —digna est sententia!—
    et amores teneros
    iam venentur retia.
5   Voto nostro serviamus—
        mos est iste numinum!

75

1.   Let's forget our studies—
    it is pleasant to fool around—
    and seize the sweet hours
    of tender youth.
    It is appropriate for the old   5
    to focus on serious matters.
    But joyful playfulness
    is appropriate for the young.
    Ref. Time passes quickly.
    Kept in by study
    our tender youth prompts us
    to fool around.

2.   The spring of our life is slipping by,
    our winter hurries toward us.
    Our life suffers loss:
    worry saps the body,
    blood dries up, the heart grows weak,   5
    joys diminish.
    Old age already scares us
    with its troupe of diseases.
    Ref.

3.   Let's imitate the gods
    —a worthy sentiment!—
    and let our nets now hunt
    for tender love.
    Let's work on what we wish for—   5
    that's what the gods do!

Ad plateas descendamus
　　et choreas virginum
Ref.

4.　Ibi, quae fit facilis,
　　est videndi copia.
　　Ibi fulget mobilis
　　membrorum lascivia,
5　dum puellae se movendo
　　gestibus lasciviunt.
　Asto videns, et videndo
　　me mihi subripiunt.
　Ref.

76

1.　Dum caupona verterem　vino debachatus
　　—secus templum Veneris　eram hospitatus—
　　solus ibam prospere　vestibus ornatus,
　　plenum ferens loculum　ad sinistrum latus.

2.　Almi templi ianua　servabatur plene,
　　ingredi non poteram,　ut optavi bene.
　　Intus erat sonitus　dulcis cantilenae,
　　aestimabam plurimae　quod essent Sirenae.

3.　Cum custode ianuae　parum requievi;
　　erat virgo nobilis,　pulchra, statu brevi.
　　Secum dans colloquia　in sermone levi,
　　tandem desiderium　intrandi explevi.

Let's go down to the piazzas
where the girls are dancing.
Ref.

4. There's plenty to look at there
and it's easy to do!
There you find the sensual movement
of gleaming limbs,
as the girls sway and gesture   5
suggestively.
I stand there watching and as I watch,
they steal my senses from me.
Ref.

76

1. As I turned away from the inn, after overindulging in wine — I was lodged near the temple of Venus — I was making my way unaccompanied, expensively dressed and carrying a full purse on my left side.

2. The door of the blessed temple was well guarded;
I was not able to go in, as I very much wanted to do.
Inside there was the sound of sweet singing.
I thought it was a crowd of Sirens.

3. I rested a little while with the doorkeeper; she was a young noblewoman, beautiful and short of stature. After chatting with her in a bantering vein, I eventually achieved my goal of getting inside.

4. In ingressu ianuae   sedens invitatus
   ab hac pulchra virgine   sum interrogatus:
   "Unde es, o iuvenis,   hucce applicatus?"
   Cui dixi: "Domina,   vestri comitatus."

5. "Quae est causa, dicito,   huc tui adventus?
   Qualis ad haec litora   appulit te ventus?
   Duxit te necessitas   et tua iuventus?"
   Dixi: "Necessario   venio detentus.

6. Intus et exterius   asto vulneratus
   a sagitta Veneris.   Ex quo fui natus,
   telum fero pectoris   nondum medicatus,
   cursu veni tacito,   quo sim liberatus.

7. Incessanter rogo te,   virgo ter beata,
   ut haec verba Veneri   nunties legata."
   Ipsa mota precibus,   fortiter rogata,
   nuntiavit Veneri   verba destinata:

8. "Sauciorum omnium   salus o divina,
   quae es dulcis praepotens   amoris regina,
   aegrum quendam iuvenem   tua medicina
   procurare studeas,   obsecro, festina!"

9. Iussu sacrae Veneris   ductus in conclavi.
   Cernens eius speciem   fortiter expavi.
   Flexis tandem genibus   ipsam salutavi,
   "Salve," dicens, "inclita   Venus, quam optavi."

10. "Quis es," inquit, "iuvenis,   qui tam bene faris?
    Quid venisti, dicito,   quomodo vocaris?

4. While sitting in the entranceway, as I had been invited to do, I was asked by this beautiful young woman: "Where are you from, young man, to have landed here?" I said to her, "My lady, I am from the same county as you."

5. "Tell me, what is the reason for your coming here?
    What wind brought you to these shores?
    Was it necessity and your youth that brought you?"
    I said: "It is in the clutches of necessity that I come.

6. I stand before you, wounded internally and externally
    by an arrow of Venus. I carry a shaft in my heart
    from the time I was born and am not yet healed.
    I have come here secretly to be set free.

7. I beg you again and again, thrice blessed maiden,
    to take this message to Venus as my envoy."
    Moved by my entreaties and importunate requests,
    she reported to Venus the message I wished to convey:

8. "You, who are the heavenly salvation of all who have been wounded and the all-powerful queen of sweet love, strive to look after a sick young man with your medicine and, please, hurry!"

9. At the bidding of holy Venus, I was led into her chamber. When I saw her beauty, I was filled with awe. Finally, I knelt down and greeted her: "Hail, renowned Venus, whom I have longed to meet."

10. "Who are you, young man, "she said, "who speak so well? Tell me, why have you come? What is your name?

Es tu forte iuvenis   ille dictus Paris?
Ista de quo retulit,   cur sic infirmaris?"

11. "Venus clementissima,   felix creatura,
cerno quod praeterita   noscis et futura.
Ipse sum miserrimus,   res iam peritura,
quem sanare poteris   tua levi cura."

12. "Bene," inquit, "veneris,   noster o dilecte
iuvenis, aptissime   sodes nostrae sectae.
Si tu das denarios   monetae electae,
dabitur consilium   salutis perfectae."

13. "Ecce," dixi, "loculus   extat nummis plenus,
totum quippe tribuam   tibi, sacra Venus.
Si tu das consilium,   ut sat sim serenus,
tuum in perpetuum   venerabor genus."

14. Ambo iunctis manibus   ivimus mature,
ubi stabant plurimae   bellae creaturae.
Omnes erant similes,   unius naturae
et unius habitus   atque vestiturae.

15. Nobis propinquantibus   omnes surrexere,
quas ut salutavimus   responsum dedere:
"Bene vos veneritis,   velitis sedere?"
Venus inquit: "Aliud   volumus explere."

16. Innuens his omnibus   iubet ire cito.
Pariter remansimus   in loco munito
solis quiescentibus;   strato redimito
plura pertractavimus   sermone polito.

Are you perhaps the young man—the one called Paris?
Regarding what my attendant told me—why are you so
ill?"

11. "Most merciful Venus, most propitious of beings, I
understand you know the past and the future. I am in
the most wretched state; my fate is all but sealed. But
you can cure me with your tender care."

12. "You are most welcome, my charming young man,
you will make a most suitable member of our group.
If you give money of good coinage,
you will be counseled to perfect health."

13. "Here is my purse," I said, "full of coins.
I will give you all of it, holy Venus.
If you give me counsel that will put me at ease,
I will venerate your lineage forever."

14. Without delay the two of us went hand in hand
where many beautiful creatures were standing.
They were all alike, with the same mannerisms,
the same appearance, and the same dress.

15. They all got up as we approached,
and when we greeted them, they answered:
"Welcome! Would you care to have a seat?"
Venus said: "We have other business to attend to."

16. She signaled to them all to leave right away.
We remained together in the room, made secure
for a couple resting alone; on a decorated couch
we had a sophisticated discussion of many topics.

17. Exuit se vestibus   genitrix Amoris,
     carnes ut ostenderet   nivei decoris.
     Sternens eam lectulo   fere decem horis
     mitigavi rabiem   febrici doloris.

18. Postmodum transivimus   ire balneatum
     in hortanum balneum   Iovi consecratum.
     Huius aqua balnei   me sensi purgatum
     omnibus languoribus   beneque piatum.

19. Ultra modum debilis   balneo afflictus,
     fame validissima   steteram astrictus.
     Versus contra Venerem,   quasi derelictus,
     dixi, "Vellem edere,   si quis inest victus."

20. Perdices et anseres   ductae sunt coquinae,
     plura volatilia,   grues et gallinae,
     pro placentis ductus est   modius farinae.
     Praeparatis omnibus   pransus sum festine.

21. Tribus, reor, mensibus   secum sum moratus.
     Plenum ferens loculum   ivi vir ornatus,
     recedens a Venere   sum nunc allevatus
     nummis atque vestibus   sic sum pauperatus.

22. Terreat vos, iuvenes,   istud quod auditis!
     Dum sagittam Veneris   penes vos sentitis,
     mei este memores   quocumque vos itis,
     liberi poteritis esse,   si velitis.

17. Cupid's mother took off her clothes
to reveal flesh of snow-white beauty.
Laying her down on the bed, I relieved
the frenzy of my feverish pain for almost ten hours.

18. Afterward we went over to bathe
in the garden baths dedicated to Jupiter.
I felt myself cleansed by the water of this bath
and fully released from all my sickness.

19. Feeling unusually weak from the bath,
I was smitten with enormous hunger.
I turned to Venus and, like a homeless beggar, said:
"I would like to eat, if there is any food around."

20. The kitchen's store of partridges and geese was brought
to us and more fowl—cranes and chickens, and a mea-
sure of flour for cakes came too. When everything was
ready, I ate in greedy haste.

21. For three months, I think, I stayed there with her.
It was with a full purse I went there, a rich man,
but now, as I leave Venus, I have been relieved
of my money and my clothes and so made a pauper.

22. Young men, may what you have heard scare you!
When you feel Venus's arrow within you,
remember me, wherever you go;
you can be free should you so choose!

77

1.   Si linguis angelicis   loquar et humanis,
   non valeret exprimi   palma, nec inanis,
   per quam recte praeferor   cunctis Christianis,
   tamen invidentibus   aemulis profanis.

2.   Pange, lingua, igitur   causas et causatum;
   nomen tamen dominae   serva palliatum,
   ut non sit in populo   illud divulgatum,
   quod secretum gentibus   extat et celatum.

3.   In virgultu florido   stabam et amoeno
   vertens haec in pectore,   "Quid facturus ero;
   dubito, quod semina   in arena sero,
   mundi florem diligens;   ecce iam despero.

4.   Si despero merito,   nullus admiretur,
   nam per quandam vetulam   rosa prohibetur,
   ut non amet aliquem,   atque non ametur,
   quam Pluto subripere,   flagito, dignetur!"

5.   Cumque meo animo   verterem praedicta,
   optans, anum raperet   fulminis sagitta,
   ecce retrospiciens   laeta post relicta,
   audias quid viderim,   dum morarer ita.

6.   Vidi florem floridum,   vidi florum florem,
   vidi rosam Madii,   cunctis pulchriorem,
   vidi stellam splendidam   cunctis clariorem,
   per quam ego degeram   fidens in Amorem.

77

1. Were I to speak with the tongues of angels and of men,
    I could not adequately express my glorious victory,
    which, despite the envy of my uninitiated rivals,
    rightly places me above all other Christians.

2. So, my tongue, tell of the causes and their effect
    but keep my mistress's name shrouded
    so that what is kept secret and hidden from people
    is not broadcast among the general populace.

3. I was standing in a pleasant, flowering grove,
    pondering the following: "What am I going to do?
    I fear that in loving the world's choicest flower,
    I am sowing seeds in sand; see, I am already despairing.

4. If my despair is justified, no one should be surprised,
    for some old crone is preventing my rose
    from loving anyone and from being loved;
    may Pluto see fit to carry her off—that's my prayer!"

5. As I pondered all the above in my mind, wishing
    that a thunderbolt might carry off the old woman,
    hear now what I saw, as I lingered there, reflecting
    on joyous affairs later abandoned.

6. I saw a flower in bloom, I saw the choicest of flowers.
    I saw the rose of May, fairer than all others.
    I saw a gleaming star that outshone all the rest,
    that made me spend my days putting my trust in Love.

7. Cum vidissem itaque   quod semper optavi,
    tunc ineffabiliter   mecum exultavi,
    surgensque velociter   ad hanc properavi,
    hisque retro poplite   flexo salutavi:

8. "Ave formosissima,   gemma pretiosa!
    Ave decus virginum,   virgo gloriosa!
    Ave, lumen luminum!   Ave, mundi rosa,
    Blanziflor et Helena,   Venus generosa!"

9. Tunc respondit inquiens   stella matutina:
    "Ille qui terrestria   regit et divina
    dans in herba violas   et rosas in spina
    tibi salus, gloria   sit et medicina!"

10. Cui dixi: "Dulcissima,   cor mihi fatetur,
    quod meus fert animus,   ut per te salvetur,
    nam a quodam didici,   sicut perhibetur,
    quod ille qui percutit   melius medetur."

11. "Mea sic laedentia   iam fuisse tela
    dicis? Nego; sed tamen   posita querela,
    vulnus atque vulneris   causas nunc revela,
    ut te sanem postmodum   gracili medela."

12. "Vulnera cur detegam,   quae sunt manifesta?
    Aestas quinta periit,   properat en sexta,
    quod te in tripudio   quadam die festa
    vidi; cunctis speculum   eras et fenestra.

13. Cum vidissem itaque,   coepi tunc mirari,
    dicens: 'Ecce mulier   digna venerari!
    Haec excedit virgines   cunctas absque pari,
    haec est clara facie,   haec est vultus clari!'

7. So when I saw what I had always longed for,
   I was filled with indescribable joy
   and getting up I hurried swiftly toward her
   and on bended knee greeted her with these words:

8. "Hail, precious gem, loveliest of women!
   Hail, glorious maiden, most renowned of them all!
   Hail, light of lights! Hail, rose of the world!
   My Blanchefleur, my Helen, my noble-hearted Venus!"

9. Then the Morning Star in answer to me said:
   "May he who rules both realms, the earthly and divine,
   who puts violets in the grass and roses on thorns,
   be your salvation, your glory and your balm!"

10. I said to her: "Sweet mistress, my heart tells me
    what my mind reports—that it will be saved by you,
    for I learned from someone that, as the saying goes,
    the one who strikes the blow best heals the wound."

11. "You say that it was a weapon of mine
    that hurt you? I deny it! Still, put your reproach aside
    and show me now your wound and tell me its cause
    so that I then can heal you with a gentle remedy."

12. "Why should I uncover wounds that are clear to see?
    Five summers have gone; the sixth approaches fast
    since I saw you joyfully celebrating on some feast day.
    You were both a mirror and a window for us all.

13. As soon as I saw you, my admiration for you began.
    I said: 'There's a woman worthy of veneration!
    She outstrips all others—a peerless maiden—
    radiant in overall appearance and radiant in her looks!'

14. Visus tuus splendidus   erat et amoenus,
     tamquam aer lucidus,   nitens et serenus.
     Unde dixi saepius: 'Deus, Deus meus,
     estne illa Helena,   vel est dea Venus?'

15. Aurea mirifice   coma dependebat,
     tamquam massa nivea   gula candescebat,
     pectus erat gracile,   cunctis innuebat,
     quod super aromata   cuncta redolebat.

16. In iocunda facie   stellae radiabant,
     eboris materiam   dentes vendicabant,
     plus quam dicam speciem   membra geminabant.
     Quidni si haec omnium   mentem alligabant?

17. Forma tua fulgida   tunc me catenavit,
     mihi mentem, animum   et cor immutavit,
     tibi loqui spiritus   ilico speravit;
     posse spem verumtamen   numquam roboravit.

18. Ergo meus animus   recte vulneratur.
     Ecce Venus graviter   mihi novercatur.
     Quis umquam, quis aliquo   tantum molestatur,
     quam qui sperat aliquid,   et spe defraudatur?

19. Telum semper pectore   clausum portitavi,
     milies et milies   inde suspiravi,
     dicens: 'Rerum conditor,   quid in te peccavi?'
     Omnium amantium   pondera portavi.

20. Fugit a me bibere,   cibus et dormire,
     medicinam nequeo   malis invenire.
     Christe, non me desinas   taliter perire,
     sed dignare misero   digne subvenire.

14. Your looks were bright and charming,
    shining and serene like a sunlit sky.
    That's why I often said, 'My God, my God—
    is she Helen or is she the goddess Venus?'

15. Your golden locks hung marvelously,
    your throat gleamed like a bank of snow,
    your breast was slender and affirmed to all
    that its fragrance surpassed all perfumes.

16. Stars radiated in your happy face;
    your teeth rivaled ivory in their hue.
    The twinned beauty of your limbs exceeds my telling,
    No wonder these qualities cast a spell on everyone.

17. Your resplendent beauty enthralled me then
    and worked a change on my mind, soul, and heart.
    My spirit hoped to speak to you there and then
    but opportunity never turned my hope into reality.

18. So my heart is well and truly wounded.
    See how seriously Venus abuses me!
    Who is ever troubled by anything as much as the man
    who hopes for something and is cheated of his hopes?

19. I have always carried an arrow buried in my heart.
    It has made me sigh thousands and thousands of times,
    saying, 'Creator of all, how have I sinned against you?'
    I have borne the burdens of all the world's lovers.

20. Food, drink, and sleep—they all passed out of my life.
    I can find no cure for my misfortunes.
    Do not allow me, Christ, to die like this, but rather see
    fit to provide a poor wretch the help he deserves.

21. Has et plures numero   pertuli iacturas,
    nec ullum solacium   munit meas curas,
    ni quod saepe saepius   per noctes obscuras
    per imaginarias   tecum sum figuras.

22. Rosa, videns igitur,   quam sim vulneratus,
    quot et quantos tulerim   per te cruciatus,
    nunc, si placet, itaque   fac, ut sim sanatus,
    per te sim incolumis   et vivificatus.

23. Quod quidem si feceris,   in te gloriabor,
    tanquam cedrus Libani   florens exaltabor.
    sed si, quod non vereor,   in te defraudabor,
    patiar naufragium   et periclitabor."

24. Inquit rosa fulgida: "Multa subportasti,
    nec ignota penitus   mihi revelasti,
    Sed quae per te tulerim   numquam somniasti.
    Plura sunt quae sustuli   quam quae recitasti.

25. Sed omitto penitus   recitationem,
    volens talem sumere   satisfactionem,
    quae praestabit gaudium   et sanationem,
    et medelam conferet   melle dulciorem.

26. Dicas ergo, iuvenis,   quod in mente geris.
    An argentum postulas,   per quod tu diteris?
    Pretioso lapide   an quod tu orneris?
    Nam si esse poterit,   dabo quicquid quaeris."

27. "Non est id quod postulo   lapis nec argentum,
    immo praebens omnibus   maius nutrimentum,
    dans impossibilibus   facilem eventum,
    et quod maestis gaudium   donat luculentum."

21. These and more are the troubles I have suffered
     and no solace lends comfort to my sorrows,
     except that again and again in the dark of night
     I am with you in imagined dream encounters.

22. So, my Rose, now that you see how I have been
     wounded, the number and the magnitude of the
     agonies I have endured because of you, bring me back
     to health now, if you will and make me whole again and
     restored to life.

23. If you do this, I will pride myself on you,
     I will flourish and rise up like a cedar of Lebanon.
     But if—though I do not fear it—I am deceived in you,
     I will be wrecked and my life will hang in the balance."

24. My shining rose said: "You have had much to endure
     nor is what you have revealed entirely unknown to me.
     But you have never dreamed what I suffered for you.
     What I have endured is more than your account.

25. But I will refrain entirely from recounting it all,
     for I wish to exact such amends from you
     as will provide joy and healing
     and apply a balm sweeter than honey.

26. So tell me, young man, what you have in mind.
     Do you want money to enrich yourself
     or to adorn yourself with a precious gem?
     If it can be done, I will give you whatever you ask for."

27. "It is not a gem or money I ask for but rather that
     which provides greater sustenance than anything else
     and an easy solution to an impasse
     and bestows shining joy on those who are sad."

28. "Quicquid velis, talia   nequeo praescire,
tuis tamen precibus   opto consentire.
Ergo quicquid habeo,   sedulus inquire,
sumens si quod appetis   potes invenire."

29. Quid plus? Collo virginis   brachia iactavi,
mille dedi basia,   mille reportavi,
atque saepe saepius   dicens affirmavi
"Certe, certe istud est   id quod anhelavi."

30. Quis ignorat amodo   cuncta quae sequuntur?
Dolor et suspiria   procul repelluntur,
paradisi gaudia   nobis inducuntur
cunctaeque deliciae   simul apponuntur.

31. Hic amplexus gaudium   est centuplicatum,
hic meum et dominae   pullulat optatum,
hic amantum bravium   est a me portatum,
hic est meum igitur   nomen exaltatum.

32. Quisquis amat itaque   mei recordetur
nec diffidat illico,   licet amaretur.
Illi nempe aliqua   dies ostendetur,
qua poenarum gloriam   post adipiscetur.

33. Ex amaris equidem   grata generantur;
non sine laboribus   maxima parantur.
Dulce mel qui appetunt   saepe stimulantur;
sperent ergo melius   qui plus amarantur.

28. "Whatever it is you want I cannot guess
    but I am eager to consent to your request.
    So, don't hold back, whatever I have, ask about it
    and if you can find anything you desire, take it!"

29. In short, I threw my arms around her neck,
    gave her a thousand kisses, and received a thousand
    and I kept repeating again and again:
    "This, this is definitely what I have yearned for."

30. Who does not know everything that followed?
    Pain and sighs were banished.
    We were introduced to the joys of paradise
    and all manner of delights were put at our disposal.

31. Now we experienced a hundredfold the joy of em-
    bracing, now my lady's desires grew apace along with
    mine, now I carried off the lovers' prize, now accor-
    dingly my name was exalted.

32. So let every lover keep me in mind and not give up
    right away though his experiences are bitter.
    The day will dawn for him
    when he will eventually win glory for all his pain.

33. From bitter experiences happy times are born;
    the greatest goals are not achieved without effort.
    Those who seek sweet honey are often stung;
    so let those embittered by love hope for better days.

78

1.   Anni novi redit novitas,
    hiemis cedit asperitas.
    Breves dies prolongantur,
    elementa temperantur
5   subintrante Ianuario.
    Mens aestu languet vario
    propter puellam quam diligo.

2.   Prudens est multumque formosa,
    pulchrior lilio vel rosa.
    Gracili coartatur statura,
    praestantior omni creatura.
5   Placet plus Franciae regina.
    Mihi mors est iam vicina,
    nisi sanet me flos de spina.

3.   Venus me telo vulneravit
    aureo, quod cor penetravit.
    Cupido faces instillavit.
    Amor amorem inspiravit
5   iuvenculae, pro qua volo mori.
    Non iungar cariori,
    licet accrescat dolor dolori.

4.   Illius captus sum amore,
    cuius flos adhuc est in flore.
    Dulcis fit labor in hoc labore,
    osculum si sumat os ab ore.
5   Non tactu sanabor labiorum,

78

1. The newness of a new year is returning,
    winter's harshness is giving way.
    The short days are getting longer
    and the elements milder,
    as January creeps in.   5
    My heart languishes with fluttering passion
    for the girl I love.

2. She is sensible and very beautiful,
    lovelier than the lily or the rose.
    Though short and of slender build,
    she stands out from every other creature.
    She pleases the eye more than the Queen of France.   5
    I feel death is now close by
    unless I am cured by the thorn's flower.

3. Venus has wounded me with her golden arrow.
    It pierced through to my heart.
    Cupid slowly thrust in his torch.
    Love breathed into me love
    for the young woman, for whom I am ready to die.   5
    There is none dearer with whom I would be united,
    though pain be heaped on pain.

4. I have been captivated with love for one
    whose flower is still in bloom.
    Sweet is the effort involved in this task
    if her mouth takes a kiss from mine.
    I will not be healed by the touch of her lips   5

nisi cor unum fiat duorum
et idem velle. Vale, flos florum!

79

1.   Aestivali sub fervore,
quando cuncta sunt in flore,
totus eram in ardore.
Sub olivae me decore
5   aestu fessum et sudore
    detinebat mora.

2.   Erat arbor haec in prato
quovis flore picturato,
herba, fonte, situ grato,
sed et umbra, flatu dato.
5   Stilo non pinxisset Plato
    loca gratiora.

3.   Subest fons vivacis venae;
adest cantus philomenae,
Naiadumque cantilenae.
Paradisus hic est paene;
5   non sunt loca, scio plene,
    his iocundiora.

4.   Hic dum placet delectari
delectatque iocundari
et ab aestu relevari,

unless the hearts of both become one
and our wishes the same. Farewell, choicest flower!

79

1. In the summer heat,
   when everything was in bloom,
   I was all afire.
   I was passing the time
   under a beautiful olive tree,   5
   worn out by the heat and the hard work.

2. This tree was in a meadow
   embroidered with every kind of flower.
   and made attractive by grass, a spring and the setting;
   shade and a breeze were also provided.
   Plato's pen could not have depicted   5
   a more agreeable scene.

3. A lively spring flowed past below
   and there was the singing of a nightingale
   and the songs of the Naiads.
   It was a virtual paradise here;
   there are no places, I know full well,   5
   more pleasant than this.

4. While I was enjoying my delight at the scene,
   and taking delight in my pleasure
   and in my escape from the heat,

cerno forma singulari
5   pastorellam sine pari,
      colligentem mora.

5.   In amorem visae cedo,
      fecit Venus hoc, ut credo.
      "Ades," inquam, "non sum praedo,
      nihil tollo, nihil laedo,
5   me meaque tibi dedo,
      pulchrior quam Flora!"

6.   Quae respondit verbo brevi:
      "Ludos viri non assuevi.
      Sunt parentes mihi saevi;
      mater longioris aevi
5   irascetur pro re levi.
      Parce nunc in hora."

80

1a.   Aestivali gaudio
      tellus renovatur,
    militandi studio
      Venus excitatur.
5   Gaudet chorus iuvenum,
    dum turba frequens avium
      garritu modulatur.
    Ref. Quanta sunt gaudia
      amanti et amato
    sine fellis macula

I saw a shepherdess
of striking beauty gathering mulberries,   5
unaccompanied.

5. I gave way to love at the sight of her;
    Venus did this, I believe.
    "Come to me," I said, "I'm not a bandit.
    I won't take anything from you or hurt you in any way.
    I offer you myself and what is mine,   5
    you who are fairer than Flora!"

6. She replied in a few words:
    "I am not accustomed to a man's games.
    My parents are harsh;
    my mother, who is quite old,
    will get angry over even a trifling matter.   5
    Stop this now in time!"

80

1a. Summer's joy
     brings renewal to the earth
     and Venus is animated
     with a zeal for campaigning.
     All the young men rejoice,   5
     while a large flock of birds
     sings and chatters.
     Ref. How great are the joys
     for the man who loves and is loved in return,
     when he is united with his beloved

       dilectae sociato!
5   Iam revernant omnia
       nobis delectabilia;
         hiems eradicatur.

1b. Ornantur prata floribus
         varii coloris,
      quorum delectatio
         causa fit amoris.
5   Gaudet chorus iuvenum,
      dum turba frequens avium
         garritu modulatur.
      Ref.

2a. In calore vivido
      nunc reformantur omnia,
      hiemali taedio
      quae viluere languida.
5   Tellus ferens gramina
      decoratur floribus
      et vestiuntur nemora
      frondosis arboribus.
      Ref.

2b. Amorum officiis
      haec arrident tempora;
      geminatis sociis
      restaurantur foedera.
5   Festa colit Veneris
      puellaris curia.
      Propinat Amor teneris,
      amaris miscens dulcia.
      Ref.

and there is no trace of bitterness.
All the things that delight us   5
are now in bloom again;
winter has been banished.

1b. The fields are adorned
     with flowers of varied hue,
     and our delight in them
     prompts us to love.
     The young men rejoice,   5
     while a large flock of birds
     sings and chatters.
     Ref.

2a. In the life-giving warmth
     everything that turned stark
     and dormant in winter's tedium
     dresses itself anew.
     The earth puts forth new grass   5
     adorned with flowers
     and the woods are clothed
     with the trees' burgeoning branches.
     Ref.

2b. This season smiles
     on the preoccupations of love;
     partners are paired off
     and their vows renewed.
     The young women   5
     celebrate the festival of Venus.
     Love proffers the young
     a draft that is bittersweet.
     Ref.

81

1. Solis iubar nituit   nuntians in mundum,
   quod nobis emicuit   tempus laetabundum.
   Ver quod nunc apparuit   dans solum fecundum,
   salutari meruit   per carmen iocundum.
   Ref. Ergo nostra contio
           psallat cum tripudio   dulci melodia.

2. Fugiente penitus   hiemis algore,
   spirat aether tacitus   aestu gratiore.
   Descendente caelitus   salutari rore
   fecundatur funditus   tellus ex humore.
   Ref.

3. Sol extinctus fuerat,   modo renitescit.
   Frigus invaluerat,   sed modo tabescit.
   Nix, quae nos obruerat   ex aestu liquescit;
   qui prius aruerat   campus revirescit.
   Ref.

4. Philomena stridula   voce modulatur.
   Floridum alaudula   tempus salutatur.
   Anus, licet vetula,   mire petulatur
   lasciva iuvencula   cum sic recreatur.
   Ref.

81

1. The sun's beams have shone brightly, announcing to the world that the season of joy has darted forth for us. Now that spring has appeared, making the earth fruitful, it deserves to be greeted with a joyful song.
Ref. So let our group
sing and dance to a sweet melody.

2. With winter's chill completely routed,
the upper air quietly breathes a welcome warmth.
As the life-giving dew comes down from heaven,
the moisture renders the earth completely fertile.
Ref.

3. The sun had been hidden but is now beaming.
The cold had strengthened, but is now abating.
The snow buried us but the warmth is now melting it.
The fields, once parched, are now turning green again.
Ref.

4. The nightingale sings with her piercing voice;
the lark greets the season of flowers.
An old woman, despite her age, is surprisingly frisky
when a pert young woman kicks up her heels so much.
Ref.

82

1. Frigus hinc est horridum,
    tempus adest floridum.
    Veris ab instantia
    tellus iam fit gravida,
5   in partum inde solvitur,
    dum florere cernitur.
    Ref. Oooaiae!
    Amoris solamine
    clerus scit diligere
    virginem plus milite!

2. Sol tellurem recreat,
    ne fetus eius pereat.
    Ab aeris temperantia
    rerum fit materia,
5   unde multiplicia
    generantur semina.
    Ref.

3. Mons vestitur floribus
    et sonat a volucribus.
    In silvis aves concinunt
    dulciterque garriunt
5   nec philomena desinit—
    iacturam suam meminit.
    Ref.

82

1. The horrible cold has gone.
   The season of flowers is here.
   The land, impregnated now
   by spring's insistent presence,
   is loosening up to give birth   5
   as we see it bursting into flower.
   Ref. Oooaiae!
   A cleric knows better than a knight
   how to cherish a maiden
   with the solace of love.

2. The sun gives life again to the earth
   so that its offspring may not perish.
   The mildness of the air
   gives body to plants
   and this generates   5
   a multiplicity of seeds.
   Ref.

3. The hill is clothed in flowers
   and filled with the sounds of birds.
   In the woods the birds are singing
   and chattering pleasantly
   and the nightingale never ceases—   5
   she is recalling her loss.
   Ref.

4. Ridet terrae facies.
colores per multiplices.
Nunc audite, virgines:
non amant recte milites,
5   miles caret viribus
naturae et virtutibus.
Ref.

5. Thymus et Lapathium
inierunt hoc consilium:
"Propter formam milites
nobis sunt amabiles."
5   "De quibus stulta ratio
suspensa est solutio."
Ref.

6. "Sed in curtibus milites
depingunt nostras facies
cum serico in palliis,
colore et in clipeis."
5   "Quid prosunt nobis talia,
cum forma perit propria?
Ref.

7. Clerici in frigore
observant nos in semine,
pannorum in velamine,
deinde et in pyxide."
5   Mox de omni clerico
Amoris fit conclusio.
Ref.

4. The earth's face is smiling
    with a wide array of colors.
    Now listen to me, maidens:
    knights do not love you properly.
    A knight is lacking in the strength   5
    of his manhood and in the virtues.
    Ref.

5. Thyme and Sorrel
    began a discussion:
    "Because they are handsome
    knights deserve our love."
    "In matters where the reasoning is foolish,   5
    no conclusion can be drawn."
    Ref.

6. "But in courts knights
    embroider our faces
    with silk on their cloaks,
    and paint them on their shields."
    "Of what use to us are such images   5
    when our own beauty has gone?
    Ref.

7. Clerics in winter's chill
    look after us with their seed,
    a covering of clothes,
    and a box of toiletries."
    Soon after this Love's decision   5
    was made in favor of every cleric.
    Ref.

83

1. Saevit aurae spiritus,
        et arborum
   comae fluunt penitus
        vi frigorum.
5   Silent cantus nemorum.
   Nunc torpescit, vere solo
        fervens, amor pecorum.
   Semper amans sequi nolo
        novas vices temporum
10   bestiali more.
        Ref. Quam dulcia
            stipendia
            et gaudia
            felicia
5   sunt haec horae
            nostrae Florae!

2. Nec de longo conqueror
        obsequio;
   nobili remuneror
        stipendio,
5   laeto laetor praemio.
   Dum salutat me loquaci
        Flora supercilio,
   mente satis non capaci
        gaudia concipio;
10   glorior labore.
        Ref.

83

1. The wind's breath bites savagely
    and the trees' foliage
    is all floating down
    with the sharpness of the frosts.
    The singing in the woods has gone silent.   5
    Love among the flocks,
    fervent only in springtime,
    is now dormant.
    Always ready for love, I refuse
    to follow the changes of the seasons
    as do the animals.   10
    Ref. Ah, how sweet
        the rewards
        and how happy
        the joys
        of the time   5
        with my Flora!

2. I make no complaints
    about my long service;
    I am rewarded
    with a noble recompense
    and take joy in my joyous reward.   5
    When Flora greets me
    with her eloquent eyebrow,
    such is the joy I conceive
    that my heart cannot contain it;
    I revel in the pain.   10
    Ref.

3. Mihi sors obsequitur
   non aspera.
 Dum secreta luditur
   in camera
5 favet Venus prospera.
Nudam fovet Floram lectus;
 caro candet tenera,
virginale lucet pectus,
 parum surgunt ubera
10 modico tumore.
  Ref.

4. Hominem transgredior
   et superum
 sublimari glorior
   ad numerum,
5 sinum tractans tenerum
cursu vago dum beata
 manus it et uberum
regionem pervagata
 descendit ad uterum
10 tactu leviore.
  Ref.

5. A tenello tenera
   pectusculo
 distenduntur latera
   pro modulo.
5 Caro carens scrupulo
levem tactum non offendit.
 Gracili sub cingulo
umbilicum praeextendit

3.   My lot
is not a harsh one.
When we fool around
in a private room,
Venus smiles favorably.   5
The bed caresses Flora's naked body;
her tender flesh is radiant,
her young chest gleams
and her breasts rise slightly,
swelling moderately.   10
Ref.

4.   I surpass mankind
and exult that I have been elevated
to the level of the gods
when I touch her tender bosom
and my hand happily follows   5
its roaming course
and, having covered
the area of the breasts,
moves down with gentler touch
to her tummy.   10
Ref.

5.   From her delicate
little breasts,
her tender flanks stretch down
evenly.
Her flesh is unblemished,   5
and offers no roughness to a light touch.
Beneath her slender waist
her navel rises

paululum ventriculo
10   tumescentiore.
     Ref.

6.   Vota blando stimulat
        lenimine
   pubes, quae vix pullulat
        in virgine
5   tenui lanugine.
Crus vestitum moderata
   tenerum pinguedine
levigatur occultata
   nervorum compagine,
10   radians candore.
     Ref.

7.   O, si forte Iupiter
        hanc videat,
   timeo, ne pariter
        incaleat,
5   et ad fraudes redeat,
si vel Danes pluens aurum
   imbre dulci mulceat,
vel Europes intret taurum,
   vel Ledaeo candeat
10   rursus in olore.
     Ref.

where her stomach
swells up a little higher.   10
Ref.

6.   Her pubic region
excites desires
with its seductive softness,
which in the maiden
has scarcely grown a sheen of down.   5
Her tender thigh,
smooth and moderately plump,
conceals the linking
of the sinews,
and gleams radiantly.   10
Ref.

7.   Oh if Jupiter
should chance to see her,
I fear he would warm
with like passion
and resort to his tricks,   5
whether he might rain down as Danaë's gold
and soothe her with his sweet shower,
or take the form of Europa's bull,
or gleam white again
as Leda's swan.   10
Ref.

84

1. Dum prius inculta
coleret virgulta
aestas iam adulta
hieme sepulta
5   vidi
viridi
Phyllidem sub tilia.
       Vidi
        Phyllidi
10 quaevis arridentia.
       Invideo
       dum video.
Sic capi cogit sedulus
       me laqueo
15   virgineo,
cordis venator, oculus
visa captus virgine.
    Ref. Hei morior!
sed quavis dulcedine
       mors dulcior.
Sic amanti vivitur,
5 dum sic amans moritur.

2. Fronte explicata
exiit in prata
ceu Dionae nata
venerit legata.
5   Videns

84

1. Now that winter was dead and buried,
   and summer, fully fledged,
   was pervading the copses
   it had earlier shunned,
   I saw   5
   Phyllis
   under a green linden.
   I saw
   everything smiling
   at Phyllis.   10
   I wanted to have her
   when I saw her.
   My eye, the heart's huntsman,
   captivated by the sight of her,
   eagerly forced   15
   my entrapment
   in the maiden's net.
   Ref. Ah! I am dying!
   But death is sweeter to me
   than any sweetness!
   Such is the life of a lover
   when he dies like this for love.   5

2. With unfurrowed brow
   she stepped out into the field
   as if she were Dione's daughter
   come to me on a mission.
   When I saw her,   5

347

invidens
huc spe duce rapior.
Ridens,
residens
10   residenti blandior.
Sed tremula
virguncula
frondis in modum tremulae
ut primula
15   discipula
nondum subducta ferulae
tremit ad blanditias.
Ref.

3.   Respondendi metus
trahit hanc ad fletus.
Sed raptura laetus
Amor indiscretus
5   meam
in eam,
ut pudoris tangere
queam
lineam,
10   manum mittit propere.
Dum propero
vim infero
posti minante machina
nec supero,
15   nam aspero
defendens ungue limina
obserat introitus.

I wanted to have her
and hurried over,
hope leading me to her.
Smiling, I sat down beside her
and began flattering her,   10
as she sat there.
But the young girl, trembling
like a trembling leaf,
like a beginning
pupil,   15
who has not yet flinched at the cane,
trembled at my flattering words.
Ref.

3. Fear of replying
    brought her to tears.
    But Cupid, who is indiscreet
    and delights in seduction,
    quickly moved   5
    my
    hand to her
    so that I could touch
    the line
    of her maidenhead.   10
    I made haste
    and applied force,
    my battering ram threatening her doorway;
    but I was unsuccessful;
    for she defended the threshold   15
    with sharp nails
    and barred my entry.

Ref. Ha morior!
Sed haec michi penitus
      mors dulcior.
Sic amanti vivitur
5   dum sic amans moritur.

4.   Tantalus admotum
    non admittit potum!
    Sed ne tamen totum
    frustret illa votum,
5   suo
        denuo
iungens collo brachium
        ruo
        diruo
10 tricaturas crurium.
      Ut virginem
      devirginem
me toti totum insero.
      Ut cardinem
15   decardinem,
duellum istud refero;
   sic in castris milito.
   Ref.

Ref. Ah I am dying!
but to me this death
is extremely sweet.
Such is the life of a lover,
when he dies like this for love.   5

4.   Tantalus does not get to drink
the water brought near his lips!
However, to prevent her
from frustrating my wishes entirely,
I once again wrapped my arm   5
around her neck,
pulled her down,
and pushed apart
her intertwined legs.
To deflower   10
the virgin,
I thrust myself fully inside her.
To unhinge
the hinge of her door,
I renewed the attack.   15
That is the way
I conduct my campaign on active service.
Ref.

85

1. Veris dulcis in tempore
   florenti stat sub arbore
   Iuliana cum sorore.
       Dulcis amor,
   Ref. qui te caret hoc tempore,
       fit vilior.

2. Ecce florescunt arbores,
   lascive canunt volucres,
   inde tepescunt virgines.
       Dulcis amor,
   Ref.

3. Ecce florescunt lilia,
   et virginum dant agmina
   summo deorum carmina.
       Dulcis amor,
   Ref.

4. "Si viderem quod cupio—
   pro scribis sub Exilio,
   vel pro regis filio."
       Dulcis amor,
   Ref.

85

1. In the pleasant springtime
    Juliana stands with her sister
    under a tree in bloom.
    Sweet Love,
    Ref. anyone without you at this time,
    is the worse off for it.

2. See! The trees are blooming,
    and the birds are singing sensuously,
    which makes the women warm for love.
    Sweet Love,
    Ref.

3. See! The lilies are beginning to bloom
    and groups of young women are offering
    songs to the highest of the gods.
    Sweet Love,
    Ref.

4. "If only I could see what I long for—
    I would choose him over all the scribes down in Silos
    or even the king's son."
    Sweet Love,
    Ref.

86

1. Non contrecto
   quam affecto.
   Ex directo
   ad te specto,
5   et annecto,
   nec deflecto
   cilia.
   Ref. Experire, filia,
   virilia
   semper sunt senilia
   labilia,
5   sola iuvenilia
   stabilia.
   Haec sunt utensilia
   agilia,
   facilia,
10   gracilia,
   fragilia,
   humilia,
   mobilia,
   docilia,
15   habilia,
   Caecilia,
   et si qua sunt similia.

2. Post fervorem
   caeli rorem,
   post virorem

86

1. I am not fondling
    the girl I am trying to win;
    I am looking straight
    at you,
    fastening my eyes on you   5
    and not deflecting them.
    Ref. Try out my manhood,
                girl,
    old men's are always
                floppy,
    only young men's are   5
                firm.
    This equipment is
    always ready,
    versatile,
    slender,   10
    fragile,
    low-hanging,
    easily roused,
    smart,
    and capable,   15
    Cecilia,
    and so on and so forth.

2. After the fervor
    the lilies offer
    heaven's dew

album florem,
5   post candorem
dant odorem,
    lilia.
Ref.

87

1.   Amor tenet omnia,
mutat cordis intima,
quaerit Amor devia.
Amor melle dulcior
5   felle fit amarior.
Amor castus est sed tamen cupidus,
    frigidus et calidus
      et tepidus.
Amor audax, pavidus
10   est fidus atque perfidus.

2.   Tempus est idoneum,
quaerat Amor socium;
nunc garritus avium.
Amor regit iuvenes,
5   Amor capit virgines.
Vae senectus, tibi sunt incommoda!
    Va t'an oy! Iuvencula
    Theoclea
    tenet me gratissima
10   tu pestis, dico, pessima.

after the greenness
comes the white flower,   5
after the whiteness,
lilies give off their fragrance.
Ref.

87

1.   Love controls everything.
     He changes the inmost feelings of our hearts.
     Love seeks out byways.
     Love becomes sweeter than honey
     and more bitter than gall.   5
     Love is chaste but libidinous,
     hot and cold
     and in between.
     Love is bold and timid,
     faithful and treacherous.   10

2.   The time is right
      for Love to seek a companion.
     Now the birds are chattering.
     Love rules young men.
     Love captivates young women.   5
     A curse on old age! All you have is problems.
     Away with you! A delightful young woman,
                    Theoclea,
     holds me in thrall.
     As for you, you are a cursed plague!   10

3.   Rigidus et gelidus
     numquam tibi socius!
     Dormit dolens saepius
     in natura frigidus —
5   nihil tibi vilius!
Venus, tenes iuvenes in gaudio.
     Sana si coniunctio,
          quam diligo,
     tuo fit imperio,
10   quicquid melius sit, nescio.

4.   Amor volat undique.
     Captus est libidine
     iuvenis iuvenculae;
     quae sequuntur, mentio.
5   Si qua sine socio,
illa vero caret omni gratia.
     Tenet noctis infima
          sub intima
     cordis in custodia;
10   sic fit res amarissima.

5.   Amor simplex, callidus,
     rufus, amor pallidus.
     Turbidus in omnibus,
     Amor est placabilis.
5   Constans et instabilis
Amor artis regitur imperio.
     Ludit Amor lectulo
          iam clanculo;
     noctis in silentio
10   fit captus Amor laqueo.

3.   An old man, unbending and cold as ice,
can never be your companion!
He sleeps, often sorrowful,
frigid in his manhood—
there is nothing more distasteful to you!   5
Venus, you keep young men happy.
If a successful uniting
with the girl I love
takes place at your command,
I know of nothing better!   10

4.   Cupid comes flying in from any quarter.
A young man is seized with desire
for a young woman;
I will not give a true account of what happens next.
If there is any girl without a mate,   5
she is excluded from all favorable regard.
She keeps darkest night
deep down inside her,
guarded in her heart;
such is her bitter plight.   10

5.   Love is straightforward and devious.
Love is red-faced and pale.
Though turbulent in all things,
Love can be placated.
Steadfast and fickle,   5
Love is controlled and ruled by art.
Love plays in bed
secretly;
in the silence of the night
Love is captured in a trap.   10

359

88

1. Amor habet superos   —Iovem amat Iuno—
   motus premens efferos   imperat Neptuno.
   Pluto tenens inferos   mitis est hoc uno.
   Ref. Amoris solamine   virgino cum virgine;
   aro non in semine,   pecco sine crimine

2. Amor trahit teneros   molliori nexu,
   rigidos et asperos   duro frangit flexu;
   capitur rhinoceros   virginis amplexu.
   Ref.

3. Virgo cum virginibus,   horreo corruptas
   et cum meretricibus   simul odi nuptas,
   nam in istis talibus   turpis est voluptas.
   Ref.

4. Virginis egregiae   ignibus calesco
   et eius cotidie   in amorem cresco.
   Sol est in meridie   nec ego tepesco.
   Ref.

5. Gratus super omnia   ludus est puellae,
   et eius praecordia   omni carent felle;
   sunt quae praestat basia   dulciora melle.
   Ref.

88

1. Love rules the Gods—Juno loves Jupiter—he suppresses Neptune's savage emotions and tells him what to do. Only Love can soften the heart of Pluto, ruler of the dead.
    Ref. Regarding the solace of love, I remain a virgin
    with a virgin.
    I plow but do not sow, I sin but do no wrong.

2. Love draws along the young and innocent with his gentle bond. Those who are rigid and resistant he harshly bends and breaks. The unicorn is captivated by a maiden's embrace.
    Ref.

3. I am a virgin among virgins. I have a horror of tainted women. I hate married women as well as courtesans, for with such women the pleasure is shameful.
    Ref.

4. I burn with passion for an excellent young woman, and my love for her grows daily. The sun is at its midday high, and I am far from lukewarm.
    Ref.

5. Pleasing beyond all else is love play with my girl;
    her heart is entirely without gall;
    the kisses she gives me are sweeter than honey.
    Ref.

6. Ludo cum Caecilia, nihil timeatis —
   sum quasi custodia fragilis aetatis,
   ne marcescant lilia suae castitatis.
   Ref.

7. Flos est; florem frangere non est res secura.
   Uvam sino crescere, donec sit matura.
   Spes me facit vivere laetum re ventura.
   Ref.

8. Volo tantum ludere, id est: contemplari,
   praesens loqui, tangere, tandem osculari.
   Quintum, quod est agere, noli suspicari!
   Ref.

9. Quicquid agant ceteri, virgo, sic agamus,
   ut quem decet fieri, ludum faciamus.
   Ambo sumus teneri; tenere ludamus!
   Ref.

88a

1. Iove cum Mercurio Geminos tenente
   et a Libra Venere Martem expellente
   nata est Caecilia Tauro iam latente.

2. Natus ego pariter sub eisdem signis.
   Par pari coniunctus sum legibus benignis,
   Paribus est ignibus, par accensus ignis.

6.   I play with my Cecilia but have no fear—
     I am, as it were, the guardian of her tender years,
     ensuring that the lily of her chastity does not wither.
     Ref.

7.   She is a flower; picking a flower is not free from risk.
     I am allowing the grapes to grow until they are ripe.
     Hope makes me happy about the future.
     Ref.

8.   I want only to play: that is, to look at her,
     to talk with her, to touch, and finally to kiss.
     The fifth stage, having sex, don't suspect me of that!
     Ref.

9.   Whatever others may do, my girl, let us ensure
     that the play we have is as it should be.
     We are both innocent; let our play be innocent.
     Ref.

88a

1.   When Jupiter and Mercury were in Gemini and Venus
was driving Mars out of Libra, that is when Cecilia was
born, Taurus being then hidden.

2.   I was also born under the same signs. I am linked with a
partner, like to like, by favorable conditions; each is
fired by an equal passion for the other.

3. Solus solam diligo,   sic me sola solum,
    nec est cui liceat   immiscere dolum,
    non in vanum variant   nostra signa polum.

4. Obicit "ab alio,"   forsitan, "amatur,"
    ut quod "solus" dixerim,   ita refellatur;
    sed ut dictum valeat,   sic determinatur.

89

1a.   Nos duo boni
       sub aere taetro.
        — Sint tibi toni
       sub celeri metro! —
5   Tempore soni
       stant pecora retro.

1b.   Herba tenella
       flore coronatur.
       Rosa novella
       rubore notatur:
5   nigra puella
       veste coornatur.

2a.   Tunica lata
       succincta balteo.
       Circumligata
       frons filo rubeo.
5   Stat inclinata
       sub alto pilleo.

3.	I alone love her and her alone and it is likewise with her, and neither one of us can deceive the other. It is not for nothing that our signs move across the sky together.

4.	Someone objects: "Perhaps she is loved by another" so that my saying "alone" is thereby refuted. But it is determined that my words should remain as stated.

89

1a.	"We are two fine lads here
	under a gloomy sky.
	—Play the music
	in a fast-paced measure!—
	When there's noise 5
	the animals stand back.

1b.	The tender grass
	is crowned with flowers.
	A fresh young rose
	stands out for its redness:
	there is a girl there 5
	wearing a dark cloak.

2a.	Her wide tunic
	was cinched with a belt.
	Her head was bound
	with a red band.
	She stood leaning to the side 5
	under a high cowl.

2b. Labor mutavit
puellae faciem
 et alteravit
eiusdem speciem,
5 decoloravit
eam per maciem.

3a. Ducit puella
gregem parvulum
 et cum capella
caprum vetulum, .
5 et cum asella
ligat vitulum.

3b. Polus obscura
nube tegitur.
 Virgo matura
. mox egreditur,
5 voce secura
nos alloquitur:

3c. 'Ecce raptores
temerarii,
 gregis pastores
conducticii,
5 fabulatores
vaniloquii.

3d. Abominantur
opus manuum;
 lucra sectantur.
Amant otium
5 nec meditantur
curam ovium.

2b. Hard work had left its trace
on the girl's face
and altered
her appearance,
making her pale   5
and thin.

3a. The girl was in charge of
a small flock
and an old billy goat
along with a nanny goat
and she had tied a calf   5
to a small she-ass.

3b. The sky was covered
with a dark cloud.
Ripe for marriage,
the young woman stepped out
and addressed us   5
fearlessly:

3c. 'Here we have
brash bandits
as hireling
shepherds,
boastful   5
storytellers.

3d. They hate
working with their hands;
it's profit they are after.
They like taking it easy
and they give no thought   5
to looking after their sheep.

4a.   Provida pactis
est turba pastorum.
    Copia lactis
non ordine morum
     rebus contractis
stat utile forum.

4b.   Nec res succedunt
nec locus in tuto:
    vellera cadunt
de spinis in luto;
     palam accedunt
lupi cane muto.'

5a.   Aspero verbo
tractans de practica
    valde superbo
vultu frenetica
     ore acerbo
cessavit rustica.

5b.   Vellem ut scires
pastorum carmina.
    Dum viri vires
non habes femina,
     numquam aspires
ad viri culmina.

6a.   Est tua cura
labor feminae.
    Solum tu cura
laborem feminae.
    Virgo, mensura
filum stamine.

4a.   Most shepherds
      are looking out for a deal.
      But the market works well
      when deals are struck
      based on the quantity of milk,   5
      not on customary arrangement.

4b.   Things are not going well
      and this is not a safe place:
      the sheep's wool, caught on thorns,
      is falling in the mud; wolves are openly
      approaching the flock   5
      and the dog is not barking.'

5a.   Having harshly criticized
      our way of doing things
      like a fanatic
      with a very superior look,
      the peasant girl   5
      ended her tirade.

5b.   I would like you to get to know
      shepherds' songs.
      Seeing that, as a woman,
      you don't have a man's strength,
      you should never aspire   5
      to the heights a man can reach.

6a.   Your concern
      is woman's work.
      Concern yourself only
      with woman's work.
      Young woman, adjust   5
      your thread to fit your web.

6b.   Gere, puella,
morem pecori!
Languet asella,
stupent teneri;
5   iungit capella
latus lateri.

6c.   Parvula fides
sociis otium;
garrula rides
magisterium.
5   Subdola strides
contra pretium.

6d.   Sumus pastores
nos egregii,
procuratores
gregis regii,
5   soli cantores
soliloquii."

90

1.   Exiit diluculo   rustica puella
cum grege, cum baculo,   cum lana novella.

2.   Sunt in grege parvulo   ovis et asella,
vitula cum vitulo,   caper et capella.

3.   Conspexit in caespite   scholarem sedere:
"Quid tu facis, domine?   Veni mecum ludere."

6b. Look to the needs
of your animals, girl!
The she-ass is sick
and the young stand there gaping;
the nanny goat offers her rear   5
to the billy goat.

6c. Your untrustworthy remarks
are of no concern to me and my companion;
with your idle chatter you mock
those who can teach you.
With intent to deceive   5
you stridently attack what is valuable.

6d. We are fine
shepherds,
guardians
of the king's flock,
the lonely singers   5
of a soliloquy."

90

1. A country girl set out at dawn
with her animals, her crook, and her newly shorn wool.

2. In her small herd there were a sheep, a she-ass,
a heifer, a bullock, a billy goat, and a nanny goat.

3. She noticed a student sitting on the grass.
"What are you doing, sir? Come play with me."

91

De Sacerdotibus

1. Sacerdotes, mementote:
    nihil maius sacerdote,
    qui, ditatus sacra dote,
    ruga caret omnis notae.

2. Mementote tot et tanti,
    quid ingratum sit Tonanti
    ad virtutem vos hortanti,
    cum sic ait: "Este sancti!

3. Sanctus ego; sancti sitis,
    conformari si velitis
    mihi, qui sum vera vitis,
    qui sum pius, qui sum mitis!"

4. Oboedite summo vati,
    sacerdotes consecrati!
    Ad hoc estis ordinati,
    sacris aris mancipati.

5. Corpus Christi vos tractatis.
    Quod si digne faciatis,
    non expertes castitatis,
    ore, corde, Deo gratis,
5   cum electis et beatis
    in conspectu maiestatis
    regnaturos vos sciatis.

91

Concerning Priests

1.　Remember, priests,
　　there is nothing more important than a priest,
　　for, once endowed with his sacred status,
　　he is free from the blemish of any reproach.

2.　You who are so many and so important,
　　remember what displeases the Thunderer,
　　when, urging you on to virtue,
　　he says: "Be holy!

3.　I am holy; be holy,
　　should you wish to be like me,
　　for I am the true vine,
　　I am pious, I am gentle."

4.　You who are consecrated priests,
　　obey the supreme prophet.
　　It was for this that you were ordained,
　　made servants of the sacred altar.

5.　You handle the body of Christ.
　　If you do this appropriately,
　　observing, of your own free will,
　　chastity before God in your words and thoughts,
　　be assured that you will reign,　　　　　　5
　　along with the chosen and the blessed,
　　in full view of his majesty.

6. O quam fortis armatura,
   qua vestitur vestra cura,
   sed, si forte contra iura
   faciatis, ruitura!

7. Nota vobis est scriptura:
   cum offertis Deo tura
   si mens vestra non sit pura,
   non sunt illi placitura.

8. Miserorum contemptores
   si vos estis contra mores
   vel altaris mercatores,
   fures estis, non pastores.

9. O sacerdos, dic, responde
   cuius manus sunt immundae,
   qui frequenter et iocunde
   cum uxore dormis, unde

10. mane surgens missam dicis,
    corpus Christi benedicis,
    post amplexus meretricis
    minus quam tu peccatricis!

11. Scire velim causam, quare
    sacrosanctum ad altare
    statim venis immolare,
    dignus virgis vapulare.

12. Vapulare virgis dignus,
    dum amoris tantum pignus
    corvus tractas et non cygnus,
    iam non heres sed privignus.

6. Ah, how strong is the armor
    in which your office is invested;
    but should you chance to act
    contrary to what is prescribed, it will collapse.

7. Well known to you is the passage in scripture:
    if, when you offer incense to God,
    your heart is not pure,
    the offering will not please him.

8. If, contrary to Christian tenets,
    you despise the wretched
    or sell altar services,
    you are thieves, not pastors.

9. You, my priest, tell me, answer—
    you, whose hands are unclean,
    who often and happily
    sleep with your wife, from whose side

10. you get up in the morning, say mass,
    and consecrate the body of Christ
    after lying in the arms of a whore,
    though she is less of a sinner than you are.

11. I should like to know the reason
    why you have no hesitation in coming
    to offer sacrifice at the holy altar
    when you deserve to be beaten with rods.

12. You deserve to be beaten with rods
    when, black as a raven, not white as a swan,
    you handle so great a pledge of love—
    no longer as a son but as a stepson.

13. Dignus morte, dignus poenis
    ad altare Christi venis
    cum foetore, cum obscaenis
    osculando fictis genis.

14. Plenus sorde, plenus mendis
    ad auctorem manus tendis,
    quem contemnis, quem offendis,
    meretricem dum ascendis.

15. Castitatis non imbute,
    sed immundus corde, cute,
    animarum pro salute
    missam cantas, o pollute!

16. Quali corde quo vel ore
    corpus Christi cum cruore
    tractas, surgens de foetore,
    dignus plagis et tortore?

17. Quali vultu, quali fronte,
    non compulsus—immo sponte—
    ore, corde, lingua sonte,
    de tam sacro bibis fonte?

18. Miror ego, miror plane,
    quod sub illo latet pane
    corpus Christi, quod profanae
    manus tractant illae mane.

19. Miror, nisi tu mireris,
    quod a terra non sorberis,
    dum, quod saepe prohiberis,
    iterare non vereris.

13. You deserve punishment, you deserve death,
    when you come to Christ's altar
    with a fetid smell and with cheeks
    made repulsive by kissing.

14. Full of sin and full of flaws,
    you stretch out your hands to your Maker,
    whom you despise, whom you offend
    when you mount your whore.

15. It is not as one imbued with chastity
    but rather unclean in heart and body
    that you, polluted priest,
    say mass for the salvation of souls!

16. What is the state of your heart, the state of your
    mouth when you take up the body of Christ along with
    his blood after getting up from your fetid bed? You
    deserve to be beaten and tortured!

17. What face do you put on, what effrontery is yours
    when, under no compulsion—rather, of your own free
    will—though guilty in word, heart, and tongue,
    you drink from so sacred a source?

18. I am amazed, absolutely amazed,
    that in that bread there lies concealed
    the body of Christ, which those polluted hands
    touch in the morning.

19. I am amazed if you are not amazed
    that you are not swallowed by the earth
    when you show no fear to do again
    what you are repeatedly forbidden to do.

20.   Forte putas manus mundas,
      cum frequenter fundis undas?
      Quas frequenter quamvis fundas,
      tam foetentes non emundas.

21.   Lava manus, aquas funde;
      quamvis clarae, quamvis mundae,
      quamvis fusae sint abunde,
      numquam purgant eas undae.

22.   Purgamentum vis audire?
      Si reatum vis finire,
      mox divinae cessant irae,
      nec te potest impedire.

23.   Si cor scissum, cor contritum
      habes, neque iuxta ritum
      lectum petis infrunitum,
      numquam erit requisitum.

24.   Sed reatum cum deploras
      et adire mox laboras,
      quod plorandum esse noras,
      Deum magis inhonoras.

25.   Nihil valet hic ploratus,
      nec dimissus est reatus,
      sed est magis augmentatus,
      Deus magis irritatus.

20.   Perhaps you think your hands are clean
      when you pour water over them again and again?
      But though you pour water on them again and again,
      you cannot entirely clean hands so filthy.

21.   Wash your hands, pour water over them;
      however limpid, however clean,
      however abundantly you pour it,
      water can never wash them clean.

22.   Do you wish to hear what will clean them?
      If you choose to end your sinning,
      divine anger soon ends and sinfulness
      can no longer be an impediment for you.

23.   If you are crushed and contrite in your heart
      and stop chasing after mindless sex
      as is your wont,
      the matter will never be investigated.

24.   But when you repent your sinful behavior
      and subsequently seek to return
      to what you came to understand is deplorable,
      you dishonor God even more.

25.   Such repentance is invalid
      and your sin is not forgiven
      but rather is the more increased,
      and God is even more provoked.

92

De Phyllide et Flora

1. Anni parte florida,   caelo puriore,
    picto terrae gremio   vario colore,
    dum fugaret sidera   nuntius aurorae,
    liquit Somnus oculos   Phyllidis et Florae.

2. Placuit virginibus   ire spatiatum,
    nam soporem reicit   pectus sauciatum;
    aequis ergo passibus   exeunt in pratum,
    ut et locus faciat   ludum esse gratum.

3. Eunt ambae virgines   et ambae reginae,
    Phyllis coma libera,   Florae compto crine.
    Non sunt formae virginum,   sed formae divinae,
    et respondent facie   luci matutinae.

4. Nec stirpe, nec facie,   nec ornatu viles,
    et annos et animos   habent iuveniles,
    sed sunt parum impares   et parum hostiles,
    nam huic placet clericus,   et huic placet miles.

5. Non eis distantia   corporis aut oris.
    Omnia communia   sunt intus et foris,
    Sunt unius habitus   et unius moris.
    Sola differentia   modus est amoris.

92

Phyllis and Flora

1. It was the season when flowers are in bloom, the sky was clear and the earth's bosom was dappled with a range of colors, when the harbinger of dawn put the stars to flight and Sleep relinquished the eyes of Phyllis and Flora.

2. The young women decided to go for a walk, for a wounded heart keeps drowsiness at bay; so keeping in step with one another, out they strode to the meadow, so that the locale might add to the pleasure of their diversion.

3. Off they went, both young and both noblewomen. Phyllis's hair was loose, while Flora's was bound up. They looked like goddesses, not young women and in appearance they were like the morning light.

4. Both were of distinguished birth, appearance, and dress, and both were young in years and spirit but they differed a little and there was rivalry between them, for Flora loved a cleric and Phyllis loved a knight.

5. They were not very different in overall or facial appearance. They were alike in all respects, inside and out. They had the same style of dress and same disposition. The only difference was in their manner of loving.

6. Susurrabat modicum   ventus tempestivus.
    Locus erat viridi   gramine festivus
    et in ipso gramine   defluebat rivus
    vivus atque garrulo   murmure lascivus.

7. Ad augmentum decoris   et caloris minus
    fuit secus rivulum   spatiosa pinus,
    venustata folio,   late pandens sinus,
    nec intrare poterat   calor peregrinus.

8. Consedere virgines   herba sedem dedit,
    Phyllis iuxta rivulum,   Flora longe sedit.
    Et dum sedit utraque,   dum in sese redit,
    amor corda vulnerat   et utramque laedit.

9. Amor est interius   latens et occultus,
    et corde certissimos   elicit singultus.
    Pallor genas inficit,   alternantur vultus,
    sed in verecundia   furor est sepultus.

10. Phyllis in suspirio   Floram deprehendit
    et hanc de consimili   Flora reprehendit,
    altera sic alteri   mutuo rependit.
    Tandem morbum detegit   et vulnus ostendit.

11. Iste sermo mutuus   multum habet morae,
    et est quidem series   tota de amore.
    Amor est in animis,   amor est in ore.
    Tandem Phyllis incipit   et arridet Florae:

12. "Miles," inquit, "inclite,   mea cura, Paris,
    ubi modo militas   et ubi moraris?
    O vita militiae,   vita singularis,
    sola digna gaudio   Dionaei laris!"

6. The early morning wind rustled gently.
    The surroundings were gay with fresh green grass
    and through the grass there flowed a stream,
    lively and playful with gurgling chatter.

7. To enhance the beauty of the spot and reduce the heat
    there was a spreading pine tree beside the stream,
    made lovely by its foliage and extending its protection
    far and wide, preventing the heat from penetrating.

8. The young women sat down, the grass furnishing
    a seat; Phyllis sat near the stream, Flora farther away.
    As they sat there and withdrew into themselves,
    Love wounded their hearts, causing them both pain.

9. Love lay obscurely concealed inside them, eliciting
    from their hearts unmistakable sobbing.
    Pallor spread over their cheeks, their expressions kept
    changing, but shame kept their passion buried.

10. Phyllis caught Flora in a deep sigh, and Flora chastised
    Phyllis on similar grounds, each getting her own back
    on the other. Finally each revealed what ailed her and
    uncovered her wound.

11. This conversation they had took a considerable time
    and the series of exchanges was entirely about love.
    Love was in their hearts and love was on their tongues.
    Finally Phyllis began the debate, smiling at Flora.

12. "Renowned knight," she said, "Paris, my love, where
    are you campaigning now, where are you serving? Ah,
    the military life, life without peer, you alone are worthy
    of the joy of Venus's domain!"

13. Dum puella militem   recolit amicum,
Flora ridens oculos   iacit in obliquum
et in risu loquitur   verbum inimicum:
"Amas," inquit, "poteras   dicere mendicum.

14. Sed quid Alcibiades   facit, mea cura,
res creata dignior   omni creatura,
quem beavit omnibus   gratiis Natura?
O sola felicia   clericorum iura!"

15. Floram Phyllis arguit   de sermone duro,
et sermone loquitur   Floram commoturo,
nam "Ecce virgunculam,"   inquit, "corde puro,
cuius pectus nobile   servit Epicuro!

16. Surge, surge, misera,   de furore foedo!
Solum esse clericum   Epicurum credo;
nihil elegantiae   clerico concedo,
cuius implet latera   moles et pinguedo.

17. A castris Cupidinis   cor habet remotum,
qui somnum desiderat   et cibum et potum.
O puella nobilis,   omnibus est notum,
quam sit longe militis   ab hoc voto votum.

18. Solis necessariis   miles est contentus;
somno, cibo, potui   non vivit intentus.
Amor illi prohibet,   ne sit somnolentus;
cibus, potus militis   amor et iuventus.

19. Quis amicos copulet   nostros loro pari?
Lex, natura sineret   illos copulari?
Meus novit ludere,   tuus epulari.
Meo semper proprium   dare, tuo dari."

13. While Phyllis recalled her friend the knight, Flora laughed and rolled her eyes and with a smile spoke jeeringly: "You might as well have said," she remarked, "you love a beggar.

14. But what is Alcibiades, my love, up to,
    a creature worthier than all creation,
    whom Nature blessed with all her charms?
    Ah, the only blessed status is that of clerics!"

15. Phyllis scolded Flora for her harsh words
    and spoke in terms calculated to upset her:
    for she said: "Here is a pure-hearted young maiden,
    whose noble heart is slave to an Epicurean!

16. Pull yourself up, poor wretch, from your foul passion!
    A cleric, to my mind, is simply an Epicurean.
    I grant the cleric no elegance,
    for his body bulges with a mass of fat.

17. His heart is far removed from Cupid's camp,
    for it is sleep he longs for and food and drink.
    My noble friend, it is well known to all
    how different from these desires are those of a knight.

18. A knight is happy with the bare essentials;
    his life is not focused on sleep, food and drink.
    Love keeps him from feeling sleepy.
    Love and youth are a knight's food and drink.

19. Who could pair our friends in the same team?
    Would law or nature allow them to be joined together?
    My friend knows how to flirt, yours how to eat.
    Mine is always giving, yours always taking."

20. Haurit Flora sanguinem   vultu verecundo,
     et apparet pulchrior   in risu secundo,
     Et tandem eloquio   reserat facundo,
     quod corde conceperat   artibus fecundo.

21. "Satis," inquit, "libere,   Phyllis, es locuta
     multum es eloquio,   velox et acuta,
     sed non efficaciter   verum prosecuta
     ut per te praevaleat   lilio cicuta.

22. Dixisti de clerico,   quod indulget sibi.
     Servum somni nominas   et potus et cibi.
     Sic solet ab invido   probitas describi.
     Ecce, parum patere,   respondebo tibi.

23. Tot et tanta, fateor,   sunt amici mei,
     quod numquam incogitat   alienae rei.
     Cellae mellis, olei,   Cereris, Lyaei;
     aurum, gemmae, pocula   famulantur ei.

24. In tam dulci copia   vitae clericalis,
     quod non potest aliqua   pingi voce talis,
     volat et duplicibus   Amor plaudit alis,
     Amor indeficiens,   Amor immortalis.

25. Sentit tela Veneris   et Amoris ictus,
     non est tamen clericus   macer et afflictus,
     quippe nulla gaudii   parte derelictus,
     cui respondet animus   dominae non fictus.

26. Macer est et pallidus   tuus praeelectus,
     pauper et vix pallio   sine pelle tectus.
     Non sunt artus validi   nec robustum pectus,
     Nam dum causa deficit,   deest et effectus.

20. Blood suffused Flora's embarrassed face
    and she appeared lovelier with a benign smile.
    Finally, with great eloquence she revealed
    what she had artfully devised in her resourceful mind.

21. "You have spoken rather freely, Phyllis," she said,
    "and you are very quick, and sharp with your eloquence
    but you have not effectively pursued the truth;
    by your account, the hemlock surpasses the lily.

22. You said of the cleric that he is self-indulgent.
    You call him a slave of sleep, drink and food.
    rectitude tends to be described by the envious.
    Allow me a moment and I will give you an answer.

23. My friend possesses so many fine things, I confess,
    that he never envies what belongs to another.
    He has storerooms of honey, oil, wheat, wine;
    gold, precious stones, and goblets are at his disposal.

24. Amid the sweet abundance of clerical life,
    abundance such that no tongue can describe it,
    Love wings his way and applauds with both his wings,
    Love that never falters, Love that never dies.

25. Though he feels Venus's spears and Cupid's shafts,
    the cleric is not emaciated or distressed,
    for there is no kind of joy of which he is deprived
    and his feelings are genuinely at one with his mistress's.

26. Your chosen one is pale, emaciated
    and poor, and barely covered with an unlined cloak.
    His limbs are weak and his upper body puny,
    for when the cause is lacking, so too is the effect.

27. Turpis est pauperies   imminens amanti.
    Quid praestare poterit   miles postulanti?
    Sed dat multa clericus   et ex abundanti;
    tantae sunt divitiae   reditusque tanti."

28. Florae Phyllis obicit: "Multum es perita
    in utrisque studiis   et utraque vita.
    Satis probabiliter   et pulchre mentita
    sed haec altercatio   non quiescet ita.

29. Orbem cum laetificat   hora lucis festae,
    tunc apparet clericus   satis inhoneste,
    in tonsura capitis   et in atra veste,
    portans testimonium   voluptatis maestae.

30. Non est ullus adeo   fatuus aut caecus,
    cui non appareat   militare decus.
    Tuus est in otio,   quasi brutum pecus;
    meum tegit galea,   meum portat equus.

31. Meus armis dissipat   inimicas sedes,
  ·   et si forte proelium   solus init pedes,
    dum tenet Bucephalam   suus Ganymedes,
    ille me commemorat   inter ipsas caedes.

32. Redit fusis hostibus   et pugna confecta,
    et me saepe respicit   galea reiecta.
    Ex his et ex aliis   ratione recta
    est vita militiae   mihi praeelecta."

33. Novit iram Phyllidis   et pectus anhelum
    et remittit multiplex   illi Flora telum:
    "Frustra," dixit, "loqueris   os ponens in caelum
    et per acum niteris   figere camelum.

27. Poverty hanging over a lover is a source of shame.
    What can a knight offer his lady when she asks?
    The cleric gives many gifts from his abundant store;
    so great is his wealth, so great are his revenues."

28. Phyllis made this rebuttal: "You are well informed
    about both careers and both lifestyles. You have lied
    about them plausibly and eloquently but this debate
    will not end on this note.

29. When the dawning of a feast day brings joy to the
    world, the cleric makes his appearance in rather dis-
    reputable fashion, his tonsure and dark clothing testi-
    fying to his gloomy pleasures.

30. There is no one so foolish or so blind that the handsome
    bearing of a knight is not apparent to her. Living a life
    of ease, your lover is like a beast of the field; mine wears
    a helmet, mine rides a horse.

31. My lover destroys enemy strongholds by feats of arms
    and if he happens to join battle alone and on foot
    while his Ganymede holds his Bucephalus,
    in the midst of the slaughter he thinks of me.

32. With the enemy routed and the fighting over, he comes
    home, pushes back his helmet, and gazes at me again
    and again. For these and other reasons I have rightly
    given my preference to a knight's way of life."

33. Flora perceived Phyllis's anger and her heaving bosom
    and fired back at her with a hail of missiles: "You speak
    in vain when you turn your face against heaven and are
    striving to transfix a camel with a needle.

34. Mel pro felle deseris   et pro falso verum,
    quae probas militiam   reprobando clerum.
    Facit amor militem   strenuum et ferum?
    Non! immo pauperies   et defectus rerum.

35. Pulchra Phyllis, utinam   sapienter ames,
    nec veris sententiis   amplius reclames!
    Tuum domat militem   et sitis et fames,
    quibus mortis petitur   et inferni trames.

36. Multum est calamitas   militis attrita.
    Sors illius dura est   et in arto sita,
    cuius est in pendulo   dubioque vita,
    ut habere valeat   vitae requisita.

37. Non dicas obprobrium,   si cognoscas morem,
    vestem nigram clerici,   comam breviorem.
    Habet ista clericus   ad summum honorem,
    ut sese significet   omnibus maiorem.

38. Universa clerico   constat esse prona;
    et signum imperii   portat in corona.
    Imperat militibus   et largitur dona.
    Famulante maior est   imperans persona.

39. Otiosum clericum   semper esse iuras.
    Viles spernit operas,   fateor, et duras.
    Sed cum eius animus   evolat ad curas,
    caeli vias dividit   et rerum naturas.

40. Meus est in purpura,   tuus in lorica.
    Tuus est in proelio,   meus in lectica,
    ubi gesta principum   recolit antiqua,
    scribit, quaerit, cogitat,   totum de amica.

34. You are giving up honey for gall and truth for falsehood in approving a knight's life and criticizing the clergy. Is it love that makes a knight restless and wild? No! it is his poverty and lack of resources.

35. My lovely Phyllis, I do wish you would love sensibly and rail no more against accurate observations! Your knight is governed by hunger and thirst, which lead men to seek the road to death and hell.

36. A knight's misfortune is very disheartening. A man who puts his life in uncertain balance so that he can win the simple necessities of life experiences a harsh and confining fate.

37. If you knew the cleric's way of life, you would not call his sober dress and rather short hair disreputable. These traits bestow high distinction on the cleric to mark him out as more important than the rest.

38. It is well known that everything defers to the cleric; he carries the symbol of his power on his crown. He gives orders to knights and is generous with gifts. The one giving the orders is greater than the lackey.

39. You swear that the cleric is always idle. He shuns mean and grueling tasks, I confess. But when his mind soars to what are his concerns, he analyzes the paths to heaven and the nature of the universe.

40. My lover is dressed in purple, yours in a breastplate. Yours is on the battlefield, mine in a litter, where he recalls the deeds of leaders of the past, and writes, queries, and reflects only about his lady friend.

41. Quid Dione valeat   et amoris deus,
    primo novit clericus   et instruxit meus.
    Factus est per clericum   miles Cythereus.
    His est et huiusmodi   tuus sermo reus."

42. Liquit Flora pariter   vocem et certamen,
    et sibi Cupidinis   exigit examen.
    Phyllis primum obstrepit,   acquiescit tamen
    et probato iudice   redeunt per gramen.

43. Totum in Cupidine   est certamen situm.
    Suum dicunt iudicem   verum et peritum,
    quia vitae noverit   utriusque ritum.
    Iamiam sese praeparant,   ut eant auditum.

44. Pari forma virgines   et pari pudore;
    pari voto militant   et pari colore.
    Phyllis veste candida,   Flora bicolore;
    mulus vector Phyllidis,   erat equus Florae.

45. Mulus quidem Phyllidis   mulus erat unus,
    quem creavit, aluit,   domuit Neptunus;
    Hunc post apri rabiem,   post Adonis funus
    misit pro solacio   Cythereae munus.

46. Pulchrae matri Phyllidis   et probae reginae
    illum tandem praebuit   Venus Hiberinae
    eo quod indulserat   operae divinae.
    Ecce, Phyllis possidet   illum laeto fine.

47. Faciebat nimium   virginis personae:
    pulcher erat, habilis   et staturae bonae,
    qualem esse decuit   quem a regione
    tam longinqua miserat   Neptunus Dionae.

41. As for the powers of Dione and the god of love, my cleric was the first to learn and teach about them. From being a cleric he became a Cytherean knight. By these and similar arguments your case is refuted."

42. Flora simultaneously ended her speech and the debate and called for Cupid's judgment on the issue. Phyllis objected at first but then agreed and after approving the judge, they returned over the grass.

43. The debate now rested entirely in Cupid's hands.
They pronounced their judge to be true and skilled
because he knew the routines of both lifestyles.
They now made ready to go to hear his decision.

44. The girls were of equal beauty and equal modesty;
they campaigned with equal fervor and equal flourish.
Phyllis was all in white, Flora wore a bicolored dress;
Phyllis rode a mule, Flora a horse.

45. Now Phyllis's mule was a unique creature
whom Neptune had created, fed, and broken in.
This was the mule he sent as a gift to comfort Venus
after the boar's mad charge and the death of Adonis.

46. Eventually, Venus gave him to Phyllis's beautiful mother, the upright noblewoman Hiberina for devoted service to the goddess's work. The happy outcome was that now Phyllis owned him.

47. He did much to enhance Phyllis's dignity:
He was handsome, responsive, and well proportioned,
as befitted an animal Neptune had sent Dione
from so distant a region.

48. Qui de superpositis   et de freno quaerunt,
  —quod totum argenteum   dentes muli terunt!—
  sciant quod haec omnia   talia fuerunt,
  qualia Neptunium   munus decuerunt.

49. Non decore caruit   illa Phyllis hora,
  sed multum apparuit   dives et decora.
  Et non minus habuit   utriusque Flora,
  nam equi praedivitis   freno domat ora.

50. Equus ille domitus   Pegasaeis loris
  multum pulchritudinis   habet et valoris.
  Pictus artificio   varii coloris;
  nam mixtus nigredini   color est oloris.

51. Formae fuit habilis   aetatis primaevae,
  et respexit paululum   tumide, non saeve.
  Cervix fuit ardua,   coma sparsa leve,
  auris parva, prominens   pectus, caput breve.

52. Dorso pando iacuit   virgini sessurae
  spina, quae non senserat   aliquid pressurae.
  Pede cavo, tibia   recta, largo crure,
  totum fuit sonipes   studium Naturae.

53. Equo superposita   radiabat sella,
  ebur enim medium   clausit auri cella,
  et cum essent quattuor   sellae capitella,
  venustavit singulum   gemma quasi stella.

54. Multa de praeteritis   rebus et ignotis
  erant mirabilibus   ibi sculpta notis:
  nuptiae Mercurii   superis admotis,
  foedus, matrimonium,   plenitudo dotis.

48. If any ask about the trappings and reins
    —what the mule's teeth chewed was pure silver!—
    they should know that all these things were such
    as befitted a gift from Neptune.

49. Phyllis was then not lacking in dignity; she appeared
    very rich and attractive. Flora matched her on both
    counts, for her reins controlled the mouth of a richly
    appointed horse.

50. The horse, controlled by the reins of Pegasus,
    was very beautiful and very valuable.
    It was mottled with a patchwork of hues,
    for black mingled with the color of the swan.

51. It was in splendid condition and of a young age
    and its looks were a little proud, but not fierce.
    It had a steeply rising neck, its mane lightly tossed,
    short ears, a prominent chest, and a short head.

52. Along its curving back stretched its spine for the young
    lady to sit on; it had felt no weight before this. Hollow
    of hoof, straight of shin, broad of thigh, the steed was
    all in all a masterpiece of Nature.

53. Set on the horse's back was a gleaming saddle,
    for a frame of gold enclosed its ivory core
    and since the saddle's corners rose to four peaks,
    each was encrusted with a starlike gem.

54. Many scenes from past events dimly known
    were sculpted there with wonderful carvings:
    the marriage of Mercury, the deities in attendance,
    the contract, the wedding ceremony, the rich dowry.

55. Nullus ibi locus est   vacuus aut planus,
    habet plus, quam capiat   animus humanus.
    Solus illa sculpserat,   quae spectans Vulcanus
    vix haec suas credidit   potuisse manus.

56. Praetermisso clipeo   Mulciber Achillis
    laboravit phaleras   et indulsit illis;
    ferraturam pedibus,   et frenum maxillis,
    et habenas addidit   de sponsae capillis.

57. Sellam texit purpura,   subinsuto bysso,
    quam Minerva, reliquo   studio dimisso,
    acantho texuerat   et flore narcisso
    et per tenas margine   fimbriavit scisso.

58. Volant equis pariter   duae domicellae,
    vultus verecundi sunt   et genae tenellae.
    Sic emergunt lilia,   sic rosae novellae,
    sic decurrunt pariter   duae caelo stellae.

59. Ad Amoris destinant   ire paradisum.
    Dulcis ira commovet   utriusque visum;
    Phyllis Florae, Phyllidi   Flora movet risum.
    Fert Phyllis accipitrem   manu, Flora nisum.

60. Parvo tractu temporis   nemus est inventum.
    Ad ingressum nemoris   murmurat fluentum.
    Ventus inde redolet   myrrham et pigmentum;
    audiuntur tympana   citharaeque centum.

61. Quicquid potest hominum   comprehendi mente,
    totum ibi virgines   audiunt repente:
    vocum differentiae   sunt illic inventae—
    sonat diatessaron,   sonat diapente.

55. No place was left empty or undecorated; there was
    more than the human mind could grasp. Unaided,
    Vulcan had carved these scenes but as he gazed at them
    he scarcely believed that his hands could have done it.

56. Setting aside Achilles's shield, Vulcan had worked
    on the trappings with devoted care,
    iron horseshoes for the hooves, a bridle for its jaw,
    and reins made from his wife's hair.

57. Purple material with a linen lining covered the saddle.
    and into it Minerva, abandoning her other pursuits,
    had woven acanthus and narcissus flowers
    and split the edges to create a tasseled fringe.

58. The two damsels galloped onward side by side.
    Their looks were modest and their cheeks tender.
    Just so do lilies or young roses spring up
    or two shooting stars flash across the sky together.

59. Their goal was to reach the garden of Love. A mild
    pique animated both their faces. Phyllis provoked a
    smile from Flora, and Flora from Phyllis. Phyllis carried
    a goshawk on her wrist, Flora a sparrow hawk.

60. After a short time they reached a grove. At its entrance
    a stream murmured past. The breeze coming from
    there smelled of myrrh and spice; the sound of tam-
    bourines and a hundred lyres could be heard.

61. Suddenly the maidens began to hear there
    every sound that the human mind can imagine.
    Different pitches were encountered there—
    perfect fourths and fifths were to be heard.

62. Sonant et mirabili   plaudunt harmonia
    tympanum, psalterium,   lyra, symphonia.
    Sonant ibi phialae   voce valde pia,
    et buxus multiplici   cantum edit via.

63. Sonant omnes avium   linguae voce plena:
    vox auditur merulae   dulcis et amoena,
    corydalus, graculus,   atque philomena,
    quae non cessat conqueri   de transacta poena.

64. Instrumento musico,   vocibus canoris,
    tunc diversi specie   contemplata floris,
    tunc odoris gratia   redundante foris
    coniectatur teneri   thalamus Amoris.

65. Virgines introeunt   modico timore,
    et eundo propius   crescunt in amore.
    Sonat quaeque volucrum   proprio rumore,
    accenduntur animi   vario clamore.

66. Immortalis fieret   ibi manens homo.
    Arbor ibi quaelibet   suo gaudet pomo.
    Viae myrrha, cinnamo,   flagrant et amomo.
    Coniectari poterat   dominus ex domo.

67. Vident choros iuvenum   et domicellarum,
    singulorum corpora   corpora stellarum.
    Capiuntur subito   corda puellarum
    in tanto miraculo   rerum novellarum.

62. The sounds of tambourine, harp, lyre and hurdy-gurdy could be heard, keeping time in wonderful harmony. There too viols gave out their sacred tones and a box-wood pipe emitted its tune through its many openings.

63. All the birds' tongues were singing at full pitch—you could hear the blackbird's voice, sweet and pleasant, the crested lark, the jackdaw, and the nightingale, which did not cease to lament the pain she had endured.

64. From the musical instruments and tuneful voices and from contemplating the beauty of the varied flowers and the charming fragrance that wafted from them the young ladies assumed that here was the chamber of tender Love.

65. The maidens went in rather timidly
and as they got closer, their love grew stronger.
Every bird sang its own song.
Their hearts were set on fire by the diverse sounds.

66. A person who remains there would become immortal. Every tree there delights in its fruit. The paths are fragrant with myrrh, cinnamon and cardamom. You could guess the owner from the property.

67. They saw groups of young men and damsels dancing, their bodies all gleaming like stars. The girls' hearts were immediately captivated by such wondrous new sights.

68. Sistunt equos pariter   et descendunt, paene
    oblitae propositi   sono cantilenae.
    Sed auditur iterum   cantus philomenae
    et statim virgineae   recalescunt venae.

69. Circa silvae medium   locus est occultus,
    ubi viget maxime   suus deo cultus:
    Fauni, Nymphae, Satyri,   comitatus multus
    tympanizant, concinunt   ante dei vultus.

70. Portant vina manibus   et coronas florum.
    Bacchus Nymphas instruit   et choros Faunorum.
    Servant pedum ordinem   et instrumentorum
    sed Silenus titubat   nec psallit in chorum.

71. Somno vergit senior   asino praevectus,
    et in risus copiam   solvit dei pectus.
    Clamat "vina!" Remanet   clamor imperfectus;
    viam vocis impedit   vinum et senectus.

72. Inter haec aspicitur   Cythereae natus.
    Vultus est sidereus,   vertex est pennatus,
    Arcum laeva possidet   et sagittas latus.
    Satis potest conici   potens et elatus.

73. Sceptro puer nititur   floribus perplexo;
    stillat odor nectaris   de capillo pexo.
    Tres assistunt Gratiae   digito connexo,
    et Amoris calicem   tenent genu flexo.

74. Appropinquant virgines   et adorant tutae
    deum venerabili   cinctum iuventute.
    Gloriantur numinis   in tanta virtute.
    Quas deus considerans   praevenit salute.

68. They halted their steeds side by side and dismounted, almost forgetting their mission from the sound of the music. But they heard again the nightingale's song, and at once the girls' passions were rekindled.

69. About the middle of the wood there was a secluded spot, where the god was fervently worshipped; fauns, nymphs, satyrs—a full company—were beating drums and singing in unison before the god.

70. They brought wine and garlands of flowers. Bacchus was instructing the nymphs and groups of fauns. They kept the dancing in time with the music but Silenus was tottering and his singing out of time.

71. Leading the group on an ass, the old man was falling asleep and the god let out a burst of laughter from his chest. Silenus shouted "Wine!" but his call was incomplete; wine and old age blocked the path for his voice.

72. The son of Venus could be seen in their midst. His face was like a star, his head bore wings. His left hand held a bow, arrows at his side. It could readily be seen he was powerful and exalted.

73. The young man leaned on a staff bound with flowers; the fragrance of nectar wafted from his combed hair. The three Graces were there, their fingers intertwined; on bended knee they held up Love's chalice.

74. The maidens drew near and, feeling quite safe, worshipped the god, surrounded by venerable youths. They exulted in the great power of his divine presence; looking closely at them, the god greeted them first.

75. Causam viae postulat,   aperitur causa,
    et laudatur utraque   tantum pondus ausa.
    Ad utramque loquitur: "Modo parum pausa,
    donec res iudicio   reseretur clausa."

76. Deus erat; virgines   norunt deum esse;
    retractari singula   non fuit necesse.
    Equos suos deserunt   et quiescunt fessae.
    Amor suis imperat,   iudicent expresse.

77. Amor habet iudices.   Amor habet iura;
    sunt Amoris iudices   Usus et Natura.
    Istis tota data est   curiae censura,
    quoniam praeterita   sciunt et futura.

78. Eunt et iustitiae   ventilant vigorem,
    ventilatum retrahunt   curiae rigorem:
    secundum scientiam   et secundum morem
    ad amorem clericum   dicunt aptiorem.

79. Comprobavit curia   dictionem iuris,
    et teneri voluit   etiam futuris.
    Parum ergo praecavent   rebus nocituris
    quae sequuntur militem   et fatentur pluris.

75. He asked the reason for their journey, the reason was revealed, and both were praised for daring to undertake so onerous a task. He said to them both: "Just rest a little while until this difficult case is resolved by a judicial decision."

76. He was a god; the maidens knew he was a god;
it was unnecessary to go over all the details again.
They left their horses and lay down to rest, exhausted.
Love told his judges to reach a precise decision.

77. Love has judges, Love has laws;
Love's judges are Common Practice and Nature.
The court's entire reviewing process is vested in them,
since they know the past and the future.

78. They went off and vigorously aired the case. After airing they brought back the court's firm ruling: in view of his knowledge and way of life, they declared the cleric was better suited for love.

79. The court approved their legal finding and decreed that it should hold for the future too; so women who pursue a knight, affirming his greater worth, take insufficient precaution over what might come to harm them.

93

1. Hortum habet insulsa   virgo virginalem.
   Hunc ingressus virginem   unam in sodalem
   spe robustus Veneris   elegi principalem.

2. Laetus ergo socia   elegantis formae,
   —nil huic laudis defuit,   nil affuit enorme.
   Cum hac feci geminum   cor meum uniforme.

3. Est amore dulcius   rerum in natura
   nihil et amarius   conditione dura,
   dolus et invidia   amoris sunt scissura.

4. Cum Fortuna voluit   me vivere beatum,
   forma, bonis moribus   fecit bene gratum,
   et in altis sedibus   sedere laureatum.

5. Modo flos praeteriit   meae iuventutis,
   in se trahit omnia   tempus senectutis;
   inde sum in gratia   novissimae salutis.

6. Rhinoceros virginibus   se solet exhibere;
   sed cuius est virginitas   intemerata vere,
   suo potest gremio   hunc sola retinere.

7. Igitur quae iuveni   virgo sociatur,
   et me senem spreverit,   iure defraudatur,
   ut ab hac rhinoceros   se capi patiatur.

93

1. An unattractive young woman has a garden for young women. I entered it and, buoyed with hope for sex, I chose one young woman as my chief companion.

2. I was delighted with my elegant companion—she lacked no praiseworthy quality and had no egregious fault. With her I made my heart, once solitary, a twin.

3. There is nothing in the world sweeter than love and, with its harsh nature, nothing more bitter too. Deceit and envy are what tear love asunder.

4. When Fortune wanted me to live a happy life, she made me well liked for my appearance and good character and set me on a lofty seat, crowned with laurel.

5. Now the flower of my youth has passed and old age draws everything to itself; so I am in the state of grace of my ultimate salvation.

6. The unicorn customarily shows himself to young unmarried women; but only a woman whose virginity is truly unstained can keep him on her lap.

7. So the virgin who associates with a young man and rejects me as an old man is rightly deprived of the privilege whereby the unicorn allows her to capture him.

8. In tritura virginum   debetur seniori
    pro mercede palea,   frumentum iuniori.
    Inde senex aream   relinquo successori.

94

1. Congaudentes ludite,
    choros simul ducite!
    Iuvenes sunt lepidi,
    senes sunt decrepiti!
Ref.   Audi, bel' amia,
    mille modos Veneris
        dat chevaleria.

2. Militemus Veneri
    nos qui sumus teneri!
    Veneris tentoria
    res est amatoria!
Ref.

3. Iuvenes amabiles
    igni comparabiles.
    Senes sunt horribiles,
    frigori consimiles.
Ref.

8. In the threshing of young women, the reward owed to
    the old man is chaff; the grain goes to the young man.
    So as an old man I leave the threshing floor to the next
    man.

94

1. Join in the rejoicing and have fun!
    Lead out troupes of dancers all together.
    Young men are full of life,
    old men are past it!
    Ref. Listen, my lovely,
       knighthood confers
       a thousand ways of lovemaking!

2. Let's campaign in the service of Venus,
    we who are young.
    The tents of Venus's camp
    are bowers of love.
    Ref.

3. Young men deserve your love—
    we are as hot as fire!
    Old men make you shudder—
    they are as cold as ice!
    Ref.

95

1. Cur suspectum   me tenet domina?
   Cur tam torva   sunt in me lumina?
   Testor caelum   caelique numina:
   quae veretur   non novi crimina.
   Ref. Tort a vers mei ma dama!

2. Caelum prius   candebit messibus,
   feret aer   ulmos cum vitibus,
   dabit mare   feras venantibus,
   quam Sodomae   me iungam civibus.
   Ref.

3. Licet multa   tyrannus spondeat,
   et me gravis   paupertas urgeat,
   non sum tamen,   cui plus placeat
   id, quod prosit,   quam quod conveniat.
   Ref.

4. Naturali   contentus Venere
   non didici   pati sed agere.
   Malo mundus   et pauper vivere
   quam pollutus   dives existere.
   Ref.

5. Pura semper   ab hac infamia
   nostra fuit   terra Britannia.
   Ha, peream,   quam per me patria
   sordis huius   sumat initia!
   Ref.

95

1.   Why does my mistress view me as suspect?
    Why are the looks she directs at me so grim?
    I testify before heaven and its holy inhabitants:
    of the crimes she fears I have no knowledge.
        Ref. My lady does me wrong!

2.   Sooner will the sky gleam white with crops,
    the air bear elms loaded with vines,
    the sea provide wild animals for men to hunt
    than I will join the citizens of Sodom.
        Ref.

3.   Though a tyrant may make me many promises
    and oppressive poverty weigh hard on me,
    I am nonetheless not the kind to prefer
    what is profitable to what is right.
        Ref.

4.   Happy with natural sex,
    I did not learn to play the passive but the active role.
    I prefer to live clean and poor
    than be defiled and rich.
        Ref.

5.   Our beloved Brittany has always been
    unsullied by this disgrace.
    Ah, may I rather die than be the cause
    for our country's initiation into this vice!
        Ref.

96

1. Iuvenes amoriferi,
    virgines amplexamini!
        Ludos incitat
        avium concentus.
5   *Ref.* o vireat,
            o floreat,
            o gaudeat
    in tempore iuventus!

2. Domicelli, surgite,
    domicellas quaerite!
        Ludos incitat
        avium concentus.
        Ref.

3. Cum ipsam intueor . . .

97

1. "O Antioche,
    ur decipis me
    atque quasi servum reicis me?
        Quid agam?
5   Quid faciam?
    Dolo lugeo,
        fleo;

96

1. Young men with your hearts full of love,
   embrace the maidens!
   The singing of the birds
   prompts games of love.
   > *Ref.* O may youth show its vigor,   5
   >   flourish
   >   and rejoice
   >   in its season!

2. Up you get, young masters!
   Seek out young mistresses!
   The singing of the birds
   prompts games of love.
   Ref.

3. When I look at her . . .

97

1. "O Antiochus,
   why deceive me
   and spurn me like a slave?
   >   What am I to do?
   >   What can I do?   5
   Your trickery has made me lament
      and weep;

luctus est doloris,
fletus mali moris.
10   Pereo!

2.   Heu me miserum
    passum naufragium!
Astragis suscipior ad ostium.
      Video,
5   doceo
    lyram, manu tango,
      amo.
    Amor est flos floris,
     lyra est decoris.
10   Gaudeo!

3.   'Post tristitiam fient gaudia;
    post gaudium erit tristitia.'
      Sunt vera proverbia,
      quae fatentur talia.
5   Dicta veritatis,
        dicta claritatis
        amantur.

4.   Ab Astrage lecto suscipior
   et in maris fluctibus relinquor.
      Tharsia nascitur,
      mater deicitur
5   pulchra cum maerore;
    Tharsia cum flore
         nutritur.

my lamenting is for my pain,
my weeping for your evil ways.
     I am dying.   10

2.   Ah poor wretch that I am,
      I suffered shipwreck!
      I was welcomed at Astrages's home.
             I saw her,
               taught her   5
      the lyre, and touched her with my hand,
               and fell in love.
      My love is the flower of the flower,
      her lyre-playing a thing of beauty.
           I rejoiced.   10

3.   'After sadness there will be joys;
      after joy there will be sadness.'
      The proverbs that tell us this
      are true.
      Sayings that are true   5
      and clear
      are loved.

4.   Astrages welcomed me to her bed
      and left me in the waves of the sea.
      Tharsia was born
      but her beautiful mother
      was sent down below and mourned.   5
      Tharsia received excellent
         nursing.

5.   Frugibus fames hinc tollitur.
     Strangolio, Dionysiadi committitur
          flos floris.
          Doleo!"
    <five lines missing?>

6.   Lycoridis hic moritur.
   Ex aere species ostenditur.
         Traditur
         invidia
5   flos amoris Tharsia
         servo.
   Nautae eam liberant,
   servum quoque fugant
         gladio.

7.   Apollonii nata venditur
      et a lenone emitur.
      Pretium proponitur:
      sexaginta nummos.
5   Cotidie pretium haec redemit,
     virgo tamen mansit
       precibus.

8.   Apollonio natam quaerente
   Dionysiadem videt flentem.
      Sepulchrum monstratur,
      mors ut videatur
5   natae.
      "Quid non flent mei oculi?
       Tharsia nunc vivit
        filia!"

5. Then cereals began to appease her hunger.
   The choicest flower
   was entrusted to Strangolius and Dionysias.
   I grieved."
   \<five lines missing?\>

6. This is where Lycoris died.
   The bronze statue was pointed out.
   Because of envy
   Tharsia, the flower of love,
   was handed over   5
   to a slave.
   Sailors set her free
   and put the slave to flight
   with their swords.

7. Apollonius's daughter was sold
   and a pimp bought her.
   The price offered:
   sixty silver coins.
   Every day she brought in her purchase price;   5
   nonetheless, thanks to her entreaties
   she remained a virgin.

8. When Apollonius came searching for his daughter
   he saw Dionysias weeping.
   He was shown a tomb
   so that his daughter's death
   might appear to be real.   5
   "Why do my eyes shed no tears?
   Tharsia, my daughter,
   is still alive!"

9.   Puppes litori approximantur.
      Tum cito vera inveniuntur
      Tharsia lyrante coram Tyrio.
            Haec prius despicitur,
5   postea cognoscitur.
            Post multa opposita
            nata fuit reddita
                  patri.

10.   Voce caelesti Iohannis in insula
      Astrages regi fit cognita.
      Astrages cognoscitur;
            Tharsia maritatur
5   Arfaxo.
            Leno destruitur,
      Strangolius deicitur
                  omnibus.

98

1.   Troiae post excidium
      dux Aeneas Latium
      errans fato sequitur.
      Sed errat feliciter,
5   dum in regno taliter
      Didonis excipitur.
      Si hospes felicior,
      hospita vix largior
      aliqua percipitur!

9. The ships draw near the shore.
   Then the truth is soon revealed
   as Tharsia plays the lyre for Apollonius.
   Tharsia, once despised,
   is recognized. 5
   After many setbacks
   the daughter is restored
   to her father.

10. A heavenly voice on the island of Saint John
    informs the king about Astrages.
    Astrages is recognized;
    Tharsia marries
    Arfax. 5
    The pimp is laid low,
    and Strangolius killed
    by the populace.

98

1. After the destruction of Troy
   Aeneas, the leader, driven by fate,
   made his wandering way to Latium.
   He became fortunate in his wanderings
   when he received such a welcome 5
   in Dido's kingdom.
   If the guest was fortunate,
   a more generous hostess
   can scarcely be imagined.

2. Troas actos per maria
   Dido suscepit Tyria,
   passisque tot naufragia
   larga pandit hospitia.
5 Et Aeneam intuita
   simplex miratur, quod ita
   laeta nitescat facies,
larga crispata sit caesaries.
   Mox ad sororem properat,
10 eique clausam mentem reserat:

3. "Anna, dux,
      mea lux,
iste quis sit ambigo.
      Quis honor,
5   quis color,
vultu vix intelligo.
      At reor,
      vereor,
hunc nostra conubia
10   poscere.
      Id vere
portendunt insomnia.

4. Ecce, quam forti pectore,
   Amoris quasi facie!
   Heu, sors hunc quae per bibula
   Scyllae traxit pericula!

5. Si Sychaei
     coniugis mei
        Hymenei

2.   Tyrian Dido took in the Trojans,
    who had been driven over the seas,
    and extended generous hospitality
    to people who had suffered so many shipwrecks.
    As she gazed at Aeneas,   5
    she guilelessly marveled that his face
    beamed with such joy
    and that his curly locks were so abundant.
    Then she hurried to her sister
    and disclosed her hidden feelings to her: 10

3.   "Anna, light
    and guide of my life,
    I cannot tell who this man is.
    I can scarcely deduce his lineage
    or what his true colors are   5
    from his face.
    But I think
    he is going to ask me
    to marry him,
    I fear.   10
    This is really
    what my dreams portend.

4.   How stouthearted a figure he presents,
    with a face almost like Cupid's!
    Alas, for the fate that drew him
    past the thirsty dangers of Scylla.

5.   If it did not entail
    detracting from,
    straining,

pacti fidei
5   non detraherem,
        non cogerem,
        non laederem,
huic uni me forsan subdere
possem culpae. Me prius perdere
10   velit Iupiter
            turpiter
            fulmine
        de culmine
deiectam Carthaginis
15 quam regina se novis
    Dido committat dominis."

6.   Anna refert: "Assiste,
        mi soror, nec resiste
    amori blando. Si iste
    iungetur tibi suisque
5   extollet te virtutibus,
    Carthago crescet opibus."

7.   His accensa Phoenissa
        in furores Elissa,
    venandi sub imagine,
    effusa nimbi turbine,
5   antro cum duce latuit,
    eique se supposuit.

8.   Propositionibus
    tribus dux expositis
    syllogizat; motibus

or harming my adherence
to my marriage vows   5
to my husband
Sychaeus,
I could perhaps
succumb to this one transgression.
May Jupiter sooner choose   10
to kill me with a thunderbolt
casting me down
shamefully
from the summit of Carthage,
than that Queen Dido should entrust herself   15
to new masters!"

6.   Anna replied: "Go along with
love's charm, my sister
and do not resist it. If this man
marries you and his qualities
make you more powerful,   5
Carthage will be enriched."

7.   Phoenician Dido,
fired to a raging passion by these words,
under the pretext of hunting,
hid in a cave with the Trojan leader
during a stormy downpour   5
and lay with him.

8.   The Trojan leader
set out his three propositions
and drew his conclusion.

fallit haec oppositis;
5   sed quamvis cogentibus
argumentis utitur,
tamen eis brevibus
tantum horis fallitur.

9.   Et sic amborum in coniugio
laeta resplenduit aetherea regio;
nam ad amoris gaudia
rident, clarescunt omnia.

99

1.   Superbi Paridis   leve iudicium,
Helenae species   amata nimium
fit casus Troiae   deponens Ilium.

2.   Hinc dolens Aeneas   quaerit diffugium,
ascendit dubios   labores navium,
venit Carthaginem,   Didonis ad solium.

3.   Hunc regno suscipit   Dido Sidonia,
et plus quam decuit   amore saucia
moras non patitur   iungi conubia.

4.   O Amor improbe,   sic vincis omnia,
sic tuis viribus   redduntur mollia,
et morti proxima   sunt tua gaudia.

She tried to elude him with opposing moves,
but though she applied   5
compelling arguments,
she was nonetheless double-crossed by them
in just a few moments.

9. And so it was that the heavens shone happily
at the union of these two,
for everything smiles and brightens
over the joys of love.

99

1. The carefree judgment of proud Paris
and Helen's beauty, loved all too well,
led to the fall of Troy and sack of Ilium.

2. Grief-stricken by this, Aeneas sought escape,
embarked on the perilous travails of a voyage
and came to Carthage, Dido's realm.

3. Sidonian Dido welcomed him into her kingdom
and, wounded with love more than was seemly,
could not wait to be united with him in matrimony.

4. O unfeeling Love, so it is that you conquer everything,
that everything is rendered weak by your strength,
and that your joys are close to death.

5. Aeneas igitur   aegre corripitur,
    et in Italiam   ire praecipitur,
    quod amans audiens   Dido concutitur:

6. "Aenea domine,   quid est quod audio?
    Didonem miseram   dabis exitio?
    Quam dura praemia   pro beneficio!

7. Nudum exceperam   egentem omnium.
    Deos offenderat   nostrum conubium.
    Quid agam, nescio;   mors est consilium."

8. "Anna, quid audio,   soror dulcissima?
    Iam volant carbasa   ora finitima!
    Abrumpe miserae,   Mors, haec asperrima!"

9. Heu, Dido nobilis   spreta relinquitur
    atque Laviniae   thalamus sequitur
    et Anna propere   pro maga mittitur.

10. "O ensis perfidi,   fortiter ilia
    mea pertransiens   deme suspiria!"
    Amantes miseri,   timete talia.

11. Aeneas audiens   iam in Italia,
    in quanta obiit   Dido miseria,
    et quod dispersa sit   eius familia,

12. mox crines dissipat   cum veste serica.
    Qui fortis viderat   tot damna bellica,
    tunc demum clamitat   voce tyrannica:

13. "Non haec credideram,   Dido, quod audio,
    quod interficeres   te meo gladio,
    ut essem, heu, tibi   mortis occasio.

5. With difficulty Aeneas was set on the right path
   and ordered to make his way to Italy.
   but when his lover, Dido, heard this she was shattered:

6. "My lord Aeneas, what is this I hear?
   Are you going to send poor Dido to her death?
   What a cruel reward for my kindness!

7. I took you up naked and in need of everything.
   Our marriage offended the gods.
   I don't know what I am to do. Death is my plan."

8. "Anna, dearest sister, what am I hearing? The sails
   are already flapping at the neighboring shores.
   Death, end these cruel sounds for one so wretched!"

9. Noble Dido was, alas, spurned and abandoned
   and marriage sought with Lavinia.
   Anna was hastily sent to fetch a sorceress.

10. "Sword of the unfaithful one, with all my strength
    run through my bowels and end my sighs."
    Unhappy lovers everywhere, fear a like fate.

11. When Aeneas, now in Italy, heard
    of the depth of Dido's despair when she died
    and of the scattering of her household,

12. he tore his hair and his silken garment.
    He who had bravely seen so many losses in war
    at last cried out with his kingly voice:

13. "I would not have thought possible, Dido, what I hear–
    that you killed yourself with my sword
    so that I might be the cause of your death.

14. Naves refeceras   quassas naufragio,
    et me susceperas   plus quam hospitio
    et sublimaveras   in regni solio.

15. Tu mihi fueras   vitae subsidium,
    sed ego sum tibi   mortis exitium.
    Quam detestabile   est hoc commercium!

16. Quamvis essem pauper   procul a patria,
    praeponebar tamen   in tui gratia
    Iarbae nobili,   quem tremit Libya.

17. Quam saepe commovet   me clara facies,
    dulcis anhelitus,   grata caesaries,
    membrorum omnium   miranda species!

18. Pro his exciderant   a corde penitus
    dolores patriae   et graves gemitus
    gentis, et coniugis   et patris obitus.

19. Non semper utile   est diis credere,
    nec, quicquid ammonent,   velle perficere;
    nam instigaverant   me te relinquere.

20. Dido, possideas   sedes Elysias,
    et inter gaudia   Aeneam audias
    pro beneficio   reddentem gratias!"

14. You repaired my shattered ships,
    and welcomed me in a more than hospitable manner
    and elevated me to the throne of your realm.

15. You provided me with life-supporting aid
    but I proved a cause of deadly destruction to you.
    How despicable an exchange this was!

16. Though I was poor and far from my homeland,
    thanks to your graciousness, I was preferred
    to noble Iarbas, before whom Libya trembles.

17. How often was I moved by your bright face,
    your sweet breath, your lovely hair
    and the wonderful beauty of all your limbs.

18. These qualities completely made me forget
    my country's agony and the heavy groans
    of my people and the deaths of my wife and father.

19. It is not always helpful to put one's trust in the gods
    or to choose to carry out whatever they advise,
    for they were responsible for my abandoning you.

20. Dido, may you dwell in your Elysian abode
    and in the midst of your happiness hear Aeneas
    offering his thanks for your kindness."

99a

Urit amor Paridem; vult Tyndaridem, rapit illam.
Res patet, hostis adest; pugnatur; Pergama cedunt.

99b

Praebuit Aeneas et causam mortis et ensem;
   ipsa sua Dido concidit usa manu.

100

1.   O decus, o Libyae regnum, Carthaginis urbem!
       O lacerandas fratris opes, o Punica regna!

2a.   O duces Phrygios,
       o dulces advenas,
       quos tanto tempore
       dispersos aequore!
5   Iam hiems septima
           iactaverat
           ob odium
               Iunonis,
       Scyllea rabies,

99a

Love burns Paris; he wants Helen and carries her off.
The deed is discovered, the enemy arrives, war ensues, Troy
    gives way.

99b

Aeneas provided both her reason and her sword for death;
but Dido herself used the sword and died by her own hand.

100

1.   O gem and royal seat of Libya, city of Carthage! Alas for
      my brother's cursed wealth! Alas for the Punic realm!

2a.   Alas for the Phrygian leaders,
      my dear guests,
      scattered so long
      over the deep!
      It was now the seventh winter   5
      that had buffeted them
      thanks to Juno's hatred
      when the raging fury of Scylla,
      the bloody gore

10   Cyclopum sanies,
            Celaeno pessima
                    traduxerat
                    ad solium
                    Didonis.

    2b.   Quid me crudelibus
            exercent odiis,
            arentis Libyae
            post casum Phrygiae
5   quos terrae naufragos
                    exceperam?
                    Me miseram,
                        quid feci,
            quae meis aemulis,
10   ignotis populis
            et genti barbarae
                    Sidonios
                    ac Tyrios
                        subieci!

    3.   Ai dolant!
                    Ai dolant!
                    Iam volant
                    carbasa!
5   Iam nulla spes Didonis.
            Vae Tyriis colonis!
            Plangite, Sidonii,
            quod in ore gladii
                    deperii
10   ob amorem Phrygii
                    praedonis!

430

of the Cyclopes,   10
and the dread Celaeno
brought them
to the throne
of Dido.

2b. Why do they now treat me
with cruel hatred,
when I welcomed them
to my land
as shipwrecked guests   5
in arid Libya
after the fall of Troy?
Ah, poor wretch that I am!
what did I do
in making the people   10
of Sidon and Tyre
subject to my rivals,
an unknown people
and a barbarous race?

3.   Alas, they are hewing!
Alas, they are trimming!
Already the sails
are fluttering!
Now Dido has no hope!   5
Alas for the Tyrian settlers!
Weep, people of Sidon,
for my death
at the bite of a sword
for the love   10
of a Phrygian pirate!

4a.   Aeneas, hospes Phrygius,
       Iarbas, hostis Tyrius,
       multo me temptant crimine,
       sed vario discrimine.
5   Nam sitientis Libyae
       regina spreta linquitur,
       et thalamos Laviniae
       Troianus hospes sequitur!
         Quid agam misera!
10   Dido regnat altera!
         Ai, vixi nimium!
         Mors agat cetera!

4b.   Deserta siti regio
       me gravi cingit proelio,
       fratris me terret feritas
       et Numidum crudelitas.
5   Insultant hoc proverbio:
       "Dido se fecit Helenam,
       regina nostra gremio
       Troianum fovit advenam!"
       Gravis conditio,
10   furiosa ratio,
       si mala perferam
       pro beneficio!

5a.   Anna, vides,
       quae sit fides
       deceptoris perfidi?
       Fraude ficta
5   me relicta
       regna fugit Punica!

4a.   Aeneas, my Phrygian guest,
      Iarbas, and my enemy in Tyre,
      assail me with many wrongs
      that pose different dangers.
      The queen of thirsty Libya   5
      is spurned and abandoned
      and my Trojan guest is pursuing
      marriage with Lavinia!
      What am I to do, wretch that I am?
      Another Dido is to be his queen.   10
      Ah, I have lived too long!
      Let death see to the rest!

4b.   A region made desert by thirst
      hedges me in with grim war.
      My brother's savagery
      and the cruelty of the Numidians terrify me.
      They insult me with this saying: 5
      "Dido has made a Helen of herself.
      Our queen fondled on her breast
      the Trojan stranger."
      It is unfair
      and an insane reckoning   10
      if I suffer punishment
      in return for my kindness.

5a.   Anna, do you see
      the nature of the perfidious deceiver's
      trustworthiness?
      He made up a fraudulent story,
      abandoned me,   5
      and is now fleeing my Punic realm!

Nil sorori
nisi mori,
soror, restat, unica.

5b.   Saevit Scylla,
        nec tranquilla
se promittunt aequora.
        Solvit ratem,
5   tempestatem
nec exhorret Phrygius.
        Dulcis soror,
        ut quid moror,
aut quid cessat gladius?

6a.   Fulget sidus Orionis,
        saevit hiems Aquilonis,
                Scylla regnat aequore!
        Tempestatis tempore,
5   Palinure,
                        non secure
        classem solvis litore.

6b.   Solvit tamen dux Troianus!
        Solvat ensem nostra manus
        in iacturam sanguinis!
        Vale, flos Carthaginis!
5   Haec, Aenea,
                fer trophaea,
        causa tanti criminis!

7.   O dulcis anima,
        vitae spes unica,
                Phlegethontis,

434

My one and only sister,
nothing remains for your sister
but to die.

5b. Scylla is raging
and there is no promise
of calm seas.
But the Phrygian
is setting sail   5
and does not fear the storm.
My dear sister,
why am I delaying?
why is my sword slow to act?

6a. The constellation of Orion gleams brightly,
the stormy north wind is raging,
Scylla rules over the deep!
In stormy conditions,
Palinurus,   5
it is not safe for you to have the fleet
set sail from the shore!

6b. The Trojan leader is setting sail nonetheless!
So let my hand set free the sword
that will cause my blood to flow!
Farewell, flower of Carthage!
Aeneas,   5
cause of this great wrong,
bear this as your trophy!

7.   Ah, my sweet soul,
my only hope for life!
Go shortly on your way

Acherontis
5   latebras
ac tenebras
mox adeas
horroris
nec pyrois
10   te circulus
moretur!
Aeneam sequere,
nec desere
suaves illecebras
15   amoris,
nec dulces nodos Veneris
perdideris,
sed nostri conscia
sis nuntia
20   doloris!

101

1.   Pergama flere volo   fato Danais data solo,
       solo capta dolo,   capta redacta solo.

2.   Ex Helicone sona,   quae prima tenes Helicona,
       et metra me dona   promere posse bona!

3.   Est Paris absque pare;   quaerit, videt, audet amare.
       Audet temptare   furta, pericla, mare.

to the hidden recesses
and horrific   5
darkness
of Phlegethon
and Acheron
and don't let
the circle of fire   10
give you pause!
Go follow Aeneas
and don't give up
on the sweet enticements
of love   15
and don't forsake
the pleasant entanglements of Venus
but remember
my pain
and proclaim it!   20

101

1. I want to weep for Troy, given up to the Greeks by Fate
   alone, taken only by trickery and, once taken, razed to
   the ground.

2. Sing out from Helicon, first ruler of Helicon,
   and give me the power to bring forth good verse!

3. Paris has no peer; he seeks, sees, and dares to love.
   he dares risk a theft, dangers, and the sea.

4. Vadit et accedit,   clam tollit, clamque recedit;
   nauta solo cedit,   fit fuga, praedo redit.

5. Tuta libido maris,   dat tura Libidinis aris,
   civibus ignaris,   quod parat arma Paris.

6. Post cursus Helenae   currunt Larissa, Mycenae,
   mille rates plenae   fortibus absque sene.

7. Exsuperare ratus   viduatorem viduatus;
   foedere nudatus   foederat ense latus.

8. Graeco ductori   prohibet dolor esse timori
   pro consorte tori   vincere sive mori.

9. Pergama dia secus   figit tentoria Graecus,
   impetitur moechus   et fabricatur equus.

10. Plena malae prolis   parit hostem machina molis.
    Destruitur dolis   tam populosa polis.

11. Tradunt cuncta neci,   praedaeque cupidine caeci
    obfirmant Graeci   pectora clausa preci.

12. Hinc ardent aedes,   hinc detruncat Diomedes
    per varias caedes   brachia, crura, pedes.

13. Multatur caede   praedo Paris a Diomede
    seque suae taedae   reddit alumna Ledae.

14. Femina digna mori   redamatur amore priori
    reddita victori   deliciisque tori.

4.   He comes, draws near, stealthily steals and stealthily withdraws. He quits the land by ship; flight ensues; he returns home a pirate.

5.   The man's lust is protected; he offers incense on the altar of Lust, while the citizens are unaware that he, Paris, is preparing for war.

6.   Chasing after Helen come Larissa and Mycenae, a thousand ships full of brave soldiers—no old men.

7.   The man robbed of his wife plans to overcome the robber; stripped of his marriage bond, he binds his sword to his side.

8.   Grief prevents winning or dying for his bedmate from being a source of fear for the Greek leader.

9.   The Greeks pitch tents near divine Troy, an attack is launched against the adulterer, and a horse is built.

10.   Full of evil offspring, the huge contrivance spawns the enemy. The city of so many is destroyed by trickery.

11.   The Greeks destroy everything and, blinded by lust for booty, their hearts close to pleas for mercy.

12.   Here buildings are ablaze, there Diomedes hacks off arms, legs, and feet in an orgy of slaughter.

13.   Diomedes's slaughter punishes Paris's piracy and the daughter of Leda returns to her marriage.

14.   A woman who deserves to die finds love again from her earlier love, when restored to the victor and to the bed's delights.

15. Saeva, quid evadis? non tradita cetera tradis!
  Cur rea tu cladis non quoque clade cadis?

16. Si fueris lota, si vita sequens bona tota,
  non eris ignota, non eris absque nota.

17. Passa modo Paridem —pateris iam—Thesea pridem;
  es factura fidem ne redeas in idem?

18. Rumor de veteri faciet ventura timeri.
  Cras poterunt fieri turpia sicut heri.

19. Femina victa mero quod inhaereat ebria vero,
  nec fieri spero nec fideiiussor ero.

20. Expleta caede superadditur Hecuba praedae.
  Tractatur foede, cogitur ire pede.

21. In facie Dorum, crinem laniata decorum,
  subsequitur lorum per theatrale forum.

22. Vivit, at invita, quia vivit paupere vita,
  et planctus inita vociferatur ita:

23. "Iuno, quid est quod agis? Post tantae funera stragis
  totne putas plagis addere posse magis?

24. Ergo reoccides hos quos occidit Atrides?
  Ergo reoccides quos obiisse vides?

15. Hell-kite, why do you escape? Not betrayed yourself, you betray the rest. As cause of the disaster, why don't you fall in the disaster too?

16. If you are unblemished, if the rest of your life is entirely admirable, they will always know you; you will not be exonerated.

17. You, who recently partnered Paris and before that, Theseus, are suffering now! Are you going to pledge not to return to the same pattern?

18. Rumors about the past will create fears for the future. Yesterday's misdeeds can be repeated tomorrow.

19. I do not expect, and refuse to guarantee, that a woman once overcome by wine, will, when drunk, adhere to the truth.

20. The slaughter finished, Hecuba is added to the booty. She is treated shamefully, forced to go on foot.

21. Before the eyes of the Dorians, her lovely hair savagely torn, she is led by a leash through the forum for all to see.

22. Still alive, but unwillingly so because she lives an impoverished life, she begins her lament, crying out as follows:

23. "Juno, what are you doing? After so much slaughter do you think that to so many blows you can add more?

24. So will you kill again those whom Atrides killed? Will you kill again those who you see have died?

25. Nullum iam reperis,   nullum, nec sic misereris;
    immo persequeris   reliquias cineris!

26. Nemo rebellatur,   et Iuno belligeratur,
    bellaque sectatur   sanguine mucro satur!

27. Me, me, Iuno, feri!   Feriendo potes misereri!
    Fac obitu celeri   corpus anile teri!

28. Usque modo flevi   casus incommoda laevi;
    Quod superest aevi   corripe fine brevi.

29. Perstitit ira dei   dare cetera perniciei;
    miror quod sit ei   mentio nulla mei.

30. Nemo mei meminit,   gladius qui cetera finit,
    mecum foedus init;   me superesse sinit.

31. Concutit ossa metus,   fit spiritus irrequietus,
    dum renovat fletus   denuo cura vetus.

32. Urbs retro sublimis   et abundans rebus opimis
    una fit e minimis   adnihilata nimis.

33. Urbs celebris dudum,   dum terminat alea ludum,
    ecce solum nudum,   pastus erit pecudum!

34. Vae tibi, Troia, peris!   iam non mihi Troia videris,
    Iamiam bobus eris   pascua, lustra feris.

35. Urbs fortunata,   si posses vincere fata,
    vel possent fata   segnius esse rata!

25. You find no one left now, no one, and still show no pity; rather you hound the remnants of their ashes!

26. No one is fighting back and Juno battles on. The point of your sword, dripping with gore, still chases after war.

27. Hit me, Juno, hit me! You can show compassion by hitting me. See to it that this old woman's body is crushed by a swift death!

28. Up till now I have merely bewailed the blows of a grim fate. Make a quick end to what is left of my life!

29. God's anger persisted in consigning everything else to ruin. I wonder if he has forgotten me.

30. No one remembers me; the sword, which ends everything, has made a treaty with me; it allows me to survive.

31. Fear shakes my bones and my soul knows no rest, while an old love renews my weeping once more.

32. A city, once lofty and overflowing with rich abundance, has become one of the least, completely annihilated.

33. Long a populous city until a throw of the dice ended the game, now will be an empty field, pasture for cattle.

34. Alas for you, Troy, you are dying! You no longer look like Troy to me. Soon you will be pasture for oxen, a haunt for wild animals.

35. A city blessed by fortune, if only you could conquer fate or if fate could have been fulfilled more slowly.

36. Regna beata satis,   urbs primae nobilitatis,
         dives honoratis   dantibus atque datis!

37. Regna beata satis,   donec nocuere beatis
         praeda voluptatis   et male fausta ratis!

38. Urbs bona, plena bono   foris, intus, cive, colono,
         praedita patrono,   praeditus ille throno!

39. Plena potentatu,   celeberrima, digna relatu,
         felicissima tu   principe, cive, statu.

40. Curia personis,   urbs civibus, arva colonis,
         terra suis donis,   horrea plena bonis.

41. Si commendemus,   quae commendare solemus:
         cultus supremus,   rus, ager, unda, nemus.

42. Potum vineta,   pastum dabat area laeta,
         merces moneta   navigiumque freta.

43. Urbs vetus et clara,   bona valde, tam bona, rara,
         tam bona, tam cara   fit pecualis hara.

44. Dives ab antiquo,   dum fato fertur iniquo,
         deperit in modico,   fit nihil ex aliquo.

45. Causa rei talis   meretrix fuit exitialis,
         femina fatalis,   femina feta malis."

36. A realm comfortably off, a city of the highest nobility, rich in honored donors and gifts.

37. A realm comfortably off until its prosperity was harmed by booty sought by lust and a fateful ship.

38. A fine city, filled inside and out with good citizens and farmers, a city endowed with a patron and a patron endowed with a throne!

39. A bustling city, powerful, worthy of report, you were most fortunate in your leader, citizenry, and standing.

40. Your court, filled with courtiers, your city with citizens, your fields with farmers, your land with gifts, and your granaries with supplies.

41. If we were to commend what we usually commend, your agriculture is outstanding—the countryside, fields, water, and woodland.

42. The vineyards provided drink and the productive threshing floors food, trade brought in coin and the narrows shipping.

43. A city old and famous, a city of such rare excellence, a city so fine and so beloved becomes a cattle range!

44. Rich from ancient times until it was carried off by an unjust fate and perished quickly; from something it becomes nothing.

45. The cause of such a disaster was a doom-laden courtesan, a femme fatale, a woman pregnant with evil."

102

Versus

1. Fervet amore Paris,   Troianis immolat aris;
   fratribus ignaris   scinditur unda maris.

2. Temptat Tyndaridem,   favet illa, relinquit Atridem,
   prompta sequi Paridem,   passa perire fidem.

3. Aequora raptor arat,   tenet, affectu quod amarat.
   Se res declarat,   Graecia bella parat.

4. Contra Dardanidem   res provocat ista Tydidem.
   Incitat Aeacidem   Pallas ad illud idem.

5. Argos nudatur,   classis coit, unda minatur,
   hostia mactatur,   aura quieta datur.

6. Passa freti strepitus   Phrygium rapit ancora litus.
   Obstruit introitus   Hector ad arma citus.

7. Ilios arma gerit,   Helenam sua Graecia quaerit;
   fraus aditus aperit,   hostis ab hoste perit.

8. Sub Danaum pube,   telorum territa nube,
   infremit urbs Hecubae,   flant resonantque tubae.

102

Metrical Verses

1. Burning with love, Paris sacrifices on the Trojan altar;
   unknown to his brothers, his ship cleaves the waves.

2. He tries to win over Helen, she favors him, and leaves
   Menelaus, ready to follow Paris, allowing her marriage
   pledge to die.

3. The abductor plows the seas, holding what he has
   loved. The deed becomes known; Greece prepares for
   war.

4. This rouses Diomedes against Paris.
   Pallas prompts Achilles to take similar action.

5. Argos is stripped of its men, the fleet assembles, the
   sea threatens, a victim is sacrificed, and a gentle breeze
   provided.

6. After trials at sea, they anchor on the Phrygian coast.
   Hector quickly takes up arms and blocks their way in.

7. Ilios takes up arms, Greece wants her Helen back;
   a trick opens access to the gates; enemy slays enemy.

8. Facing the Greek warriors and terrified by the hail of
   weapons, Hecuba's city cries out; trumpet blasts rend
   the air.

9.   Miles ad arma fremit,   vitae fraus Hectora demit,
      urbem pugna premit,   Troia sub hoste tremit.

10.   Ars nisi ditaret   Danaos numenque iuvaret,
      murus adhuc staret,   qui modo rege caret.

11.   Quaeritur ars, fit equus,   latet intra viscera Graecus.
      Fit Priamus caecus,   ducitur intro pecus.

12.   Flendo Sinon orat,   Ithacus fallendo laborat,
      machina claustra forat,   urbem flamma vorat.

13.   Credula fallaci   flammae subiecta voraci,
      passa dolos Ithaci   Troia fit esca faci.

14.   Ars urbem tradit,   urbs in discrimina vadit,
      ignis edax radit   Pergama, Troia cadit.

15.   Urbis opes lacerae   flammis alimenta dedere,
      igni cessere   moenia, claustra, serae.

16.   Argis exosa   iacet Ilios, ante iocosa,
      inclita, formosa,   nunc rubus, ante rosa.

17.   Igni sublatus   fugit, omnia ferre paratus
      firma classe ratus   te, Cytherea, satus.

18.   Tellus fatalis   petitur navalibus alis.
      Obviat ira salis   peste, furore, malis.

19.   Pestem concepit   mare, fluctus surgere coepit,
      puppibus obrepit   spuma, procella strepit.

9. Soldiers roar for arms, a trick robs Hector of his life,
   fighting crushes Troy, trembling before the enemy.

10. Had guile not enriched the Greeks and a deity not
    assisted them, the walls of Troy, which now lack its
    king, would still stand.

11. The Greeks resort to trickery, build a horse, and hide in
    its innards. Priam proves blind and the beast is brought
    inside.

12. Sinon weeps and begs — the Ithacan contrives deceit,
    the contrivance pierces the walls; fire consumes the city.

13. Trusting a trickster, engulfed in voracious fire, a victim
    of the Ithacan's ploys, Troy becomes fuel for flames.

14. A trick betrays the city, the city walks into the danger,
    all-consuming fire rakes the citadel, Troy falls.

15. The wealth of the devastated city fuels the flames,
    walls, barriers, and locks all give way before the fire.

16. Hated by the Argives, Ilios, once joyous, renowned,
    and beautiful lies there, now a briar, earlier a rose.

17. Out of the fire, he flees, ready to endure all dangers,
    your son, Venus, confident in his stout ship.

18. On their ships' wings they make for the land assigned
    by fate. The sea's wrath obstructs their path with
    monsters, storms and other ills.

19. The sea spawns destruction, the waves get bigger;
    foaming brine sweeps over the deck in a howling gale.

20. Flat Notus insanus,   insurgit turbo profanus,
    navita Troianus   utitur arte manus.

21. Hinc quasi delira   pelagi succingitur ira,
    stat prope mors dira,   stat procul inde lira.

21a. Dux errat pelago,   rotat illum mortis imago.
    Obvia Carthago   dat loca certa vago.

21b. Didonem caecat furor,   et se crimine faecat;
    se feriendo necat;   dux fugit, alta secat.

22. Rebus sublatis,   currentibus ordine fatis,
    regnis optatis   utitur arte ratis.

23. Pacem vestigat,   sed eum lis dira fatigat;
    et furor instigat   et nova pugna ligat.

24. Pugna praedatur,   furit in Turnum, dominatur,
    viscera scrutatur   sanguine mucro satur.

25. Coepta luens sceleris   te victum, Turne, fateris.
    Obrutus ense peris,   praeda cibusque feris.

26. Aeneae cedit   victoria, pugna recedit.
    Pugnae succedit   gloria, paxque redit.

27. Sub vinclo fidei   post inclita facta trophaei
    regia nupsit ei   virgo favore dei.

20. The south wind blows madly, a fearsome whirlwind arises; the Trojan crew put their skilled hands to work.

21. Then they are surrounded by the mad rage of the sea—grim death is at hand, cultivated land far away.

21a. Aeneas is driven off course, a vision of death sends him spinning. Carthage lies ahead, a safe haven for the wanderer.

21b. Blinded by passion, Dido stains herself with sin; she commits suicide; Aeneas flees, cleaving the deep.

22. After losing everything, when fate has run its course, he reaches the desired realm, with his seamanship.

23. He searches for peace but grim strife wears him down; turmoil prompts him; a new war binds him.

24. He wins spoils in the fighting; he furiously defeats Turnus; his sword, sated with blood, pierces Turnus's innards.

25. Paying for wrongs committed, Turnus, you admit your defeat. You die, slain by the sword, prey and food for wild animals.

26. The victory goes to Aeneas, the fighting fades away. Glory follows the fighting and peace returns.

27. After his famous victory, the princess pledges her loyalty and marries Aeneas with God's blessing.

Abbreviations

AH = Guido M. Dreves; Clemens Blume, eds., *Analecta Hymnica* (Leipzig, 1886, 1920)

B = The *Carmina Burana* manuscript (Munich clm 4660 and 4660a)

BNP = Hubert Cancik and Helmuth Schneider, eds., *Brill's New Pauly* (Leiden, 2002–2010)

CCSL = Corpus Christianorum, Series Latina (Turnhout)

DMLBS = *Dictionary of Medieval Latin from British Sources* (Oxford 1975–2013)

EDB = *Eerdmans Dictionary of the Bible* (Grand Rapids, Mich., 2000)

H-S-B = Alfons Hilka, Otto Schumann, and Bernhard Bischoff, eds., *Carmina Burana* (Heidelberg, 1930–1970)

L&S = C. T. Lewis and C. Short, eds., *A Latin Dictionary* (Oxford, 1879)

MW = Otto Prinz, Johannes Schneider et al., eds., *Mittellateinisches Wörterbuch* (Munich, 1967–)

OLD = P. G. W. Glare, ed., *Oxford Latin Dictionary* (Oxford, 1983)

PL = J-P Migne, ed., Patrologia Latina (Paris, 1841–1855)

P-W = Georg Wissowa, ed., *Paulys Realencyclopädie der classischen Altertumswissenschaft* (Stuttgart, 1909–1972)

TLL = *Thesaurus Linquae Latinae* (Leipzig, Berlin, 1900–)

Note on the Text

More than half the poems in the Benediktbeuern manuscript *(B)* are found nowhere else, but more than three hundred manuscripts scattered over Europe include one or more of the *Carmina Burana* poems, often in more complete and less corrupt versions. The standard edition, by Alfons Hilka, Otto Schumann, and Bernhard Bischoff (H-S-B), which includes both the original poems (1–228) and the poems added later (1*-26*), offers readings from many of these other witnesses. Bischoff added useful textual notes to CB 1 to 186 at H-S-B 1.pt.3.191–212. CB 7* to 15* and 26* are found in seven leaves of the *Fragmenta Burana,* now bound as a separate manuscript (clm 4660a) but included in Bischoff's facsimile edition of the *Carmina Burana.* Benedikt K. Vollmann brought out a single volume of Latin text, German translation, and commentary that adheres closely to *B,* resorting to readings from other manuscripts or to conjectures only when *B*'s readings are manifestly incorrect.

This text has a negative critical apparatus. The base text is that of H-S-B. Only deviations from this text are recorded. This is done by citing the names of the editors or other scholars who first adopted or suggested them. *B*'s reading is always cited when a different reading from that of H-S-B is adopted. The abbreviations used in the Notes to the Text are indicated at the beginning of that section. It should be borne in mind that in his extensive critical apparatus Schumann frequently suggested readings that he did not adopt.

ORTHOGRAPHY AND RHYMES

The policy of Dumbarton Oaks Medieval Library is to follow the norms of classical Latin orthography. As a result, where the manuscript has *e,* this has been expanded, where necessary, to *ae* or *oe* to conform with classical norms; thus the manuscript's *fede mense* becomes *foedae mensae.* While this use of classical spelling is helpful for those unfamiliar with Medieval Latin orthography, there is a serious drawback in the case of rhythmical poetry, which is almost always rhymed, in that it tends to conceal many rhymes. Medieval writers wrote *e, ae,* and *oe* all as *e,* because they were all pronounced as *e.* So readers should bear in mind that *festae* and *maeste* provide a perfect two-syllable rhyme both with one another and with *veste.* Another common deviation from classical spelling found in medieval manuscripts occurs with the interchangeability of *i* and *y* in certain words, as in *girare/gyrare* and *sydus/sidus.* In these cases too the classical spelling has been adopted.

The only exception to this policy is found in reporting manuscript readings in the Notes to the Text. Accordingly, if *B* has *mense* (= *mensae*), then it is reported as *mense* in the Notes to the Text. On the other hand, if a scholar emends a text to read *mense* (meaning *mensae*), then the emendation is recorded in the Notes to the Text as *mensae;* however, if it means *mense* (the ablative of *mensis*), it is printed as *mense.*

By DOML policy, the Latin texts follow the norms of classical Latin orthography. For consistency, the Middle High German ones have been standardized to the so-called classical form of the language. Accordingly, the German texts established by Vollmann have been normalized by applying principles like those employed by Christoph Cormeau in the standard edition of the songs of Walther von der Vogelweide (Berlin, 1996).

Notes to the Text

Schu = Schumann
Tr = Traill
Voll = Vollmann

ORIGINAL COLLECTION

9.2.2	dissimiliter *B Voll*: missam viliter *Schu*
9.5.5	sic Ephranitas diceres *Tr*: nec Effronitas (Efranitas *Voll)* dicere *B Voll*: nunc Ephranitas dicere *Schu*
9.5.6	postea similes *Tr*: potes simile *B Voll*: potestis simile *Schu*
11.1	Nummus . . . summus *B Voll*: summus . . . Nummus *Schu*
14.2.7	hac *Tr*: hec *B Schu Voll*
15.5.11	invaria *B Schmeller Voll*: in varia *Schu*
16.2.3	tamen *Schmeller*: enim *B Schu Voll*
16.3.4	conspice *Bojanga*: legimus *B Schu Voll*
17.1.7–8	obdurans . . . curans *Herkenrath*: obdurat . . . curat *B Schu Voll*
17.1.12	dissolvis *Herkenrath*: dissolvit *B Schu Voll*
17.2.7–8	obumbrata et velata *Patzig Voll*: obumbratam et velatam *B Schu*
17.3.9	cordis *B Voll*: corde *Schu*
21.3.6	reverentur *FO: stanzas 2 to 5 omitted by B Voll*: reverentur *Schu*
25.3	*See Notes to the Translation.*
31.4.6	me *Voll*: non *B Schu*
31.5.6	quid luerit *Tr*: quis fuerit *B Schu Voll*
31.8.1	Croesi *Schmeller*: Resi *B Voll*: Beli *Schu*
39.6.12	Sanctum *Tr*: Sanctum Isra(h)el *B Schu Voll*
41.4.4	pugna *B Voll*: cursus *Schu*
41.7.1	venti *Strecker*: fluctus *Schu*: B fructus *Voll*

41.7.4   sepelitur *Strecker*: deglutitur *B Schu Voll*

41.7.5   deglutitur *Strecker*: sepelitur *B Schu Voll*

41.15.2   recepit *Strecker*: excepit *Schu*

41.21.2   et Pilatus *Strecker*: Spurius qui *B Schu Voll*

41.21.4   lota *Strecker (See Juvenal 6.464)*: lata *B. Schu Voll. See Notes to the Translation.*

41.25.4   dives. *Strecker*: sacer *B* Voll: saccus. *Schu*

41.25.6   pellitur *B Strecker Voll*: tollitur *Schu*

42.14.4   mare falsum fit *Tr*: mare salsum est *B Schu Voll*

43.1.4   et *Voll*: ut *B Schu*

43.2.2   lates *Tr*: latet *B Schu Voll*

43.5.5   sed si de qua *Voll*: de qua sed di *B Schu*

43.5.6   huius *Tr*: cuius *B Schu Voll*

43.8.3   principalium mente *Tr*: principatus per mentis *Voll*: principatus mentis *B Schu*

43.8.4   miseria *Voll*: in serie *B Schu*

45.3.1   si rodere *B Voll*: quos rodere *Schu*

46.1.4   quaerens *Tr*: querit *B Schu Voll*

46.5   *Lines so ordered Tr*: 2, 1, 3, 4 *in B Schu Voll*

46.5.5   hinc *Tr*: hic *B Voll*: hoc *Schu*

46.9.5   gusta *Tr*: gustu *B Schu Voll*

46.10.6   valet *suggested by Schu*: venit *B Schu Voll*

49.12.3   habitet *Tr*: habitat *B Schu Voll*

49.12.4   hoc *Tr*: hanc *B Schu Voll*

50.2.4   de stercore pauperem ac caeno *Bischoff*: de paupere pauperem a ceno *B Voll*: de pulvere pauperem a caeno *Schu*

50.5.1   Turcomili *Heraeus*: Hircomili *B Schu Voll*

            atque Trogoditae *Tr*: Turgo et Editae *B Schu Voll*

50.12.2   ter centum Templarii *Tr*: Templarii ter centum *B Schu Voll*

50.14.1   navita *Peiper*: navica *B Schu Voll*

51a.*Ref.*2 ymas *Peiper Voll*: ysma *B Schu*

53.6.3   hanc *Tr*: ac *B Schu Voll*

54.5.12   Hamadryades *Schmeller*: adriade ades *B*: Adryades *Schu*: Adriades *Voll*

57.6.5   istis *Tr*: illis *B Schu Voll Walsh*

58.2.10   Arcas *Tr*: Arcus *B Voll*: Argus *Schu Walsh*

58.6.2   verno *suggested by Schu*: nro *B*: nostro *Schu Walsh*

59.1.3   nubilo *Sedgwick Bischoff Walsh*: iubilo *B Schu Voll*

59.1.4   frondem pansat *Tr*: fronde pausat *Sedgwick Walsh*: fronde pausa
        B Schu Voll

59.3.3   libitum *Herkenrath Bischoff Voll Walsh*: libidum *B*: liquidum *Schu*

59.6.1   Dione *Bischoff*: Clyope *B Schu Voll Walsh*

59.7.1   puris *Tr*: ludis *B Schu Voll*

59.7.2   pudice *B (according to Bischoff) Voll Walsh*: iudice *Schu*

59.7.3   temeritas *Walsh suggested by Schu*: emeritas *B Schu Voll*

60.1a.3   sede revinctae suavi *Tr*: federe iuncto mari *B Voll*: foede revinc-
        tae lari *Schu*

60.1a.6   inde perire *Bischoff*: ire perinde *B Schu Voll (B and Voll have this as*
        1b.1)

60.1b.1   At tu diligis quidem *added by Tr*: ire perinde libet *B Voll*: *Schu* has
        a lacuna

60.1b.3   hic *Tr*: hec *B Schu Voll*

60.1b.5   amator *Tr*: amaror *B Schu Voll*

60.4.1   effluis *Tr*: affluis *B Voll*: affligis *Schu*
        in meritum *B*: immeritum *Schu Voll*

60.5c.1   quaeris inique *Tr*: ueris inique *B*: quaesivique *Schu*: quaerens
        tuique *Voll. See Notes to the Translation.*

60.7a.1   rem *added by Tr*: te *added by Schu*

60.7a.5   nos *added by Tr*: omitted by *B Schu Voll*

60.8c.2–3   pira structa luet *B Voll*: lyra, spreta luget *Schu*

60.9.3   natando *Tr*: notanda *B*: nutando *Schu Voll*

60.10.7   reclude *B Spanke Bischoff Voll*: retrude *Schu*

60.11.3   hunc tu *Tr*: hunc *suggested by Schu*: hanc *B Schu Voll*

60.11.4   cum *Tr*: et *B Schu Voll*

60.11.8   ius tenebam *Patzig Heraeus*: iustum rebar *B Schu Voll*

60.11.9   ut bearer *added by Tr*

60.12.7   vis transponere *Tr*: vi transponeres *B Schu Voll*

60.12.8   et . . . conterere *Tr*: ut . . . contereres *B Schu Voll*

60.15.3   obnixerim *Tr*: obnixeram *B Schu Voll*

60.15.4   hinc *Tr*: hic *B Schu Voll*

60.16.5   intercipe *Peiper Bischoff*: interripe *B Schu Voll*

60.21b.3   haec noctis *Tr*: mentis *B*: et membra *Schu*: conventis *Voll*

60.23.3   omen *Tr*: omne *B Schu Voll*

60.25.1   amore . . . linit *Tr*: auroris . . . lenit *B*: furores . . . lenit *Schu Voll*

60.26.3   supplici *Tr*: suplicis *B Voll*: supplicis *Schu*

61.1a.2   Teieridum *B Voll*: Teiorum *Schu*

61.1a.4   verno *Tr*: in verno *B Schu Voll*

61.1b.2   me *Tr*: vita me *B Schu Voll*

61.1b.3   si decus *Tr*: sed decus hoc *B Schu*: sed eius hoc *Voll*

61.1d.3   vitae *Heraeus Voll*: vita *B Schu*

61.1d.4   alit spes *Voll*: alit et spes *B Schu*

           stabilis *Heraus*: habilis *B Schu Voll*

61.3.3   sibi *B Voll*: verbi *Schu*

61.6c.4   sic valent *B Voll*: sed squalent *Schu*

61.7.3   eo *Tr*: mea *B Schu Voll*

61.7.4   quo *Tr*: quam *B Schu Voll*

61.9b.1   istaec *Tr*: hec *B Schu Voll*

61.9b.3   non . . . fors *Voll*: num . . . sors *B Schu*

61.11b.5   vi rotundi *Voll*: vi iocundi *B Schu*

61.13b.4   alterare *Voll*: alterari *B*: tolerare *Schu*

62.1.12   pignora *B Voll Walsh*: pondera *Schu*

62.3.4   gaudio *Tr*: ipsum gaudio *B Schu Voll Walsh*

62.4.1   Orpheus *B Dronke Voll*: Morpheus *Schmeller Schu Walsh*

62.4.5   per se molendinorum *Tr*: molendinorum *B Schu Voll*: molendi-
           nariorum *Walsh*

62.5–6   *In B Schu Voll Walsh stanza 6 precedes 5.*

62.5.6   ne sic *Tr*: me *B*: ne *Schu Voll Walsh*

62.6   et gratior *Tr*: *omitted by B Schu Voll Walsh*

63.4a.6   hoc *Tr*: in hoc *B Schu Voll*

65.2a.3   Erythraeus *suggested by Schu*: Euricteus *B Schu Voll*

65.4a.1   Veneri *Tr*: veteri *B Schu Voll*

65.4b.1   veteri *Tr*: Veneri *B Schu Voll*

65.7b.1   opus ture *Tr*: onus mire *B Schu*: opus mire *Voll*

65.7b.2   meam *Tr*: eam *B Schu Voll*

65.10a.4   multiformi *Voll*: multiformis *B Schu*

67.1a.4   mundi quae *Meyer Wollin McDonough*: mundique *B Schu Voll Walsh*

68.5.1   beari spes, halitus *Tr*: beati spes alitur *B*: beati spes, halitus *Schu Walsh*: beat Tispes alitur *Voll*

70.4b.3   hoc meum *Voll*: que meum *B*: . . . meum *Schu*: sic mecum *Walsh*

70.5a.1   prae ceteris *Walsh*: sed ceteris *B Schu Voll*

71.6a.1   infelix *Bischoff Walsh*: felix *B Voll*: fidelis *Schu*

72.2a.7   amoris *McDonough*: amori *B Schu Voll Walsh*

72.2a.12   furoris *McDonough*: furori *B Schu Voll Walsh*

74.2.6   cuius omnis regio *Walsh suggested by Schu*: qui sublato bravio *B Voll*: *Schu has lacuna*

75.1.7–8   res est . . . ludere *Herkenrath Walsh*: *Schu has a lacuna*: *no lacuna B Voll*

75.3.3   amores *Walsh*: amoris *B Schu Voll*

75.3.4   venentur retia *Peiper Walsh*: venantur *ocia B*: venantur retia *Schu*: venari otia *Voll*

76.2.4   aestimabam plurimae *Sedgwick Bischoff Walsh*: aestimabant plurimi *B Schu Voll*

76.3.3   secum dans *Bischoff Walsh suggested by Schu*: secundans *B Schu Voll*

76.8.1   sauciorum *Sedgwick Walsh*: secretorum *B Schu Voll*

76.12.2   sodes *Strecker*: sedes *B Schu*: sedis *Voll*: cedes *Walsh*

76.19.3   quasi *Bischoff Walsh*: quamvis *B Schu*: tamquam *Voll*

76.21.2   ivi *Tr*: ubi *B Schu*: fui *suggested by Bischoff*: sibi *Voll*: vixi *Walsh*

76.21.3   recedens *Voll Walsh suggested by Schu*: residens *B Schu*

76.21.4   vestibus *Peiper Voll Walsh*: *omitted by B*: *Schu indicates lacuna* pauperatus *Walsh suggested by Schu Bischoff*: preparatus *B Schu Voll*

77.5.3   laeta *B Voll*: sata *Schu*: laete *Dronke*

77.5.4   morarer ita *Herkenrath Schu*: morararet icta *B Voll Dronke*

77.6.4   fidens in *Tr*: semper in *B Voll*: lapsus in *Schu*: sentiens *Walsh*

77.13.3   excedit *Strecker Voll Walsh*: extendit *B*: exscendit *Schu*

77.18.2   Venus *Walsh suggested by Schu*: *omitted by B Voll*: vita *Schu*

77.20.3   desinas *B Bischoff Voll Walsh*: destinas *Schu*

77.22.3   nunc si *Dronke Walsh*: si *B Voll*: dicens *Schu*

77.31.2   meum *Schmeller Voll*: mecum *B Schu*

78.1.1   redit *Patzig Walsh*: rediit *B Schu Voll*

79.6.3 saevi *Spanke Bischoff Walsh*: suevi *B Schu Voll*

81.3.2 frigus *Meyer Bischoff Voll Walsh*: prius *B Schu*

81.4.4 lasciva *B Schmeller Voll*: lascivit *Meyer Schu*

82.1.3 *B has* instantia *Bischoff Walsh or* inflantia *Schu or* infantia *Voll*
instantia *Bischoff Walsh*: *B unclear*: inflantia *Schu*: infantia *Voll*

82.Ref.2 amoris solamine *Walsh*: amor insolabile *B Schu*

82.6.1 curtibus *Bischoff*: cordibus *B Voll*: cortinis *Schu*: cursibus *Walsh*

83.5.7 gracili *Schmeller McDonough*: gracilis *B Schu Voll*

84.4.14–15 ut cardinem decardinem *Tr*: ut cardinem determinem *Voll Schu, and (without* ut) *B*: cardinem, ut determinem *Walsh*

85.3.2 virginum dant agmina *Spanke*: virgines dant agmina *B Voll*: virgines dant gemina *Schu*

85.4.1 viderem *Spanke*: viterem *E*: vitarem *Schu*. *See Notes to the Translation.*

87.1.6 castus est sed tamen cupidus *Tr*: caecus caret pudicitia *B Schu Voll*

87.3.1 rigidus et gelidus *Tr*: frigidus et calidus *B Schu*: frigidus nec calidus *Voll*

87.3.6 tenes *Tr*: tenet *B Schu Voll*

87.3.7 si *Tr*: sic *B Schu Voll*

87.4.3 iuvenis *Voll*: iuvenes *B Schu*

87.4.5 qua *Schmeller*: q; *B*: quae *Schu Voll*

87.4.6 gratia *Patzig*: gaudio *B Voll*: gloria *Schu*

87.4.9 cordis in *B Voll*: cardinis *Schu*

87.5.3 turbidus *Voll*: tu curtis *B*: truculens *Schu*

88a.4.3 valeat *B Voll*: maneat *Schu Walsh*

89.1a.5 soni *Patzig*: toni *Voll*: solis *B Schu*

89.1b.6 coornatur *Tr*: coronatur *B Schu*: coram datur *Voll*

89.3c.1 raptores *Herkenrath*: pastores *B Schu Voll*

89.4a.1 pactis *Schmeller*: pastus *B Schu Voll*

89.4a.2 pastorum *Herkenrath*: polorum *B Schu Voll*

89.4a.5 contractis *Tr*: atractis *B Voll*: attractis *Schu*

89.6a.3 solum tu cura *Tr*: *B has* solum cura *with a small lacuna between the words*: solum *and lacuna Schu*: solum cura *Voll*

89.6a.4 laborem femine *Voll*: labor femine *B*: *Schu has a lacuna*

89.6c.2 sociis Voll: socus *B Schu*: secus *Bischoff*

91.2.3 vos *Tr*: nos *Schu*: *stanza omitted by* B *Voll. See Notes to the Translation.*

91.9.1 dic *Tr*: hic *Schu*: huc *B Voll*

92.11.1 iste *B Voll*: ille *Schu Walsh*

92.30.4 tegit *B Voll*: terit *Schu Walsh*

92.47.4 Neptunus *B Voll*: Nereus *Schu Walsh*

92.53.1 radiabat *B Voll. Walsh*: faciebat *Schu*

92.53.4 quasi *Schu Walsh*: velut *B Voll*

93.1.1 insulsa *Tr*: insula *B Schu Voll Walsh*

93.1.3 Veneris *Herkenrath Walsh*: virginis *B Schu Voll*

94.*Ref*.3 dat chevaleria *Tr*: da chevaleria *Bartsch*: da hizevaleria *B*: hahi zivaleria! *Schu*: da—hi!—zevaleria *Voll*

95.5.2 terra Britannia *Raby Walsh*: Briciavvia *B Schu Voll*

95.5.3 per me *Peiper Voll Walsh*: perimit *B Schu*

95.5.4 sumat *Schmeller Voll Walsh*: sumant *B Schu*

97.2.3 ostium *Schmeller*: hostium *B Voll*: hospitium *Schu*

97.6.1 Lycoridis *suggested by Schu*: Liocardadis *B Schu Voll*

97.6.2 ostenditur *Peiper*: monstratur *B Schu Voll*

97.8.1 Apollonio natam quaerente *Voll*: Apollonio natam querentem *B*: Apollonius natam quaerens querentem *Schu*

97.8.8 filia *Bischoff*: sileam *suggested by Schu*: sileant *B Schu Voll*

97.9.2 tum cito vera *Voll*: vera *B Schu*

97.9.3 Tharsia lyrante *Voll*: Tharsiam lyrantem *B Schu*

98.2.6 simplex *Schmeller*: supplex *B Schu Voll*

98.5.4 pacti fidei *Tr*: pacti rei *B Schu Voll*

98.5.5 detraherem *Schmeller Bischoff Voll*: retraherem *B Schu*

98.5.15 quam regina se novis *Voll*: *omitted by* B: *Schu indicates lacuna*

99.8.3 miserae, Mors, haec *Tr*: miseram mors est *B*: miseram lucem *Schu*: misera mors est *Voll*

99.9.1 Heu, Dido *Peiper*: Dido *B Schu Voll*

99.12.3 tyrannica *Tr*: yranica *B^{pc}*: hyrcanica *Voll*: ironica *Peiper Schu*

99a.1 urit *Wollin*: armat *B Schu Voll*

99a.2 Pergama *Wollin*: menia *B Schu Voll*

99b.2 *See Notes to the Translation.*

100.2b.1 quid *B (later hand)*, *Schmeller*, *Voll*: qui *B Schu*

100.3.1 and 2 ai *Tr*: hai *B Voll*: achi *Schu*

101.17   pateris iam *B Voll*: Paridem modo *Schu*

102.12.2   machina claustra forat, urbem flamma vorat *Tr*: ignis ligna vorat. machina saxa forat *B Voll*: urbem flamma vorat, machina claustra forat *Schu*

102.21.1   hinc *B Voll*: huc. *Schu*

102.21.2   lira *B*: lyra *Schu*: pira *Voll*

Notes to the Translation

1

Rhythmical pattern: 6x(7pp+4x6p)

The theme is the corrupting power of money, especially when it comes to securing advancement within the church and winning lawsuits.

1.2	The Latin could also mean "makes an impious man pious."
1.4	Money can buy professional advice or, possibly, money is a substitute for advice.
2.2	*Confusio* means both "confusion" and "shame," "disgrace."
4.7	The clergy *(clericis)* served in a wide variety of clerical positions, assisting and advising kings and members of the nobility, as well as holding public office as judges.
5.1	Compare Luke 6:38, "Date, et dabitur vobis" (Give and it shall be given unto you).
5.2	*auctoritas:* used of a quotation from an authoritative source, such as the Bible or a classical author.
5.9	The curious phrase "sancta dat" probably echoes Acts 13:34, "dabo vobis sancta David," which the New English Bible translates as "I will give you the holy promises made to David."
6.4	Codrus was a poor man who lost everything in a fire (Juvenal, *Satires* 3.203–11). He came to symbolize any very poor man; compare CB 19.5.8.
6.5–6	The poet is engaging in wordplay with *foedus* (pact) and *defoedare* (defile).
6.7–10	"Ablative" etymologically suggests taking away, while "dative" suggests giving; so the "ablatival men" are the judges who accept bribes and the "datival men" are those who bribe. "Genitive" suggests anything to do with generation, and here we should understand "acts" *(actus)* rather than "men"; see Frantzen in Van Poppen and Frantzen, "Der Genitivus," 181. On the punning use of grammatical terms, a popular feature of Latin poetry in the twelfth century, see Ziolkowski, *Alan of Lille's Grammar of Sex.*

2

Meter: Dactylic hexameters

A dialogue on the theme of Horace, *Epistles* 1.2.56: "Semper avarus eget" (The avaricious man is never satisfied).

3

Rhythmical pattern: 3x(7pp+6p); *Ref.* 6p+7pp+6p
Author: Walter of Châtillon
Date: ca. 1162

A lament for the moral decline of the world. Stanzas 2 and 3 focus on the growth of avarice and the decline of liberality, while stanza 4 deals with the corrosive effect of cupidity on trust; stanza 5 returns to a general condemnation of these tendencies.

3.1   Medieval students had to learn Latin as a foreign language much as students do today by learning the forms of the verbs, nouns, and so on—largely by repetition. Here we have "I give, you give, I gave, to give." Compare the opening of 172.

4.1   *Cupido* denotes strong desire in all its forms, including avarice, gluttony, and lust and so, unlike "avarice," looks forward to the theme of this stanza as well as backward.

4.5–6   Though many medieval readers viewed Dido sympathetically, she was also seen as the embodiment of *libido* (lust); see Desmond, *Reading Dido,* 84.

4

Rhythmical pattern: 2x(8pp+7p), 2x(9p+8pp)

Like the Hebrew captives in Babylon, the Church is depressed. Stained by the world's sins, it has resorted to simony. Avarice is the root of all the world's wrongdoing.

Stanza 1 is inspired by Psalms 136(137):1–2.

1.2   *Vox exultationis* (voice of joy), a recurring phrase in the Psalms, as at 41(42):5, must refer to the music normally produced by the instruments. Here, poetically, it assumes the role of the Hebrews. Alternatively, we could posit an error and read *vox exulationis*, which would link the phrase to the protesting Hebrews themselves.

1.4   Jerome tells us that Babylon means *confusio:* see his *Interpr. Nom. Hebr.* CCSL 72, p. 159 (Lagarde, 80, 15) or PL 23.775.

5

Meter: Correlative Leonine hexameters (see below)

The unusual layout of this poem reflects its perversely ingenious construction. It comprises eighteen pairs of hexameters, with each hexameter comprising five words. Since the last word always rhymes with the second word (i.e., the caesura), the hexameters are Leonine hexameters. While reading horizontally produces satisfactory meter, it produces little or no sense. Sense is obtained by reading each word in the top line with the corresponding word in the line below.

After a few general maxims, the poem moves on to the general decline in morals and then (stanzas 5–16) focuses on the array of problems plaguing an unnamed abbey and its surrounding community, with blame being placed on the current abbot. Praise seems reserved for the previous abbot, Gerald, for whom a place in paradise is requested.

This poem survives in at least eleven other manuscripts. Not surprisingly, the name in line 17 varies (Gerard and Bernard are also found). It is unclear to us today whether the name refers to the abbot mentioned in 5 or an earlier abbot. *B* and three other manuscripts have a somewhat different version of line 17, which includes no name: "He studied under learned men, was a model of virtue; he established rules, ruled like a bishop, and accumulated honors"; for Latin text, see H-S-B 1.1.7.

6

Rhythmical pattern: 4x8pp

The poet laments that the decline in learning has turned the world upside down. Respect for learning has changed to contempt. The young behave as if they have the wisdom of their elders. Over-reaching in human behavior is likened to absurd behavior in the animal world. Old men and supposedly respectable young women exhibit the lack of sexual constraint commonly associated with young men. Virtue in short is turning into vice. People need to prepare themselves for Judgment Day.

The poem belongs to the "World Upside-down" topos (see Curtius, *European Literature,* 94–98), which leads into a list of *adynata* (impossible things).

6.1   On Gregory and other proper names, see the Index of Proper Names (vol. 2 of the present work, DOML 49).

6.4   A small Greek coin, a sixth part of a drachma.

8.1–2   At Luke 10:39–40 Mary sits and listens to Jesus, while Martha is distracted by her many tasks.

12.3   Compare Matthew 7:21.

For a more extended discussion of this poem, see Bisanti, *Poesia d'Amore,* 29–39.

7

Meter: Dactylic hexameters

A collection of quasi-proverbial comments about nobility. Their inclusion here was probably inspired by the apparent breakdown in normal behavior patterns described in poem 6.

8

Rhythmical pattern: 4x8p, 3x7pp, 6p
Author: Walter of Châtillon

This attack on the failings of the higher echelons of the Church is a minor masterpiece.

1.5   Bede interprets the "daughters of Zion" (Song of Songs 3:11) as the souls of the faithful in heaven; see Bede, *Opera Exegetica,* CCSL 119b, p. 241, lines 435–36, or PL 91.1127).

2.2   A benefice is an ecclesiastical living or prebend.

2.5–7   For Simon and Gehazi, see the Index of Proper Names.

3.3   The bride of Christ is the Church.

3.5   For *altaria* as altar fees, see *DMLBS,* "altare" 2d.

4.3   The Syrian is Naaman, with whose leprosy Elisha cursed Gehazi.

4.7–8 On Christian bodies as temples for the Holy Spirit, see I Corinthians 6:19.

5.5–6 The leech's two daughters (Proverbs 30:15) were identified allegorically in the *Glossa Ordinaria* as avarice and lust (PL 113.1113).

6.1 Ecclesiastes 12:1.

6.7–8.7.8 Juvenal 14.109.

7.7 Parodic allusion to the introit for the first Sunday after Easter: "quasi modo geniti infantes . . . ," which is closely modeled on 1 Peter 2:2.

8.3 *Epicurus* is here a disparaging term, referring not to the ancient philosopher himself but to any contemporary, who might be termed a *gourmand,* or glutton, for this was the view generally held of the philosopher in the medieval world.

9

Rhythmical pattern: 6x8pp

Despite the scriptural passages condemning simony, the practice still flourishes.

5 On Abraham and Ephron/Ephran, see "Ephron" in the Index of Proper Names.

10

Rhythmical pattern: 4x8p (stanza 1, 2x8p)

This poem is largely about the prevalence of simony among the Church hierarchy. Unusual is the prominence of Simon himself, whose role as a magician perhaps allows him to be omnipresent, nudging individuals into simoniacal behavior; see further on him in the Index of Proper Names.

1.2 Compare Isaiah 40:3 and Matthew 3:3.

2.3 By *vita* here, the poet means eternal life.

3.2 Christ is quite frequently referred to as *Deus* in Medieval Latin; see examples cited in *DMLBS,* "deus" 3a.

3.3 Compare Mark 8:34.

5.1 The prelates' behavior makes them ineligible for eternal life.

6.4   Readers would be expected to supply *latronum* (of thieves) after *spelunca* from the famous passage about Christ and the money changers described at Matthew 21:13, Mark 11:17, and Luke 19:46. (The next line confirms this.)

8.3   On the king of the south, see Daniel 11:5–6.

8.4   That is to say, money opens all doors.

10.2–3   Christ tells how the guest unsuitably attired for the king's son's wedding is brusquely bound hand and foot and thrown out into the darkness (Matthew 22.11–14). At Revelation 2.10 Christ promises: "Be faithful till death and I will give you the crown of life." Though originally a *diadema* meant a headband, by the Middle Ages it was understood as a crown.

12.2   *iusum* is a Vulgar Latin form of *deorsum* (down, downward) that came into use in Late Antiquity. It survives as the Italian *giù*.

11

Meter: Leonine hexameters

This collection of adages about the power of money to influence or even control most aspects of human society is remarkable for the fact that the adages are all specifically about *nummus* (*pecunia* is difficult to fit into a hexameter) and that the great majority have some form of *nummus* in first or second place. The collection is also remarkable for its popularity; it is found in fifty-five manuscripts besides *B* itself.

5   *Black priors:* Benedictine priors.

21–22   The snow-white lamb is the innocent victim. Money, however, supports the opposing party, the black lamb.

30   Pepper, like all imported spices, was very expensive at this time.

12

Rhythmical pattern: 4x(6pp+6pp), 6pp, 6pp, 6pp
Only two rhymes (*-ium* and *–io*) are used throughout.

The theme of this poem is very unusual. It argues that when detractors malign someone, they and the target of their attack become emotionally closer. The poet compares their relationship to that of lovers after a quarrel, which ultimately has the effect of enhancing their longing for one another. So it is that the poet gathers "grapes" from his detractors' "thorns" (Matthew 7:16).

2.2   The perfect *fulsit* is used in the timeless aoristic or gnomic sense to express a general truth.

13

Meter: (1–3, 5) Dactylic hexameters; (4) Elegiac couplet

This collection of observations about envy was no doubt prompted by the preceding poem, for detractors were traditionally thought to be motivated by envy. With 2 compare Horace, *Epistles,* 1.2.57–60, and with 5, *Dicta Catonis,* 2.13.1.

2.2   Sicily is often associated with oppressive rulers in ancient history. Dionysius I (ca. 432–367 BCE), tyrant of the city Syracuse there, though a great soldier and a man of culture, was the archetypal tyrant of the Greek world.

14

Rhythmical pattern: 8x(4pp+6pp)
Author: Philip the Chancellor

The first in a group of poems about the fickleness of Fortune and how she creates instability.

Fortune is instrumental in helping some reach the top of her revolving wheel, only to be brought down when they fall out of favor, and others take their place. So it was with Troy, Greece, and Rome, and Darius and Pompey. Fortune's favor would be most welcome if only it were lasting.

1.13–14   Psalms 112(113):7.
1.15–16   Juvenal 7.197: "Si Fortuna volet, fies de rhetore consul" (If Fortune wants, she will turn you from a teacher into a consul).
3.7–8   Ancient literature is full of advice about choosing a middle course. Here Philip may be recalling the Sun's advice to Phaethon: "medio tutissimus ibis" (Ovid, *Metamorphoses* 2.137).

4.7–8   By the twelfth century, though the greatness of Rome's name still remained as a distant vision, the infighting of its inhabitants and the corruption of the Roman Curia had greatly tarnished the image of contemporary Romans.

15

Rhythmical pattern: 6x(6pp+6pp)
Author: Philip the Chancellor

This rather difficult poem praises *stabilitas* (steadfastness). While not ostensibly about Fortune, which is not mentioned, the theme is relevant, for *stabilitas* is man's moral protection against the destabilizing effects of Fortune documented in poem 14.

To be steadfast we need to avoid making commitments to take actions that we may later feel to be immoral (stanza 1). This means that we need to reflect carefully *beforehand* (stanza 2). The beginning steps are therefore of vital importance. However, the follow-through is even more important (stanza 3). This is where the lack of steadfastness proves disastrous (stanza 4). Steadfastness, while unwavering in itself, involves flexibility, which may include changing location without altering one's goal.

1.1–2   The opening lines constitute a deliberate twist on the famous quote from Horace (*Epistles* 1.11.27) that points out that moving to a more attractive location does not necessarily improve one's sense of well-being.

1.7–12   This unusually difficult passage reflects Philip's thoughts on *synderesis* (later discussed at length in his *Summa de bono*), a scholastic term for what is more generally known as conscience.

1.8   For *consilium* used in a legal context in the sense of instigation or abetment, see *DMLBS,* "consilium" 2a.

3.1–2   Horace, *Epistles* 1.2.40.

16

Rhythmical pattern: 4x(7pp+6p) but sometimes with extra syllables

This poem describes the revolving nature of the wheel of Fortune from the point of view of one who has just suffered a fall from the top.

1.3–4   See *Dicta Catonis* 2.26.2 for this depiction of *Occasio* (Chance, Fortune). Fortune is beautiful as she approaches, but once she has passed, we see that the back view is much less attractive. The hairiness/baldness aspect is also important, for one can catch her hair as she comes, but there is nothing to grasp when she leaves. For the illustration of the wheel of Fortune in the *Carmina Burana* manuscript, see the facsimile edition by Berhard Bischoff, fol. 1r; Vollman, *Carmina Burana,* plate 1; or Jones, *Carmina Burana: Four Essays,* plate 1 (b&w). The illustration is described below in notes to CB 18a.

3.4   Bojanga's *conspice* gives us the needed rhyme.

17

Author: Possibly Philip the Chancellor
Rhythmical pattern: 4x(4p+4p+7pp)

The speaker in this poem has experienced a sharp decline in his fortune similar to that described in poem 16. While the capricious nature of Fortune often gives the impression that she is playing a game, the recurrence of *ludus* (game) in both stanzas 1 and 2, together with the reference to his bare back, suggests that the speaker's sudden misfortune is due to his gambling; see the recurring theme in the drinking and gambling poems below (CB 187–226).

    This poem provides the text for the opening and closing chorus of Carl Orff's *Carmina Burana* cantata.

2.10   *per ludum:* this can refer either to the cruel sport of Fortune or to the gaming at which the speaker lost his clothes and should probably be understood both ways.

3.4–5   For *affectus* in the sense of *effectus* (success), see *MW,* "affectus" 2.

3.4–6   The speaker has been reduced to a level no better than that of a serf. The service is probably owed to a human master rather than to Fortune herself, as Vollmann's translation implies.

3.9   Literally, "make a strike on the strings."

3.10   There is a play here with *sors,* which is used throughout this poem as a synonym for *Fortuna.* However, since *Sors/Fortuna* is

476

the subject of the sentence, *per sortem* can hardly mean "by Fortune" and so must be used in the idiomatic sense of the phrase "randomly" or "arbitrarily."

18

Meter: (1–3) Elegiac distichs; (4, 5) Dactylic hexameters

Proverbial observations about Fortune.

2   = Ovid, *Tristia* 5.8.15–18.

18a

This clever Leonine hexameter, added by a later hand, succinctly sums up the message of the famous illustration of the wheel of Fortune, which graces the first folio of *B* in the codex as it is bound today: a wooden wheel with a crowned *Fortuna* seated inside it, holding an opened scroll in each hand. *Regnabo* is found beside the climbing figure on the left, *regno* beside the crowned king seated at the top, *regnavi* beside the falling king at the right, and *sum sine regno* near the figure lying under the wheel. (Since the first *regno* is a verb and the second a noun, they form a permissible rhyme.)

19

Rhythmical pattern: 3x(7pp+6p), 5pp, 7pp+6p
Author: Walter of Châtillon (ca. 1160–1180)

1.3–5   Horace maintains that virtue is the midpoint between opposing vices (*Epistles* 1.18.9).

2.2   *Dicta Catonis,* prologue 6.

5.5   Proverbs 13:7, "One pretends to be rich, although he has nothing." Codrus (sometimes spelled Cordus) is a poor poet who loses what little he had in a fire (Juvenal, *Satires* 3.203–9).

The humor here lies in the fact that the advice offered by Walter to a man who shows himself warm and friendly to everyone, namely, to be more discriminating, is traditionally offered to a wealthy patron or potential patron, for it is revealed in the last line that the man in question is penniless and, presumably, a beggar, but in Walter's eyes rich in everything that matters.

20

Meter: (1, 4) Dactylic hexameters; (2) Leonine hexameters; (3) Two dactylic hexameters followed by a pentameter
Authors: (3.1) Horace, *Epistles* 1.18.9; (3.2–3) Ovid, *Remedia Amoris* 323–24; (4.1) Horace, *Satires* 1.2.24, slightly changed; (4.2) Juvenal, *Satires* 14.109

1.1   Est modus in verbis = Horace, *Satires* 1.106.
1.3–4   *do, das* and *teneo, tenui.* These and similar reminiscences of the classroom, which crop up quite frequently in Medieval Latin poetry, remind us that for all these medieval poets Latin was a foreign language that had to be learned in school.

The proverbial observations reflect themes in poem 19.

21

Rhythmical pattern: 7p, 7pp, 8pp, 2x(7p+7p+8pp), 4pp, 4pp, 3p, 8pp, 4pp, 4pp, 8pp, 7p
Author: Philip the Chancellor

Christ forgives us our sins. Adam's sin passed sinfulness on to all mankind. We are not necessarily punished here on earth for our sins. Punishment may be postponed till Judgment Day. The prelates are to blame. Their pursuit of money sets an evil example for everyone.

1.2   John 14:6.
1.17   John 5:8.
2.8–12 There is a difficulty here with *translato,* which agrees with *palato,* whereas we would expect it to agree with the venom *(fel).* However, besides meaning "palate," the Latin word can mean more generally "taste." If we think of taste in more physical terms, such as saliva, then the process whereby the poison could be passed on to succeeding generations becomes more understandable.

3.2   Isaiah 11:2.

3.5   *castitatis* is a genitive of description tantamount to an adjective modifying *timor.* On pious fear see Augustine, *City of God* 14.9.

3.6   The two manuscripts that have this stanza read *reverentur.*

3.8   Compare 1 Corinthians 5:7, "Expurgate vetus fermentum" (Get rid of the old leaven); *vetustatis* is a genitive of quality or description, equivalent to an adjective; see Blaise, *Manuel,* §85.

3.9   The bridegroom is Christ. Compare Matthew 25:1–13.

4.2   Christ is the judge on Judgment Day.

4.5–6   Compare Matthew 7:16.

4.13–15 Matthew 3:12.

5.1   Psalms 15(16):6, "Lineae ceciderunt mihi in praeclaris" (the lines have fallen for me in pleasant places). The lines, here rendered by *funiculus,* are used by surveyors to demarcate plots of land. By extension, they refer to the lot that human beings inherit, as children of God. Augustine interprets this passage allegorically: "Just as the possession of priests and Levites is God, so it has happened that the boundaries of what I possess lie in your glory." *Enarratio in Psalmos,* CCSL 38, p. 91.

5.4   "This sea" alludes, by a familiar allegory, to our life here on earth with all its imperfections: so Hugh of St. Victor, *Adnotatiunculae in Threnos:* "Quid per mare, nisi vita saecularis accipitur" (What is understood by "the sea" if not our life on earth?) (PL 175.292).

5.13   Luke 16:13, "non potestis servire Deo et Mammonae" (You cannot serve God and Mammon).

22

Rhythmical pattern: Rhyming short lines in no discernible pattern
Author: Philip the Chancellor
Note: CB 21, 26, 27, are attributed to Philip in other manuscripts. For the attribution of CB 22, 23, 29, and 33–36 to Philip, see Traill, "Cluster of Poems."

Be an active Christian: preach the faith, do good works, avoid harmful pleasures, and think of the joys of your life in heaven.

11–12   Leviticus 5:8. The dove in this passage was interpreted allegori-
        cally to mean preaching, while the act of turning the dove's
        head back to its wings was thought to mean turning preaching
        into action; see H-S-B 2.1.36.

43   "Homeland" is heaven.

23

Rhythmical pattern: 9x8pp
Author: Philip the Chancellor

This poem offers advice to aspiring teachers. They need to think about,
and live by, what they teach. If they are to become priests, they should not
be thinking about money or any form of vice. If they intend to be monks,
they need to be on their guard against temptation. The last line of each
stanza is taken from a well-known hymn.

1.3   Presumably, by the "letter" Philip means the literal interpreta-
        tion of the Bible, which was a prerequisite for understanding
        the allegorical (or figural) interpretation.

1.9   The first line of a hymn on the Blessed Martyrs often attributed
        to Saint Ambrose (*AH* 50, p. 19).

2.6   For *coniunx* as "companion," see L&S, "coniunx" 2.

2.9   The first line of stanza 2 of *(A)eterni Christi munera;* see note 1.9.

3.7   The story of Samson and Delilah is told in Judges 16. Though
        the Vulgate does not call Delilah a prostitute, commenta-
        tors such as Rupert of Deutz did not hesitate to do so (PL
        167.1043A): compare also CB 31.3.9–10 below.

3.8   *ut = utinam* and expresses a wish.

3.9   This is the opening line of a hymn in honor of a martyr; see *AH*
        51, p. 130.

24

Rhythmical pattern: 4p+4p+7pp
Usually the first two segments rhyme and the final letter in each line is *a*.

The poem warns that since the possessions and pleasures of this world are not lasting, we need to shun the desires of the flesh and focus on the joys of the hereafter.

6   With *fugit, transit velut, umbra,* compare Job 14:2, "fugit velut umbra."

11   With *carnis desideria,* compare Galatians 5:16, "desiderium carnis."

25

Meter: Hexameters, of which 1, 2, 4, and 5 have Leonine rhymes
Authors: (1) Poeta Astensis, *Novus Avianus,* 5.35; (3) Ovid, *Epistulae ex Ponto* 4.3.35; (6–7) Horace, *Epistles* 2.1.262–63

B's reading in line 3 (followed by Schumann and Vollmann) is *omina.* However, I have adopted the reading of most editors of the *Epistulae ex Ponto: omnia.*

26

Rhythmical pattern: Descort
Author: Philip the Chancellor

Mankind, why provoke God with your sinful behavior? Better to repent and be prepared when the bridegroom (Christ) comes.

1.11–13   On the fig tree, see Mark 11:13–20.

3   Here Philip has combined the stories of the inappropriately dressed wedding guest (Matthew 22:11–13) and the foolish virgins who did not take oil for their lamps when they went to see the bride and groom (Matthew 25:1–13).

4.3   Compare Apocalypse 3:20.

27

Rhythmical pattern: Descort
Author: Philip the Chancellor

It is good to put your trust in the Lord. Avoid the pursuit of financial gain and seek forgiveness for your sins. Otherwise, on Judgment Day you may be sent to hell. Blessed are those who avoid sin and worldly affairs.

1.1–4	Compare Psalms 117(118):8–9.
1.18–19	Compare Genesis 3:19.
2.7–8	Compare Matthew 8:12, 13:42, 4:30.
2.17–20	Matthew 3:12.
3.11	Matthew 5:6.
3.16	For the story of the talents, see Matthew 25:14–30.

28

Meter: Leonine hexameters, often with one-syllable rhymes
Author: Otloh of Saint Emmeran (11th century)

The lines are arranged alphabetically by first word, and it is for this reason that *B*'s *Risus* has been changed to *Nisus*.

3	We should focus on ensuring an eternal life.
4	Otloh is thinking of Christ's words at Matthew 5:28.

29

Rhythmical pattern: 6x7pp, 2x4pp, 6x7pp
Author: Philip the Chancellor

Philip chastises Pamphilus (whose name means "Promiscuous Lover") for angering God by wallowing in the mire of lust. Sex can become an addiction. So when a woman tries to seduce him, the safest course is to flee.

1.1	Compare Psalms 39(40):3.
1.4	Anyone who is not preparing himself for eternal life is wasting time.
2.12–14	On the Hydra and Antaeus (the son of Earth), see "Hercules" in the Index of Proper Names.
3.7	The Egyptian woman refers to Potiphar's wife, who tried to seduce Joseph; Joseph, however, broke away from her, leaving his cloak *(pallium)* in her hands (Genesis 39:2).

30

Rhythmical pattern: 7pp, 3pp+4pp, 7pp, 6p, 3pp+4pp, 6p
Author: Probably Philip the Chancellor

When I was young I could do whatever my heart desired. "Try anything" was my watchword. Now I want to make recompense for my sins.

31

Rhythmical pattern: 2x(5pp+3p+4pp), 2x(7pp+6p)
Author: Probably Philip the Chancellor

As I approach the evening of my life, I wish to make amends for the sins of my youth. I need to face the fact: I will reap what I sowed. I did not come to a fork in the road, for I neither abjured Venus nor did I sleep with others' wives. "Chase after prostitutes" was the advice I followed. It was Scripture, not the bean pods, that put me on the right track. The story of Dinah warns that a well-established vice is hard to shake. If I go back to my bad old ways, I will deserve death. I am changing my ways, leaving the byways of Venus for the Royal Road. If I have all the attributes of the heroes of old, but do not give up prostitutes, it means nothing. So I ask for God's grace to pardon me, a sinner.

2.7   *falso . . . opere* (falsely): on the analogy of *magno opere (magnopere)*.
3.1–10   The fork in the road is the "crossroads" where Hercules has to make his choice. Reference to the *bivium,* where the young man has to choose between good and evil, became a cliché of medieval biography. The last two lines constitute an ironic Christian recasting (with Delilah as prostitute) of Cato's comment when he saw a young man emerging from a brothel: "Bravo! As soon as vile lust inflates the veins, it is right for young men to come down here, and not screw other men's wives" (Horace, *Satires* 1.2.31–35). Philip's remark that he did not *steal a wife's* embraces shows he is thinking of this passage. On Delilah as a prostitute, see note above on 23.3.7.
3.10   *Sexus,* like "manhood," can denote gender or the genitals; see *DMLBS,* "sexus" 1a and d. Both meanings seem intended here.

4.1   The bean pods were the pigs' food that the Prodigal Son, in re-
duced circumstances, would have been glad to eat had they
been offered to him (Luke 15:16).

5.1–10   When Dinah, Jacob's daughter, went out to chat with some
women in Canaan, Shechem, the local prince, saw her and
raped her (Genesis 34:1–2). Medieval exegesis took a dim view
of Dinah; she was seen as allegorically representing those souls
that tend to wander where they should not, attracted by worldly
glitter; see, for instance, Peter of Riga, *Aurora,* Part 1: Genesis
1023–24.

6.4–2   "A fool who repeats his folly is like a dog returning to its vomit"
(Proverbs 26:11).

7.7   On his journey to the promised land Jacob asks permission to
pass through the land of the Amorites, promising to keep to
the royal road without turning to the left or the right (Num-
bers 21:22).

8.4   The literal translation "give me Cicero" needs to be expanded to
"give me the eloquence of Cicero" to harmonize with the other
examples.

9.2, 9.8   The two instances of *rei* constitute legitimate rhymes, as the
first is the genitive of *res, rei* f. thing and the second the genitive
of *reus, rei* m. sinner (in apposition to *mei*).

For more detailed discussion of this poem, see also Traill, "Biblical Exege-
sis," 335–41.

32

Meter: Leonine hexameters
Author: (1) Unknown; (2) Otloh of Saint Emmeran

1   Various attempts to explain human suffering.
2   The power of God's grace.

33

Rhythmical pattern: 5x8pp, 4pp, 4x8pp
Author: Philip the Chancellor

484

Philip advises a recently appointed bishop to feel shame for his youthful foolishness only if he fails to grow out of it, and urges him to develop the qualities expected of a bishop. He should protect the poor, be generous, and punish the wicked. He should not take bribes or misuse church funds, and he should be judicious in the company he keeps. He should be truthful and accept sound advice with a good grace and be modest and abstain from evil.

1.1	Compare Horace *Epistles* 1.16.36.
2.4	On the sterile tree, see Matthew 3:10.
6.1	Isaiah 38:1.
7.1–2	I Thessalonians 5.22.

34

Rhythmical pattern: Descort
Author: Philip the Chancellor

In this general lament about corruption in the Church, Philip argues that the leadership's sickness affects the lower orders to the general detriment of society. The devil has taken his seat at the very center. God needs to come with his avenging sword!

1.1	Zion is often used allegorically for the Church.
2.5	Matthew 24:12.
2.8–12	Legally appointed guardians of children whose fathers had died could, and not infrequently did, abuse their powers and essentially strip the child of his inheritance; compare Juvenal, *Satires* 1.46–47. Though there is no word for guardian (or heir) in the Latin, their relationship is revealed by the words *pupillus* (a boy who is an orphan or under the care of a guardian) and *impio*, which implies that a man's actions violate a duty he has.
3.3	Matthew 21:13, "You are making it (the temple) a den of thieves" (*speluncam latronum*).
3.6	*princeps Babylonis*, the Devil.
3.12–13	Compare Matthew 21:12.

35

Rhythmical pattern: 9x7pp
Author: Philip the Chancellor?

The poet muses on the changing status of individuals as they make their way through life. He urges his fellow bishops not to take him as a model but to keep their passions under control.

1.1–2   *Magnus* (big) and *parvus* (small) have irregular comparative and superlative forms. Here the poet uses them to illustrate the vicissitudes and anomalies of life as they affect the individual.

3.1–2   Though the poet could here be addressing four nonidentical groups, it seems best to assume with Vollmann that he is addressing a single group, his fellow bishops. There are no overwhelming reasons for attributing this poem to Philip the Chancellor, though its subject matter (advice to bishops), was one of his favorite topics. Since the poet here seems to assume the persona of a bishop who repents his misuse of the office and we know that Philip was never a bishop, there are reasons to doubt the attribution. However, elsewhere Philip speaks in the persona of the Virgin Mary, and in several poems in the persona of Christ; so the objection is not conclusive.

3.6   For the foolish virgins who failed to bring oil for their lamps, see Matthew 25:1–13.

36

Rhythmical pattern: Sequence
Author: Philip the Chancellor

Philip tells office bearers in the Church that no one should be refused confession, but reminds them that confession without contrition is ineffective (stanzas 1a–b). He counsels them if they are seeking higher office to pursue virtue by fostering the innocent, checking wrongful behavior, judging fairly, supporting the needy, and exalting the humble (2a–b). They should remember that more is expected from those with more responsibility and to beware of setting a bad example to their flocks. However, if they slip up and sin, they should not despair, for no one should be denied the chance to repent (3a–b).

37

Rhythmical pattern: 3x(8pp+7p), 7p, 8pp, 7p
Author: Philip the Chancellor?
Date: 1187–1188

This poem comments on a crisis that affected the Grandmont order of monks in the period 1185 to 1188. The order comprised choir monks, who devoted themselves entirely to spiritual matters, and lay brothers, who worked in the fields and controlled the finances and administration of the abbey. Theoretically, the prior, a choir monk, had overall charge, but the growing numbers and power of the lay brothers led to heated disagreements, and in 1185, the lay brothers deposed the prior, Guillaume de Treignac, of the mother house in Grandmont in the Limousin and appointed a choir monk, Étienne, from the Vincennes cell of the order to replace him. The French king, Philip Augustus, convened an assembly in Vincennes to resolve the dispute, without success. The situation was further complicated by the fact that Grandmont lay in the western part of France controlled by Henry II of England, who favored the lay brothers, while Philip favored the choir monks. For a more detailed account, see Hutchison, *Hermit Monks*, 67–82.

The first two stanzas list reversals of the natural order of things (compare CB 6): the fleece that remains dry when all around it is soaked with dew, the destructive power of an insignificant moth, a talking ass, a cart before the ox, and bases set at the top of columns instead of capitals.

Our poet clearly views the subjection of the choir monks to the will of the lay brothers as a similar, unnatural reversal.

1.1–2 At Judges 6:36–40 Gideon asks God for assurance that Israel will win the upcoming battle. The following sign would assure him: if a fleece placed on the threshing floor should become moist with dew, while everything around it remains dry. The next morning the fleece is indeed moist and everything else dry. To make doubly sure, the next evening Gideon asks God to keep the fleece dry while letting everything around become moistened. This also happens. Gideon is reassured and wins his battle. It is at first unclear which "sign" the poet here has in mind—a failed version of the first night, indicating that God was withholding his approval, or the successful outcome of the second night. A dry fleece surrounded by dry ground would not be a violation of the natural order of things, whereas the dry fleece surrounded by moist ground of the second night certainly is, and it is with such reversals of what is natural and "right" that stanzas 1 and 2 are concerned. So the reference is to the dry fleece of the second test.

1.3–4   Job 13:28 and Matthew 6:19.

1.5–6   Matthew 3:12.

1.7   Balaam's ass speaks to her master at Numbers 22:28–30.

1.8–9   This seems to be a variant of a familiar proverb, which, in English, involves putting the cart before the horse.

2.3–4   The austerity of the Grandmontines won them many admirers and donors, including the kings of England and France. Daughter cells sprang up all over France in the latter part of the twelfth century.

2.5–6   The new *plantatio* appears to refer to the new regime under Etienne (see above), resulting from the recent seizure of power by the lay monks.

3.1–4   The *sanctum sacerdotium* refers to the choir monks. *Unctio regalis* (royal unction) is probably poetic language for an anointed king and could refer to either Philip or Henry. The lay brothers are referred to by "a beast of burden."

3.7–8   Compare John 10:1, "He who does not enter the sheepfold by the door . . . is nothing but a thief and a robber." The venal favor probably refers to Henry's generous financial support.

4.1–2   The life of the choir monks.

4.3–4   The comparatively uneducated lay brothers are being referred to here.

4.5   Their *tirocinium* is their new (usurped) role as masters.

4.7   Presumably, some rule passed by the new prior, Étienne.

5.1–9   The fool is probably Prior Étienne, and the rhetorician the ousted Prior Guillaume.

5.8   For *assumptus de stercore,* compare 1 Samuel 2:8 and Psalms 112(113):7.

6.1   *regis filiam:* Schumann and Vollmann suggest a comparison is intended between the handing over of the monastery to the lay brothers and the fate of the king's daughter, Tharsia (see notes on CB 97 below), in the novel *Apollonius, King of Tyre,* but this seems highly unlikely. More probably, the reference is to Alys, the hapless daughter of Louis VII, betrothed to Richard the Lionheart and kept for twenty years in the custody of his father, who, his biographer says, "had not been able to resist the opportunity to seduce her" (Gillingham, *Richard I, 5*). If she accompanied Henry II to France at some point between 1185 and 1188 and was sent to Grandmont for temporary safekeeping and subsequently returned to Henry, this would account for the heated, but judiciously vague, rhetoric of the last stanza, the addressee of which would then be either Henry or the prior of Grandmont. Unfortunately, we have almost no information on the whereabouts of Alys in this period and substantial gaps in the movements of Henry in France.

38

Meter: Leonine hexameters with single-syllable rhymes
Author: Otloh of St. Emmeran (11th century)

Maxims on the importance of a proper education.

39, 39a, 39b

Rhythmical pattern: Free
Author: Unknown, but of German origin

This may once have been a single, longer poem, several of whose stanzas have been lost. The surviving stanzas do not provide a coherent sequence and so have been rearranged into three segments.

39

The poet laments the moral decline of the world, where the clergy act like wolves rather than shepherds and the secular magnates have no regard for the laws. Everything is topsy-turvy. The Church has sunk the world's ship. Strife has sown the seeds of death. Life is insecure. Some of the clergy are in love with money. It is a case of the blind leading the blind. The bishops have armed themselves to tackle their prey. Their concerns have become entirely secular. Laws have been set aside. The monks are just as bad.

2.1–2   Rachel and Leah were often interpreted allegorically to repre-
         sent, respectively, the contemplative and active aspects of the
         Church. Here then Leah perhaps represents the orders who
         engaged more with the world, like the Augustinians and Pre-
         monstratensians, or even the Cistercians, who did not shrink
         from physical labor. These and similar orders grew very rapidly
         in the twelfth century. Hence, "Leah finds favor." Rachel would
         then stand for the Benedictine and other more reclusive or-
         ders. However, it may be, as Schumann suggests (H-S-B 2.1.66),
         that Rachel stands for the Church in general, for it is unclear
         from the biblical narrative (Genesis 29 and 30) what the sin
         (scelus) was that caused Rachel to be infertile. Schumann won-
         ders if we are perhaps to see it in the behavior of her father,
         Laban, who violated his contract with Jacob by giving him
         Leah as his wife rather than Rachel, for the notion of inherited
         guilt is enshrined in the Ten Commandments (Exodus 20:5).
         In terms of the allegory, the sin would be the perception that
         the Benedictine order had drifted away from the ideals of its
         founder and been corrupted by simony and avarice. For further
         discussion, see Bisanti, *Poesia d'Amore*, 39–43.

2.6–7   Rahab was interpreted allegorically as prefiguring the Church,
         so Rupert of Deutz (PL 167.537C). The "ship of the world" is an
         extension of the familiar allegory of the ship of state. The poet
         seems to be blaming the Church for the world's plight.

3.3–4   On Albinus and Rufinus; see "Albinus" in the Index of Proper
         Names.

3.12   Since the only form of cremation allowed "within the camp" un-
         der Jewish law was that of whole animals or animal parts in sac-
         rificial offering, these words equate church leaders with ani-
         mals; see 4.1–2.

4.1   *Cornuti* means "equipped with horns" but can also refer to the
         projecting "horns" of a miter. The devil is also often depicted
         with horns, e.g., in the early thirteenth-century *Codex Gigas.*

4.2   The *canes muti* (dogs that fail to bark) of Isaiah 56:10 were inter-
         preted allegorically in the *Glossa Ordinaria* as prefiguring the
         bishops.

4.3–12   These lines describe bishops dressed for combat. A good num-
         ber of bishops participated in the crusades. Prior to the twelfth
         century, canon law had vigorously prohibited the clergy from
         taking up arms and engaging in war. However, as L. Duggan,
         Armsbearing and the Clergy, 102–44, points out, three factors
         brought about dramatic changes in this doctrine in the twelfth
         century: the crusades, the rise of the military-religious orders,
         and the theory of the just war. However, *iure imperiali* (5.12)
         suggests that the poet is referring to Frederick Barbarossa's at-
         tempts to retain control of his lands in Italy. If so, then the
         principal target of stanza 4 is likely to be Rainald of Dassel,
         archbishop of Cologne, who was Frederick's archchancellor of
         Italy and commander in chief of the emperor's army there un-
         til his death in 1167. No doubt many would see the archbishop's
         prominent role in the war as contravening even the more re-
         laxed standards of the middle of the twelfth century.

4.10   That is, a rear view of Fortune, hence a sign of bad luck; com-
         pare note on CB 16.1.4.

4.11   The humeral veil is a long piece of cloth draped over the shoul-
         ders and worn as a liturgical garment.

5.10   Compare Ephesians 5:16.

6.2   Schumann notes that *vates* often means "bishop" from the fifth
         century onward; see also Blaise, *Dictionnaire,* s.v. 2.

6.8–9   *Iura* refers to Roman law, and *canones* and *decreta* to canon law.

6.10–11 Ezekiel 20:21, "exacerbaverunt me" (they provoked me — God
         speaking).

6.12   Isaiah 1:4, "blasphemaverunt Sanctum Israel" (they have blas-
        phemed the Holy One of Israel).

7.1–4   The black monks are the Benedictines, who wear a black habit.

7.5–6   The white monks are the Cistercians, who wear white choir
        robes.

7.7–12 These brothers are the Premonstratensians, an order of canons
        regular, who often preached and performed pastoral duties in
        parishes close to their abbey. As priests they were "revered as
        fathers." They are often called Norbertines *(Norpertini)* after
        their founder, Saint Norbert, or the White Canons, from the
        color of their robes. The order was founded in Prémontré in
        eastern France in 1120 and grew rapidly.

39a

This fragment consists of the second and fourth stanzas as they occur in
the manuscript. It reminds mankind that they are merely ash, to which
their bodies will soon return. The entire world is vanity. Creatures grow
and pass away. It is only man's spirit that can live with God.

2.1   Compare Ecclesiastes 1:2 and 12:8.

39b

Advice to a priest: when you are about to celebrate mass, clean the old
leaven from your heart and keep in mind the words of Psalms 42(43),
which opens *Iudica me* (Judge me).

1.4–5   On "old leaven," see note on CB 21.3.8.
1.8   Compare Psalms 42(43):1.

40

Meter: Hexameters (1: caudate; 2 and 3: Leonine)

Man's talents are God's gifts. Diligence is eventually rewarded. We should
strive to bring joy to others.

1.1   Prevenient grace is divine grace bestowed prior to any individu-
         al's decision or action and, according to Augustine, cannot be
         resisted.

41

Rhythmical pattern: 2x(8p + 8p + 7pp)
Author: Walter of Châtillon
Date: 1179

This satire is found in at least eleven manuscripts, of which *B* is by far the
most eccentric.

  Walter's patron, William, archbishop of Reims, attended the Third Lat-
eran Council (March 1179) in Rome. Walter seems to have accompanied
him and delivered *In Domino confido,* a satire in mixed prose and verse as
part of the *Laetare* Sunday entertainment there; see Walter of Châtillon,
Shorter Poems, xcvi–xcvii. CB 41, which purports to reflect Walter's experi-
ences when dealing with the papal bureaucracy and is highly critical of the
corruption of the Roman Curia, would have been performed probably in
Reims among other places. The criticism, though no doubt seriously in-
tended, is delivered in an engagingly lighthearted manner. The rollicking
rhythm is well adapted to the subject matter. The marine metaphors begin
early and are maintained throughout.

1.1   Isaiah 62:1.
1.3   Isaiah 45:8.
2.2   Lamentations 1:1.
2.4–5   Isaiah 62:4.
3.4   *bithalassus* refers to a dangerous stretch of water, usually at a nar-
         row strait or a peninsula, where "two seas" meet. Here it refers
         specifically to the strait between the toe of Italy and Sicily,
         where mythical monsters Scylla and Charybdis were thought
         to lurk.
5.1   Syrtes, Scylla, and Charybdis are all found together at Virgil, *Ae-
         neid* 7.302.
6.2   Franco was the papal chamberlain from 1174 to 1179.
8.6   Psalms 121(122):4.

493

10.6   There is a discussion of *actio finium regundorum* (legal terms tend to retain old spellings) regarding border disputes between landowners at *BNP* 5.428–29. However, *finis* could also be used of a legal remedy *(actio)* or a concept in general; so the phrase could be used of an action to determine which court was competent to judge a given case or which law applied in a given instance.

13.3   A Bezant is a Byzantine gold coin.

13.5   Walter often uses *parcitas* (meanness) as a synonym for *avaritia* (greed, miserliness) when he is reminding sponsors or patrons of the blessedness of *largitas* (generosity); see his *Shorter Poems,* xliv.

14.4   In an attempt to ingratiate themselves with their victim, the officials address him in broken French.

15.3   The Council of Tours in May 1163, where Alexander III was recognized as the rightful pope by the kings of England and France.

16.5–6   These lines combine Matthew 16:19 with Psalms 149:8. The audience will probably think of the penances imposed by Pope Alexander III on Henry II for his involvement in the murder of Becket and on Frederick Barbarossa for precipitating the schism of 1159 to 1177.

17.2   *di carnales* is an anagram of *cardinales.*

17.5   *in fine lectionis* (at the end of the reading/lesson). The context suggests that this phrase was used as a formula to introduce a summarizing account like our "to cut a long story short" or "at the end of the day."

19.5–6   Walter is humorously alluding to Psalms 18(19):3, "Dies diei eructat verbum et nox nocti indicat scientiam" (One day speaks to another, night to nighttime imparts knowledge).

20.3   Compare Matthew 23:24 for swallowing camels.

21.4   Juvenal 6.464: "ad moechum lota veniet cute" (she will come to her lover with her skin cleansed).

21.5–6   Juvenal 5.2–3: "monstrum nulla virtute redemptum a vitiis" (a monster whose vices are redeemed by no virtue).

27.1   The only time when Alexander III, Peter of Pavia, and Franco were all in Rome together was from February to July 1179; see also the introductory notes to this poem.

29 Though the first half of this stanza flatters the pope, the second half clearly implies that he is not a true worshipper of God. This criticism of the pope may reflect Walter's personal experience, for he seems to have unsuccessfully applied for financial support from the pope during an earlier visit to Rome between November 1165 and August 1167; see his *Shorter Poems,* lxxxvi–lxxxviii.

29.5–6 For the story of Elisha and Gehazi, see the Index of Proper Names under Gehazi.

30.5–6 Compare Psalms 38(39):2, "posui ori meo custodiam" (I have put a guard on my mouth).

42

Meter: 4x(7pp+6p) Goliardic stanzas
Author: Walter of Châtillon
Date: ca. 1170

Particularly noteworthy in this lively denunciation of the corruption of the ecclesiastical establishment in Rome is the open attack on the pope (presumably, Alexander III) in stanzas 12 to 14; for more on this poem, see Walter of Châtillon, *Shorter Poems,* lxxxviii–lxxxi and 196–203.

2.4 Literally, "The face is not the (outer) skin of the heart."

4.1 The play with *mundus* (world) and *mundus* (clean) is a cliché of Medieval Latin poetry. The added play with *caput* and *capit* gives it a certain freshness.

9.2 Besides being round and silver, many coins had a cross on them. Vollmann points out that in addition to its general meaning (used in the translation here) *placet* was recognized as a way of closing a deal, rather like the American "It's a deal!" and a handshake.

9.3 *Placet* here is from *placare* and so a legitimate rhyme with the preceding *placet.*

12.4 As Apollo flays him alive for his hubris, Marsyas screams, "Non est . . . tibia tanti" (Ovid, *Metamorphoses* 6.386).

13.2   *Papare*, while literally meaning "to be pope," has overtones (with its object) of "poping it over," i.e., "appropriating" and a word-play on classical Latin *pappare* (to gobble down).

13.3–4   The French verb *payer* (to pay) is derived from *pacare* (appease). Though today the *a* sounds as in English "pay," it must originally have sounded as in "pat." The imperative *paies* has two syllables; so if you cut off ("si vis apocopare") the second (un-stressed) syllable, the two imperatives sound as in modern French *papa*.

14.1   A *bulla* was actually a seal. In time *bulla* (bull) came to be applied to a document bearing the papal seal.

14.4   The clearly erroneous reading *mare salsum est* of most manu-scripts appears to have been reached in two stages: (1) *falsum* was misread as *salsum* (*f* and *s* are readily confused in medieval scripts, and *salsum* is a standard epithet of *mare*); (2) a scribe, noticing that *fit* made no sense—since the sea *is* salty it cannot *become* salty—changed *fit* to *est*.

Causa can mean either the case one presents for a petition, or, on its way to becoming French *chose* and Italian *cosa,* more gen-erally, "thing," as in "your ship is sunk and everything is lost."

15–17   *Bursa* and *loculus,* besides meaning "purse," were also used in medical Latin to designate purse-shaped bodily organs, such as the scrotum or the bladder. While on one level Walter is certainly talking about the fate of the petitioner's purse, line 15.4 indicates that he expects his audience to catch the double entendres. The "physic" implied might involve prostitutes or treatment for what is today seen as the urinary problems caused by an enlarged prostate.

43

Rhythmical pattern: Lay

The complex rhythmical structure of stanzas 1 to 4 is repeated in stan-zas 5 to 8.4. Lines 8.5–6 constitute a coda. Stanzas 1, 4, 5, and 8.1–4 are in goliardic rhythm (7pp+6p), but some lines do not observe the normal cae-sura after 7pp.

Date: The date and overall context of this poem are unclear, but the pervasive gloom suggests the schism of 1159 to 1177. The mood recalls that of Walter of Châtillon's poem about the Antichrist, *Dum contemplor animo* (1171/72).

The corruption in Rome reflects the sickness of the world at large. Rome is unable to provide the leadership needed. The Prince of Darkness has moved to fill the vacuum and is finding many followers. The very underpinnings of the state are threatened, but perhaps the source (a noble family?) from which it has drawn strength in the past will help it now. The poet appeals to this source to put an end to the vices that plague the world and bring happier times, but the poem ends with little hope.

1.3–4   Rome is like the foolish virgins who have no oil for their lamps when the Bridegroom (Christ) comes (Matthew 25:1–13).

4.4   *Fluxa* is ablative singular.

5.1   *rerum coniectura* (the combination of things) is a philosophical way of referring to the world.

6.4   For *opere* as *quasi* adverb (like *magnopere*), see *DMLBS,* "opus" 1f.

8.8   A reference to the centurion in Matthew 8:5–10, of whom Christ says, "Truly I tell you: nowhere in Israel have I found such faith." Since Israel was often understood allegorically to mean the Church, the last lines can be interpreted to mean that there is no one in the Church who inspires confidence.

44

This prose satire on corruption in Rome mimics the simple language of the Bible, quoting well-known passages in very different contexts. The scene is the well-guarded gateway leading to the papal chambers. Not even Christ himself is to be admitted unless he offers the guards money. When a poor man comes, he has to sell everything he has to raise money for the needed bribes, but it is not enough and he is ignominiously thrown out. A rich man comes and offers money to the guards, the chamberlain, and the cardinals. The pope becomes ill when he hears of this, but a "pill" of gold and silver soon cures him.

3   There is a pun, since a contemporary humorous etymology of *Roma* was *Rodens manus.*

45

Meter: Leonine hexameters

1   A fifteen-line poem on corruption in Rome that focuses especially on the pope. It points out that there is little difference between the pope and the emperor in this regard.

2, 3   Single-line maxims on the same theme.

3   There is a play here with *manus rodit,* for it is usually in the order *Rodit manus* to emphasize the perceived character of the city.

46

Rhythmical pattern: Essentially 6x8pp but with occasional lines of 7p

    The rhythmical irregularities of this poem, the first of a series on crusading, suggest that it was written in Germany.

Though the overall subject matter, a call to join the crusade (almost certainly the Second Crusade of 1145–1149), is clear enough, the precise significance of certain stanzas and, more generally, the sequence of thought are often hard to grasp.

1   The crusaders are likened to Faith, who, in Prudentius's *Psychomachia* (21–29), is disheveled and unarmed when she goes to confront Idolatry. Perhaps *Gratia* here = Holy Writ (Ephesians 6:10–17).

2.2   The biblical phrase "daughter of Babylon," like "daughter of Sion," is a normal way of saying "city of Babylon, Jerusalem, etc."; see Blaise, *Dictionnaire,* "filia." By the twelfth century, Babylon had been more or less abandoned for hundreds of years, and the reference is presumably to Baghdad, by now a major city and cultural center, a mere fifty-three kilometers from the site of Babylon.

2.3–4   Psalms 136(137):8–9. This was generally taken allegorically in medieval interpretations to mean "nipping in the bud tendencies to sin." However, in the context of the Second Crusade it probably should be understood literally as referring to the anticipated slaughter of the Saracens in the Holy Land.

2.5–6   The old crime was the pillaging of Jerusalem by Nebuchadnez-
         zar, king of Babylon, in 597 BCE and refers to the series of de-
         portations of leading Jews to Babylon (597–582 BCE) and
         the Babylonian Captivity commemorated in Psalms 136(137),
         which ended in 538 BCE.

3.1–4   The "Whore of Babylon" is described in Revelation 17 and 18.
         The gold cup she carries is full of "obscenities and the foulness
         of her fornication" (17:4).

4.1–6   This stanza quotes from a contemporary prophecy: "Cum as-
         cenderis ad costam tetragoni sedentis aeterni . . . pones vex-
         illa tua rosea usque a extremos labores Herculis, quia erexit te
         Christus in artemonem navis, in capite cuius est velum triangu-
         latum" (When you land on the coast of the everlasting seated
         rectangle . . . you will set your rose-colored banner at the [site
         of the] remotest labors of Hercules, because Christ has raised
         you up as the foremast of his ship, at the top of which there is a
         triangular sail); see H-S-B 2.1.95. This was interpreted to mean
         that the arrival at Constantinople of Louis VII, who led the
         Second Crusade along with the German emperor, Conrad III,
         would signal the end of Muslim power in the Mediterranean as
         far west as Spain.

4.1   Unlike the prophecy itself, CB 46 does not identify the *princeps
         principum*.

4.3   The rectangle may refer to the Iberian Peninsula, roughly so
         shaped.

4.3–4   Schumann interprets the "eternal, seated tetragon" as the Byz-
         antine emperor and the "coast" as Constantinople.

5.1   Schumann understood the *quem* as interrogative, but it seems
         better, with Vollmann, to take it as a relative pronoun, refer-
         ring to the *princeps principum*.

5.6   *Pacis visio* (vision of peace) is a patristic translation of "Jerusa-
         lem."

6.1   *Confusio* = Babylon; see CB 4.1.5.

6.6   Compare Ecclesiastes 7:14, "Considera opera Dei" (Consider
         God's handiwork). Presumably, the poet is urging the Muslims
         to abandon Edessa.

7 Heretics ("demon worshippers," here Muslims) are like statues, devoid of speech, reasoning, and freedom to move as they wish. Compare Psalms 114(115):4–8 and 134(135):15–18.

8 Crusaders have the protection of the True Cross, which, though destined to be lost in the Third Crusade, was still in Jerusalem at this time.

9 This stanza suggests that these are the ordinary soldiers accompanying the knights who go into church for mass.

9.1–4 Compare Luke 14:23.

9.5–6 Compare Psalms 33(34):9.

10 This stanza is based on the incident recorded at Matthew 15:2–28 and Mark 7:24–30 involving a Syro-Phoenician (i.e., non-Jewish) woman, who asks Christ to cure her daughter, who is tormented by a demon. Christ answers that he "was sent to the lost sheep of the house of Israel and to them alone." After an exchange about dogs eating the crumbs that fall under the master's table, he tells the woman her daughter is well.

11 The *campus libertatis* probably refers to Golgotha, the site of Christ's crucifixion, which liberated mankind from mortality. See "Liberation" at *EDB* 808. The market in Jerusalem where eternal life can be purchased appears to refer metaphorically to the promise made by the pope that any crusaders who die fighting to protect Jerusalem from the Muslims will have their sins instantly forgiven and so will go straight to heaven.

13.5–6 Compare Matthew 7:6.

14.1–2 John 14:2, "In my father's house there are many mansions."

15.1–2 Matthew 20:16.

47

Rhythmical pattern: 6p, 3x7pp, 6p, 7pp, 2x(4p+4p+7pp), 3x8p, 2x8p, 2p
Author: Philip the Chancellor
Date: Late 1187

This poem is a call to join the Third Crusade to recapture Jerusalem from the Muslim forces led by Saladin. In 1187 Guy of Lusignan, king of Jerusalem, led his army out of the city against the Muslims, suffered a crushing defeat at the Horns of Hattin, and became a prisoner of Saladin. Less than a month later, in October 1187, Saladin captured Jerusalem. The news of the disaster may have precipitated the death of the ailing pope Urban III. His successor, Gregory VIII, promptly issued a call for a crusade to recapture the city. It is in this context that Philip wrote this poem, whose allusive nature has caused many difficulties. On the historical background, see Phillips, *Crusades,* 138–50. In recent years musicologists have argued that CB 47 is to be dated to the Fifth Crusade. For a defense of the traditional dating and a more detailed examination of this poem, see Traill, "Philip the Chancellor and the Third Crusade."

1.2	The Lord's second cross is the capture of Jerusalem by Muslim forces.
1.3	Christ's new wounds are: (1) the loss of the True Cross (1.4), which was carried into battle and lost at Hattin; (2) the violence presumed to have been done to his tomb (1.5–7). In fact, the tomb was unharmed. Saladin saw its economic potential and preserved it to be visited by pilgrims for a fee.
1.4	Christ's cross is often referred to as a tree.
1.7	Lamentations 1.1.
1.8	Saladin emptied the city of its Christian population, freeing the elderly and those who could pay their ransom, and enslaving those who could not.
1.9	The goat is a symbol of the infidel; the Lamb is Christ.
1.11	Zion, the bride, is the Church. On Ananias, see "Hananiah" in the Index of Proper Names.
1.13	On *cornu David* see Psalms 131(132):17. *Cornu* appears to mean "power," and David symbolizes Israel but at the same time is a *figura* (allegory) for Christ. David's power is bent low because Jerusalem has been captured.
1.14 and 17	Philip, like Walter of Châtillon, was fond of rhyming the same word when used with different grammatical functions; compare 3.14 (verb) and 17 (noun) below.
2.7	*Pars totalis* probably here means "the entire region"; however, *pars totalis* can be viewed as a paradox ("the part that is the whole"), referring perhaps to Christ or Christianity.
2.7–10	The royal land is the Kingdom of Jerusalem; just as Moses was

the leader of the Jews, so Guy of Lusignan was the leader of Christian Jerusalem. His subjects lament his helplessness because he is now a prisoner of Saladin.

2.8 Compare Exodus 1:14.

2.16–17 Christ.

3.1–2 All who have taken the cross, i.e., become crusaders.

3.4–5 Augustine interprets the roaring lion cubs of Psalms 103(104) as evil demons.

3.8 According to Augustine on Psalms 119, the land of Kedar denotes spiritual darkness; see also Jerome, *Hebr. Nom.*, CCSL 72, p. 63: "Cedar 'tenebrae' vel 'moeror.'" Here it seems to refer to the sinful world in which we live.

3.13 Babylon here is not the city on the Euphrates but the realm of the devil.

3.15–17 A reminder of the pope's promise that all crusaders who die fighting for Jerusalem will win a martyr's crown and go straight to heaven. *Componere* is used specifically of preparing a body for burial; for the water of life, see Revelation 21:7. On *pugna/pugna* see 1.14 above.

47a

Rhythmical pattern: as in 47
Author: Philip the Chancellor?

This poem, which clearly has nothing to do with poem 47, seems to have become attached to the latter because the melody is the same for both; see Clemencic, *Carmina Burana*, 55–60. Poem 47a advocates a code of amorality, which at first seems humorous, but the last five lines show that that humor is sardonic and that he is merely adopting these attitudes to show their barrenness.

1.6 Ovid, *Amores* 3.4.17.

1.8 Compare Luke 10:37.

1.9 Compare note on 47.1.14.

1.11–12 The poet is not necessarily thinking of cases in canon law, for judges in civil courts too were usually drawn from the educated class, which was largely clerical.

2.6   By sitting on the fence, one can play both sides, eventually fa-
        voring the party offering the larger bribe.

2.8   Thais is a standard name for a courtesan in ancient comedy.

48

Rhythmical pattern: 4(p)p+6pp, 5pp, 2x(4(p)p+6pp), 5pp, 3x(4(p)p
+6pp); *Ref.* 5pp
Date: After October 1187

Like CB 47 this is a call to join the Third Crusade.

The prophecy in the psalms has been fulfilled. The Saracens have de-
filed the Holy Sepulcher (stanza 1). May God destroy his enemies. The
widow of Zarephath mourned for the two sticks she lost and always will
mourn until she finds them (2). Just as the Shunamite woman called for
Elisha to revive her dead boy, we need an Elisha today if the Church is to
regain the cross it has lost (3). Crusaders are assured of salvation if they re-
flect on their sins (4). We need to hurry to assist Christ. He chose to de-
stroy Jerusalem so that we could wash away our sins in this way. He really
does not need our help, for he is all-powerful (5).

1.1–5   Psalms 73(74):7, "They set fire to your sanctuary, tore down and
        polluted the abode of your name." But see note on CB 47.1.3.

Ref. and 2.1 Compare Psalms 67(68):2, "You disperse them like smoke; you
        melt them like wax near fire. The wicked perish at the presence
        of God."

2.7–10 Zarephath (or Sareptha) was a Phoenician town, now Surafend.
        There Elijah sojourned with a starving widow who had almost
        no food or fuel. See 3 (1) Kings 17:10–12. The two sticks were
        held to prefigure the cross.

3.1–6   See 4 Kings (2 Kings) 4:18–37; the mouth-to-mouth resuscita-
        tion appears in verse 34: "posuitque os suum super os eius."

3.4   For this unusual use of *met = ipse,* see H-S-B 1.3.198.

48a

This is the second stanza of a three-stanza *alba* by Otto von Botenlauben
(probably 1177–1244). The *alba* was a subgenre of love lyric that was popu-

lar in medieval literature. It depicts lovers who have spent the night together but now have to part, for dawn is breaking. Given that the rhythmical patterns of 48 and 48a are identical and that the similarity in length and content of the unusually short refrains is striking, coincidence is out of the question; one poem was modeled on the other. Scholars have debated which poem came first; see Vollmann, *Carmina Burana,* 988–89. The Latin poem, which appears to reflect the situation in the early stages of the Third Crusade (late 1187–1188?), borrows much from poem 47 and could have been written much later, inspired both by 47 and by Otto's alba.

49

Rhythmical pattern: 4x(7pp + 6p) with some variations, e.g., 2.4: 8pp + 7p
   The extra syllables point to German authorship; see Norberg, *Versification,* 185.
Date: September 1187?

This call for men to take the cross and go fight in the Holy Land is hard to date, for the apparent reference to the imminent fall of Tyre while Jerusalem appears safe (stanza 6), seems to rely as much on biblical prophecy as on contemporary events (see notes below). After his victory at Hattin and before moving against Jerusalem, Saladin captured all the coastal cities of the kingdom of Jerusalem except Tyre, whose fall now seemed inevitable. It was saved by the unexpected arrival of Conrad of Montferrat, who rallied morale and skillfully organized the defense of the city. Saladin abandoned the siege of Tyre and turned his attention to Jerusalem itself, which soon surrendered (Phillips, *Crusades,* 136). So the poem fits the situation of September 1187 even if a more realistic assessment must have suggested that optimism about Jerusalem was misplaced.

   The poet focuses on young men (stanza 2), urging them to remember their Creator (Ecclesiastes 12:1), while the old are dismissed—their days are over. The young are reminded that joining the crusade will free them from sin and the devil's clutches (stanzas 4–5). Tyre's fall is imminent but Jerusalem has the Lord's protection (6). Those who take the cross will be saved on Judgment Day (7–10). Just as there was a temple in heaven for

Lazarus, who rose from the dead, so there will be one for the crusaders (11–12).

1.1–3	Ephesians 5:14.
2.1	Ecclesiastes 12:1.
2.4	The reference is to Matthew 3:10 or Luke 3.9, where the unproductive fig tree is to be cut down.
3.1	Compare 2 Chronicles 36:17.
4.1–2	Matthew 6:33.
4.3	Galatians 5:24.
4.4	Psalms 50(51):3.
5.3	Compare Galatians 6:14.
5.4	The Enemy (*hostis*) is the devil.
6.1	For Jacob's dream of the ladder reaching up to heaven, see Genesis 28:12–15.
6.3	Regarding Tyre, compare Ezekiel 26–28, especially 27:36, "Destruction has come upon you and you shall be no more." Tyre was often understood allegorically to allude to paganism or heresy and hence Islam.
6.4	Calvary; compare Psalms 67(68):16, "mons Dei, mons pinguis."
9.3	The Enemy is the devil.
12.1	On Lazarus, see John 11:1–43. For the doctrine that Christian bodies are temples of the Holy Spirit, see 1 Corinthians 19.

50

Rhythmical pattern: 4x(7pp+6p) with some irregularities
Date: 1188

The poet sadly recounts the events in the Holy Land since June 1187. Raymond III, count of Tripoli, allied himself with Saladin and brought in Turkish troops who occupied Galilee (stanzas 1–3). After the roster of Saladin's allies drawn from the eastern Mediterranean, North Africa, and the Near East, the poet tells how they brutally attacked the Christians (4–7). The king of Jerusalem, Guy of Lusignan, and the Templars set out to oppose him but, vastly outnumbered, were defeated at Hattin. The king was captured and the Templars beheaded (8–12). Acre fell without a fight but

Tyre was saved (13–14). The land trodden by Christ, where he was baptized and crucified, and favored by God, is now in the hands of Saladin (15–18). The world should lament this disaster (19–21). God punishes the wicked, raises up the humble, and welcomes the repentant. He punished the Israelites by giving the ark to the Philistines and then the Philistines by making them return it to the Israelites with gifts. So let us repent and offer God gifts so that he may give us what we ask for (22–25).

2.4   Psalms 112(113):7.

3.1–4   For the complicated and rapidly changing situation in the Holy Land at this time, see Phillips, *Crusades,* 132–33. Regarding Raymond's role here, he says (p. 132): "Rumors that Raymond had allowed the Muslims through his lands forced him to renounce his agreement with Saladin and swear homage to King Guy."

4–6   This list of the forces supposedly assembled by Saladin is largely fictional. Besides the Muslim forces actually assembled by Saladin, the poet has added the names of peoples and places between Turkey and India and between Mauretania and Egypt that appear as "enemies" in Roman and biblical history.

5.2   Following the Mauritanians and Getulians, *Barbari* almost certainly refers specifically to the Berbers rather than vaguely to "barbarians."

6.3   The Quadi were a subgroup of the Suebi, a Germanic tribe.

12.1   Guy was released by Saladin after a year's imprisonment. The fragment of the True Cross, which the Latins had carried into battle, was lost at Hattin.

13.3   Acre surrendered in the summer of 1187.

14   Tyre is *Sur* in Phoenician and Hebrew, and *Suris* is a Latinization of *Sur.* The chance arrival of Conrad of Montferrat, who quickly and efficiently organized the defenses of Tyre, saved the city. Saladin abandoned the siege and turned his attention to Jerusalem.

16.1   Matthew 14:24–27.

16.2   Matthew 14:17–21.

16.3   John 1:29–34.

16.6   The story that the Jordan flowed backward at the touch of
          Christ's body is not biblical but found in Sedulius, *Carmen Pas-*
          chale 2.162–65.
19.3   Matthew 15:26–27.
19.4   Revelation 16:6.
20.2   Jeremiah 6:26.
21.4   Compare Psalms 13(14) and 52(53):3.
22.3   Luke 1:52.
23–24   Compare 1 Kings (1 Samuel): 4–6. The Philistines defeated the
          Israelites in battle and captured the Ark of the Covenant. They
          were then smitten with tumors and a plague of rats. They fi-
          nally decided to return the Ark to the Israelites together with
          some gifts.

51

Rhythmical pattern: 4x8p; *Ref.* 3(p)p, 4x7(p)p

This seemingly simple but ultimately rather puzzling poem is perhaps best
seen through the lens suggested by Vollmann: while the poet is lamenting
the plight of the world around him, he presents it in terms drawn from the
book of Genesis.

Adam's eating of the apple (stanza 1.1–2 and Genesis 3:1–7) banished us
from Paradise (1.4 and Genesis 3:23–24); Mankind's sinfulness and the gen-
eral decline (2.1–4, 3.1–2, and Genesis 4:8–24); humans became captives of
the devil (4.1) and mortal (4.2–4 and Genesis 3:19).

*Ref.*3   Gihon is where Solomon was crowned; see 3 Kings (1 Kings)
           1:33–40.
*Ref.*4   Sion/Zion is Jerusalem.
3.3   *Limatura* here means a creation made from "mud," that is, man
           (Genesis 2:7). "Those on high" appear to be God and the "sons
           of the gods" mentioned at Genesis 6:2, just before God decides
           to eliminate mankind except for Noah (Genesis 6:5–8).
4.2   Man is in exile here on earth, as his "homeland" is in heaven.

51a

Rhythmic pattern: 4x8p; *Ref.* 3pp, 4x7pp
Date: 1168/69

This poem reflects the alliance forged in 1168 between Amalric I, king of Jerusalem from 1163 to 1174, and the Byzantine emperor, Manuel I Comnenus, for the purpose of a joint invasion of Egypt. Amalric then promptly invaded Egypt in October and captured Bilbais and marched to Cairo. However, sufficient Muslim reinforcements arrived in time to cause him to return to Jerusalem.

The Byzantine emperor prepares for war (stanza 1). Amalric's victory in Bilbais (2). Pray for Amalric's success and the pagan king's destruction (3).

The refrain is a mixture of Greek and Latin. It is an adaptation of the *Trishagion,* as used in the Western Church in the Improperia of Good Friday. The Greek, jumbled in *B,* has been normalized somewhat.

2.3   The "shared inheritance" is clearly the Holy Land, as Schumann notes (H-S-B 2.1.112), and more specifically Jerusalem. *Sors* can refer to allotted land and here is seen as the land allotted by God to all Christians, both Latin and Greek, for protection. Spreckelmeyer, *Kreuzzugslieder,* 78, was the first to see that it should be translated here as "inheritance."

3.4   It is unclear who is meant by the "pagan king," but we probably have to think of Shirkuh, the Kurdish general whose arrival in Egypt prompted the departure of Amalric.

52

Rhythmical pattern: Variable
Date: Before 1187

This poem is found in two twelfth-century Limoges manuscripts besides *B.*

Everyone should participate in the festivities except the monk who castrated himself (stanza 1). Let's sing a victory song to God who rescued Jerusalem from the pagans (2). This festival celebrates the victories over the Philistines, Amalekites, and the descendants of Hagar, and the rescue of the city by the Christians. This is God's beloved city, where Christ chose to be crucified for mankind and where the apostles received the Holy Spirit (3). Fire comes every year as a sign of divine favor. The city is destined to be highly honored and much visited (4). The Holy City is the home of the Ark of the Covenant, is hospitable to the poor, and is a safe refuge (5). It outshines the sun and moon and is holier than any other city. Areuna chose a good site (6).

1.1   Solignac Abbey, near Limoges, was founded by Saint Eligius in the seventh century.

1.3   The Latin of this line has caused head-scratching. If Serracus is a monk, nothing about him is known. If the letters are meant to mean *serra cum* (with a saw), the reference is unclear.

1.5   Aeacus was a judge of the underworld.

2.3 and *Ref.* The festival appears to celebrate the capture of Jerusalem by the Crusaders on July 15, 1099, but other victories of Jewish history are also remembered.

*Ref.*3   In the temple of Dagon, the god's statue was found broken after the Ark of God was placed near it (1 Samuel 5:1–4).

3.4   At Pentecost tongues of fire brought the Holy Ghost to the Apostles (Acts 2:1–4).

4.1   The only explanation offered for this line is that there was a belief that a fiery phenomenon similar to that observed at Pentecost occurred every year thereafter (H-S-B 1.2.114.)

6.3   Araunah's threshing floor became the site of the Temple; see *EDB* 87.

53

Rhythmical pattern: Variable
Author: A cleric close to Wichmann, archbishop of Magdeburg
Date: Not long after July 24, 1177

This poem celebrates the Treaty of Venice (1177) that ended the schism of 1159 to 1177 and the key role played in the negotiations by the archbishop of Magdeburg.

The year 1177 ended almost twenty difficult years of schism (stanzas 1–2). Wichmann brought about this agreement, whereby the emperor and the pope put an end to the *error* (3–4). Rome should rejoice that the pope reached the "harbor of peace." With the help of three others, Wichmann ended the strife (5–6). The Church should rejoice, for achieving this peace is like the return of the Jubilee year. Jerusalem should also rejoice (7–9).

1.11–2   "Simon's (i.e., Peter's) ship": the Church.

2.5   Compare Matthew 24:12.

3.2   Wichmann of Seeburg, archbishop of Magdeburg 1154 to 1192.

3.8   *Error* can mean "mistake" but also "heresy," an ambiguity which can be useful in situations where interested parties differ in their view of certain key events; compare 4.6.

4.1–4   This stanza evokes the doctrine of two swords, which was based on interpretations of Luke 22:38 and played an important role in the debate over the balance of power between the papacy and the various secular leaders. The two swords were interpreted to represent power in the spiritual sphere (the prerogative of the pope) and in the temporal sphere (the prerogative of the secular kings and emperors). There was often disagreement as to whether the secular leaders held their positions independently or at the pope's pleasure. Here Alexander III and Frederick Barbarossa are portrayed as allies in the fight against the grave *error*. This is a diplomatic recasting of the reality, for the schism was caused by Frederick, who refused to accept Alexander as pope and recognized instead a series of antipopes. Also, the use of the comparative form *maior* (greater) in the sense of the positive has the diplomatic advantage of suggesting that there were errors on both sides.

5.1–6   The helmsman is the pope, the storm the schism, the crew the Church, and the harbor the peace treaty. The right hand is that of Frederick.

7.4   Psalms 101(102):14, "You will arise and have mercy on Zion . . . for the time has come."

9.4   Compare Zechariah 9:9.

53a

Rhythmical pattern: Varied
Author: Supporter of Pope Alexander III
Date: Soon after July 4, 1187

This poem also reflects the Treaty of Venice, but the tone is triumphalist, for it represents the viewpoint of the Alexandrine party. The two stanzas may be a complete poem or the surviving part of a longer one. The poet sees Pope Alexander III as a shrewd master of the hunt, who has trapped various birds and animals, all of whom were viewed as allegories or metaphors for heretics.

1–2   Psalms 10(11):1; Rabanus Maurus sees the birds flying to the
       mountains as a metaphor for followers of a heretic (PL
       112.1001B).
2.1–2 The most commonly used metaphor for heretics was the foxes
       that damage vineyards (Song 2:15 and Judges 15:4–5); see Alan
       of Lille, *Distinctiones Dictionum Theologicalium* (PL 1011A).
3.3   For snakes as a metaphor for heretics, see the *Glossa Ordinaria*
       (PL 113:491C).

54

Rhythmical pattern: Irregular, with some sections in prose

This incantation takes the form of an exorcism, whether for a specific unnamed individual (3.6 *homini*) or for mankind in general is unclear.

The poet, assuming the role of the exorcist, tells all the *daemonia* to come when summoned and obey him (stanza 1). He then addresses all who support the devil and exorcizes them (2). He tells them to stop harassing mankind, to appear before him and then go down to hell (3). They will go down to meet their punishment, while humans will be saved (4). He then exorcizes the various groups, mainly minor divinities of the Greco-Roman world, such as dryads, satyrs, and penates, and asks God to save us (5–6).

2.3   The snake here is the devil.
2.5–6 Compare Apocalypse 12:3–4.

2.7   The *sigillum Solomonis* is a five–pointed star used in magic; see *Lexikon des Mittelalters*, 3.1414.

2.7–8   The names Gordan, Ingordin, and Ingordan are thought to have their origin in magic words.

2.13–14   The names of the three wise men do not appear in the biblical source (Matthew 2:1–12) but belong to later tradition.

2.15–18   1 Samuel 16:23.

5.3   Tetragrammaton refers to the four-lettered Hebrew name for God, which is often transliterated as *jhwh*.

5.18–19   In the Vulgate, Paul is called *vas electionis* (Acts 9:15) "vessel of choice"; this gave rise to analogous constructions, as here "vessel of Christianity," i.e., a Christian.

55

Meter: Leonine hexameters

The words make no sense. They are a fragment of a longer poem written in "devil-speak," which survives in several versions. Only in the form transmitted here do the first five syllables presented seem recognizable as Latin ("so many bitter things"). For further details, see Hilka, *Zur Geschichte eines lateinischen Teufelspruches*.

Though CB 55 has traditionally been regarded as a separate piece, it may be intended as a concluding magic incantation to assist in the exorcism of the demons of CB 54.

LOVE POEMS

Besides meaning "joyful song," *iubilus* refers more specifically to sequences and descorts (see Meter, Rhythm, and Rhyme in the Introduction), which constitute the first subgroup of the large "Love Poems" section of the *Carmina Burana*. Many of the poems in this section open with the signs of spring (trees sprouting leaves, flowers springing up, birds singing, and so on) before turning to the theme of love; these descriptions can be brief or quite extended. (Note that CB 103–131a of subgroup 4, and subgroups 5 to 9, appear in volume 2 [DOML 49]).

Subgroups in the Love Poems

CB

56

Rhythmical pattern: Descort; *Refs.,* both 2x7pp

The sun moves from Aries into Taurus; it is time to banish sadness and to turn to the joys of love (stanzas 1–2). A student of Minerva, I entered Venus's school and saw a woman second only to Helen in beauty. I have never seen a woman more noble and beautiful and less fickle. If I earn her love, I am blessed (3–4). Look favorably on me, Venus; I am shifting my allegiance from Minerva to you (5).

1.2–5   The coming of spring is announced here quite succinctly in astrological terms. The sun moves into Taurus about April 20.

*Ref.*1 (and 2)   Compare *Omnia vincit Amor* (Virgil, *Eclogues* 10.69).

5.8–9   The choice between Venus (love interests) and Minerva (the need to study) is a recurring theme in Medieval Latin love lyric; compare Walter of Châtillon, *Shorter Poems,* 62–63.

57

Rhythmical patterns: (1–7) Descort; (8a, b) 2x(8p+7pp)

The first seven stanzas, listing the signs of spring, constitute a fairly typical opening for a love poem. They focus on the resistance offered by Winter (stanza 1) and the efforts of the pagan deities Hymen (2–3), Venus (4), Thetis and Ceres (5), and the Sun (7) to help usher in the activities of spring. The fertilizing of the earth by rain is analogous to the fertilizing of females by males (6). Phrison sang the preceding poem to a princess who was on her way to be married (8a). A dwarf reported this to the bridegroom and was mutilated for his pains (8b).

3.5–8   Thanks to Hymen, the natural world is able to reproduce. These lines seem inspired by the opening poem of Martianus Capella's *De Nuptiis Philologiae et Mercurii,* where Hymen plays a prominent role. *in hoc* = because of this.

4.4   The first syllable of *suo* coalesces with the second, so that the run of lines of 8pp is not interrupted.

5.1–4   Thetis encourages sea fishing to resume in earnest, as does *Sol* in stanza 7.

5.5–8   Once Proserpine is restored to Ceres, the crops will grow again.

6   Traditional Greco-Roman mythology saw the natural process of the earth being fertilized by rain in human terms; so the earth was seen as female (mother earth) and the rain god was male (Zeus/Jupiter).

7.1   *Sol,* the Roman sun god equated with Helios and later with Apollo, was familiar to the medieval world from his role in Ovid, *Metamorphoses* 2. The sun is in Pisces from February 20 till March 20.

7.6   Juno allies herself here with Winter and the North Wind; hence, *turbidae* (compare 3.6 *turbini*). Fulgentius, *Mitologiae* 1.3, identifies her with *aer;* that is, the lower part of the sky, where clouds and mists gather. By dispelling the clouds and stormy weather, the sun brings calm and beauty to Juno *(aer).*

8a and b   These stanzas suggest an episode in a contemporary romance, now lost, whose characters and plot were presumably familiar to the audience; compare CB 97, a summary of the Apollonius romance. CB 57 as we have it may be only a segment of a longer poem.

58

Rhythmical pattern: Descort

The spring opening of this poem expands on the theme of birdsong by focusing on birds for most of the poem (stanzas 1–5). First, the nightingale and blackbird remind us of Ovid's tragic tale of Procne and Philomena (stanza 1). Present too are Jupiter and Juno as the sky gods, par excellence, Venus and Cupid to promote reproduction, and various mythological figures associated with woodlands (2). The birds' sensuous movements enliven the picture of the crowded assembly (3). Then follows a catalog of birds, their noisy joy being strangely soothing (4–5). Springtime is a joyful and colorful season enhanced by the warmth of the sun (6).

1.8–18   On the mythological background, see the Index of Proper
         Names under "Philomena."

2.7–13   The mythological figures seem to have been chosen to repre-
         sent different aspects of the life of birds: Jupiter and Juno rep-
         resent the upper and lower regions of the sky, respectively; Cu-
         pid and Venus the drive to mate and reproduce; Arcas,
         huntsmen; Narcissus and Faunus, plant and animal life.

2.10   Arcas (see the Index of Proper Names) and his mother, Callisto,
         become the Little Bear and Great Bear constellations, respec-
         tively, at Ovid, *Metamorphoses* 2.507.

2.11   For Orpheus with plectrum, see Ovid, *Metamorphoses* 10.150,
         and for horned Faunus, Ovid, *Heroides* 5.137–38.

4.1–15   For a similar catalog of birds, see CB 133.

4.2   The eagle is probably called "gift-bearing" because it carries
         large prey in its talons that can be easily spotted by humans.

6   Rather surprisingly, the poem does not turn to human love as
         one of the features of spring, unless we assume it to be implied
         by *laetitia* (6.1).

59

Rhythmical pattern: 4x(7pp+6p); *Ref.* 6p, 7pp+6p

It is late March. The poet sees a group of young women. The sky is clear and leaves are burgeoning on the linden tree in homage to Venus (stanza 1). The valley is rich in flowers and the birds are singing (2). The women are naked and wreathed with flowers (3). As he moves toward them, a young servant girl reveals herself suggestively, and the poet desires her (4). Flora and Phyllis discuss whether a chaste or an unchaste woman is to be preferred (5). Flora maintains that the pagan goddesses are in agreement with scripture on the issue (6). The poet brings back the news to young virgins (7).

The difficulties of this complex poem are enhanced by a number of textual problems. Even where scholars agree on what readings to adopt, they differ widely on how individual lines should be translated. The interpretation offered here is a shortened and updated version of Traill, "Carmina Burana 59."

1.2–4	These lines appear to date the scene to the spring equinox, in late March.
1.4	For *pansare,* the frequentative of *pandere,* see the entry for *pansare* in *DMLBS*. *Pansat* seems preferable to Walsh's *pausat,* which has naked women seeking shade from the sun in northern Europe in late March.
2.1	Here, as at 6.3 and elsewhere, *flagrare* is an alternative form for *fragrare* (to be fragrant).
3.3	Here *occulta* presumably designates the private parts, normally concealed.
3.4	That is, Dido too could appear naked with impunity. For the view of Dido here as shameless seductress, see note on CB 3.4.5–6 above. *Inulta* plays on Dido's famous words at Virgil, *Aeneid* 4.659: *Moriemur inultae* (we shall die unavenged).
4.2	The *arcum Cupidineum* refers to her pubic area (Vollmann) but also to the effect—like that of Cupid's bow—that it has on the poet.
5.1–2	Phyllis and Flora engage in a similar debate about love in CB 92.

The language here *(quaestio, potior quae dignitas)* is legal and, more specifically, reflects that of Gratian's *Decretum,* the first part of which considers the relative standing *(dignitas)* of the various sources of canon law with a view to determining which is to prevail *(quae potior?)* in the case of conflict, while the second part discusses thirty-six cases *(causae)* by way of a series of *quaestiones.* While the answer to the question "Which is to be preferred—the chaste or unchaste woman?" might seem fairly straightforward, Gratian cites authorities who maintain that *castitas* can actually be enhanced by rape *(Decretum Gratiani* C.32 q 5). Hence the question, which at first glance just seems silly, is not without serious ramifications and therefore *honesta.*

5.4   The poet is probably parodying here the rather ponderous way in which lawyers (including Gratian) state the obvious.

6.3–4   Flora may be thinking of the Leviticus 21:10–13, where instructions are given regarding the high priest: he is to marry a virgin and have the oil of anointment poured over his head.

6.4   *quam (amans) in infinito:* that is, than one who loves a nonvirgin.

7.2–3   If these lines are punctuated (or recited) with the break placed after *actibus* rather than *futuris,* then they could mean:

1. May they flourish and prosper in chastity (reading *pudice*) *for* sexual intercourse to come. Brazenness does not lead to salvation.

2. May they flourish and prosper, made chaste (reading *pudicae*) *by* sexual intercourse to come (see on 5.1–2 above). Brazenness . . .

7.4   While *iocunditas* can mean spiritual joy, it can also refer to the joy of sex. In the courtly love tradition, *joi* had a number of meanings, but above all "it represents the erotic pleasure derived from the verbally imagined physical union and the expected sexual gratification from the game of love" (Lazar, "Fin' amor," 77). *Spes* (hope) is virtually a technical term among the troubadour poets. The consummation of their hope *(spes adulta)* was *joi (jocunditas).* Understood in this light the words have a sexual but still fairly refined implication. *Spes* could also be used of children in whom parents placed their hopes; so the last line could mean "May their grown-up (virgin) daughter be a source of joy to those dear to her (that is, her parents)." However, it could also mean "May the young virgin, ripe for marriage, fall to the men she loves as a source of sexual joy." It seems likely that the poet was expecting his readers to be reminded of the notorious verse (1 Corinthians 7:36), which can be accurately translated as follows: "If anyone thinks that he is acting improperly toward his virgin because she is ripe for marriage, and if something must be done, he may do what he wants; there is nothing wrong in it, if she marries." Precisely what Paul meant by the passage is unclear; see Suggs, Sakenfeld, and Mueller, *Oxford Study Bible,* 1454, for three alternative translations of this passage. What is most relevant here, however, is its clear potential for a risqué interpretation that condones premarital sex with a virgin.

60

Rhythmical pattern: Lay

Though this poem is presented as a single poem in *B,* H-S-B printed it as two separate poems, CB 60 (stanzas 1–16) and 60a (17–26), because the woman addressed in the latter part seems completely different from the woman in the earlier part. However, in 1950 J. A. Huisman, *Neue Wege,* 66–77, demonstrated that Walther von der Vogelweide's *Leich* (lay) (1.1 in Cormeau's edition) has exactly the same complicated structure as the two parts together. The conclusion that one poem is a *contrafactum* (that is, a rhythmically identical copy) of the other seems inescapable. This also makes it very difficult to believe that 60 and 60a do not constitute a single poem. Although Huisman thought that Walther's *Leich* was the earlier of the two, it is now generally held to be the *contrafactum.* For a more detailed study of this complex poem, see Traill, "Mal d'amour," 95–112.

The speaker sees himself as tied to his beloved (stanza 1a), but she keeps running off to entertain other admirers (1b). She is not there when he needs her (2). When he visits her, she brusquely dismisses him and pays no heed to his reproaches (3–4). He tells the sad tale of their affair (5a). He gave up all other women for her. She became his lover but soon was chasing after another (5bc). Now even Glycerium will offer him no solace (6). His silence has merely brought him grief; it is time to tell the truth (7a). He loved her beyond all others, but she forgot him (7b). He is overwhelmed with conflicting emotions. She will pay for her crimes on the funeral pyre (8a–c). Her inconstancy overwhelms him (9). He begs her to love those who are devoted to her (10). She cultivates his enemies and remains unimpressed by his love songs and fidelity (11). She promised that their lives would be as one but has no qualms about transferring her affections (12). Her dishonest behavior shows her to be mad (13–14). It would do no good for him to keep silent. He begs Venus to punish her, not him (15–16). But Cupid and the coming of spring have changed his heart (17–18). He longs for her kisses; no other woman comes close to her in his affections (19). His bed awaits, but she does not come (20). He asks his "princess" for a rendezvous at sunset (21). He describes her beauty and insists that he will never cease to sing her praises (22–23). He hopes that sex will be the reward for his song and sees an opportunity for devoted service (24–25). He asks the woman to look favorably on the prayer of her suppliant (26).

1a The bird is a nightingale. Ambrose (*Hexaemeron* 5.24.8) recounts that the nightingale is so devoted to hatching her eggs that she refuses to leave her nest and sings to relieve the tedium. Pliny maintains that she sings for fifteen days without stopping and would rather die singing than be outmatched by a rival (*Natural History* 10.43); see Pfeffer, *Change of Philomel,* 20–21.

1b Comparison with the *contrafactum* indicates a line is missing in *B* at the beginning of this stanza; so a line that fits the rhythm and rhyme has been added.

3 Roman poets frequently refer to the *salutatio* (morning greeting of a patron or social superior) as a burden.

4.1 See *MW* 3.1128, lines 46–57, for examples of *effluere* = "to devote oneself to" with phrases like *ad res illicitas.* For *meritum* = *quaestus,* see *TLL* 8.819, line 42.

4.4 *minans* from *minare* (to drive), not *minari* (to threaten).

5b *Diludium* (interlude, break) is a rare word; so it is fairly certain that our poet is imitating Horace's *diludia posco* (*Epistles* 1.19.47), where Horace calls for a break in the hostile exchanges between rival poets and himself.

5c.1 The initial letters of stanzas were usually left to be filled in later in red ink. In this case the initial Q was not added. *Gratiam inire* (to come into favor) is a common expression (see *OLD*, "inire" 6b), and *ini* is a well-attested alternative for *inii* (compare Statius, *Thebaid* 1. 69 and 8.107).

6a.3 Glycerium ("Sweetie Pie") is a standard name for a courtesan in Roman and medieval comedy.

7a.1, 7a.4 *rem* and *nos* have been added to supply the missing syllables.

8, 9 The speaker's anger is such that he gets quite carried away. The contemplated punishment is remarkably severe: to be burned (alive?) on a pyre. The charge, not made explicitly but unmistakably, is prostitution. At this point we seem a long way from the world of courtly love.

10.6 *Obnoxios;* the plural form suggests the world of Roman comedy, where a lover might contemplate with equanimity sharing a courtesan with a small number of other clients, as in Terence's *Andria.* However, the *meaning* of the word ("in thrall to") suggests the world of courtly love and the abject relationship of the lover to his lady.

10.7 There is no agreement over who the *secretarii* are. They appear in Andreas Capellanus, *De Amore* 1.E.268 (Walsh): "Amoris tui secretarios noli plures habere," which Walsh translates as "Do not have too many privy to your love." Vollmann, however, considers that the *secretarii* refer to those admitted to the *secretum* (the lady's bedroom) and thinks the line essentially means "Don't take on several secret lovers." Spanke thinks that they are the equivalent of the *losengeors* (flatterers), the bane of the troubadours. Since in our poem the *secretarii* seem to be rivals of the *obnoxii* for the lady's affections, it is probably best to see them as the lady's advisers (flatterers in the eyes of the troubadours).

11.9 This line has been added because the *contrafactum* indicates that a four-syllable line is missing before the closing line of the stanza.

12.3   This is a virtual quotation of Horace, *Epistles* 1.18.3, where "a path out of the public eye" describes the choice not to go in for politics or mercantile pursuits. Here, however, *fallentis vitae* may refer to the uncertainties common to all lives or, possibly, to a clandestine affair.

14b.4   The *Bacchanaria* was a female devotee of Dionysus (Bacchus), often portrayed as in an ecstatic frenzy.

16   *Lamia* was a female monster. It translates the Hebrew mythological monster Lilith at Isaiah 34:14.

17–26   Hilka and Schumann judged that this part of the poem could not be about the woman of the first part because the poet's attitude to her has entirely changed. However, the evidence of the *contrafactum* confirms *B*'s presentation of this poem as a single poem of twenty-six stanzas. The poet's explanation for the *volte-face,* a not uncommon feature of vernacular poems of courtly love, is given in stanza 17.

17.1   "Cupid turns my mind/heart around" would be a very strange way in Medieval Latin lyric to signal the beginning of a love affair. The phrase really only makes sense if Cupid is intervening to change the poet's attitude toward the woman he has so rancorously described. Cupid's threatening aspect too makes little sense if this is a different love, but it is an appropriate way of indicating his anger toward the attitude the poet has so far displayed.

18   The *contrafactum* indicates two lines are missing here; see Huisman, *Neue Wege,* for sexual desire being signaled by inflated veins (compare Horace, *Satires* 1.2.31–35).

19a   For Nature singling out the beloved for favorable treatment, compare CB 67.1–2.

19b   Compare 5b above.

22a and b   These sections are devoted to a common feature of medieval love poetry, the *descriptio puellae,* a detailed account of the woman's beautiful features. Compare CB 67 for a longer description.

22c   The *contrafactum* indicates that a third versicle is missing here.

23.1   Maenalus was a mountain sacred to Pan in Arcadia. It was believed to have prophetic powers and was consulted for advice in love affairs; see Virgil, *Eclogues* 8.22–24.

25.3   *Veneris* is better understood as an objective genitive (in the sense of "sex") after *incitamentum* rather than as a (redundant) subjective genitive.

26   Martianus Capella, *De Nuptiis Philologiae et Mercurii* 1.6, describes *Sophia* (Wisdom) as *intemeratior* (purer) than all other maidens.

The second part of this poem shows the influence of the vernacular courtly love tradition. This is clear when the poet addresses the woman as *proles regia* (21a.1), and in the closing stanza when he calls her *intemerata virginum, serena,* and *generosa* and refers to himself as her suppliant. However, even the first part, which evokes the world of Roman comedy and satire, shows some evidence of this same tradition, as when the poet addresses the woman as *a virgo inclita* (a distinguished young lady [2d.1]), when he refers to the *salutatio* (the morning greeting expected of social inferiors [3.2]), and when he sees himself as among *obnoxios* (those in thrall to her) at 10.6. The subject matter of the two sections, namely, the lover's despair at the treatment he is receiving followed by the realization that he derives a kind of joy from his self-effacement, is found in many Provençal and Old French lyrics. There is even a classical precedent (and probable model) for the lover's *volte-face* from hate to love, albeit an ironic and humorous one, in Ovid, *Amores* 3.11. However, in CB 60 the man's reactions seem to be excessive in both parts, and it is probably best to view the poem as an ironic commentary on the folly of lovers. For more detailed commentary, see Traill, "Mal d'Amour."

61

Rhythmical pattern: *Da capo* sequence

Comparison of this poem with its parody, CB 195, shows that as originally written it was a *Da capo* sequence, comprising two identical groups of stanzas: B 2a–b = 9a–b; C 3 = 10; D 4a–b = 11a–b; E 5 = 12 (now missing); F 6a–d = 13a–c (d missing); G 7 = 14. These two groups are introduced by two nonidentical sections, A 1a–d and H 8a–b. The *Carmina Burana* manuscript contains an additional six stanzas that seem not to have been part of the original version and are excluded from the text here and the text of the H-S-B edition, where they are relegated to the notes. Vollmann includes all the stanzas in his text.

The signs of spring have heightened the poet's confidence in his professional skill and his hopes that his lady will consent to be his lover (stanza 1). His lady's smile and kindness lift his spirits and increase his desire (2). Her attentions make him a better poet (3). Her beauty is more than mortal. He seeks release from his despair (4–5). Just as it was love at first sight when Apollo saw Daphne, so the poet fell in love with his lady. Her charms are magnetic. Just as Paris was a brilliant warrior, so the poet has shone with his feasts (6). The resistance of his lady troubles him. No matter which of her suitors she chooses, she should accept his praise (7–8). He has been fired with love since he first saw her. But she resists her young admirer (9). He is infatuated with her and would rather have her acceptance of him than be made king of the world (10–11). Her smile has given him hope, but if she cannot love him, then perhaps she can change him (13a–b). But if there is discord between them, he will leave (13c). He asks her to give meaning to her signs of affection and yield to love's play (14).

1a.1–2 In line 2, the poet is probably thinking of Ovid, *Tristia* 2.363–64, where Ovid speaks of the love poetry of the Tean bard (Anacreon) in the drunken setting of the symposium. Unlike the Archpoet (191.16–18) and Anacreon and his followers, this poet does not need wine to fuel his inspiration; the exuberance of spring itself provides prompting enough (1a.4).

1b.2 The line has two syllables too many in *B; vita* was probably added by a scribe who understood *vel* in the sense of "or" rather than "even."

2a.1–2 These poetically phrased lines are difficult to render in convincing English. The point is that the lady's noble birth is apparent in her disarming smile, which banishes the poet's sadness and sense of insecurity.

2a.3 The moth is a symbol of destructiveness.

3.4 *Doctus* (learned) is often used approvingly of poets.

5.4 That is, when I first saw you.

6c   Here the poet compares himself with Paris (Priam's son), the great lover of mythology, whom medieval authors often portrayed as a great soldier. The poet has tried to impress his lady (and others) with expensive banquets, as he ruefully explains, and this has brought about his financial difficulties described in stanza 7. Schumann needlessly changes *B*'s *sic valent* to *sed squalent*.

7.1   Either *florenti* or *desolatio* could refer to the state of his love life. However, the sense of the stanza as a whole requires *florenti* to refer to his love life and *desolatio* to his financial losses due to his elaborate banquets.

9b.1   *B*'s *haec* leaves the line one syllable short; for *iste* in the sense of "this of mine" in Medieval Latin, see *DMLBS*, "iste" 5.

9b.6   *Tenero* suggests the poet is young and inexperienced.

13a   Here Jupiter's smile would appear to mean the smile on Jupiter's face; for other denotations of the phrase, see note on 73.1a.3 below.

62

Rhythmical pattern: Descort

Just as a light breeze blows away the clouds, so music can sway a wavering heart and make it turn to love (stanza 1). The Evening Star induces sleep (2). Sleep brings calm to our cares and relief to our pain. It is on a par with love for the joy it brings us (3). Sleep can be induced by music (4), a full stomach (5), or sex (6).

This is generally reckoned to be one of the finest poems in the *Carmina Burana*. There is a close parody of it among the drinking poems (CB 197). The parody is based on only these six stanzas, and it ends, like CB 62, with a suitable punch line. The parody enables us to correct the ordering of the stanzas in *B*, which places stanza 6 before stanza 5. The fact that the parody has no stanzas corresponding to *B*'s stanzas 7 and 8 suggests that these stanzas, which are much indebted to the earlier stanzas, are later additions by another poet or a separate poem altogether. They are printed here as 62a.

3.4 Since *B*'s *ipsum* adds clutter and two extra syllables (compare 197.3.2), it is omitted.

4.1 By a simple metonymy, Orpheus here stands for music and resumes the theme of stanza 1. Though Vollmann prints *Orpheus* in his text, he states in his notes that Morpheus is the right reading. However, it seems very likely that Morpheus would have been known to medieval readers, as he is to us today, only from Ovid, *Metamorphoses* 11.635–70, where he has the responsibility of creating images only of *human figures* (638: "hic solos homines imitatur") in dreams; Phantasos, on the other hand, is responsible for rocks, water, trees, and all lifeless things (642–43).

4.2–5 Music creates in our minds a series of images. The simple country scenes evoked here all portray static movement.

4.5 *Per se* has been added because the parody and awkward rhythm indicate that the line in *B* is two syllables short; *lenti* (slow) is a possible alternative.

5 As Vollmann has shown, this stanza is indebted to a physiological theory put forward by William of St-Thierry's *De Natura corporis et animae*. Of digestion he says: "There also rises from this process of digestion a subtle, sweet vapor, which gently touches the brain and presses against its lobes so that it lulls all its actions; this is sleep. . . . The soul resting within, with all functions of the senses shut down, turns over within itself the past, present and future, and this constitutes dreams"; see PL 180.698C–D for the Latin text, and McGinn, *Three Treatises,* 109, for the translation.

5.2 William of St-Thierry also divides the brain into three compartments, as many others as far back as Galen did before him, with imagination in front, reason in the middle, and memory at the back; see McGinn, *Three treatises,* 114.

5.8 The organs involved in digestion were thought to be servants of the higher organs—the senses and the brain.

6.2–4 The warm fuzziness often felt after sexual intercourse.

6.6 A punch-line ending.

62a

Rhythmical pattern: Descort

The first stanza, with the couple under a tree and a nightingale singing, looks very like the opening of a typical love poem. It gets quickly to the point: sex is better than resting. Stanza 2, which appears indebted to *Vacillantis trutinae* (CB 108), meditates on the uncertainties that are the lot of a lover.

Arguments against these lines belonging to CB 62 (though they are presented as such in *B*) are the following:

1. The parody of 62 (CB 197) has only six stanzas.

2. Both the original (without these stanzas) and the parody end in a suitable punch line.

3. Lenzen (*Überlieferungsgeschichtliche,* 92–94) argues that much of 62a consists of weak imitations of material from well-known twelfth-century lyrics, including 62 itself, pointing out that *post Veneris defessa commercia* (2.14) falls intolerably flat after *post blanda Veneris commercia* (62.6.1).

1.3–4   with *suave . . . suavius,* etc., compare 62.6.5–6.

2.4–5   compare 108.2a.3–5: *navicula / levis in aequore, dum caret ancorae / subsidio.*

2.6   with *(animus) fluctuat* compare *mens . . . fluctuat* (108.1a.3).

2.14   See argument 3 above.

63

Rhythmical pattern: Sequence with refrain
Author: Philip the Chancellor

Hercules achieved fame by slaying many monsters but undercut his heroism by falling for Iole. Though love mars fame and wastes time, lovers ignore this and slave away in the service of Venus (stanza 1a and refrain). Hercules killed the Hydra and carried the world on his shoulders but was tamed by a girl (1b). He killed Cacus, Nessus, and Geryon and brought Cerberus up from the underworld but was captivated by a girl (2a). He yielded to Venus's gentle power, though he killed the giant snake that guarded the Apples of Hesperides, broke off the horn of the river god

Achelous, killed the Erymanthian boar, the Nemean lion, and Diomedes, who owned man-eating horses (2b). He defeated the wrestler Antaeus (3a). Such were the Labors of Hercules, but he became captivated by a woman, and this detracts from the glory of his deeds (3b). The poet intends to be braver than Hercules by fleeing from Venus, which is the best way to beat her (4a). His love affair with Lycoris has been pleasant but is now ending, for he is going to turn to other pursuits (4b).

For the stories associated with the various names, see the Index of Proper Names under "Hercules."

2a.3	As a centaur, Nessus is both physically *duplex* (biform) and morally *duplex* (duplicitous) in his dealings with Hercules.
2a.10	Cacus and Cerberus both had three heads; Nessus was part man, part horse; and Geryon was a three-bodied giant. Iole's smile, in contrast, was *simplex* (single and straightforward).
2b.4	The guardian of the rich garden refers to the giant snake that guarded the Apples of the Hesperides.
3a	Philip is playing with two different verbs (*vinco, vincere* [to conquer], and *vincio, vincire* [to bind]), many of whose forms look identical.
4a.11–12	For the same conceit, compare CB 29.3.14 and 31.8.9, and Alan of Lille, *De Planctu Naturae* 9.71: *fugiendo fugatur.*

63a

Meter: Leonine hexameter

This advice addressed to a youth about avoiding homosexual rape perhaps had a proverbial significance about the need to react appropriately to warning signs.

For *actus* in the sense of "sexual act," see Adams, *Sexual Vocabulary,* 205.

64

Meter: Dactylic hexameters
Author: Ausonius

In a *tour de force,* Ausonius lists the Twelve Labors of Hercules in the traditional order, devoting only a single hexameter to each. Its inclusion here is perhaps intended to comment on CB 63, which refers somewhat allusively to several of Hercules's labors as well as to some of his deeds outside the canonical twelve labors.

1   Cleonae (mod. Klenia) a small town near Nemea.

For a succinct account of each labor, see under "Hercules" in the Index of Personal Names.

65

Rhythmical pattern: Sequence

At any time of year the poet depends on only one deity for his salvation (stanzas 1–2a). The Graces have indicated their favor and Venus in human form has smiled on him (2b). His lover, though a virgin, long pretended to be a married woman. Losing her virginity has not made her reluctant to have more sexual encounters (3a). The poet has hung up his fetter and is free and ready to have sex with her (3b). He would show the symptoms of a lover if his love was unrequited, but that is not the case (4a–5b). She has brightened his life and he worships her (6a–7b). She is joyful, beautiful, and witty and shows signs of her love (8a–9b). His poems spread her fame all over the world. Anyone in a similar situation is asked to pray that the poet's love will endure and he will reciprocate (10a and b).

This is one of the most difficult poems in the *Carmina Burana.* Dronke, *Medieval Latin,* 1.300, has called it "deliberately obscure." There is no generally accepted overall interpretation.

1   The word *(eucrasis -is)* I have translated as "rhythm" is a Latinized Greek word meaning "harmonious mixture," a medical term usually denoting the situation when the four humors are in proper balance.

2a   These names for the Sun's four horses—Philogaeus (Earthlover) denotes winter; Erythraeus (Ruddy), spring; Actaeon (Gleaming), summer; and Lampas (Shining), fall—appear in Fulgentius, *Mitologiae* 1.12. They differ from those given at Ovid, *Metamorphoses* 2.153–54.

2a.7   The one deity is of course Venus, but she is blended here with the Venus in human form, the *virgo* (2b.6).

2b   On Pasithea, Euryale, and Euphrosyne, see "Graces" in the Index of Personal Names.

2b.7   *Allotheta* is a very rare word, scarcely to be found in Latin dictionaries. It could be used to describe various grammatical misusages, but that meaning does not seem appropriate here. Peter Helias, *Summa* 1.1003, line 22, tells us that *allotheta* is "a general name for all figures of speech." Vollmann translates it as "allegorist," but that seems dubious. It is better to see the word as the personification Allegory, who warns the reader to understand allegorically key elements in what follows. Unfortunately, there are a number of ambiguities that make it hard to determine the literal meaning of the Latin, far less the correct allegorical interpretation. Most probably, however, *Allotheta* is a way of referring to the poet's lover, as the conjectural translation of this word in this passage in *MW* 1.484.31–34 suggests: "one who changes his sex," presumably by cross-dressing, that is, a transvestite.

3a   The bearded Venus, sometimes called *Aphroditus,* is attested in a number of ancient statues, figurines, and literary texts. She was female in form and dress but had a beard and male genitalia (often revealed by a raised skirt). Macrobius tells us "men sacrifice to her in women's dress, women in men's dress" (*Saturnalia* 3.8.2). Most scholars seem to agree that just as *Dione nudula* and the "certain woman" are blended at 2b.6, so too are the bearded Venus and the poet's *virgo* in 3a. Dronke, *Medieval Latin,* 1.300, assumes a homosexual partner or, perhaps more precisely, a transvestite. Vollmann, on the other hand, considers the partner to be female and holds that her bipartite nature consists in her continued pretense to be a *virgo,* when she is in fact sexually active. It should be noted that *virgo,* though rarely applied to males in classical Latin, was increasingly so used in Late and

Medieval Latin; also, the use of feminine pronouns or adjectival forms to suggest male effeminacy is a familiar practice in many societies.

3a.3–4   *Renovare* in religious contexts can mean "make (a deity) present" by some ritual practice. So at the divine level, "renovata maturo tumultu" refers to the god's epiphany prompted perhaps by the crowd of worshippers hurrying to his sanctuary, while on the human level, it refers to the arrival of the *virgo* from the crowded city streets.

3a.6   For a similar use of *mentiri,* compare Virgil, *Eclogues* 4.42.

3a.14   *Natura* means both "nature" and "genitalia" (*OLD,* "natura" 15).

3b.5   "Venus" may here also refer to the *virgo,* and "Adonis" may be genitive of *Adon* and refer to the poet; compare CB 6*.1.

3b.6   Cithaeron is a mountain close to Thebes. Its associations are with the worship of Bacchus rather than Venus. Presumably, this is the poet's error for Cythera (*i* and *y* are frequently confused in medieval manuscripts), which had an important cult of Venus.

3b.9   Apollo becomes enslaved at the sight of Daphne (CB 61.6a.1–2), who did not return his love.

3b.10   The identity of Apollo's cohort is not obvious. However, Apollo is often identified with the sun, and if we understand *immobili* to agree with *cohorti* instead of (or in addition to) *Delio,* then his *immobilis cohors* would be the fixed stars.

3b.14   There is clearly a double entendre here, since *ianua / porta* can refer to the vulva or the anus; see Adams, *Sexual Vocabulary,* 89.

6b.1   The verb *colo,* which means "worship" as well as "to cultivate (a friendship)," neatly continues the identification of the *virgo* with the deity.

7a.2   The same effect is produced by *confiteor,* which can mean "acknowledge" in a general sense but has a special religious application, as in *confiteor Christum.*

7b   No one has been able to make sense of this line as it stands in *B*. *Mire* seems wrong, as it does not provide a two-syllable rhyme with *mature.* The substitution of *ture* (frankincense)—for which *mire* would be an easy error paleographically—solves the problem and is appropriate both for the deity (as incense) and for the *virgo* (as perfume). The manuscript's *eam* has been changed to *meam* because a word cannot rhyme with itself (unless used in a grammatically different manner).

9a.1   For *flosculus* = choicest or best of anything, see *DMLBS,* "flosculus" 2.

10b.6   On the Jubilee year see, note at CB 123.6.4.

66

Meter: Leonine hexameters with single rhymes

This poem seems to comment on the opening of CB 65 by pointing out that the names of the Sun's horses also reflect the different segments of the day.

1, 8   The classical spelling "Erythraeus" does not scan but would have been written "Erythreus" in Medieval Latin. The *-eus* could have been construed as two shorts or (as here) a long diphthong. The initial *E* was actually short but has to be long here; medieval poets were often vague about the correct quantity of vowels in Greek words.

67

Rhythmical pattern: Sequence
Author: Peter of Blois (canonist)

When the heavenly powers created the world, Nature knew what she was going to do. She had long been thinking of my woman and devoted her best work to creating her (1a–b). She lavished many gifts of beauty on her (2a–b). Her eyes, wrinkle-free brow, playful laughter, and eyebrows are all exquisite, as are her nose, lips, and teeth (3a–b, 4a–b). Her complexion is a pleasant mix of pink and white tones. In presenting Coronis as a gift to the world, Nature also made her a trap for the unwary (5a–b).

The core of this poem is a well-worn cliché: the *descriptio puellae,* or the detailed listing of a woman's attractive features. What distinguishes this poem from other instances of this *topos* is the playfully extravagant open-ing, where he tells us that his Coronis is the culmination of Nature's work in creating the world.

The first two stanzas (1a–b) draw their inspiration and some of their lan-guage from Bernard Silvestris's *Cosmographia.* The first book *(Megacosmos)* opens with Nature's complaint about the formlessness of primordial mat-ter *(Silva).* *Noys* (Intelligence) agrees, and the two goddesses assist Silva in differentiating itself into the elements of fire, earth, water, and air. It will be seen that stanza 1a.1–5 of CB 67 neatly summarizes these processes. The *globo veteri* refers to the original, undifferentiated state of *Silva,* the *superi* are *Natura* and *Noys,* the *rerum faciem* is *Silva* differentiated into the four elements, and the *mundi seriem* is the array of created phenomena.

1a.4   I formerly argued ("Notes on CB 62 and CB 67," 149–51) that *quae* refers to *rerum faciem* but am now persuaded that *Natura* is its postponed antecedent.

1a.7   The notion that Nature lavished special care (1b) on the poet's girl is in itself a topos, but backdating her intention to do so to the beginning of creation is Peter's original touch. His *praecon-ceperat* wittily alludes to the *concepta,* which Bernard has Nature say she will have to abandon (1.1.10) if something cannot be done about Silva's formlessness. Bernard does not tell us what these *concepta* were (although he probably refers to her longing for the creation of mankind); so Peter supplies the answer: the creation of Coronis!

3a–5a   A model *descriptio puellae* is given in Geoffrey of Vinsauf's *Poetria Nova* 562–99; see Faral, *Arts,* 214–15, for the Latin text, and Geoffrey's *Poetria,* ed. Nims, 36–37, for the English translation.

3a.3   The lily is a symbol of whiteness, as the rose is of redness or pinkness; compare 5a.6 below.

5a.6   See on 3a.3.

5b.1   In Greek mythology, Coronis was a young woman of Thessaly beloved by Apollo. Pregnant by him with Asclepius, she had an affair with another and Apollo killed her but rescued his son from her womb; see Ovid, *Metamorphoses* 2.542–632.

68

Rhythmical pattern: Descort

It is a sunny spring morning with the birds singing and the flowers dancing (stanzas 1–2). Venus favors lovers and the cold winds have gone (3–4). The hot kisses of my girl lead me to hope for more (5). Happy is he who chances on such a mix of nectar and honey that lulls our senses to sleep! (6).

1.1	The references to the planets here suggest the time of day rather than the season. Mercury is visible for only a short time, just before sunrise and just after sunset. Since the Sun is banishing Saturn, it is clearly early morning. The season is indicated in 1.2–3.
1.2	On Jupiter's smile, see note on 73.1a.3 below.
4.4	The planet Saturn was associated with gloom and winter. "Jupiter" was often used by metonymy for sky.
4.10	The sun is in Taurus from April 20 till May 20.
5.1	*Beare* (to bless) seems to be used in Medieval Latin love poetry as a euphemism for "to grant sexual favors," as at CB 70.2.8 and 73.6a.2. For this use of the infinitive, see Blaise, *Manuel,* §327.

69

Rhythmical pattern: Descort

Summer has departed. The birds no longer sing. The trees are bare and the flowers have gone (stanza 1). But no frost can cool my ardor. I am tortured by love. If only I could have one kiss! (2). A kiss from her lips makes me feel immortal; her hair and hands are beautiful. Everything about her is perfect! (3).

While spring is the time par excellence for love, it is not unusual for poets to point out, as here and in CB 83, that their love is just as fervent in winter.

2.5	*amare* is the subject of *studet.*
3.1–21	Some of the details of the *descriptio puellae* here (the fact that she draws the eyes of everyone, her playful laugh, her slightly full

lips) are so similar to CB 67.3b and 4b that it is reasonable to suppose that it influenced this poem.

70

Rhythmical pattern: Lay

The bulk of this poem takes the form of a conversation between the poet and his lover. It opens with the poet's description of the setting for his talk with Thisbe (stanza 1). Wondering if his lover can be won over by his arguments (2), he decides he has to try (3). He tells of the passion that burns him like a flame; only she can save him from his misery (4a–b). She replies that in love constancy and patience are what count, and he needs to find another love, for she is not interested in a furtive affair (4c, 5a–c). He replies that only she can extinguish his fire. It is up to her whether he lives or dies (6a–b, 7a). She asks why she should risk her life. Her family has her closely watched. She fears unfriendly gossip (7b, 8a–b, 9, 10). He dismisses her fears. He will take care of the watchers (11a–b). She wavers and then agrees to submit to Venus's yoke (12a–b). He tells her that Venus's yoke is liberating and that her joys are sweet (13, 14a–b). She surrenders herself to him (15).

1.4	The name Thisbe was known to medieval poets mainly because of the famous story in Ovid, *Metamorphoses* 4.55–166, where the exotic Greek genitive (Thisbes) was available to them at line 115.
2–3	As Vollmann points out, these stanzas must be understood as an interior monologue that ends with "So let's begin with these words."
3.4	Proverbial; compare Terence, *Phormio* 203, and Virgil, *Aeneid* 10.284.
5a.3	*Famulantia* is a rare word. See *MW* 4.76.50–52, where it is interpreted as "female servant."
5b	Compare Ovid, *Remedia Amoris* 462: "successore novo vincitur omnis amor" (every love is vanquished by its successor).
11b.1	Stilbon is another name for Mercury, who put Argus to sleep.

71

Rhythmical pattern: Sequence

1b   Just as Phoebus (in 1a–b) is used by metonymy for the sun, so Cybele is used for the earth, and Bacchus (Semele's son) for the grapevine.

For a short account of the mythological background to these names and figures, see the Index of Proper Names.

72

Rhythmical pattern: Sequence
Author: Peter of Blois (canonist)

Despite its disturbingly violent subject matter, this poem shows the high level of skill and polish that we associate with Peter of Blois. The exquisite ending turns what at first seems to be a rape scene into what we can regard only as rough sex. For a detailed analysis of this poem, its companion piece CB 84, and their author, see Traill, "Rough Sex."

    The poet expresses his thanks to Venus for granting him the victory he has now achieved after a long campaign (stanzas 1a–b). He had completed the first four stages of love and was eager for the culminating stage, but Coronis was very reluctant and wept profusely (2a–b). Her tears only increased his desire and he renewed his pleas (3a–b). Coronis curls up and crosses her legs but he binds her arms and forces himself upon her (4a–b). Both enjoyed the encounter and Coronis kissed her lover, sighed, and fell asleep (5a–b).

2a.1–2   The five stages (or "lines") of love crop up frequently in Medieval Latin love poetry.

2a.8   At this point Peter (mentally) switches his narrative tense to the historic present for the sake of vividness; hence the use of the future perfect here. Though English also uses the historic present, particularly in this kind of excited narrative, the change here seems rather abrupt; so I have postponed it to 2b in the translation.

2a.9   In Medieval Latin *de cetero* often means "in the future" (see *DMLBS*, "ceterus" 4a).

2b.6   With *repagula,* compare *ianua* at 4a.9 below, and see note on *portae* at 65.3b.14.

73

Rhythmical pattern: Sequence

1a.1   *Cronos* (Saturn) symbolizes winter. As a Greek name, one would expect it to decline and show an ablative ending *(Crono)* here. However, that would create a hiatus, which this poem rigorously avoids. The poet seems to have chosen to treat it like an indeclinable biblical name.

1a.3   The *risus Iovis* can mean "the smile of Jupiter" or "radiant sky," or it can refer to the name of the urn in which the mildness of spring was stored; see Martianus Capella, *De Nuptiis Philologiae et Mercurii* 1.16–17. The second and third meanings seem most relevant here. Compare CB 68.1.2.

1b.1–2   *Cynthius* is an epithet of Apollo, since he was born on Mount Cynthus in Delos. *Coma rutilante* could also be taken as an ablative of means (with his russet hair, that is, his beams).

1b.3–4   The ancients divided the sky into two sections: the *aether* above the clouds and the *aer,* the air up to and including the clouds, where the weather happens. Fertility generally needs a combination of sun, rainfall, and gentle winds.

2a.3–4   This is the silver urn in which spring was stored; see note on 1a.3 above.

3b   Since both *philomena* and *luscinia* can mean nightingale, it is best to assume that *philomena* here means swallow, as it does at Cassiodorus, *Variae* 8.31.

9.3   A clear-cut instance of Venus and Dione denoting the goddess's harsher and pleasanter aspects, respectively.

74

Rhythmical pattern: 2x(7pp+6p), 2x(7pp +7pp+6p)

Spring has come with all its joys (stanza 1). As the world heats up, Venus warms my heart (2). The nymphs and satyrs are responding appropriately and the nightingale is singing (3). The flowers are out and the crickets are chirping (4). The man who has a lover is lucky; the man without a lover is wretched (5).

2.1   On *Risu Iovis* see note at 73.1a.3.

4a   Compare 73.a, where the Dryads, Satyrs, and Napaean nymphs are listed.

75

Rhythmical pattern: 4x7pp, 2x(8p+7pp); *Ref.* 2x(7pp+6p)

The poet urges his companions to stop studying and enjoy themselves (stanza 1), for they are in the spring of their lives and winter is approaching with all its troubles (2). They should do as the gods do and go after what they want. He urges them to go and watch the girls dancing (3), for the sensuous swaying of their limbs takes his breath away (4).

1.2   Horace, *Odes* 4.12.25: "dulce est desipere in loco."

1.7–8 These lines are missing in the manuscript. Herkenrath's emendation neatly fills the gap.

2.5–8 Walsh points out that these lines are clearly indebted to Juvenal, *Satires* 10.217–19: "minimus gelido iam in corpore sanguis / . . . circumsilit agmine facto / morborum omne genus."

4   The final stanza shows considerable skill in evoking the suggestive movements of the dancing girls and the effect on the young men watching.

76

Rhythmical pattern: 4x(7pp+6p), equivalent to Goliardic stanza

This tongue-in-cheek satire describes a young man's visit to a well-appointed brothel as if it were a visit to a temple of Venus.

Stopped at the entrance to the temple of Venus, the narrator explains to the female doorkeeper his need to enter (stanzas 1–7). He is admitted to the presence of Venus, who asks his name and why he has come. When the man explains his desperate medical condition, Venus welcomes him and promises excellent counseling on proper payment (8–12). The man gives up his purse, and they proceed to a room full of beautiful women, who invite him to sit, but Venus says they have other business to do (13–15). Left alone in a private room, they enjoy conversation for a while. Then Venus strips and lies down on the couch, and for the next ten hours the man alleviates his raging fever (16–17). After this they have a bath and an excellent meal (18–20). The man stays there for three months. When he leaves, his money and rich apparel are gone. His story should be a warning to all who hear it (21–22).

4.4   *Vestri comitatus* could also mean "one of your company." Peter Stotz kindly pointed out to me that *unde* here could be understood as "why?" "for what reason?" and that the answer could be taken to mean "for your companionship" (genitive of cause).

5.3   For *et* in the sense of *vel*, see Blaise, *Dictionnaire,* s.v. 4.

12.2   *sodes* is an alternative form for *sodalis* (*DMLBS,* "sodes"); for the history of the development of this meaning, see Stotz, "Zur Geschichte eines Bedeutungssprungs."

13.1   On *loculus* see note on 21.2 below.

16.4   The poet is playing on the ambiguity of *pertractare,* which here can mean "discuss" or, more literally, "touch, paw."

18.2   Garden areas and bathing facilities were not uncommon in medieval brothels; the distinction between public baths and brothels tended to be blurred; see Rossiaud, *Medieval Prostitution,* 4–5.

19–20   Food and drink were often served in brothels. Rossiaud, *Medi-*

eval Prostitution, 5 notes: "The managers found the kitchen nearly as profitable as the bedroom."

21.2 *Loculus,* besides meaning "purse," can also mean "scrotum" (*DMLBS,* "loculus" 3); both meanings are probably intended here. For similar play with this ambiguity, see Walter of Châtillon, *Shorter Poems,* 46n and 139n.

22.2 Northcott ("Some Functions," 16) suggests that the somewhat surprising use of the preposition *penes* (here = "in") indicates wordplay with the plural of *penis* but does not explain how. If so, it should make some appropriate sense when taken in apposition with *vos.* Adams, *Latin Sexual Vocabulary,* 36, points out that *penis* was actually used in an affectionate way, so that *vos penes* as a vocative is close to "you guys." This suits the context admirably.

22.4 The poem ends on a suitably ambiguous note. Ostensibly, it means "you can save yourselves from my misfortune." However, since *liber* can mean "not practicing restraint, licentious" (*OLD,* "liber" 11b), it can also mean "you can do as I did."

77

Rhythmical pattern: 4x(7pp+6p) Goliardic stanza

The poet has won a glorious victory. Here is his story. As he stood in a pleasant grove, he reflected on how foolish he was to pursue an impossible dream, for an old woman zealously guarded the woman he loves (stanzas 1–4). Suddenly he saw a beautiful flower (his beloved). Filled with joy, he ran up to her and on bended knee greeted her as his Helen (5–8). When she replies politely, he tells her that she must be the one to save him, as it was she who wounded him. She denies wounding him and asks him to show her his wound. He says his wounds are clear to see. It has been more than five years since he first saw her (9–12). He tells her he found her a peerless beauty. All her features are perfect (13–16). He wanted to speak to her but no opportunity arose. This is how he has been wounded. He cannot eat, drink, or sleep and asks Christ to help him (17–20). His only solace is that in dreams he imagines himself with her. He asks her to restore him to life; if she does not do so, he may die. She says that she has suffered too (21–24). She wants to help him and asks what will give him joy. Does he want money or precious stones? He says he wants a solution that will bring joy. She tells him not to hold back but to take what he wants (25–28). He then embraces her and they kiss, becoming more and more intimate until eventually he wins his prize. His experience should encourage others not to give up. Worthwhile goals are not achieved without effort (29–33).

Walsh points out that this poem has been variously interpreted as a serious love poem and as primarily humorous. He rightly argues that we should not restrict ourselves to this dichotomy. It would have been natural for Medieval Latin poets, steeped as they were in the traditions of Ovidian love poetry and Roman comedy and satire, to treat the courtly love tradition with a certain degree of humor even when paying tribute to it. CB 60 is a striking example of this tendency.

1.1	Compare 1 Corinthians 13:1.
1.4	There is a pun in "profanis," which can mean "pagan" or "uninitiated."
2.1	The poet here echoes the opening of Venantius Fortunatus's famous hymn: *Pange, lingua, gloriosi;* see Walsh, *Hymns,* 96–101.
2.1–4	Discretion is a recurring feature in courtly love poetry because of the fear of harmful gossip. In particular, the mistress's name is not to be mentioned.
3.1	The sighting of the beloved usually takes place in a *locus amoenus* (attractive location). Here, of course, it is by no means the first sighting, as we learn in stanza 12.
3.3–4	Sowing seed in sand was a proverbial expression of futility.
4.4	The reference to Pluto's abduction of Persephone (Proserpine) to live with him as queen of the underworld is witty not only because of the contrast between Persephone and the old crone but also because it amounts to saying "To hell with her!"
5.3	*laeta* probably, though not definitely, refers to love affairs.
5.3–4	In his discussion of this poem, Dronke, *Medieval Latin,* 1.318–31, reads *moraret icta* with *B* (319), which he interprets to mean that the chaperon was indeed struck by lightning (323). However,

Vollmann translates the same words to mean that a brewing storm was delaying its bolts of lightning. Scribes often confuse *r* and *t*, and *morarer ita* gives excellent sense.

6.2 *Madius,* an alternative form for *Maius,* is useful here because it has the needed extra syllable. The blending of the attractive woman with the rose finds extended allegorical expression in the *Roman de la Rose.*

6.4 *Fidere in* with accusative is common in Medieval Latin, particularly in the case of believing in a divinity.

8 Vollmann points out that the terms in which the woman is addressed are those often applied to the Virgin Mary.

9.1 The Morning Star is Venus and so applicable to the beloved, but this too is a name given to Mary.

10.4 This proverbial notion is as old as Greek mythology, as the story of Telephus (who was wounded by Achilles and could be healed only by his spear) illustrates.

12.4 Probably inspired by 1 Corinthians 13:12, "Videmus nunc per speculum in aenigmate, tunc autem facie ad faciem" (At present we see only puzzling reflections in a mirror, but one day we shall see face to face). The beloved was at once a mirror whereby one can see God dimly and a window through which one can see him clearly.

15–16 Another example of the *descriptio puellae* topos; see note on CB 67.3a–5a above.

18.2 The verb *novercari* first appears in Late Latin; from the stereotypical view of a stepmother *(noverca),* as reflected, for instance, in fairy tales, it means "to act maliciously."

19 Compare *Pamphilus* 1: "Vulneror et clausum porto sub pectore telum."

30.1 This device, common in Medieval Latin poetry, sidesteps describing the details of a sexual encounter. It finds its origin in Ovid; compare *Amores* 1.5.25: "cetera quis nescit?"

31.4 Compare Psalms 148:13.

33.3 This proverbial expression was generally used to warn about possible negative consequences of indiscriminate sexual encounters.

78

Rhythmical pattern: Irregular; lines of 7, 8, 9, or 10 syllables
Probably of German origin.

1.5   In the twelfth century, Europe was still operating on the Julian
         calendar, whose lack of precision had by this time caused it
         to fall some eight days behind a more precise reckoning; so
         January 1 was actually January 9 in Gregorian terms, by which
         date days had been getting longer for eighteen days. Even so, it
         does seem rather early to be announcing the passing of win-
         ter's harshness. More probably, the year is being viewed here in
         terms analogous to a life, with spring marking the beginning
         and winter the end.

2.1–5   A short *descriptio puellae.*

3.1–2   A golden arrow inflicted passionate love on the victim, while a
         lead arrow caused aversion to love.

79

Rhythmical pattern: 4x8p, 6p

This pastourelle has close affinities with Walter of Châtillon's at *Shorter Poems,* no. 32, and his parody of the genre (*Shorter Poems,* no. 17). Besides the single rhyme of the first five lines of each stanza, the sixth line of every stanza shares the same rhyme.

4.5   *Sine pari* occurs often in pastourelles, where it seems to mean
         "unaccompanied," but it can also mean "peerless."

80

Rhythmical pattern: Sequence with refrain; some irregularities

81

Rhythmical pattern: 4x(7pp+6p); *Ref.* 7pp, 7pp+6p

4.3–4   The frisky old woman recalls similar old women in Neidhart's
         Sommerlieder 1 and 3, suggesting a German origin for this poem.

82

Rhythmical pattern: 6x7pp; *Ref.* 4x7pp; many irregularities

The advent of spring provides the occasion for a debate between two
young women about the comparative merits of a knight and a cleric as a
lover, as in the much longer and more sophisticated poem 92, which ap-
pears to have inspired this poem. Several of the details of the signs of
spring are indebted to *Hiemale tempus, vale.* The rhythmical irregularities
and the apparent Germanism in line 1 suggest a German origin.

1.1   *Hinc est* is strange Latin but perhaps a Germanism.
4.6   There is wordplay with *natura*, which, besides meaning "nature"
         or "character," can (like the English "manhood") also denote
         the genitalia.
6.6   The beauty that is gone could also refer to that of the knight
         who might well perish in war.
7.4   A *pyxis* was a small box or chest, often decorated, that would
         contain valuables, such as money, spices, or perfumes.

83

Rhythmical pattern: 2x(7pp +4pp), 2x(7pp+8p), 7pp, 6p; *Ref.* 4x4pp, 2x4p
Author: Peter of Blois (canonist)

It is wintertime and the livestock show no interest in mating (stanza 1).
But the poet is always ready for love and much enjoys his time with Flora
(2). They enjoy sexual play in a secluded room, where she lets him run his
hands over her body, which he describes in detail (3–6). Such is her beauty
that if Jupiter were to see her, he would seek to seduce her by resorting to
his trickery (7).

84

Rhythmical pattern: 4x6p, 2x(2p+3pp+7pp), 2x(4pp+4pp+8pp), 7pp; *Ref.* 2x(4pp+7pp), 7pp
Author: Peter of Blois (canonist)

The poet's eye is captivated by Phyllis sitting under a tree (stanza 1). When she steps into the field, he approaches her, sits beside her, and starts flattering her. The girl begins to tremble and cry. When he touches her sexually, she uses her nails to reject his advances (2–3). He responds by pushing her down and forcing her legs apart and entering her (4).

While the subject matter of this poem disturbingly describes a rape, the poet shows remarkable skill. In many ways it can be regarded as an outdoor version of poem 72 *(Grates ago Veneri)* but without the saving grace of that poem's closing stanza. It shares enough striking similarities with 72 to confirm Walsh's conclusion that both poems were written by the same poet; see further on both poems in Traill, "Rough Sex and Rape." Its juxtaposition with 83 confirms the attribution.

1.1–4   The poet shows his skill in the opening lines by employing the unusual rhyme *-ulta* four times.

Ref.   *B* and *V* (a Vatican manuscript that contains this poem) record the refrain with minor differences, but only after the first stanza. The differences led Schumann (followed here) to conclude that *B*'s version belongs after stanza 3, as its line 2 rhymes with 3.17 (which otherwise does not rhyme), and that *V*'s version belongs after stanza 1, as its line 2 rhymes with 1.17. Unfortunately, if there were corresponding variations in line 2 of the refrain for stanzas 2 and 4, they have not survived.

4.12, 4.15 It was a fashion among poets of the late twelfth century to create new compound verbs with the prefix *de* to mean "undo . . ." as in *virginem devirginem* and at Walter of Châtillon's *Shorter Poems,* 24.3.6 *rosa derosatur.*

85

Rhythmical pattern: 3x8pp; *Ref.* 4pp, 8pp, 4pp

How the coming of spring affects young women. This poem is found again at CB 159.

3.3   By "highest of the gods" the women presumably mean Amor.

4   Following Spanke (Review, 39) and Dronke ("Latin Songs," 29–
          32), I have chosen to follow the much older (11th century) Es-
          corial manuscript *(E)* for the last stanza, which gives expres-
          sion to the sentiments of Juliana. Dronke's suggestion that this
          last stanza was changed for a readership in South Tyrol, where
          the reference to Silos and the fame of its scriptorium would
          not be recognized, is highly likely. *B*'s version is written from a
          male point of view with little originality:

Si tenerem, quam cupio,	If I held the woman I long for
in nemore sub folio	in a glade beneath the foliage,
oscularer cum gaudio.	I would kiss her joyfully.

4.2–3   "I would choose" has to be supplied in English to fill out the
          meaning implied.

86

Rhythmical pattern: 6x4p, 3pp; *Ref.* 4x(7pp + 4pp), 8x4pp, 8pp

The speaker praises his sexual "equipment" with a string of adjectives and asks Cecilia to sample it (stanza 1 and refrain). He apparently goes on to describe the growth and flowering of lilies, but there are clear sexual double entendres (2).

*Ref.*16   Vollmann substitutes *sessilia* for *Caecilia,* arguing that the unusual
           word could easily have been misheard as the (more familiar)
           girl's name. *Sessilis* means "fit for sitting on" and is so used of a
           centaur's back at Ovid, *Metamorphoses* 12.401. Turcan-Verkerk,
           "Review," 423–25, argues against this reading, as does the oc-
           currence of *Caecilia* in CB 88.

*Ref.*17   *et . . . similia.* These are the closing words of Donatus, *Ars Minor,*
           the most widely used textbook of Latin grammar for a thou-
           sand years.

2.2–7   The "dew," "white flower," and the "lily's fragrance" refer in elegant language to the different stages of the process of male ejaculation.

87

Rhythmical pattern: 5x7pp, 11pp, 7pp, 4pp, 7pp, 8pp

Love is all-powerful and brims with contradictory feelings (stanza 1). It is spring and time for the young to seek a lover. The old should not become involved in love, particularly not with my girl, Theoclea! (2). An old man makes a poor lover. Sex makes young men happy. I hope Love can unite me with my girl (3). Any girl without a mate is, deep down, very sad (4). Despite his inherent contrariness, Love can be controlled and even captured by a night of love (5).

This carefully constructed poem about the nature of love is found only in *B* and suffers from a number of serious corruptions. The fact that single-syllable rhymes are not uncommon suggests a comparatively early date, perhaps in the 1150s.

1.6   *B*'s *caret pudicitia* is clearly wrong, as the rhyme scheme requires the ending *-(id)us*. If *cupidus* is correct, then something like *castus* is required in the first half.

2.6   The old man's *incommoda* (ills) are listed at Horace, *Ars Poetica* 169–76.

2.6–3.5   The sequence of thought is difficult. It seems to run as follows: now that it is springtime, Amor should be looking for a companion with a view to assisting him in his love life; the companion should not be an old man, who would be ill-suited for love.

3.5   Venus here denotes sexual activity as well as the goddess herself.

3.7   The poet is playing with the astrological (conjunction) as well as the sexual (coupling) meanings of *coniunctio*. The implied antecedent of *quam* is *eius* (or *cum ea*).

4.4   *Mentio* (literally, "I am not revealing the truth") is here a variant of the formula for declining to go into the details of a sexual encounter; compare note on 77.30.1 above. For the active form of the verb, see Blaise, *Dictionnaire,* "mentio."

88

Rhythmical pattern: 3x(7pp+6p); *Ref.* 4x8pp

After acknowledging the power of Amor (stanzas 1–2), the poet describes his relationship with his girl (3–9). She is quite young and he sees himself as the guardian of her virginity (6). Their love play comprises the first four stages of love—seeing, talking, touching, and kissing—but falls short of the final stage (8). Since both are young and innocent, their love play should be innocent too (9).

B presents 88 and 88a as a single poem, but they appear as two separate poems in two better manuscripts. The arrangement of the stanzas in *B* (5, 9, 6, 4, 2, 1, 7, 8) differs significantly from that of the Florence manuscript *(F)*, which is followed here. While Vollmann follows *B* closely, H-S-B alters *F*'s arrangement somewhat (1, 2, 7, 4–6, 9, 8).

1.1   Ovid has Venus describe Cupid's power over the other gods at *Metamorphoses* 5.365–70.

1.2   For Neptune's love for Corone, see Ovid, *Metamorphoses* 2.569–88.

1.3   Since Latin did not use the distinctions of capitalization deployed by English, *amor* can at any time denote Cupid or simply love. Here, strictly speaking, *hoc uno* should mean "love" rather than "Cupid" because the absence of *ab* indicates that the ablative is not one of personal agency, though for speakers and writers of Latin the distinction here would have been blurred. For the story of Pluto and Proserpine (Persephone), see "Ceres" in the Index of Proper Names, and Ovid, *Metamorphoses* 359–424.

8.1–4   The five stages of love are a recurring topos of Medieval Latin love poetry.

88a

Rhythmical pattern: 3x(7pp+ 6p)

The poet describes his girl's horoscope (stanza 1), which is identical to his own. So they are protected by kindly powers and fired by the same passion for one another (1–2). They love one another without deception or un-faithfulness, no matter what others say (3–4).

On the relationship between this poem and 88, see notes to 88. The four additional stanzas in *B* that Schumann judged to be spurious and relegated to his textual notes are not printed here, but are included in Vollmann's edition of 88 as stanzas 11, 12, 15, 16.

89

Rhythmical pattern: *Da capo* sequence (see introduction to CB 61) with the second part beginning at stanza 4a

This poem presents a wide range of problems both textual and interpreta-tional. Among the most crucial is whether we should understand the en-tire poem as a song sung by a shepherd (or two shepherds) about an ex-change of words with a young woman in charge of a few animals. The alternative view is that we should understand 1b, 2b, 3b, and 5b as narrated by the poet. Vollmann inclines to the former view (though his punctuation does not accurately reflect this), while Schumann's punctuation indicates that he inclined to the latter. Vollmann's seems the more persuasive view, given the *nos* at 3b.5, which implies a shepherd speaking at that point and, presumably, in the preceding stanzas too.

The debate format reflects the form of Virgil's *Eclogues*. It is not easy to be sure how even a predominantly male medieval audience would react to the shepherd's taunting of the shepherdess to stick to "women's work," when they were well aware that women were often employed in herding animals. It is important to reflect that the unfavorable characterization of the shepherdess in 5a represents the shepherd's view, which is not neces-sarily the same as the poet's.

I do not share Vollmann's certainty that the poem must be understood allegorically, though that remains a possibility. If it is allegorical, his sug-gestion that we are to see the shepherds as symbolizing the clergy, who are to be criticized for their preoccupation with making money rather than with tending to the needs of their flocks, is more than likely. Stanza 3d may be taken to suggest such an interpretation. The difficulty is whom or what we should see in the shepherdess, and Vollmann's suggestions of such groups as the Waldensians and the Humiliati I find unconvincing. More probably, the shepherdess could represent the poor in general. Perhaps the strongest argument in favor of an allegorical interpretation of this kind is the reference to the dog that fails to bark (4b.4). This appears to allude to the *canes muti* of Isaiah 56:10, on which the *Glossa Ordinaria* comments: "Just as dogs should guard the flock, so the prelates should guard the people." Relevant here is a passage in Walter of Châtillon where he refers to prelates and priests who are more interested in making money than in looking after their flocks as *canes muti* (*Shorter Poems,* no. 55.9.2).

1a.1   Compare Virgil, *Eclogues* 5.1: "boni quoniam convenimus ambo" (since we two good fellows have met).

1a.3   Presumably, one shepherd sings and the other plays an instrument.

6c.1–2   Very difficult. I understand *parvula fides* to refer to the little confidence the men place in the shepherdess's words. Since their *negotium* is looking after their animals and *otium* is the opposite of *negotium,* the four words seem to mean that her remarks have no bearing on their work.

90

Rhythmical pattern: 2x(7pp+6p) with rhymes at caesura

The first two stanzas read like the opening of a pastourelle. The language is simple but perfectly controlled. The third stanza, however, involves two solecisms: in the first line *scholarem,* which has its natural stress on the second syllable, here needs to be stressed on the first, while the second half of line 2 is 7pp instead of 6p. Moreover, the content is rather surprising, as the male figure in a pastourelle usually belongs to a higher class than the shepherdess, and it is usually he who makes the advance. For these reasons Schumann considered the third stanza to be spurious. Despite Dronke's gallant defense of the third stanza (*Medieval Poet,* 251–57), I am inclined to agree with Schumann, Bernt, and Walsh that it is a later addition.

91

Rhythmical pattern: 4x8p

Priests are reminded of their duty to be holy. More specifically, they are enjoined to be sure that their hands are not polluted when they handle the body of Christ (4–8). A priest who sleeps with his concubine and then officiates at mass should be beaten. He is impure inwardly and outwardly. Christ's body is not to be found in the bread handled by such hands (9–18). No amount of water can wash his hands clean. While a clean and sincere break from such behavior can be met with forgiveness, if he returns to his old ways, his sin will not be remitted (19–25).

Though the poem is satirical in tone, it is perhaps not so out of place among the love poems as H-S-B suggest, because it is the priest's habit of saying mass shortly after rising from the bed of his mistress that disqualifies him from the priesthood. The poem is found in ten manuscripts, all with different numbers of stanzas variously arranged. I have followed H-S-B in accepting only twenty-five of the forty-eight attested stanzas. H-S-B print the twenty-three rejected stanzas in their critical notes. Vollmann includes in his edition only the nine stanzas found in *B* (6–12, 15, and 14), in that order.

2.3   Given the second-person plural forms in 2.1, 4.1, and 4.3, it seems more reasonable to read *vos* here. The manuscripts are divided (see H-S-B 1.2.90) and *nos* and *vos* are constantly confused.

3.1   Leviticus 11:44, "Sancti estote quoniam et ego sanctus sum" (You are to keep yourselves holy because I am holy); similarly, 1 Peter 1:15–16, which adds: "et ipsi sancti in omni conversatione sitis" (and be holy in all your conduct).

3.3   Christ is the true vine (John 15:1).

4.1   The "supreme prophet" is Isaiah, whose strictures about properly offering sacrifice to God are referred to in stanza 7.

7.1–4   The passage in question is Isaiah 1:13–15, where the Lord says that a sacrifice is an abomination to him when "manus vestrae sanguine plenae sunt" (when your hands are bloodied). The bloody hands came to be understood as standing for any kind of impurity. Peter of Celle singles out fornication in particular; see his *Sermo* 7 (PL 202.658A).

21.4   *Unda* (wave) here, as often, is a synonym for *aqua* (water).

92

Rhythmical pattern: 4x(7pp+6p); sometimes 8pp for 7pp and 7p for 6p

This famous and much loved poem survives in ten manuscripts, which show considerable variation in the number of stanzas they record (*B* ends at stanza 62, while the earliest manuscript omits all stanzas after 39) and in other details. It belongs to the class of debate poems, a popular genre in medieval literature. The *Concilium Romarici Montis* (Council of Remiremont), dated circa 1151, is the forerunner in this amusing subgenre, which debates whether a knight or a cleric makes the better lover. There is also clearly a close connection (see below) between this poem and Andreas Capellanus's *De Amore*, which is perhaps to be dated about 1186. It is hard to say which work influenced the other, but I incline to the view that the poet of *Anni parte florida* drew on the *De Amore*. If so, then Walther's estimate (*Streitgedicht*, 147) that our poem was composed at the end of the twelfth century is correct. For an extended discussion of this poem and the scholarship on it, see Bisanti, *Poesia d'Amore*, 45–82.

Two love-smitten young noblewomen, Phyllis and Flora, go for a walk across the meadow to a pleasantly shaded spot beside a stream (stanzas 1–7). Sitting apart, they muse on their loves; when they notice one another sighing, they start talking about the men they love (8–11). This leads to a debate as to whether a knight or a cleric makes the better lover. After some initial sparring (12–14) the debate proper gets underway. Phyllis, who loves a knight, attacks clerics for being excessively fond of food, and praises knights, whom she considers focused on love and youth and taking only the bare essentials in food and drink (15–19). Flora's reply emphasizes the wealth of the cleric, which can buy many things for his lady friend, and the poverty and physical weakness of the knight (20–27). Phyllis then ridicules the gloomy clothes and tonsure of the cleric, in stark contrast to the noble appearance of a knight on horseback. While the cleric does "little or nothing," the knight is fighting the enemy and thinking of his love back home (28–32). Flora replies that it is pointless to speak against the clergy, arguing that a knight's life is dangerous and his need for food and drink often leads to his death. A cleric's clothing and tonsure are symbols of his high standing. He gives orders to knights and reads, writes, and thinks about his lady friend. He has read and taught about the art of love (33–41). Flora and Phyllis then agree to submit the issue to Cupid's judgment and prepare to travel to his garden. Phyllis rides a mule and Flora a horse; their mounts and accouterments are described in detail (42–59). When they arrive at Cupid's grove, they hear musical instruments and the singing of birds. Inside the grove they see young men and women dancing. They dismount and move closer. Bacchus is instructing nymphs and fauns. Silenus is there too, drunk and sleepy (60–71). When the women reach Cupid and tell him why they have come, he submits their issue to his judges, who pronounce in favor of the cleric (72–79).

3.1   *Regina* is sometimes used of a woman of some eminence, not
       necessarily a queen or a princess; see *OLD,* "regina" 3.

6–7   The setting where the debate takes place is a *locus amoenus* (at-
       tractive spot), where erotic encounters (usually with tragic out-
       comes) often take place in Ovid's *Metamorphoses.*

12.1   Paris is depicted as something of a coward in the *Iliad* but re-
       ceives considerably more favorable treatment in the Late An-
       tique authors Dares and Dictys, the main sources for informa-
       tion about the Trojan War in the Middle Ages.

16–30 At various points in the debate, as Walsh has pointed out, there
       is clearly a close relationship between our poem and a dialogue
       between a cleric and a noblewoman in Andreas Capellanus's *De
       amore.* It is worth quoting a sample passage here in full:

> Love by its nature requires that body adornment be pleasing
> and attractive and insists that a man should be prepared to be
> generous with what he has to everyone, as the occasion de-
> mands, to show spirit against those who fight against him, to
> take delight in all the exertions in battle, and to submit to
> the unrelenting fatigue of war. The cleric, on the other hand,
> who makes his appearance adorned like a woman and with his
> head horribly shorn, can help no one with his bounty unless
> he chooses to steal the property of others. He is seen to de-

> vote himself to unrelenting idleness and to be a slave only to his belly. (1.490)

Phyllis castigates the cleric's love of food and drink in 16 and 19, his lack of generosity in 19, his unbecoming clothes and tonsure in 29, and his idleness in 30.3.

19   On the cleric's love of eating and lack of generosity, see preceding note.

20.1–2   A pale complexion was prized in women in the ancient and medieval worlds because it was characteristic of upper-class women, who did not need to work in the sun.

23   Food and wine are often designated in ancient and Medieval Latin poetry by their respective gods Ceres (Demeter) and Bacchus (Lyaeus), as at Terence, *Eunuchus* 732.

26.2   Literally, "and barely covered with a cloak that lacks a hide."

29–30   For the corresponding passage in Andreas Capellanus, see note on 16–30 above.

31.3   Jupiter chose Ganymede as his cupbearer and lover; so by referring to the knight's squire as his Ganymede, Phyllis is alluding to a general assumption that knight and squire indulged in homosexual relations when on military campaigns.

33.3   Echoes Psalms 72(73):9, "Posuerunt in caelo os suum" (They have set their mouth against heaven), a passage often given an anti-heretical interpretation; see Jeanjean, "L'utilization anti-hérétique de Ps. 72,9."

33.4   This would appear to be a humorously misremembered version of the famous phrase about driving a camel through the eye of a needle (Matthew 19:24; Mark 10:25).

37   Similar remarks are to be found about the distinctiveness of the cleric's dress in Andreas Capellanus, *De Amore* 1.493.

38.3   On the cleric's generosity see Andreas Capellanus, *De Amore* 1.494.

39.3–4   Thanks to his education the cleric is both a theologian and a man of science.

41   His reading of classical literature (especially Ovid) has taught the cleric a great deal about love.

41.3   The assertion that the cleric has become a "Knight of Venus"

thanks to his clerical status is a clever rhetorical point and a
suitable culmination of Flora's case.

44 Flora's more colorful dress and more prestigious mount reflect
the wealth of her cleric but probably also allude to her eventual
victory.

45 In Medieval Latin poetry incidents recorded in classical my-
thology are not infrequently regarded as contemporary or in
the recent past.

46 The reference is to the Hiberina of Juvenal, 6.53, where the sati-
rist's (clearly rhetorical) question "Is one man enough for Hi-
berina?" suggests her service to the goddess.

54.3 Martianus Capella's *De Nuptiis Philologiae et Mercurii* was widely
used as a textbook in medieval schools and familiarity with it
assumed.

61.4 The musical intervals *diatessaron* (perfect fourth) and *diapente*
(perfect fifth) are discussed in Martianus Capella, *De Nuptiis
Philologiae et Mercurii* 9.933–34.

63.4 For the story of the nightingale's pain, see "Philomena" in the
Index of Proper Names.

70–71 For his picture of Silenus here, our poet is indebted to two pas-
sages in Ovid: "His usual entourage thronged around Bac-
chus—Satyrs and Bacchanals; but Silenus was absent. Phrygian
countryfolk had captured him as he staggered, fuddled with
wine and years" (*Metamorphoses* 11.89–91), and "Drunken old
Silenus can scarcely remain seated on the ass's back" (*Ars Ama-
toria* 1.543-44). Vollmann believes that the laughing god (71.2) is
Cupid, but Walsh is right to insist that it must be Bacchus, for
Cupid, referred to in 69.2, is not properly introduced until 72.1.

93

Rhythmical pattern: 3x(7pp+6p/7p)

This is written out as a single poem in *B,* our sole source. Difficulties are
posed by corruptions in the text, particularly in the first stanza. Schumann
and Walsh, considering the subject matter of stanzas 4 to 8 incompatible

with what precedes, decided that CB 93 must be two poems, 93 and 93a. It is striking, however, that both parts are written not only in the comparatively unusual scheme of three goliardic lines (7pp + 6p) but in flexible goliardics, in which 7p can be substituted for 6p. Also, though the ambiguity of *virgo* (young woman, virgin) and *virginitas* raises difficulties, it is undeniable that these concepts are central to both parts. Again, the *joie d'amour, chagrin d'amour* motif outlined in 3.1–2 finds fuller expression and indeed resolution in stanzas 4 to 8. Accordingly, I believe that 93 is a single poem. The poet contrasts his life as a young man, when he was good-looking and well respected, with his present life as an old man, when his expectations in the realm of sex are considerably diminished.

1.1–3 B's *insula* can mean "island," "city block," or the town of Lille, but none of these seems very satisfactory; so it has been emended to *insulsa* (unattractive, dull). Despite the emphasis on "virginity" *(virginalem, virginem),* the setting here, where a man selects for himself a *virgo* from a group of women in a garden, suggests a brothel. Medieval brothels not infrequently had gardens (CB 76.18.2, and Rossiaud, *Medieval Prostitution,* 5). It appears then that we are dealing with young unmarried women rather than virgins. Such gardens would of course be enclosed, and it may well be, as Walsh suggests, that the "virginal garden" alludes to the "enclosed garden" of Song of Songs 4:12; but if so, and if we are right in seeing a brothel here, then the allusion is ironic.

3.3 The "envy" may refer to the malicious gossip of others, but *invidia* can also refer to the reprehensible coveting of something (or someone), as in 84.2.6, and this meaning might also be appropriate here.

6 The unicorn resting on a lady's lap in medieval paintings and tapestries is understood to indicate her virginity, as in the famous Lady of the Unicorn tapestries in the Musée de Cluny, Paris.

7–8 The argument, convoluted and dubious, seems to be that the *virgo* would not lose her privileged status as a virgin if she remained true to the old man.

94

Rhythmical pattern: 4x7pp; *Ref.* 6p, 7pp, 6p

A simple song contrasting the suitability of young and old men as potential lovers.

95

Rhythmical pattern: 4x(4p+6pp); *Ref.* 8p

The speaker has learned that his mistress suspects him of homosexual behavior; he vigorously denies this (stanzas 1–4). He would rather die than be the first to practice this behavior in Brittany (or Britain?) (5).

2	To emphasize the unwavering nature of his heterosexuality, the poet gives us a list of *adynata* (impossible phenomena), a common rhetorical device of ancient poetry; compare also Burns's "And I will luve thee still, my dear, / Till a' the seas gang dry . . . And the rocks melt wi' the sun."
2.4	For the link between Sodom and homosexuality (generally called sodomy in the Middle Ages), see Genesis 19:1–11.
4.1	Alan of Lille wrote his *De Planctu Naturae* circa 1160/65, in which Nature laments the prevalence of homosexuality. Walter of Châtillon, writing between 1160 and 1180, also complains frequently about the prevalence of the behavior.
5.2	*Britannia,* the most plausible of the emendations for *B*'s "Bricavvia," could mean either Britain or Brittany.
5.3	For *quam* in the sense of "rather than" without preceding comparative, see *DMLBS,* "quam" 7.

96

Rhythmical pattern: 2x7pp (but stanza 1 2x8pp), 5pp, 6p; *Ref.* 3x4pp, 7p

This fragment of a poem breaks off at 3.1 at the bottom of folio 49v. It must have continued, and was no doubt followed by other similar poems, now lost, on the missing folios.

97

Rhythmical pattern: Sequence (1–6). The remaining stanzas may once have also been in sequence form but are so corrupt that this is no longer evident.

This poem summarizes the plot of the Late Antique novel, *Apollonius, King of Tyre,* which was very popular in the Middle Ages. However, the summary is so sketchy and allusive that it presupposes considerable familiarity with the novel; it is more of an aide-memoire than a précis. The text is marred by many corruptions. The author's dubious Latinity makes it very difficult to suggest plausible corrections.

The novel survives in over a hundred Latin manuscripts, which can be grouped in nine redactions. There are also vernacular translations, notably in English. Plot details vary in the different versions. CB 97 appears to follow the redaction known as RA, of which a text, a translation, and a more detailed plot summary appear in Archibald, *Apollonius.*

Apollonius, king of Tyre, was a suitor for the hand of the daughter of Antiochus, king of Antioch. Antiochus, however, was in love with his daughter (not named) and was maintaining a secret, incestuous relationship with her against her will. He invited suitors for his daughter, promising to marry her to anyone who could figure out the answer to a riddle. Apollonius guessed the correct answer, but Antiochus told him his answer was wrong and plotted to kill him. Apollonius learned of the plot and escaped, embarking on a complex series of adventures, the relevant parts of which are described below. In the first five stanzas it is Apollonius himself who tells his story.

1	In guessing the correct answer to the riddle (Antiochus himself), Apollonius revealed that he knew of Antiochus's incestuous relationship.
1.2–6	Antiochus's trickery and spurning of Apollonius refer to his failure to honor his promise.
2–4	Astrages is the daughter of Archistrates, the king of Pentapolis (in Cyrene), who offers Apollonius hospitality after his ship is wrecked. She asks him to tell his story; so Apollonius tells her of his misfortunes. He also teaches her to play the lyre

and sing. Apollonius and Astrages fall in love, get married, and soon are expecting a child. Meanwhile, a ship arrives from Tyre with the news that Antiochus has died and that Apollonius is now king of Antioch and Tyre; so he and his wife set sail for Tyre. On the way Astrages goes into labor, gives birth to a daughter (Tarsia/Tharsia), but sinks into a coma and is taken for dead. She is placed in a coffin and lowered into the sea. When she is washed ashore near Ephesus, a medical student realizes that she is not dead and revives her. She is placed in the temple of Diana as a priestess for her protection.

5   In great distress Apollonius puts in at Tarsus and leaves his daughter with her nurse, Lycoris (in *B*, Liocardadis), in the care of Strangolio, whom he had encountered in an earlier stage of his travels, and his wife, Dionysias. He leaves jewelry and rich clothes for Tharsia and money for her keep.

6   When Tharsia is fourteen, Lycoris, on her deathbed, tells her who her real parents are and urges her if she is in danger to seek sanctuary at the statue of Apollonius that the people of Tarsus erected to commemorate his generosity to the city during a time of famine. One day Dionysias, noticing that the people admired Tharsia because of her rich dress and jewelry rather than her own daughter, resolves to get rid of her and tells her slave Theophilus to kill her. Pirates rescue her from Theophilus.

7   The pirates sell Tharsia to a pimp, who outbids the leading citizen, Athenagoras. Taken to a brothel in Mytilene, Tharsia begs her first client, Athenagoras, to spare her virginity, telling him her sad story. He takes pity on her and gives her a large sum of money. The same happens with the rest of her clients, so that she earns at least her purchase price every day. Soon she persuades the manager of the brothel to let her sing to her clients to earn money for the pimp instead of being a prostitute.

8   Apollonius arrives in Tarsus and is told by Dionysias that Tharsia died of a pain in the stomach. He is taken to her "tomb," where an inscription confirms her death. Apollonius is surprised that he cannot weep and wonders if this means that she is still alive.

8.1   The author has apparently used an ablative absolute construction where a nominative is required.

9   As Apollonius is returning to Tyre, a storm blows his ships to Mytilene, where he sits in the ship's bilge, mourning his daughter. Athenagoras summons Tharsia from the brothel to entertain him by playing her lyre. She tells Apollonius her life story and he recognizes his daughter. Shortly after this Athenagoras (here called Arfax) and Tharsia are married.

10   On his way back to Tyre with his daughter and son-in-law, Apollonius is advised by an angel to go to the temple of Diana in Ephesus and tell the story of his misadventures there. He does so, and Astartes recognizes her husband. For his cruelty the pimp is burned alive. Apollonius, his wife, daughter, and son-in-law sail to Tarsus, where it is revealed that Dionysias attempted to have Tharsia murdered. She and Strangolio are stoned to death by the populace.

10.1   The island is Patmos, the island of John, author of the book of Revelation (Revelation 1:9).

98

Rhythmical pattern: Descort

The poet offers a sketch of the love affair between Aeneas and Dido described by Virgil in *Aeneid* 1 and 4. Rather surprisingly, he hides the fact that the liaison is destined to end tragically. Perhaps the whole point of the poem is to lead up to the learned ribaldry of stanza 8.

1   Dido's welcome of the shipwrecked Trojans is described in *Aeneid* 1. The book ends with a banquet in their honor, at which Aeneas recounts the fall of Troy (book 2) and his subsequent adventures (book 3), and Cupid, in the guise of Aeneas's son Ascanius, makes Dido fall hopelessly in love with Aeneas.

2.3   *Naufragium* besides meaning "shipwreck" can be used of any serious misfortune. Both meanings are implied here.

3.1–5.16 This speech is a shortened recasting of Dido's speech at *Aeneid* 4.9–29. Compare, in particular, 5.8–9 with Virgil's "huic uni forsan potui succumbere culpae" (4.19).

4.3–4   These words could reflect either Dido's compassion for the dangers the Trojans have had to face or apprehension (compare 3.8) that their arrival in Carthage may prove disastrous for herself and her people.

6   Anna's speech in Virgil (4.31–53), also introduced by *Anna refert*, emphasizes the dangers of hostile neighbors and the advantages of an alliance with the Trojans.

7.2   Virgil refers to Dido several times as "Elissa." For the storm and the cave scene in Virgil, see *Aeneid* 4.160–72.

8–9   The strange intrusion of language appropriate to the description of a disputation *(propositionibus, syllogizat, argumentis)* is puzzling. It might seem at first that the poet is summarizing the famous exchanges between Aeneas and Dido—when Dido pleads with him to stay, Aeneas explains why he must go, and Dido then denounces him for abandoning her (4.305–87)—and this may be a deliberate move on the part of the poet to mislead the reader temporarily. However, the closing stanza makes it quite clear (compare *Aeneid* 4.165–67) that stanza 8 describes the activities in the cave and that the contest must be the act of lovemaking *(amoris gaudia)*, often described in medieval poetry in terms of a wrestling match *(lucta)*, hence Dido's opposing moves (8.3–4). Bischoff suggested that the "three propositions" are to be understood as referring to Aeneas's penis and testicles (see the editions of Bernt and Vollmann). While his readers are left in no doubt that Dido and Aeneas had sex in the cave, Virgil describes the scene with comparative decorum in terms of a wedding ceremony presided over by deities and meteorological phenomena. The contrast with our poem, which seems intended for a student audience, is striking.

99

Rhythmical pattern: 3x(6pp+6pp) with some irregularities, especially in the second halves of verses

This summary of the love affair of Aeneas and Dido comprises two parts by two separate authors. This is clear both from their approach to the subject matter (the second poet departing freely from the text of the *Aeneid*) and on technical grounds (see Vollmann). Correctly viewing the second part as an addition by a later poet, Schumann relegated the second part (stanzas 11–20) to his apparatus. However, it has considerable interest in its own right.

4.1	Virgil, *Eclogue* 10.69, "Omnia vincit Amor."
7.1	Though Odysseus was naked when he met Nausicaa, Aeneas was not naked when he first appeared to Dido. *Nudus* is here used figuratively in the sense of "destitute."
8.2–3	The corruptions in both these lines are unusually difficult to correct. They condense the opening and the close of Dido's speech to Anna (*Aeneid* 4.416–36), in which she asks her sister to intercede for her and beg Aeneas to stay in Carthage. In line 2, which is clearly inspired by, but quite different from, *Aeneid* 4.416–17, I have followed Schumann in adopting *ora* for *B*'s *aura*. My attempt at a solution to the difficulties presented by 8.3 assumes that *asperrima* refers not to *Mors* but to the unwelcome sounds of the Trojan fleet as it gets ready to depart.
9	While Aeneas follows his destiny in Italy, which entails war and winning the hand of Lavinia, Dido, pretending to deal with her sorrow, calls for a sorceress to use magic to ease her pain and asks for a pyre to be built to burn her marriage bed and the mementos of Aeneas.
9.2	For the use of a deponent verb in a passive sense, see Blaise, *Manuel,* §212, and *DMLBS,* "sequi" 2b.
10.1–2	Dido climbs the pyre and commits suicide with Aeneas's sword. Line 3, apparently the last line of the original poem, draws the moral from the tragic love affair.
11–20	Stanzas 1 to 10 describe the love affair primarily from Dido's point of view. It seems that a later poet wanted to give Aeneas a chance to have his say. In doing so he departs radically from Virgil's depiction of his hero, for Virgil's Aeneas does not criticize his decision to follow the advice of the gods and political considerations rather than his own personal wishes. The Aeneas who emerges from these stanzas is a decidedly more likable, sensitive, and "modern" character than Virgil's Aeneas in *Aeneid* 4.

12.3 Though *tyrannus* usually has the same negative overtones as our "tyrant," it is also used by poets in the neutral sense of "king, sovereign," as at *Aeneid* 7.266, where King Latinus applies it to Aeneas. It follows therefore that *tyra(n)nica* is a plausible emendation for *B*'s *yranica,* which avoids the awkward hiatus at the end of the line created by *ironica.* I agree with Schumann that there are no grounds for asserting that the letter after *r* was originally an *o*.

16.2 The use of the genitive singular pronouns *mei* and *tui* instead of the appropriate forms of *meus* and *tuus* was fairly common in poetry prior to the mid-twelfth century, so the use of *tui* here (if correct) suggests an earlier date for both poems.

20 In the *Aeneid* (6.450–76) Dido's shade spurns Aeneas and returns to the shade of her husband, Sychaeus.

99a

Meter: Dactylic hexameters
Author: Peter of Riga

This succinct summary of the Trojan War has recently been convincingly attributed to Peter of Riga (1140–1209); see Wollin, "Troiagedichte," especially 407–9, where he prints a text of the two lines as found in Peter's earlier work, *Colores rhetorici.* I have gratefully adopted Wollin's text, as it presents better readings than *B* for the first and second last words of the distich.

99b

Meter: Elegiac couplet

This is the epitaph that Dido, according to Ovid (*Heroides* 7.195–96), wanted inscribed on her tomb. The reading of *B* is *illa,* which Schumann and Vollmann adopt. I have followed most editors of the *Heroides* in printing *ipsa* in line 2, which underlines the fact that death was her own choice.

Meter: (1) Dactylic hexameters
Rhythmical pattern: (2–7) Sequence with corresponding stanzas (except 3 and 7)

Dido laments her own fate and that of her city. She wonders why her generous hospitality toward the hapless Trojans has been met with hatred (stanzas 1–2b). She sees the Trojan ships preparing to leave, knowing that Aeneas is looking for a marriage in Italy and that her own people are mocking her (3–4b). She tells Anna that death is her only option. Despite the prospect of poor weather, the Trojan fleet is setting sail (6a). She thrusts herself upon Aeneas's sword, bids Carthage farewell, and urges her soul to tell her story in the world below (6b–7).

1.2	Dido's brother, Pygmalion, killed her husband, Sychaeus.
2a.7–8	Virgil, *Aeneid* 1.4, "Iunonis ob iram."
3.1	*Dolare* means "to chop at, hew, trim" and no doubt refers to the preparations for departure described at *Aeneid* 4.397–400 and especially the trimming of boughs for oars implied at 399–400; Dido witnesses this activity and sighs (408–11).
3.3–4	Compare 99.8.2. It seems clear that CB 99 has influenced CB 100 or vice-versa or both have drawn on a common source. Curiously, the best manuscripts have "vocat iam carbasus auras" (the sails summon a breeze) at *Aeneid* 4.417, but perhaps some inferior manuscripts had "volat iam carbasus auris" (the sails are flapping in the breeze).
4a.2	The "Tyrian enemy" may refer to Dido's brother, Pygmalion, or it could be in apposition to Iarbas and translated as "the Tyrians' (that is, Carthaginians') enemy."
5a.8	Apparently, our poet interpreted *Aeneid* 4.436 as suggesting suicide; see on CB 99.8.3 above.
6a.5	Palinurus, Aeneas's helmsman, overcome by Sleep, fell overboard, still clutching the tiller, close to the Italian shore.
6b.4	It is difficult to understand exactly what is meant by *flos Carthaginis*—perhaps "my beautiful Carthage" comes closer to rendering its emotional impact.

6b.5–6   By *Haec . . . trophaea* Dido means Aeneas's realization that he was
           the cause of her death.

7.9   *Pyrois,* essentially a Greek word meaning "fiery," is found several
           times in Martianus Capella, where it refers to the planet Mars
           (*Thesaurus Linguae Latinae,* x, pt. 2, 2789). Here it appears to re-
           fer to Phlegethon, the underworld river of fire. For a discus-
           sion of this word and indeed this stanza, see Dauser, *"Miszel-*
           len," 95–102.

101

Meter: Elegiac couplets, each with the same rhyme in four places

This poem on the fall of Troy, whose popularity in the medieval world is
evident from the number of manuscripts (sixty-six at least) in which it sur-
vives, is something of a tour de force, for the same rhyme is used four
times in each couplet (at each caesura and line end). In addition, our poet
manages to work in a fair amount of wordplay (*solo* in stanza 1, *parat . . .*
Paris in stanza 5, *viduatorem viduatus* in stanza 7, and so forth). Boutemy,
"Le poème *Pergama flere volo*" dates the poem to the first third of the
twelfth century. It is distinguished from others on the fall of Troy by its
emphasis on Hecuba's lament and the *damnatio* of Helen. Hecuba's des-
perate, mocking lament is especially well done, particularly 23 to 31. The
closing section on Troy itself, contrasting its past glory with its present
state is repetitive and rather tedious and may have been added (or at least
added to) by a later poet or poets, though the final stanza (on Helen) seems
original.

1   *Solo* in line 1 and at the beginning of line 2 is from *solus -a -um*
           (alone, only), while *solo* at the end of line 2 is from *solum*
           (ground).

2   The deities who rule Helicon are the Muses. Calliope was the
           eldest and the one primarily associated with epic poetry.

3   Paris goes to Sparta, absconds with Helen, the wife of Mene-
           laus, and returns with her to Troy.

4   In the ancient world pirates made their living largely by kidnap-
           ping people who lived near the coast and selling them into slav-
           ery.

564

5.1   *Maris* here is the genitive of *mas maris* m. male. "The altar of lust" is presumably the altar of Venus, who favored Paris for choosing her as the most beautiful of the three goddesses (Judgment of Paris).

6.1   That is to say, Achilles, who came from Thessaly (whose chief town was Larissa), and Agamemnon, king of Mycenae, came in pursuit of Paris and Helen with their followers.

7   Menelaus is deprived *(viduatus)* and Paris is the "depriver" *(viduatorem)*. *Foedere* refers to the marriage contract that bound Helen to Menelaus; *foederare* usually used of binding people by an agreement is here used of binding on a sword.

8   The Greek leader is Menelaus. The object of *prohibet* is all of line 2, and *ductori* and *timori* are in a double dative construction.

13.2   The daughter of Leda is Helen.

15   The poet apostrophizes Helen.

17.1   Vollmann reads the line: *Passa modo Paridem, (pateris iam Thesea pridem)*. An Athenian myth has it that the Athenian hero Theseus abducted the young Helen before she was married to Menelaus. *Passa* is used in the sense of playing the passive sexual role.

21.2   *Lira,* a comparatively rare word, which denotes the ridge between two furrows, is used here for *terra* because it rhymes with *ira.*

24   *Atrides* means "son (or descendant) of Atreus" and is applicable to either Agamemnon or Menelaus.

37.2   The inauspicious ship is that of Paris, for it brings Helen to Troy.

102

Meter: Elegiac couplets; each couplet has the same rhyme at caesura and line end

Author: Peter of Riga

As Boutemy, "Le poème *Pergama flere volo*," points out, this summary of the story of Troy is indebted to CB 101 for some of its phrasing. But CB 102 goes beyond the fall of Troy to devote a dozen couplets to the story of

Aeneas (17–27). Most manuscripts omit the episode in Carthage, but *B* devotes two couplets to it and another manuscript one. Given the importance of the episode, it seemed best to include the relevant couplets in *B*, 21a and 21b (22 and 23 in Vollmann), in the text, though Schumann relegates them to his notes. Recently, Wollin ("Troiagedichte," 400–407) has convincingly confirmed the tentative attribution to Peter of Riga made by Wilhelm Wattenbach in 1892.

For the summary of the plot, the Latin alternates confusingly between the past and the present tenses. In the translation I have followed the English convention of using the present tense throughout.

2, 4	The first three rhymes are achieved by naming the heroes by their patronymics.
5.1	Argos, a town in the Peloponnese, was used by Homer and other poets to mean Greece.
5.2	The sacrificed victim is Iphigenia, the daughter of Agamemnon. The sacrifice calmed the winds but led to the murder of Agamemnon by Clytemnestra, which in turn ensured her murder by her son, Orestes.
6.1	*Ancora* is used by metonymy for "fleet" in the first half of the line but in its proper sense of "anchor" in the second.
7.2	"Trickery" combines the building of the wooden horse and Sinon's gulling the Trojans into pulling it into the city.
9.1	At *Iliad* 22.227–49, Hector is tricked into confronting Achilles for the fatal duel by Athena, who assumes the appearance of his brother Deiphobus. A more likely source, however, is Dictys Cretensis, who relates (*Ephemeris belli Troiani* 3.2–3) that Achilles fell in love with Hector's sister Polyxena and promised to end the war if Hector agreed to let Polyxena marry him. However, Achilles was so enraged when Hector killed Patroclus that he ambushed and killed a group of Trojans, including Hector, as they were crossing a river (ibid. 3.15).
11.2	Priam believes Sinon's lies about the wooden horse, which, he said, the Greeks made too big to be drawn into the city (*Aeneid* 2.187–88).

12–13   Sinon was left behind by the Greeks to trick the Trojans into pulling the wooden horse inside the city; this is described at length in Virgil, *Aeneid* 2. The "Ithacan" is Odysseus (Ulysses).

15   Here and in stanzas 19 and 27 the poet uses perfect tenses instead of historic presents.

16   The Argives are the Greeks; compare note on 5.1.

17   Aeneas was the son of Venus and the mortal Anchises.

19.1   *Pestem concepit* could also mean "caught the plague." Either way the phrase refers metaphorically to the beginning of the storm in the *Aeneid*.

21.2   Compare *Aeneid* 1.91, "Everything threatened the men with imminent death." For *lira* (literally, "the ridge between two furrows"), see *DMLBS, lira*.

22.2   After his helmsman Palinurus falls overboard, Aeneas guides the ship safely to the Italian shore near Cumae (*Aeneid* 5.868).

23–24   Not long after their arrival in Italy, war breaks out between the Trojans and some of the Italian communities under the leadership of Turnus, Aeneas's rival for the hand of Lavinia. The vicissitudes of this war, described in *Aeneid* 7–12, are ended by a duel between Aeneas and Turnus.

24.2   Literally, "His sword point, sated with gore, examines the innards [of Turnus]." The gruesome language does not reflect Virgil's description of the death of Turnus but rather the Roman practice of haruspicy, that is, the examination of the entrails of animals (usually sheep) by *haruspices* as a way of divining future events.